The Unwritten Brazilian Constitution

The Unwritten Brazilian Constitution

Human Rights in the Supremo Tribunal Federal

Edited by
Rubens Becak and Jairo Lima

LEXINGTON BOOKS
Lanham • Boulder • New York • London

Published by Lexington Books
An imprint of The Rowman & Littlefield Publishing Group, Inc.
4501 Forbes Boulevard, Suite 200, Lanham, Maryland 20706
www.rowman.com

6 Tinworth Street, London SE11 5AL, United Kingdom

British Library Cataloguing in Publication Information Available

Library of Congress Cataloging-in-Publication Data Available

Library of Congress Control Number: 2020944658

ISBN 978-1-7936-2369-0 (cloth : alk. paper)
ISBN 978-1-7936-2370-6 (electronic)

Contents

Chapter 1

The Promises of the Brazilian Constitution of 1988 and the Encounter between Human Rights and the Supreme Court

Rubens Becak and Jairo Lima

THE BIRTH CERTIFICATE

The Brazilian Constitution has been in effect since October 5, 1988, and included in its curriculum several political achievements as well as major institutional challenges. The fact that it reached 30 years of age is already a sign that the Brazilian Constitution exceeded the average life expectancy of a constitution according to the survey by Elkins, Ginsburg, and Melton.[1] However, after going through childhood and adolescence, adulthood poses more complex challenges than those experienced thus far.

The Constitution of 1988 was the result of a negotiated transition to a democratic regime; between 1964 and 1985, Brazil experienced its longest military dictatorship in history. In 1985, through an indirect election, the military left the office, and Tancredo Neves was elected. However, before taking office, Neves had a health problem and passed away before being sworn in as President. The Vice-President José Sarney took his place; he was responsible for presenting, in 1985, an amendment to the Constitution to convene a National Constituent Assembly.

Elections to choose the constituents took place in 1986, and from 1987 onward, work began on the future Constitution. Two important facts related to this Assembly are noteworthy: (a) the National Constituent Assembly in Brazil was not elected exclusively to draft the new Constitution, the deputies and senators also served roles as ordinary representatives in the Chamber of Deputies and in the Senate and (b) 1/3rd of the senators who participated in the constituent process were not elected to the National Constituent Assembly because the previous Constitution determined that election for the Senate occurred every 4 years for between 1/3rd and 2/3rd of the members of each State, alternately. Therefore, each Senator served an 8-year term. Thus, to avoid interrupting the term of 1/3rd of senators who were still in the middle of their term, the political option was to keep them in office with the right to participate in the National Constituent Assembly. However, according to previous rules, these senators had not been chosen through direct election.

Despite these two factors, the influential participation of organized civil society represented the main feature of the constitutional process of 1987/1988 through public hearings and popular initiatives. For this reason the interests of various sectors of society were considered, but were not necessarily convergent between them; however, there was strong demand to restore active participation in the political life of the country combined with demands for more rights. This broad democratic opening at that time resulted in a quite detailed and extensive constitutional text that aimed to protect the most different demands:[2] political rights, social rights, freedom of expression, independence of powers, free market, social function of property, universal healthcare, protection of indigenous people, etc.

Among the main innovations brought by the Constitution of 1988 was an extensive list of fundamental rights at the beginning of the text; article 5 of the Constitution originally contained 77 fundamental rights. Moreover, it was considered that the list was an open list because there could be fundamental rights implicit in the Constitution (article 5, § 2).[3] This open clause helps to "oxygenate" the judicial system, keeping it abreast of historical developments of the fight for new rights. Finally, for these rights not only to be declared but also to be implemented in the lives of citizens, the Constitution of 1988 established a set of institutional instruments related mainly to the judicial review on the American or Kelsenian models.

The most innovative aspect, however, was the emphasis given to the dignity of the human person in article 1. The dignity of the human person is one of the foundations of the Brazilian Republic. It represents the true axiological epicenter of the Constitution, radiating its effects over the entire legal system, and guiding the government's actions. In addition, article 3 of the Constitution established that one of the objectives of the new republic would be the "eradication of poverty and of social inequalities."

This provision represents a strong link between constitutional politics and the social reality in Brazil because the national colonial formation characterized by the ethnocide of indigenous peoples, together with slavery, can help explain the country's poor and unequal society, where the master-slave logic reigns, according to one of the great Brazilian thinkers Gilberto Freire.[4] Inequality is the characteristic feature that permeates the trajectory of Brazil's construction.[5] Even transformations due to capitalist expansion in the twentieth century did not allow for a reduction in the distance between rich and poor, as urban expansion generated by the rural exodus only replaced poverty in the countryside with the various forms of poverty in cities. Unlike the European debate in the 1980s about the Welfare State crisis, at the same time in Brazil, it did not make sense to speak of rescuing lost citizenship because until then, it had not been achieved by the majority of the population, running counter to the mechanisms of participation and the collective distribution of advantages and opportunities. Thus, the poverty and inequality that the Constitution of 1988 recognized is not limited only to the economic aspect; it is also related to the denial of rights, to discrimination (stigmatization that amplifies negative attributes) and to the exclusion of access to integrating social instruments. Therefore, along with not-having (material resources), the challenges that the new Constitution had to face also included the not-being (citizenship).

Thus, the conflation of human dignity and reduction in inequality meant that the Constitution of 1988 went beyond the restricted notion of the Constitution as the regulation of powers and recognition of fundamental rights because it was established as a directive constitution. "For the Directive Constitution Theory, the constitution is not only a guarantee of the existent, but also a program for the future. When providing lines of procedure for politics, without substituting it, the interdependency between State and society stands out: the directive constitution is a state and social constitution."[6] Thus, the distance between the textual provisions of the Constitution and the Brazilian social reality opened up space in the 1990s for a Brazilian Doctrine of effectiveness committed to the normative force of the constitution, to the judicial interpretation of the constitution and to the judicialization of constitutional issues.[7]

CONSTITUTIONAL TRANSFORMATION STRATEGIES

The notion that the Constitution represents a plan to be implemented by political institutions is present in the various provisions that compel the ordinary legislator to create public policies, such as Agricultural policy (article 187); the National Education Plan (article 214); the National Culture Plan (article 215, § 3); and the National Youth Plan (article 227, § 8, II). In other situations, the Constitution itself regulates the details of how public policy is structured: the Fund for Irrigation of Dry Regions (article 42, ADCT); the Social Emergency Fund (article 71, ADCT); the Fund for Combating and Eradicating Poverty (article 79, ADCT); and the Policy for Limiting Public Spending (article 106, ADCT). According to a study by Claudio Couto and Rogério Arantes, "After thorough examination of the 1,627 provisions of the original Charter and the application of the Methodology for Constitutional Analysis (MAC), we concluded that 30.5% of those provisions can be safely classified as policy."[8] Notably, a large extent of the constitutional text led to the regulation of matters traditionally considered to be infra-constitutional, as public policies precisely represent the political objectives of each new government and are therefore political actions that in essence should not have the same long-lasting pretense of a norm with constitutional status.

Therefore, when the Brazilian Constitution expanded its areas of regulation to encompass public policies, it raised several issues typical of constituted powers to the constitutional level. The entrenchment of the interests of various political groups that led to an extensive text that regulates matters modifiable with each new government indicates one of the reasons why the constant approval of new constitutional amendments is required.

The constitutional amendments are a mechanism of connection between the Constitution and time. Based on the notion that the Constitution corresponds to the product of the foundation of a given political community, there is a need for a certain approximation between the legal norms and collective goals. For this reason, the full immutability of the constitutional pact hinders the updating of its norms. Consequently, time further degrades the already complex reconciliation between people and the Constitution. Thus, constitutional amendments represent an opportunity for the correction and improvement of the original text based on new needs, information and political experiences. In addition, the constitutional reform process represents the idea of constitutional supremacy and the ensuing duality of democratic politics because this instrument enables identifying constitutional norms and differentiating them from infra-constitutional legislative acts.

Between 1988 and 2019, the Brazilian Constitution had been amended 112 times, that is, an average of 3.5 approved amendments per year.[9] Of the 111 Brazilian constitutional amendments, 36 sought to amend Title X of the Constitution of 1988. The text of the Constitution is subdivided into ten major sections according to topic, for example, fundamental rights (Title II), State's organization (Title III), division of powers (Title IV), taxation (Title VI), etc. Title X represents the section of transitional provisions, containing the constitutional rules that regulate provisional situations (in the Brazilian case, public policies) and regulate the institutional transition between the previous and the new Constitution. Among all Titles of the Brazilian Constitution, Title X was the object of the greatest number of constitutional amendments between 1988 and 2019.

From these data, we conclude that the high rate of amendments to the Brazilian Constitution is related to the fact that its wide scope regulates public policies that require updates with each new government. This statement is also based on the fact that almost 1/3rd of the 111 constitutional amendments had the purpose of amending Title X, which addresses transitional provisions. However, when changes in the constitution become routine practices of the constituted powers, the distinction between constitutional and ordinary politics is threatened by the banalization of the Constitution.

Furthermore, despite its importance to the structure of a dualistic constitutional order, procedural restrictions are not the only restrictions that exert some type of influence over the amending power because substantive content also seeks to perform the same restrictive functions. By predicting unamendable clauses, the constituent power determines that the initial constitutional project is not open to any changes. These limits, therefore, seek a reconciliation between the desires of permanence and of change by providing the freedom of restricted change.

The provision of substantive limits to amending power has become embodied as a tradition in Brazilian constitutional history because only the constitutions of 1824 and 1937 did not include these restrictions, the first because of its monarchical character and the second because of its authoritarian character. The Constitution of 1891 provided for the intangibility of the republican–federal form and the equality of the representation of states in the Federal Senate (article 90, § 4). These clauses were restricted to covering only the inalterability of the Federative Republic after the Constitution of 1934 (article 178, § 5); these limits were kept in the constitutions of 1946 (article 217, § 6°) and 1967 (article 50, § 1), as well as in Constitutional Amendment No. 1/69 (article 47, § 1).

With the Federal Constitution of 1988, there is an expansion of the substantive limits to constitutional amendments through, initially, the exclusion of the republic as an unamendable clause, followed by maintenance of the federation and the inclusion of direct, secret, universal and periodic voting, of the separation of powers, and of individual rights and guarantees (article 60, § 4). Note that the non-inclusion of the republic in this role interrupts the process of its frequent affirmation in time, precisely for a Constitution that emerged from a participatory process and that sought to satisfy collective interests. At the time of the creation of the Constitution of 1988, the constituents preferred to delegate to the popular will the definition of the form of government, republic or constitutional monarchy, according to the referendum held in 1993.

The main advantage associated with the stipulation of substantive limits to the amending power is to guarantee the continuity of the victorious constitutional project. Despite the possibility of amending the constitution, constituents embraced the notion of perfection of the foundational moment through the unamendable clauses. This perfectibility also serves to control eventual attempts at constitutional reform that seek to destroy the essential core of the Constitution.

The Brazilian Constitution provides that unamendable clauses cannot be the object of constitutional amendment that "tend to abolish them." It refers to a relative intangibility that protects only the suppression of what the jurisprudence of the Brazilian Federal Supreme Court (STF, for its abbreviation in Portuguese) considered to be their essential core but does not prevent the expansion or reduction in these rights. This position, therefore, grants a certain freedom of action to the representatives because they can manage the content of the entrenched clauses in different directions, as long as the content does not completely eliminate the minimum essence of these rights. However, from the moment control is taken over the constitutionality of constitutional amendments, this competence to interpret unamendable clauses is transferred to the STF because it determines whether a constitutional amendment violates, or not, unamendable clauses.[10] Such evaluation depends on the interpretation of the Judicial branch itself regarding the limit and scope of such clauses. As observed by Schwartzberg,[11] entrenchment does not guarantee protection against change but merely represents the immunization of content against popular decisions.

THE BRAZILIAN SUPREME COURT

As already stated, the Brazilian Constitution of 1988 represents an institutional framework able to restructure the relationship between powers after the military dictatorship. There is a consensus about the pivotal role of the STF as a direct consequence of the Constitution institutional arrangement. The constituents drafted the Brazilian Constitution to set an extensive system of judicial protection for fundamental rights, by means of several instruments that have strengthened access to the Judiciary. Specifically, in the case of the STF, its role was consolidated as a triple court: Constitutional Court; Court of Appeals and Criminal Court. In addition to constituent choices, STF centrality is a product of the Legislative delegation by means of constitutional amendments and ordinary legislation. Ultimately, the STF developed a decisional pattern extending its competences in favor of nonexplicit powers in the Constitution.

Regarding the form of organization of the Judiciary, the literature presents two models: the career model and the recognition model. The career model involves judges who join the judicial system when young and spend their entire career as judges, without significant party-political influences. In contrast, the recognition model selects older individuals with higher qualifications and an excellent reputation to be judges.[12] This latter model is characterized by the inclusion of political actors external to the Judicial Branch in those positions. The Brazilian judicial system primarily adopts the career system in initial instances of the Judiciary, while the Federal Supreme Court relies on the recognition model, which may lead to the inclusion of individuals who have never been a judge before.

Historically, immediately after the proclamation of the Republic in Brazil in 1889, the former Supreme Court of Justice was transformed into the current Supreme Court (STF). The Constitution of 1891 established that the STF be composed of 15 judges; this number was reduced to 11 judges in the Constitution of 1934, 1937, and 1946. At the beginning of the military dictatorship in 1965, the President of the Republic created 5 new seats–increasing from 11 to 16—to enable a majority favorable to the government in the Court. In 1969, three judges were compulsorily retired, and in that same year, the number of members was changed back to eleven judges. Finally, the Constitution of 1988 expressly confirmed the composition of the STF to consist of "eleven Justices, chosen among citizens older than 35 and younger than 65 years of age, of remarkable judicial knowledge and unimpeachable reputation." The constitutional process of nomination is initiated by the appointment of the President of the Republic, followed by approval by absolute majority of the members of the Senate after public hearing. The Justices are appointed for a life term and mandatorily retire at the age of 75. Therefore, accepting the position may mark the beginning of a long trajectory of influence on constitutional politics.

Among the several noteworthy aspects regarding the STF in the last 30 years is the fact that throughout its existence since the nineteenth century, of the 167 Justices who have seated in the Court, only 3 were women. The first female Justice of the STF was appointed in 2000 (Ellen Gracie). Currently, there are two female Justices: Carmen Lucia and Rosa Weber. On that point, notably, no political initiative to institutionally change this underrepresentation of the female gender in the STF has taken place thus far.

In addition, in 2002, the Brazilian Congress passed a law to create TV Justice, which is a public TV channel aimed to expand judicial transparency, mainly through the live broadcasting of STF decisions. Since then, hearings, oral opinions, and internal deliberations have been available on TV. This law has contributed to human rights decisions being more transparent to the general public. However, not only have the decisions become more public but individual Justices have also become famous through the daily news.

Due to the main features of the Brazilian Constitution described so far, the STF was called to interpret it several times, and it developed an unwritten understanding of the content of the fundamental rights. These decisions are not totally available to the international community because they are not translated into English. Based on this gap, we offer an original book with the main STF leading cases on human rights, with comments provided by great scholars in Brazil. The articles present a deep discussion on the characteristics of the cases and demonstrate how the STF has built legal arguments to interpret the extension of fundamental rights.

The book begins with an analysis of the rise of the STF as an important institutional actor in Brazilian politics after 1988 propelled by Professor Murilo Gaspardo of Universidade Estadual de São Paulo (UNESP). After this contextualization, twelve leading cases on human rights were selected. Unlike the United States, where cases are known by the names of the involved parties, in Brazil, cases are traditionally referred to by the subject matter of the decision.

Thus, a professor at the Universidade de São Paulo (USP), Cristina Bernardo de Oliveira, provides an analysis of a case related to the freedom of expression, involving the publication of a book with anti-Semitic content. Professors at the Universidade Federal do Paraná (UFPR), Estefânia Barboza and Melina Fachin, present a study on how the STF acted in cases that concerned the right to abortion. Lucas de Laurentiis, professor at Pontifícia Universidade Católica de Campinas (PUC-CAMP) presents a study on the decision that allowed scientific research with embryonic stem cells; in this particular case, the discussion is about an embryo's right to life. Professor Maria Paula Bucci of USP analyzes the decision of the STF that recognizes the constitutionality of racial quotas in Brazilian universities.

In 2011, the STF recognized the constitutionality of same-sex unions; Fernando Alves from Universidade Estadual do Norte do Paraná (UENP) analyzes the case. Regarding gender issues, Simone Lopes of the Universidade Federal de Juiz de Fora (UFJF) presents a study on the decision that recognizes homophobia as a crime.

In recent years, the STF was also called to rule on issues related to political rights, as was the case of party allegiance, which is analyzed by professor Orides Mezzaroba from the Universidade Federal de Santa Catarina (UFSC). In addition, another electoral issue analyzed is the decision that prohibited companies from donating to electoral campaigns, a case addressed by João Andrade Neto.

Professor Nina Ranieri at USP studies the social right to education, which was discussed at the STF on two occasions: in relation to religious teaching and to homeschooling. Still regarding social rights, Fernanda Duarte and Rafael Iório, both from "Estacio de Sá" University (UNESA), comment on the judicialization of the right to health in Brazil, especially with regard to the supply of drugs and high-cost treatments.

José Duarte Neto, also from UNESP, addresses the topic of the presumption of innocence. This discussion reaches its most controversial moment with the arrest of ex-president Lula da Silva and his request to run for office in the 2018 presidential election. The twelfth analyzed case corresponds to the decision of the STF to declare an unconstitutional state of affairs in regard to the Brazilian prison system. This study was produced by Professor Emerson de Oliveira from Universidade de Marília (UNIMAR). Lastly, the book concludes with a critical reflection on the main institutional challenges facing the STF to establish itself as guardian of human rights, developed by Flavia Santiago Lima from the Universidade de Pernambuco (UPE).

There are also several other important cases that deserve to be discussed within the international academic community. This book represents only an initial project to bring Brazil closer to studies of comparative constitutional law. As the following pages will demonstrate, the trajectory of decisions by the STF are not always consistent with each other. Just as political reality is composed of losses and gains, so is the judicial history of human rights in Brazil.

NOTES

1. According to these authors, "the median survival time (the age at which one-half of constitutions are expected to have die) is nineteen years". Elkins, Zachary; Ginsburg, Tom; Melton, James. *The Endurance of National Constitutions*. Cambridge University Press, 2009, p. 129.

2. In the Brazilian case, according to the Comparative Constitutional Project ranking, CF/88 ranks third in terms of the longest constitutional text in number of words, only behind the Constitution of India and Nigeria.

3. "The rights and guarantees expressed in this Constitution do not exclude others arising from the regime and the principles adopted by it or from international treaties the Federative Republic of Brazil signed".

4. Freire, Gilberto. *Casa-grande e senzala: formação da família brasileira sob o regime da economia patriarcal*. 48ª edição. São Paulo: Global, 2003.

5. Income inequality in Brazil is still a serious problem, as the country remains among those with the highest level of inequality, according to the World Inequality Report, 2018.

6. Bercovici, Gilberto. Revolution trough Constitution: the Brazilian's directive Constitution debate. *Revista de Investigações Constitucionais*, v. 1, n. 1, 2014, p. 9.

7. Lynch, Christian Edward Cyril; Mendonça, José Vicente Santos de. Por uma história constitucional brasileira: uma crítica pontual à doutrina da efetividade. *Revista Direito e Práxis*, v. 08, n. 2, 2017, p. 974–1007.

8. Couto, Claudio; Arantes, Rogério. Constitution, government and democracy in Brazil. *World Political Science Review*, v. 4, n. 2, 2008, p. 22.

9. The approval of a constitutional amendment in Brazil does not depend on a popular referendum, which is considered a factor that contributes to making the approval procedure more difficult, according to Donald Lutz (1994, p. 368). A constitutional amendment in Brazil is approved by the Chamber of Deputies and the Federal Senate, in two rounds of voting in each House, being approved with a 3/5 majority.

10. Lima, Jairo. *Emendas Constitucionais Inconstitucionais: democracia e supermaioria*. Rio de Janeiro: Lumen Juris, 2018.

11. Schwartzberg, Melissa. *Democracy and Legal Change*. Cambridge University Press, 2007.

12. Garoupa, Nuno; Ginsburg, Tom. *Judicial Reputation: A Comparative Theory*. Chicago: The University of Chicago Press, 2015, p. 28.

REFERENCES

Alvaredo, Facundo; Chancel, Lucas; Piketty, Thomas; Saez, Emmanuel; Zucman, Gabriel. *World Inequality Report*, 2018. Available in: https://wir2018.wid.world/files/download/wir2018-summary-english.pdf

Bercovici, Gilberto. Revolution trough constitution: the Brazilian's directive constitution debate. *Revista de Investigações Constitucionais*, v. 1, n. 1, 2014, p. 1–18.

Couto, Claudio; Arantes, Rogério. Constitution, government and democracy in Brazil. *World Political Science Review*, v. 4, n. 2, 2008, p. 1–33.

Elkins, Zachary; Ginsburg, Tom; Melton, James. *The Endurance of National Constitutions*. Cambridge University Press, 2009.

Freire, Gilberto. *Casa-grande e senzala: formação da família brasileira sob o regime da economia patriarcal*. 48ª edição. São Paulo: Global, 2003.

Garoupa, Nuno; Ginsburg, Tom. *Judicial Reputation: A Comparative Theory*. Chicago: The University of Chicago Press, 2015.

Lima, Jairo. *Emendas Constitucionais Inconstitucionais: democracia e supermaioria*. Rio de Janeiro: Lúmen Juris, 2018.

Lutz, Donald. Toward a Theory of Constitutional Amendment. *The American Political Science Review*, v. 88, n. 2, 1994.

Lynch, Christian Edward Cyril; Mendonça, José Vicente Santos de. Por uma história constitucional brasileira: uma crítica pontual à doutrina da efetividade. *Revista Direito e Práxis*, v. 08, n. 2, 2017, p. 974–1007.

Schwartzberg, Melissa. *Democracy and Legal Change*. Cambridge University Press, 2007.

Chapter 2

The Brazilian Supreme Court and Its Political Protagonism

An Overview of the STF and Its Rise to Prominence in Brazilian Politics after 1988

Murilo Gaspardo

INTRODUCTION

As part of the book *The Unwritten Brazilian Constitution: Human Rights in the Supreme Court*, the goal of this chapter is to present an overview of the rise of the Brazilian Supreme Federal Court (STF)[1] as a leading institution in constitutional politics after 1988. I will examine the increasing political participation of the judicial power, a phenomenon that is common in other countries as well, and will explain how the 1988 Constitution (and its complementary legal framework) enabled the STF to assume a leading role. I consider the political and cultural factors which aid in the comprehension of this phenomenon and finalize by addressing the paradox between the STF's contribution to the guarantee of human rights, versus the hazards that this position implies for democracy and institutional stability.

THE JUDICIAL POWER AND ITS POLITICAL ROLE: AN OVERVIEW

According to the classic doctrine of the separation of powers, the judicial power was considered politically neutral. Its function was to apply the law to specific cases, following general and abstract normative concepts as closely as possible. In the conception of the liberal state, the main role belonged to the legislative power, but the scope of its competence was restricted to a minimum, to ensure individual and economic freedom and to maintain order in social relations. The executive power, in turn, had as its fundamental functions the guarantee of external security and, internally, of order, protection of private property and the lawful execution of contracts.

During the twentieth century, and especially after World War II (taking into consideration the peculiarities of each country), the State gradually took on new social and economic functions. This tendency broadened the scope of legislative activity and, above all, increased participation of the executive power (or government), both in terms of political leadership and policy-making. With the increased recognition of human rights and the development of corresponding doctrines, the judicial power has assumed an increasingly active role in addressing social problems, striving for the common good, and guaranteeing human rights. Thus, we may observe a political protagonism of the judicial power, a phenomenon that, on different levels, takes place everywhere in the Western World.[2]

Until the constitutionalization of social rights, the law was understood as pertaining to the field of subjective rights, that is, legally protected interests, which were restricted to the private domain, while politics was the field of pure and simple interest, that is, the unprotected interests, which covered collective and indivisible goods. From the beginning of the twentieth century, there has been a "return of distributive disputes to the forefront of legal discourse, due to social constitutionalism." Thereby, the problem of collective and indivisible goods became part of the field of law.[3] This phenomenon occurred at the same time as the formation of the so-called *mass democracy*, the decline of the separation of powers and the supremacy of the parliament, in addition to the rise and expansion of the executive power.[4]

Together with the affirmation and assertion of social rights, the legal concept of programmatic norms was developed, that is, "rules of malleable and generic content, and indefinitely delayed effectiveness," perhaps due to the recognition of the restricted enforceable limits to which these social rights may be subjected.[5] In this respect, one may perceive both the legal character of social rights (with their enforceability by the courts) and the challenges for their implementation. Since social rights are clearly established in their legal capacity, so they are also deemed enforceable in the courts, albeit with the limitations that such situations present. Hence, the politicization of the judicial power means its participation in policy-making, which may or may not result in *judicial activism*. Judicial activism does not occur when such participation follows the constitutional commands; however, it does appear when the exercise of the jurisdictional function goes beyond the limits imposed by the rule of law. In other words, when the normative attributions of the constitution extend a series of political allowances to the judicial power—and it acts within these boundaries—one may perceive the constitutionally defined political role of the Judiciary. However, if the judicial power goes beyond its legal attributions and transcends its political role, it causes tension between the powers.[6] We may also note that the phenomenon of the judicialization of politics can be understood as the transference of the attributes of the so-called political powers (legislative and executive) to the judicial power, by way of the constitution and of legitimate constitutional interpretation.[7]

Having offered this general contextualization, one may ask what explains the rise of STF as an important protagonist in national politics after 1988, as well as whether its performance reveals only the politicization of the judicial power or, whether it also implies the practice of judicial activism. The Constitution of 1988 is the legal framework of the democratic transition that ended the authoritative period that started with the 1964 coup *d' etat*. It contemplates a wide range of civil, political, social, and economic rights and establishes: (a) guidelines for public policies, (b) sources of budget funds, and (c) jurisdictional guarantees for constitutional effectiveness. In addition, it strengthened the judicial power—the STF in particular—and established the Public Ministry (Public Prosecution Office) as the guardian of human rights.

In the political sphere, despite the free and periodic elections and socioeconomic advances such as price-stability, decrease in poverty, and expansion of public policies (a process that has suffered an inflection in recent years), there has been great political instability: two presidents suffered impeachment processes; there have been several cases of governmental corruption. There is also increasing frustration with unfulfilled promises of economic development and social benefits. This has led to a crisis of the executive and legislative powers' legitimacy, creating an opportunity for the expansion of the judicial power's political capabilities, which have been reinforced through the actions of politicians.

We may also observe a process of the transformation of "legal culture," through movements such as *neoconstitutionalism*, with an emphasis on juridical principles (as opposed to juridical rules) and enforcement via judicial decisions, interpretational freedom and relegation of the Judiciary as the main advocate for human rights. This can be observed in theoretical publications as well as in the legal training offered by undergraduate and graduate law schools.

In this sense, Vieira states that

> this visible process of expanding the authority of the courts around the world has gained even more pronounced contours in Brazil. The enormous ambition of the 1988 Constitution, in addition to the gradual concentration of powers within the STF's jurisdiction, which took place over the last twenty years, points to a change in the balance of the Separation of Powers system in Brazil.

> The Supreme Federal Court, which since 1988, had already accumulated the functions of constitutional court, top judicial board, and specialized jurisdiction, in the context of a legally ambitious Constitution, had its political role reinforced by the N. 3/93 and N. 45/05 Constitutional Amendments, as well as by N. 9.868/99 and N. 9.882/99 Federal Acts, becoming a singular institution in comparative terms, either considering its own history or the history of existing courts in other democracies, even the most prominent ones. *Supremocracy* is, as I call it—surely in an impressionistic fashion—the singularity of the Brazilian institutional arrangement.[8]

Thus, there is a set of normative, political, and cultural factors that explain the Brazilian STF's protagonism in national political activity after 1988, as I will discuss further below.

THE NORMATIVE FRAMEWORK OF THE BRAZILIAN CONSTITUTION

The 1988 Federal Constitution[9] presents 250 articles in its main text and 114 in the Transitional Constitutional Provisions Act (many of which were added in 2016, during Michel Temer's brief presidency, in the "New Public Budget Regime" Amendment). Between the Constitution's promulgation and March 2020, 105 Constitutional Amendments have been approved. It is an extensive, extremely detailed charter, which attempted to contemplate a diverse society's demands (many of them contradictory), presented during the transition to democracy.

In the words of Vieira and Barbosa

> the current Brazilian Constitution resulted from the broadest and most democratic pact signed in the country's history among the multiple political and institutional protagonists, sectors and social classes. The Brazilian reconstitutionalization did not follow a rupture with the ancient regime but was an essential part of the transitional process to which it lended its legal framework. Both the various democratizing forces and those which had supported and benefited from the authoritarian regime participated in the elaboration of the constituent. This explains its legally binding nature. The elaboration of this *Magna Carta* took place in a context of strong distrust, political fragmentation and in the absence of a hegemonic vision of the country itself. This situation explains why, in general, the various protagonists sought to maximize their own interests, prerogatives and aspirations, entrenching them in the constitutional body. The result of this strategy was a broad, detailed, ambitious and, in many ways, contradictory Constitution. Thus, it can be represented by the idea of a *maximizing commitment*. On the other hand, the text presents a series of regressive

> terms, based on the strong *corporatist* and *patrimonialist* aspects of the country's culture, aimed to concentrate income and power through a series of privileges and interests of bureaucratic statements and economic groups.[10]

A set of provisions originally foreseen in the 1988 Constitution contributed decisively to the politicization of judicial power and the STF's protagonism, as well as Constitutional Amendments and Federal Acts that regulate such constitutional provisions.[11] These may be organized into three categories: (1) a wide range of fundamental rights, together with guidelines for public policies, budgets, and financial sources; (2) the role, prerogatives, and powers attributed to the judicial power—and to the STF in particular—as well as to the institutions of the Public Ministry and the Public Defender's Office; (3) the constitutional control system.

The Constitution's Title II is dedicated to "Fundamental Rights and Guarantees." Its article 5 recognizes a wide range of civil rights, spread over 78 items. Article 6 establishes the following social rights: education, health, nourishment, employment, housing, transportation, leisure, security, social security, maternity and child protection, and assistance to the destitute. Article 7, with 34 items, deals specifically with the rights of urban and rural workers, and article 8 is dedicated to the right of workers unions. Finally, articles 14 and 15 contain political rights. The Constitution does not limit the list of rights and guarantees to those expressed in its text, prescribing that they "do not exclude others arising from the regime and principles adopted by it, or from international treaties to which the Federal Republic of Brazil is a part"[12] (art 5t § 2). This provision clearly indicates the wide possibilities given to the Supreme Court for the recognition of new fundamental rights.

The enunciation of social rights is complemented by a set of guidelines for the implementation of public policies, which compose the Constitutions' Title VIII, entitled "The Social Order" (Articles 193 forward). Its chapters deal with social security (health, pension, and social assistance) and education. Article 196, for instance, states that "health is the right of all and the duty of the state, guaranteed through social and economic policies which aim to reduce disease and other health problems, via equal and universal access to actions and services for their promotion, protection and recovery." Finally, there are guarantees of minimum investment of funds by a mechanism of mandatory budget, such as in article 201: "the Union will apply annually, never less than eighteen percent, and the States, the Federal District and the Municipalities, twenty-five percent, at least, of the revenue resulting from taxes, including those derived from transfers, in the maintenance and development of education."

The 1988 Constitution, therefore, due to a certain distrust of customary political process, sought to transform everything into constitutional issues, limiting the freedom of future elected representatives. Thus, "any abrupt movement made by administrators or legislators generates an incident of unconstitutionality, which, as a rule, will cascade onto the Supreme Court."[13] Such a broad set of fundamental rights and guidelines for public policies, in addition to the constitutional commandment which stipulates that "the law will not exclude the judicial power's right to assessment of injury or threat to any one right" (article 5, XXXV), would already be enough to give a great political power to STF.[14] However, there are more important elements to consider from the standpoint of the legal framework.

The administration's control system also contributes to the judicial power's politicization, because the 1988 Constitution enlarges the scope of popular action and public civil action, creating the collective *mandado de segurança* and emphasizing principles such as morality and efficiency. Such institutes have led the way for the control of administrative discretion.[15]

Brazil adopts the *Separation of Powers* system (Constitution, article 2) between legislative, executive and judicial. The latter, which is the focus of this chapter, has a complex structure (from article 92 forward), that is divided into Common Justice (State and Federal), Labor Justice, Military Justice and Electoral Justice, first instance judges, state (or regional) and higher courts, with the STF as the preeminent organ. Several prerogatives are guaranteed to the Judiciary (such as budget and administrative autonomy) and to its judges (lifelong position, the irreducibility of earnings, immovability from their positions without their consent). Although it is defined as the "guardian of the Constitution" (article 102), the STF is not just a Constitutional Court. It is within its jurisdiction to judge several kinds of actions (from article 102, I, "b" on), such as criminal offenses by high authorities, conflicts of jurisdiction etc. In addition, the STF also functions as an ordinary (article 102, II)[16] and extraordinary (article 102, III)[17] court of appeals.

Therefore, the STF has been assigned with functions that, in most contemporary democracies, are divided into at least three types of institutions: constitutional courts, specialized judicial courts (or simply diffused powers by the judicial system) and courts of appeal of last resort.[18]

The STF's power was reinforced by Constitutional Amendment N. 45/2004 (Judicial Power Reform), which, among other changes, established the Binding Precedent which, according to Ramos, "is an act of creation rather than application of the law."[19]

As provided in the Federal Constitution, Article 103 – A:

> The Supreme Federal Court may, *ex officio* or by provocation, by decision of two thirds of its members, after repeated decisions on constitutional matters, approve precedents that, from its publication in the official press, will have a

binding effect in relation to the other organs of the Judicial Power and direct and indirect public administration, at the federal, state and municipal levels, as well as revising or canceling them, as established by law.[20]

In addition to the judicial power, the constitutional conception of two other justice systems' institutions was fundamental to strengthen the STF's political role: the Public Ministry[21] and the Public Defender's Office.[22] Although they are not the only ones that may do so, these entities may refer demands which guarantee jurisdictional human rights to the court—and they possess the administrative and legal structure to do so.

The third element of the institutional framework that constitutes the protagonism assumed by the STF is the double system of Brazilian constitutional control: diffused (incidental, in the course of legal proceedings, between parties in litigation) and abstract (objective, without parties). Diffused control is exercised by all judges in all causes situations, while abstract constitutional control is concentrated in the STF. In the case of abstract control, "the final decisions of merit, pronounced by the STF, in Direct Actions of Unconstitutionality and in Declaratory Actions of Constitutionality will be effective against all, and have a binding effect in relation to other branches of judicial power, and the direct and indirect public administration, at the Federal, State and Municipal levels" (Federal Constitution, article 102, § 2). Actions of unconstitutionality can be presented to the Supreme Federal Court against legal or regulatory federal or state acts, while Constitutionality Declaratory Actions are limited to the federal ones (article 102, I). The Declaratory Action of Constitutionality, instituted by Constitutional Amendment N. 3/93, is revealed as an "anomalous kind of 'sanction' or judicial 'ratification'."[23]

There has been a great expansion of legitimate possibilities to file Direct Actions of Unconstitutionality,[24] which has made the filing of such actions quite common and politicized—for instance, when a small political party decides to plea unconstitutionality when it is defeated in a decision of the legislative branch. According to article 103 of the Constitution, the following entities have legitimate right to file Direct Actions of Unconstitutionality and Declaratory Actions of Constitutionality: I—the President of the Republic; II—the Bureau of the Federal Senate; III—the Bureau of the Chamber of Deputies; IV—the Bureau of the Legislative Assembly or Legislative Chamber of the Federal District; V—the State or Federal District Governor; VI—the General Attorney of the Republic; VII—the Federal Board of the Brazilian Bar Association; VIII—political party with representation in the National Congress; IX—union confederation or national class entities.

One may observe that abstract constitutional control includes constitutional amendments approved by the National Congress, both for formal (defective legislative process) and material reasons—in the event of a violation of the provisions of article 60, § 4th: "the proposal for an amendment to abolish: I – the federal form of State; II – direct, secret, universal and periodic vote; III – the separation of powers; IV – individual rights and guarantees." Abstract constitutional control also comprehends Direct Action of Unconstitutionality by Omission and Allegation of Disobedience of Fundamental Precept. It is also important to mention the *mandado de injunção*,"[25] because, although it is part of the diffuse control, it also can be judged by the STF in some situations.

The Direct Action of Unconstitutionality by Omission has the goal of making an effective constitutional rule. If it is judged to be valid, the STF formally acknowledges the "competent authority for adopting the necessary measures and, in the case of an administrative body, to do so within thirty days"[26] (article 102, § 2). The original interpretation of this provision by the STF was limited to the notification of the omission to the National Congress as a consequence of valid judgment, but later

> the Plenary of the Court has adopted the understanding that, in a prolonged period of omission, it is possible that the decision pronounced by the Supreme Federal Court is capable of regulating the subject, in a case of omission, during a given period or until the regulation is edited to fill the void. In these cases, the Court, without assuming an exercise typical of the legislative branch, has accepted the possibility that the judicial branch can temporarily regulate the matter.[27]

The Allegation of Disobedience of Fundamental Precept[28] can be proposed and must be considered by the STF based on the non-compliance with such precepts (article 102, § 1).

According to article 5, LXXI, of the Brazilian Constitution, the "*mandado de injunção* will be granted whenever a lack of regulatory rule makes it impossible to exercise constitutional rights and freedoms, as well as prerogatives inherent to nationality, sovereignty and citizenship." Its judgment rests with the STF "when the formulation of the regulatory norm is attributed to the President of the Republic, the National Congress, the Chamber of Deputies, the Federal Senate, the bureaus of one of the Legislative Houses, the Federal Court of Accounts, one of the Superior Courts, or the Supreme Federal Court" (Federal Constitution, article 102, I, q).[29] Within this normative framework, the STF became "responsible for having the last word on numerous substantial issues, validating and legitimizing, at times, decisions from the representative bodies, as well as others which replaced the choices of the majority." The extent of the list of constitutional matters that can be submitted to the STF's jurisdiction, in addition to its competence to control the *reforming constituent power*, cannot be compared to any other Constitutional Court.[30]

THE LEGITIMACY CRISIS OF EXECUTIVE AND LEGISLATIVE BRANCHES AND TRANSFORMATIONS IN JURIDICAL CULTURE

Political parties and unions, institutions linked to the circle of the government and parliament, were forged to channel social conflicts through the formulation of public policies and to the defense of long-term and general interests, in other words, those that affect society as a whole, through pressure and actions with these institutions. However, given the perception of limits for the government and parliament to carry out the obligations of the constitution, along with the weakening of representative democracy and the loss of representation of political parties, new social protagonists have appeared in recent decades and are organizing to fight for specific rights, as well as to seek recognition (feminists, blacks, LGBTs, etc.). Thus, non-governmental environmental organizations and social movements in general started to view the judicial power (and the STF, in particular) as a political interlocutor or a place to wage the battle for the defense of human rights.[31]

There are relevant differences in the performance of political parties and these new social protagonists. For example, to address the defense of educational rights, a political party would seek to discuss and mobilize society in order to promote a broad educational reform, which would be the topic for debate in legislative and executive elections. Meanwhile, a neighborhood association would mobilize and eventually file suit in the Public Ministry, demanding the construction of a school in the neighborhood.

Thus, the current appreciation of the judicial power can be explained as a

> response to the disqualification of politics and the demise of the democratic being within the new conditions brought about by the decadence of the Welfare State. [. . .] This Power and its institutions are thus perceived as being the reliable safeguards for equality, as well as behaving as substitutes for the State, to political parties, to family, and to religion, which would no longer be able to continue to fulfill their functions of social solidarity.[32]

This involves, among other risks, the transformation of the citizen into a client who is dependent on the State, as well as the privatization of citizenship. Despite this, it permits the possibility of a citizenship, which is parallel or proximate to the government/parliament circle, in which case the judicial power becomes a prominent arena for the struggle for the expansion of citizenship.[33]

In the case of Brazil, some factors that have contributed to this loss of confidence in the political parties and their representatives are: (a) "the inefficiency of the representative powers in adopting the normative measures"[34] necessary for the realization of the rights expressed in the Constitution; (b) successive reforms to privatize public services and to de-constitutionalize rights that occurred after the country's re-democratization process, leading those affected by these measures to seek the judicial power;[35] (c) successive corruption scandals involving leaders and political parties; (d) the growing media appeal of jurisdictional activity, particularly with the live broadcasts of the STF's sessions and the emphasis given to controversial judgments on civil rights and criminal actions involving high State officials.

In addition to the normative and political factors presented, the transformation of the legal culture itself also explains the growing political protagonism of the judicial power and the STF in particular. This transformation involves legal training and important theoretical changes, especially in constitutional hermeneutics and the contributions of the movement that is often called "neo-constitutionalism," which presents a historical, philosophical and theoretical framework. The historic landmark of neoconstitutionalism is post-war constitutionalism in Western Europe, especially with the enactment of the Bonn Basic Law, the German Constitution of 1949, and the creation of the Federal Constitutional Court, installed in 1951. In Brazil, the historic landmark is the 1988 Constitution[36] itself.

In the philosophical field, the main element was the development of post-positivism from the "historical overcoming of jusnaturalism and the political failure of positivism." Post-positivism

> seeks to go beyond strict legality, but does not disregard the positive law; seeks to undertake a moral reading of law, but without resorting to metaphysical categories. The interpretation and application of the legal system must be inspired by a theory of justice, but it cannot include voluntarisms or personalisms, especially when judicial. Within the set of rich and heterogeneous ideas that seek shelter in this paradigm-under-construction includes the attribution of normativity to the principles and the definition of their relations with values and rules, the rehabilitation of practical reason and legal arguments, the formation of a new constitutional hermeneutics, and the development of a theory of fundamental rights built on the foundation of human dignity. In this environment, a rapprochement between law and philosophy is promoted.[37]

In the field of legal theory, there are three major transformations: "a) the recognition of the normative force of the constitution, b) the expansion of constitutional jurisdiction, c) the development of a new dogma of constitutional interpretation." This new constitutional hermeneutics, in practice, means that the interpreter has greater freedom to go beyond the abstract text of the constitutional norm to address concrete legal problems. In turn, the judge is no longer the individual who just must "reveal the solution contained in the normative statement. The interpreter becomes a co-participant in the process of creating the law, completing the legislator's work, making assessments of meaning for open clauses and making choices between possible solutions."[38]

As Ávila summarizes, "neoconstitutionalism" has the following characteristics: principles instead of rules (or more principles than rules); reflection in place of subsumption (or more reflection in place of subsumption); private justice instead of general justice (or more individual and concrete analysis than general and abstract); judicial instead of legislative or executive powers (or more judicial and less legislative and executive powers); constitution replacing the legal and regulatory acts (or greater, or direct, application of the constitution as opposed to legal and regulatory acts).[39]

FINAL CONSIDERATIONS

The judicial power, conceived in the classic liberal model as "politically neutral," has assumed, in the last decades, a growing political protagonism, which is manifest in demands for the realization of social rights, in the electoral process, in the fight against corruption and in the very legislative process itself. In the STF, this phenomenon is observed in a particularly intense way. The explanations are diverse, ranging from the institutional design established by the Brazilian Constitution, the influence of currents of legal doctrine such as the so-called neoconstitutionalism, including the legitimacy crisis of the "Government/Parliament circle." Such protagonism, initially seen as an instrument for guaranteeing human rights and the democratic institutions themselves, also encountered criticism regarding its possible contribution to dysfunctionalities in democratic regimes, when manifest as judicial activism, that is, as the political performance which goes beyond the limits established by the Constitution. This is aggravated by the fact that the STF faces difficulties in operating as a collegiate body (often due to excessive demands), resulting in the predomination of monocratic decisions.

Therefore, although the STF is fundamental in "the keeping of the Brazilian Constitution," as well as imperative in the guarantee of human rights, the Court cannot be immune to controls. On the other hand, these controls should not take on an electoral nature, under penalty of denaturing its basis for legitimacy (legal reason), as well as its counter-majority nature (indispensable for the protection of minorities and the rule of law and democracy itself). Consequently, as Vieira states, there must be "a rationalization of its jurisdiction and a polishing of its deliberative process, in order to restrict the political tensions inherent to the exercise of a constitutional jurisdiction such as the one in Brazil."[40]

In the same sense, Mendes states that "(1) if democracy is not just the will of the majority, an anti-majority institution is desirable and necessary and (2) if the constitution is supreme and must be obeyed even by the legislator, there must be an external controlling agent that oversees such obedience." However, it is necessary to "reaffirm the uncertainty and fallibility of politics." as well as to "reduce expectations in relation to the constitutional court."[41] Thus, an alternative could be a "deliberative interaction" between the powers, which "does not eliminate the possibility of error, but maximizes the possibility of success." Thus, the constitutional control by the Supreme Federal Court does not need to be seen primarily as a dyke or a barrier, but may also be seen as a source of propulsion for more qualified deliberations.[42]

NOTES

1. This is the acronym in Portuguese (*Supremo Tribunal Federal*) and may appear as such in this article.
2. Vieira, 2008, p. 442–443.
3. Lopes, 2004, p. 137–170, Vianna et al., 1999, p. 15–19.
4. Castro, 2006, p. 46.
5. Castro, 2006, p. 52.
6. Ramos, 2009, p. 2. The author (2009, p. 8) identifies as *activist* the exercise of the judicial function in constitutional matters "contrary to the Constitution and the Law."
7. Ramos, 2009, p. 88.
8. Vieira, 2008, p. 444.
9. Brasil. Constituição Federal de 1988. Brasília: Congresso Nacional, 1988.
10. Vieira e Barbosa, 2018, p. 376.
11. Ferreira Filho (2009, p. 190) states that the 1988 Constitution is "largely responsible" for the phenomenon of the politics judicialization, because "it attributed to the Judicial Power, in addition to its traditional role of *legal guardian*, a new one: the legitimacy guardian."
12. Constitution, Article 5, § 3: "The international human rights treaties and conventions that are approved, in each House of National Congress, in two rounds, by three fifths of the respective members' votes, will be equivalent to the Constitutional Amendments."
13. Vieira, 2008, p. 447.

14. There are several procedural instruments foreseen in the Constitution to promote the defense of Human Rights, among which we highlight: *habeas corpus*, *habeas data*, individual and collective *mandado de segurança* (a Brazilian innovation in the constitutional field that could be translated as *writ of mandamus*).

15. For more details on the subject, see Ferreira Filho, 2009, p. 253–256. The role of the 1988 Constitution to the Judiciary in controlling elections is also a relevant issue.

16. It is incumbent upon the STF to judge, on ordinary appeal: "a) habeas corpus, writ of mandamus, habeas data and injunction order decided in a single instance by the Superior Courts, if the decision is denied; b) political crime."

17. It is incumbent upon the STF to judge, through an extraordinary appeal, the cases decided in a single or last instance, when the contested decision: "a) contradicts the provision of this Constitution; b) declare a federal treaty or law unconstitutional; c) deem a valid law or act of local government contested in light of this Constitution. d) to judge valid local act challenged in face of federal act."

18. Vieira, 2008, p. 447.

19. Ramos, 2009, p. 252. By the way, Ferreira Filho (2009, p. 245) points out that the binding precedent "are normative statements comparable to interpretive constitutional norms. This, combined with the power to restrict the effects of the declaration of unconstitutionality, reinforces the idea that the STF has assumed the role of derived constituent." A clear example of this is the Binding Precedent N. 13, in which the STF prohibited the practice of nepotism, as a result of the constitutional principle of administrative morality.

20. Constitution, Art. 103 – A, § 1: The precedent will aim at the validity, interpretation and effectiveness of specific rules, about which there is current controversy between judicial bodies or between them and the public administration that causes serious legal insecurity and relevant multiplication of processes on the same issue.

21. Constitution, Article 127. "The Public Ministry is a permanent institution, essential to the State's jurisdictional function, with the task of defending the legal order, the democratic regime and unavailable social and individual interests."

22. Constitution, Article 134. "The Public Defender's Office is a permanent institution, essential to the jurisdictional function of the State, entrusting it, as an expression and instrument of the democratic regime, fundamentally, the legal orientation, the promotion of human rights and defense, in all the degrees, judicial and extrajudicial, of individual and collective rights, in full and free of charge, to the needy, in the form of item LXXIV of 5th Art. 5 of this Federal Constitution."

23. Cf. Ferreira Filho, 2009, p. 218 and ss.

24. Previously, it was the exclusive responsibility of the General Attorney of the Republic.

25. It could be translated as *injunction*, but it is not the same as the English and American injunctions, it is a typical Brazilian institute.

26. The procedural discipline of the Direct Action of Unconstitutionality by Omission was established by Federal Act 12.063 / 2009.

27. Brazil. STF. About the Court: Judicial Review. Available at: <https://www2.stf.jus.br/portalStfInternacional/cms/verConteudo.php?sigla=portalStfSobreCorte_en_us&idConteudo=120199>. Access in: Apr. 9th 2020.

28. "In terms of the Law 9.882/99, the allegation of disobedience of fundamental precept is suited to avoid or repair grievance to a fundamental precept, as a result of an act of the public power. As a typical instrument of concentrated constitutional control, the allegation of disobedience of fundamental precept can be used, either directly or indirectly, to impugn or challenge a law or a regulation issued by a municipality, a state or the Federation. In the first but not in the second case, the action is original. That means that in the second case the action is given rise by a previous legal dispute or a concrete situation (it has an incidental character). Law 9.882/99 imposes that the allegation of disobedience of fundamental precept can only be admitted if there is no other efficient way to sane the grievance (article 4, § 1). The decision of a case of allegation of disobedience of fundamental precept can also show modulation of effects." Brazil. STF. About the Court: Judicial Review. Available at: <https://www2.stf.jus.br/portalStfInternacional/cms/verConteudo.php?sigla=portalStfSobreCorte_en_us&idConteudo=120199>. Access in: Apr. 9th 2020. See also: Supremo Tribunal Federal. Legislação Anotada – Leis Infraconstitucionais – Versão Integral. Lei Federal 9888/1999. Available at: <http://www.stf.jus.br/arquivo/cms/publicacaoPublicacaoTematica/anexo/Lei_9882.pdf >. Access in: Apr. 2nd, 2020

29. "The Constitution of 1988 acknowledged a particular meaning to the judicial review of the so-called legislator omission. The article 5, LXXI, of the Constitution expressly stipulated that the "mandado de injunção" shall be granted whenever the lack of regulation of a constitutional rule makes infeasible to practice a constitutional right or a prerogative inherent to the status nationality, sovereignty and citizenship. The "mandado de injunção" is a remedy to be used when the legislator did not comply with his/her duty to enact a law, as required by the Constitution, and this breach affects affirmed constitutional rights." Brazil. STF. About the Court: Judicial Review. Available at: <https://www2.stf.jus.br/portalStfInternacional/cms/verConteudo.php?sigla=portalStfSobreCorte_en_us&idConteudo=120199>. Access in: Apr. 9th 2020.

30. Vieira, 2008, p. 444–445.

31. In this sense, see Campilongo, 1998, p. 32–34. On the pressure of social movements over the Judicial Power, see Lopes, 1998, p. 80–81.

32. Favetti, 2003, p. 34. The author defines the judicialization of politics as the "phenomenon in which there is a transfer of political conflict from its own arena (political arena) to a legal arena." And he adds: "this phenomenon is typical of states with Separation of Powers and means the expansion of the role of the Judicial Power in the system of Power."

33. On the role of the courts, see: Santos, 1996, p. 13.

34. Ramos, 2009, p. 246.

35. Frischeisen, 2004, p. 74–77.

36. Barroso, 2006, p. 2–4.

37. Barroso, 2006, p. 5.

38. Barroso, 2006, p. 5–8.

39. Ávila, 2009, p. 2.

40. Vieira, 2008, p. 457.

41. Mendes, 2008, p. 4–5.

42. Mendes, 2008, p. 214–215.

REFERENCES

Ávila, Humberto. "Neoconstitucionalismo": entre a "Ciência do Direito" e o "Direito da Ciência." In: *Revista Eletrônica de Direito do Estado (REDE)*. Salvador: Instituto Brasileiro de Direito Público, n. 17, jan./fev./mar. de 2009. Disponível na Internet: <http://www.direitodoestado.com.br/rede.asp>.

Barroso, Luis Roberto. Neoconstitucionalismo e constitucionalização do Direito (O triunfo tardio do direito constitucional no Brasil), *Questio Iuris*, v. 2, n. 1, Rio de Janeiro, 2006. pp. 1–48.

Brasil. *Constituição Federal de 1988*. Brasília: Congresso Nacional, 1988.

Brasil. *Lei Federal No. 9882/1999* (Dispõe sobre o processo e julgamento da arguição de descumprimento de preceito fundamental, nos termos do § 1º do art. 102 da Constituição Federal). Brasília: Congresso Nacional, 1999.

Brasil. *Lei Federal 12.063/2009* (Acrescenta à Lei no 9.868, de 10 de novembro de 1999, o Capítulo II-A, que estabelece a disciplina processual da ação direta de inconstitucionalidade por omissão). Brasília: Congresso Nacional, 2009.

Brasil. *Lei Federal No. 13.300/2016* (Disciplina o processo e o julgamento dos mandados de injunção individual e coletivo e dá outras providências). Brasília: Congresso Nacional, 2016.

Brazil. Supreme Federal Court. About the Court: Judicial Review. Available at: <https://www2.stf.jus.br/portalStfInternacional/cms/verConteudo.php?sigla=portalStfSobreCorte_en_us&idConteudo=120199>. Access in: Apr. 9th 2020.

Campilongo, Celso Fernandes. Os Desafios do Judiciário: um Enquadramento Teórico. In: Faria, José Eduardo (org.). *Direitos Humanos, Direitos Sociais e Justiça*. São Paulo, Malheiros, 1998, pp. 30–51.

Campilongo, Celso Fernandes. *Política, Sistema Jurídico e Decisão Judicial*. São Paulo: Max Limonad, 2002, 193.

Castro, Marcos Faro de. Instituições Econômicas: Evolução de seus Elementos Constitucionais na Sociedade de Mercado, *Revista de Direito Empresarial, Curitiba*, v. 1, n. 6, jul./dez. 2006, pp. 41–62.

Castro, Marcos Faro de. Julgar a Economia, *Rev. TST*, v. 68, n. 1, Brasília, jan./mar. 2002, pp. 190–203.

Favetti, Rafael Thomaz. *Controle de Constitucionalidade e Política Fiscal*. Porto Alegre: Sérgio Antônio Fabris, 2003.

Faria, José Eduardo. Direito e Justiça no Século XXI: a Crise da Justiça no Brasil. *Seminário Direito e Justiça no Século XXI*. Coimbra: Centro de Estudos Sociais, de 20 de maio a 1º de junho de 2003, 40p.

Faria, José Eduardo. O Judiciário e os Direitos Humanos e Sociais: Notas para uma Avaliação da Justiça Brasileira. In: Faria, José Eduardo (org.). *Direitos Humanos, Direitos Sociais e Justiça*. São Paulo: Malheiros, 1998, pp. 94–111.

Ferreira Filho, Manoel Gonçalves. *Aspectos do Direito Constitucional Contemporâneo*. 2ª ed. São Paulo: Saraiva, 2009.

Frischeisen, Luiza Cristina Fonseca. *Construção da Igualdade e o Sistema de Justiça no Brasil: alguns caminhos e possibilidades*. Tese (Doutorado em Direito). São Paulo: Faculdade de Direito da Universidade de São Paulo, 2004.

Lopes, José Reinaldo de Lima. A Função Política do Poder Judiciário. In: Faria, José Eduardo (org.). *Direito e Justiça – A Função Social do Judiciário*. São Paulo: Ática, 1989, pp. 123–144.

Lopes, José Reinaldo de Lima. Crise da Norma Jurídica e Reforma do Judiciário. In: Faria, José Eduardo (org.). *Direitos Humanos, Direitos Sociais e Justiça*. São Paulo: Malheiros, 1998, pp. 68–93.

Lopes, José Reinaldo de Lima. Direito Subjetivo e Direitos Sociais: O Dilema do Judiciário no Estado Social de Direito. In: Faria, José Eduardo (org.). *Direitos Humanos, Direitos Sociais e Justiça*. São Paulo, Malheiros, 1998, pp. 113–143.

Lopes, José Reinaldo de Lima. Raciocínio Jurídico e Economia, *Revista de Direito Público da Economia*, v. 2, n. 8, Belo Horizonte, out./dez. 2004, pp. 137–170.

Mendes, Conrado Hübner. *Direitos fundamentais, separação de poderes e deliberação*. Tese (Doutorado) apresentada ao Departamento de Ciência Política da Faculdade de Filosofia, Letras e Ciências Humanas (FFLCH) da Universidade de São Paulo (USP). São Paulo: Universidade de São Paulo, 2008.

Ramos, Elival da Silva. *Parâmetros Dogmáticos do Ativismo Judicial em Matéria Constitucional (Tese de Titularidade)*. São Paulo: Universidade de São Paulo, 2009.

Vianna, Luiz Weneck et al. *A Judicialização da Política e das Relações Sociais no Brasil*. Rio de Janeiro: Revan, 1999.

Vieira, Oscar Vilhena. Supremocracia, *Revista Direito GV*, v. 4, n. 2, 2008, pp. 441–464. São Paulo: jul.—dez.

Vieira, Oscar Vilhena e Barbosa, Ana Laura Pereira. Do compromisso maximizador à resiliência constitucional, Dossiê 30 anos da constituição brasileira, *Novos Estudos CEBRAP*, v. 37, n. 3, 2018, pp. 375–393, Set.—Dez.

Chapter 3

Freedom of Speech

Ellwanger Case

Cristina Godoy Bernardo de Oliveira

INTRODUCTION

The Ellwanger case was a landmark to Brazilian jurisprudence because the Supreme Court decided that anti-Semitic acts constitute the crime of racism. In addition, the Court balanced the principle of the dignity of human beings with freedom of expression and stated that freedom of expression is not absolute. Although freedom of expression is important in a democracy, the equality justice and the protection of the dignity of human beings are limits to the exercise of freedom of expression.

There are many issues related to freedom of expression; consequently, this chapter will remark the most important discussions that the Supreme Court faced to decide in Ellwanger case. Furthermore, the debate about the meaning of the word "race" is relevant to understand the position of the Supreme Court regarding the scope of the term.

After the Ellwanger case, there were some anti-Semitic cases but nothing that is getting worse. The non-governmental organizations are making efforts in order to reduce anti-Semitism and prejudice in Brazil. Consequently, the historical revisionism did not strengthen in Brazil afterwards.

Finally, this chapter focuses on the case study and on the impact of the Ellwanger case. After the description of historical backgrounds, the problem related to the tension between freedom of expression and Democratic principles will be analyzed. Lastly, a review of the developments in the Ellwanger case and the anti-Semitic movement will be studied to understand the current scenario in Brazil regarding anti-Semitism.

HISTORICAL BACKGROUNDS

Siegfried Ellwanger was born in Candelária, State of Rio Grande do Sul, in Brazil. He founded the Revision Press (Revisão Editora) in 1987, which was responsible for the launch of several books that have discriminatory, anti-Semitic, and historical revisionism content, such as: *Holocaust*: *Jewish or German? Behind the Scenes of the Lie of the Century*; *No more Gas ... the end of a myth*; *SOS for Germany*; *The truth about Jewish-Catholic Dialogue in Brazil*; *Innocent in Nuremberg* etc.

Ellwanger, the founder of the Revision Press, could not finish High School due to financial problems in his family. He started to sell food that was prepared by his mother. Afterwards, he worked at a sugar factory. In 1946, he became a Marine and moved to the State of Rio de Janeiro.

In 1948, Ellwanger returned to the State of Rio Grande do Sul and he worked at an important iron and steel company. After eight years, he was invited by another iron and steel company in order to assume the position of manager.

In 1966, he founded his own iron and steel company and he became a successful businessman in the State of Rio Grande do Sul.[1]

After running his company for 20 years, Ellwanger decided to write his first book, *Holocaust*: *Jewish or German? Behind the Scenes of the Lie of the Century*, that was published in 1987. He decided to adopt a pseudonym, S.E. Castan, that caused confusion in the Jewish community because the surname Castan had Jewish origin.

The pseudonym was not a disrespectful joke against the Jews, but it was the middle name of Ellwanger, little used by him, and was his mother's surname. Palloti Press published the first edition of the book, and in spite of the impact of this book in the State of Rio Grande do Sul, Ellwanger founded his own publisher, Revision Press.

A historical data that is important to remark is the fact that the Revision Press was founded three years after the end of the Military Regime in Brazil. Therefore, this was a period that the population intended to protect freedom at all costs, after more than two decades of censorship and dictatorship.

According to the former Brazilian President, Fernando Henrique Cardoso, the return to democracy was a moment that it was *forbidden to forbid*.[2] Thus, this scenario contributed to the dissemination of the revisionism until 1996.

In addition, there are three different moments the publisher (Revision Press) went through[3]: 1) From 1987 until 1996: historical revisionism and anti-Semitic books; 2) from 1996 until 1999: Ellwanger was sued by many people and Jewish associations. Thus, he was not as explicit as previously; and 3) from 1999 until 2003: Revision Press started to publish its work on the Internet.

At each moment, the publisher went through several transformations in order to modify its objectives to avoid lawsuits. Therefore, Revision Press invited many authors, participants of nationalist and integralist movements, to cover the true scope of the publisher that was to spread anti-Semitic ideologies.

The first book that was written by Ellwanger, *Holocaust: Jewish or German? Behind the Scenes of the Lie of the Century*, had an explicit denialist content. The author argued that Germany was the real victim on account of the indemnities that it paid after World War II for crimes that were not committed.[4] In this book, there are quotes from the book of Henry Ford, entitled *International Jew*, in which Ford claims that the Germans were exploited by a gang of Jews.[5]

The quotation of other authors and the use of revisionist theory are strategies to cover the real intention of Ellwanger that is the dissemination of an anti-Semitic ideology. Thus, Ellwanger based his statements on claims of other authors to give his book a scientific look and avoid being sued.

The Revision Press published books that were written by other revisionists, such as Sérgio Oliveira and Marco Polo Giordani. These deniers mention texts like *Protocols of the Wise Men of Zion* as a resource of their books.

The book entitled *Holocaust: Jewish or German? Behind the Scenes of the Lie of the Century* is available for sale in Brazilian Amazon. In addition, there are a lot of these books in digital format nowadays. Thus, it is not difficult to read any of this denialist book in Brazil.

The activities of the Revision Press caused a lot of discussions, and in November of 1991, the prosecutor of the State of Rio Grande do Sul sued Mr Ellwanger regarding his violation of the article 20 of the Law 8.081/90: "practicing, inducing or inciting, through the media or by publication of any nature, discrimination or prejudice of race, colour, religion, ethnicity or national origin."

The Racial Crime Law, Law 7.716, is known as the Caó Law, was modified by the Law 8.081/90. Thus, the trial of the Ellwanger case was the Law 7.716 modified by Law 8.801/90. Consequently, Ellwanger was sued by the prosecution for the crime of racism.

After a public mobilization made by several collective groups, like Antiracist People's Movement (MOPAR—Movimento Popular Antirracista), the Jewish Movement, the Black Movement, and the Justice and Human Rights Movement, the Court of Justice of Rio Grande do Sul condemned Ellwanger for the practice of the crime of racism in October 1996.

The Court of Justice of the State of Rio Grande do Sul condemned Ellwanger for the crime of the article 20 of the Law 8.081/90 due to the abuse of their freedom of expression, exceeding the limits allowed by law. In addition, according to article 5, XLXII of the Federal Constitution of Brazil (FC/88), the statute of limitations never expires in the crime of racism.

The defense of Ellwanger appealed, arguing that the Ellwanger could not be condemned by the crime of racism because the Jews did not constitute a race. Thus, the statute of limitations expired because Ellwanger did not practice the crime of racism, but discriminatory acts.

In this way, the Supreme Court analyzed the Habeas Corpus (HC 82.424-2/RS) filed by the defense of Ellwanger and decided on September 2003. After an extensive debate, the Supreme Court stated: "the division of human being into races results from a process of merely political-social content. From this assumption comes racism, which in turn generates discrimination and segregationist prejudice." The decision maintained Ellwanger conviction for the crime of racism and this case was considered "a historical landmark case regarding the prohibition of antisemitism and racism directed to the Jewish ethnicity, by condemning criminal practices against the Semites."[6]

Afterwards, the debate on freedom of expression and the protection of democracy become relevant to understand why this decision of the Supreme Court is considered a landmark in the discussion related to the fight against racism.

FREEDOM OF SPEECH × DEMOCRACY

The Supreme Court decided that the division of human races is a consequence of a social and political process, but there is not a biological division. Thus, this human division is based on racist ideologies that aim to discriminate and segregate certain groups of the society. According to Professor Ronaldo Porto Macedo Júnior, "this process gives birth to racism, which in turn generates discrimination and segregationist prejudice."[7]

In addition, the moral and political standards of the Federal Constitution of Brazil could not harmonize with crimes of racism. The Democratic Rule of Law demands the protection of the dignity of the human being and the peaceful coexistence between the people of Brazil. Thus, the discrimination against Jews could not be accepted by democratic institutions in Brazil and the freedom of speech is not an absolute constitutional principle.

According to the Supreme Court, the Revision Press denied historical facts as the Holocaust spread anti-Semitic ideas and incited discrimination against Jews. Therefore, the limits of the principle of the freedom of speech were exceeded and Mr. Ellwanger is convicted for the crime of racism.

The freedom of speech is fundamental in a democracy, but it is not an absolute principle because the discrimination attacks the dignity of human beings and prejudiced ideas violate the structure of the Brazilian constitutional order. In addition, "the Justices understood that, in this case, the conduct of the petitioner in publishing books with anti-Semitic content was explicit, revealing a manifest intention to deceive, as he based himself on the wrong premise that the Jews are not only a race, but more than that, a fundamentally and genetically lesser and pernicious racial segment."[8]

Consequently, the principle of proportionality was used to resolve the apparent conflict between fundamental rights in the Ellwanger case. On the one hand, protection of the dignity of the Jews was necessary; on the other hand, freedom of expression must be guaranteed in a democracy.

The former Ministry of Foreign Affairs of Brazil, Celso Lafer,[9] was invited to participate as amicus curiae in the trial process. According to his opinion, racism is a violation of the principle of equality justice and constitutes a way of not recognizing the rights of the other in a society.

The Supreme Court decided, by 8 votes to 3, that the crime of racism is a limitation on the principle of freedom of expression and anti-Semitic ideologies are examples of the crime of racism. Thus, as Paulo Gustavo Gonet Branco stated: "Freedom of expression, therefore, may suffer a setback when its content jeopardizes a democratic education, free from prejudiced hatreds and founded on the superior intrinsic value of every human being."[10]

The three divergent votes of the Plenary of the Supreme Court are from Justices Moreira Alves, Carlos Britto, and Marco Aurélio. The three Justices understood that the crime of racism was not practiced when publishing books that denied the existence of the Holocaust, for example. Furthermore, according to Ellwanger, the real victims were the Germans because Jews are described in his book as a race that dominates other peoples. Finally, freedom of expression must be protected in a democracy, and publishing books with historical revisionist content should not be considered a crime of racism.[11]

Although the three divergent votes considered the inexistence of the practice of the crime of racism, the majority of the Supreme Court argued that the principle of equality justice and of the dignity of human beings are external limitation on freedom of expression. Thus, hate speech and the crime of racism could not be tolerated in Brazil despite the importance of the principle of freedom of expression.

In this way, the Supreme Court decided that race is not a biological criterion but a social and political criterion. Therefore, Ellwanger was convicted for the practice of the crime of racism because Jews could be considered a race and the principle of freedom of expression is not absolute. Thus, this case was important because of the explicit prohibition of anti-Semitism and racism against the Jewish ethnicity by the majority of votes of the Brazilian Supreme Court.

BRAZIL AFTER THE ELLWANGER CASE

The Ellwanger case is a leading case because of the impact of the decision of the Supreme Court on the understanding of the crime of racism. Thus, the study of the outcome of this decision in Brazil is relevant to evaluate the racism in Brazil and the judicial decisions after more than a decade of the trial of the Ellwanger case.

There were several websites that disseminated anti-Semitic ideas in Brazil, such as www.valhalla88.com and www.thitepowersp.org (these websites were offline by court order since 2012[12]). Furthermore, the site "Zylon-b Wear," the so-called non-profit organization, raised money with the sales of books to support the organizations that were Pro-white cause. The books of the Revision Press were in the catalog of the "Zylon-b Wear" with other racist contents and "remained online until mid-2008."[13]

In May 2005, a group of neo-Nazi attacked Jews in the city of Porto Alegre in the same date of the anniversary of the Nazi surrender.[14] After the attack, a seizure warrant was issued in the homes of the members of the neo-Nazi group and copies of books of the Revision Press were found with other anti-Semitic materials.[15] In 2018, three members of the neo-Nazi group were convicted for the attack and the Israeli Federation of Rio Grande do Sul, in a note, stated that the justice was done.[16]

In 2007, Federal deputy Marcelo Itagiba (PMDB/RJ) proposed a bill (Projeto 987/2007) that aims to change the article 20 of Law 7.716 in order to include the crime of the denial of the Holocaust.[17] The project was not enacted until now (April 2020) due to the manifestation of many groups that consider that the freedom of expression will be violated if this bill passes.

The Israeli Confederation of Brazil (Conib) was founded in 1948, and FGV Law worked together in a project that aimed to develop standards that could help judges to identify acts of racism on the Internet. Thus, the scope is to harmonize freedom of expression with the protection of the dignity of human beings.

In this way, a guide[18] was written to help judged to balance the two principles that are protected by the Federal Constitution: freedom of expression and the dignity of human beings. Furthermore, a tool was developed to evaluate hate speech and "this is a matrix of variables that allows the identification, evaluation and sanctioning of 'hate speech', through algorithms for identification, evaluation and, consequently, development of possible forms of punishment for hate speech and its possible derivations, incitement to racism, prejudice and violence."[19]

The "1st International Legal Forum against Discrimination" held in March 2019 in Chile aimed to debate about legal strategies to face anti-Semitic ideologies. Conib represented Brazil in this Forum and suggested the formation of a voluntary commission with experts to develop plans to face acts of discrimination against race, ethnicity, and religion.

On March 18, 2019, "Conib promoted a meeting between representatives of the Jewish community and the president in office (Hamilton Morão), in the day on which the National Day of Jewish Immigration is celebrated."[20] Thus, a non-governmental organization is developing an important role for dialogue between the Brazilian government and the Jewish community to address the problem of hate speech.

In 2017, *Devariam* magazine published a report that indicated the increase of the Brazilian *Alia* (return of the Jews to Israel). According to *Devariam* magazine, issue 33, "In 2016, 700 people lived Brazil which represents an increase of 250% since the foundation of the State of Israel"[21].

Michael Abadi stated that the political instability in Brazil, the violence, economic problems, the lack of public transparency are some causes of the departure of many Jews from Brazil[22]. The increase of Brazilian *Alia* is not temporary and will not decrease because the reasons that generate the return to Israel are getting worse in Brazil.

There are no restrictions for Brazilian Jews to the exercise of educational and religious practice. In addition, the first bilingual Jewish school started its activities in 2001. Furthermore, according to the UN Report (Antisemitism in Brazil), there is no evidence of restriction to the exercise of religious activities by Brazilian Jews. On the contrary, they celebrate several commemorative dates freely, for example, *Purim* and *Simchá Torah.*[23]

Finally, Brazil is a country where there are episodes of racist behavior, but it is not something continuous and frequent. In addition, there are websites that disseminate anti-Semitic discourse, but there are no restrictions on the rights of Jews. Furthermore, the Jewish community has had an excellent dialogue with the Brazilian government since 1980, and, since then, this relationship has strengthened.

CONCLUSIONS

The Ellwanger case is a historical landmark for judicial decisions in Brazil because the anti-Semitism practices are recognized as a crime of racism; in other words, the statute of limitation will never expire.

Furthermore, the Supreme Court decided that there is only one race in biological terms. On the other hand, the Plenary of the Supreme Court decided that the political and social meaning of race must be observed to analyze the crime of racism.

Ellwanger was convicted for the practice of the crime of racism. In this way, the Supreme Court decided that there are limits to the exercise of freedom of expression and the dignity of human beings is one of these limits. Furthermore, the freedom of expression without the protection of equality could not succeed in a democracy.

After the Ellwanger case, non-governmental organizations increased their activities in order to face the anti-Semitism in Brazil. Furthermore, there are many partnerships to define hate speech and to identify cases of practice of the crime of racism in Internet. The anti-Semitic acts are isolated, and there are no limitations to Jewish educational and religious activities in Brazil.

Finally, the increase of the Brazil *Alia* is not caused by discrimination and attacks against Jews, but due to the political, economic, and social scenario in Brazil. The street violence and the lack of public transparency are some reasons that justify the growth of the outflow of Brazilian Jews.

NOTES

1. José Luís Mousinho dos Santos Monteiro Violante, "O caso Ellwanger e seu impacto no direito brasileiro" (LL.M. thesis, PUC/SP), 10.
2. Fernando Henrique Cardoso, *A arte da política: a história que vivi*, Rio de Janeiro, 2006, 108.
3. Carlos Gustavo Nóbrega de Jesus, *Anti-semitismo e nacionalismo, negacionismo e memória: Revisão Editora e as estratégias da intolerância (1987-2003)*, São Paulo, 2006, 16.
4. S.E. Castan, *Holocausto judeu ou alemão? Nos bastidores da mentira do século*, Porto Alegre, 1987, 137.
5. S.E. Castan, *Holocausto judeu ou alemão? Nos bastidores da mentira do século*, Porto Alegre, 1987, 22.
6. Neubiana Silva Veloso Beike and Giovanna Comacio, "Antisemitism in Brazil: A report to the UN Special Rapporteur on Freedom of Religion or Belief", accessed April 11, 2020, https://www.ohchr.org/Documents/Issues/Religion/Submissions/TheBrazilianCenterofStudiesinLawandReligion.pdf.
7. Ronaldo Porto Macedo, "Freedom of expression: What lessons should we learn from US experience?", São Paulo, 2017, 279.
8. Ronaldo Porto Macedo, "Freedom of expression: What lessons should we learn from US experience?", São Paulo, 2017, 279.
9. lso Lafer, "Parecer: O caso Ellwanger: anti-semitismo como crime da prática do racismo", *Brasília*, 2004, 87.
10. Paulo Gustavo Gonet Branco, *A Jurisprudência do STF nos 20 anos de Constituição*, São Paulo, 2010, 263.
11. Ellwanger case, HC 82.424-2/RS, (Plenary of Supreme Court, 2003)
12. TJSP, Apelação Criminal n. 990.08.180555-3 (12ª Câmara de Direito Criminal do TJSP, 2012).
13. Neubiana Silva Veloso Beike and Giovanna Comacio, "Antisemitism in Brazil: A report to the UN Special Rapporteur on Freedom of Religion or Belief", accessed April 11, 2020, https://www.ohchr.org/Documents/Issues/Religion/Submissions/TheBrazilianCenterofStudiesinLawandReligion.pdf.
14. Neubiana Silva Veloso Beike and Giovanna Comacio, "Antisemitism in Brazil: A report to the UN Special Rapporteur on Freedom of Religion or Belief", accessed April 11, 2020, https://www.ohchr.org/Documents/Issues/Religion/Submissions/TheBrazilianCenterofStudiesinLawandReligion.pdf.

15. Neubiana Silva Veloso Beike and Giovanna Comacio, “Antisemitism in Brazil: A report to the UN Special Rapporteur on Freedom of Religion or Belief”, accessed April 11, 2020, https://www.ohchr.org/Documents/Issues/Religion/Submissions/TheBrazilianCenterofStudiesinLawandReligion.pdf.

16. Fernando Canofre, “Após 13 anos, júri condena 3 acusados de ataque neonazista no RS”, *Folha de São Paulo*, September 19, 2018, https://www1.folha.uol.com.br/cotidiano/2018/09/apos-13-anos-juri-condena-3-acusados-de-ataque-neonazista-no-rs.shtml#erramos.

17. Neubiana Silva Veloso Beike and Giovanna Comacio, “Antisemitism in Brazil: A report to the UN Special Rapporteur on Freedom of Religion or Belief”, accessed April 11, 2020, https://www.ohchr.org/Documents/Issues/Religion/Submissions/TheBrazilianCenterofStudiesinLawandReligion.pdf.

18. Conib, “Pesquisa da Faculdade de Direito da FGV em parceria com a Conib gera guia para análise do discurso de ódio”, November 2019, https://www.conib.org.br/pesquisa-da-faculdade-de-direito-da-fgv-em-parceria-com-a-conib-gera-guia-para-analise-do-discurso-de-odio/.

19. Neubiana Silva Veloso Beike and Giovanna Comacio, “Antisemitism in Brazil: A report to the UN Special Rapporteur on Freedom of Religion or Belief”, accessed April 11, 2020, https://www.ohchr.org/Documents/Issues/Religion/Submissions/TheBrazilianCenterofStudiesinLawandReligion.pdf.

20. Neubiana Silva Veloso Beike and Giovanna Comacio, “Antisemitism in Brazil: A report to the UN Special Rapporteur on Freedom of Religion or Belief”, accessed April 11, 2020, https://www.ohchr.org/Documents/Issues/Religion/Submissions/TheBrazilianCenterofStudiesinLawandReligion.pdf.

21. Marcus M. Gilban, “Ideologia vs. Economia: Relatos sobre a Aceleração da Aliá Brasileira”, n. 33 (August 2017), http://docvirt.com/docreader.net/docreader.aspx?bib=DEVARIM&pasta=Ano%2012%20-%20no%2033%20-%20Agosto%20de%202017.

22. Marcus M. Gilban, “Ideologia vs. Economia: Relatos sobre a Aceleração da Aliá Brasileira”, n. 33 (August 2017), http://docvirt.com/docreader.net/docreader.aspx?bib=DEVARIM&pasta=Ano%2012%20-%20no%2033%20-%20Agosto%20de%202017.

23. Neubiana Silva Veloso Beike and Giovanna Comacio, “Antisemitism in Brazil: A report to the UN Special Rapporteur on Freedom of Religion or Belief”, accessed April 11, 2020, https://www.ohchr.org/Documents/Issues/Religion/Submissions/TheBrazilianCenterofStudiesinLawandReligion.pdf.

REFERENCES

Carlos Gustavo Nóbrega de Jesus, *Anti-semitismo e nacionalismo, negacionismo e memória: Revisão Editora e as estratégias da intolerância (1987–2003)*. São Paulo: Unesp, 2006.

Celso Lafer, “Parecer: O caso Ellwanger: anti-semitismo como crime da prática do racismo”, *Brasília* a.41, no. 162 (April 2004): 53–90.

Conib, "Pesquisa da Faculdade de Direito da FGV em parceria com a Conib gera guia para análise do discurso de ódio", *Conib News*, November 2019, https://www.conib.org.br/pesquisa-da-faculdade-de-direito-da-fgv-em-parceria-com-a-conib-gera-guia-para-analise-do-discurso-de-odio/.

Ellwanger case, HC 82.424-2/RS, (Plenary of Supreme Court, 2003).

Fernando Canofre, "Após 13 anos, júri condena 3 acusados de ataque neonazista no RS", *Folha de São Paulo*, September 19, 2018, https://www1.folha.uol.com.br/cotidiano/2018/09/apos-13-anos-juri-condena-3-acusados-de-ataque-neonazista-no-rs.shtml#erramos.

Fernando Henrique Cardoso, *A arte da política: a história que vivi*. Rio de Janeiro: Civilização Brasileira, 2006.

José Luís Mousinho dos Santos Monteiro Violante, "O caso Ellwanger e seu impacto no direito brasileiro" LL.M. diss., PUC/SP, 2010.

Marcus M. Gilban, "Ideologia vs. Economia: Relatos sobre a Aceleração da Aliá Brasileira", *Devariam magazine*, n. 33 (August 2017), http://docvirt.com/docreader.net/docreader.aspx?bib=DEVARIM&pasta=Ano%2012%20-%20no%2033%20-%20Agosto%20de%202017.

Neubiana Silva Veloso Beike and Giovanna Comacio, "Antisemitism in Brazil: A report to the UN Special Rapporteur on Freedom of Religion or Belief", United Nations Human Rights Office of the High Commissioner (OHCHR), Accessed April 11, 2020, https://www.ohchr.org/Documents/Issues/Religion/Submissions/TheBrazilianCenterofStudiesinLawandReligion.pdf

Paulo Gustavo Gonet Branco. *A Jurisprudência do STF nos 20 anos de Constituição.* São Paulo: Saraiva, 2010.

Ronaldo Porto Macedo, "Freedom of expression: What lessons should we learn from US experience?", *Revista Direito GV* 13, no. 01 (April 2017): 274–302.

S.E. Castan. *Holocausto judeu ou alemão? Nos bastidores da mentira do século.* Porto Alegre: Editora Revisão, 1987.

TJSP, Apelação Criminal n. 990.08.180555-3 (12ª Câmara de Direito Criminal do TJSP, 2012).

Chapter 4

Asking "The Woman Question"

Judicial Recognition of the Right to Abortion in Brazil

Melina Girardi Fachin and Estefânia Maria de Queiroz Barboza

INTRODUCTION

In Brazil, criminal law considers abortion a crime except when the mother's life is at risk or in cases of rape. The criminalization of voluntary termination of pregnancy in an absolute manner and without allowing for the support of women reveals gender discrimination that inexorably violates the human rights of women. This has profound effects on the lives of women who face obstacles imposed on them by being a woman.

Historically, one of the impacts of this stance is the way in which the voluntary termination of pregnancy is regulated by Brazilian law; regardless of the time, women have been left out of the discussion of this topic that is so intrinsic to being a woman, which violates one of the basic principles of deliberative or procedural democracy, that is, an equal voice in the process of deliberation. The criminalization of the voluntary termination of pregnancy reiterated in force by criminal law dating back to the 1940s took place against the belief that when a woman has an abortion, she destroys "the hope of the father, the memory of a name, the guarantee of a race, the heir of a family and a citizen of the State";[1] this religious sentiment propels the condemnation of abortion. Under this view, it is evident that women are reduced to mere reproducers at the service of interests alien to them.

Currently, beyond the two exceptions that are punishable by law, it is possible to resort to voluntary termination of pregnancy in cases of anencephaly, an exception added by ADPF 54.[2] However, unfortunately, in addition to anencephaly, there are other serious pathologies that are often incompatible with social life, which legislators and jurists strive to ignore in their reasoning on the issue of voluntary termination of pregnancy.

Advances in medical studies on the prenatal diagnosis of congenital disorders[3] make room for the concept of selective termination of pregnancy. The issue of the couples' right to autonomy to decide whether to continue a pregnancy is greatly broadened when the concept of selective termination of pregnancy is considered. This is the concept used by the Federal Medical Council to justify pregnancy terminations motivated by fetal anomalies and diseases.[4]

In several countries, once the fetal diagnosis of these pathologies is made, the families are given the right to choose either continue the pregnancy or perform legal and state-assisted selective termination of pregnancy, as observed in Denmark, Sweden, Norway, France, England, Germany, and Spain. In Brazil, the only option for the selective termination of pregnancy is through preliminary injunctions in the courts.

Brazil is the country with the fourth-highest number of deliveries of anencephalic fetuses worldwide, a flagrant sign that due to restrictive legislation Brazilian women are forced to gestate despite a diagnosis of fetal nonviability.[5] Here, we find a double condemnation: Women are not allowed the option of voluntary termination of pregnancy or the selective termination of pregnancy, and their sick children who are forced upon them will not have access to the minimal infrastructure necessary to enable them to lead a dignified life.[6]

The prohibition of voluntary termination of pregnancy, therefore, is used as a means of discrimination against women. For Sílvia Pimentel, criminalization reveals double discrimination: in the first instance, it hurts all women because it hurts autonomy, rights, and fundamental freedoms; in a second instance, it discriminates more sharply and distinctly against those with scarce economic resources, thus violating the principles of justice and equity.[7]

In addition, there is a third discriminatory level related to the denial of rights that applies to adolescents, as age is another factor of vulnerability. The report "Motherhood in Childhood: Facing the challenge of adolescent pregnancy," produced by the United Nations Population Fund (UNFPA), draws very worrying conclusions regarding early motherhood and corroborates the idea that age is a discriminatory factor in regards to the voluntary termination of pregnancy and access to sexual and reproductive rights.

According to the UNFPA, 95% of adolescent births occur in poor countries; 19% of young women in these same countries become pregnant before the age of 18; girls under 15 years old account for 2 million of the 7.3 million adolescent births every year, or 20,000 adolescent births per day; of these, 70,000 adolescents die annually from causes related to early pregnancy and delivery; and 3.2 million unsafe abortive procedures are performed for adolescents each year.[8] The numbers are significant and demonstrate a disregard for the rights of women, young girls, and vulnerable girls. When the age factor is taken into account, it is noticeable that the danger to which young women are exposed only worsens. Being a woman is a risk, and being a young woman is an even greater risk.

According to Nancy Williamson, the author of that report, the harms related to early pregnancy revolve around very early marriages and stable unions, violence and gender inequality, poverty, the sexual violence and coercion that girls suffer daily, national policies that restrict access to contraception and age-appropriate sex education, and a lack of access to reproductive health services. This illustrates a scenario in which obstacles to access to human rights are created.[9]

Historically situated in a "nonplace," women are conceived as domestic beings who are docile and are raised to mother and care for others, which prevents their access to education and paid work.[10] The effects of this view on the lives of women are worrisome.

In Brazil, the rate of abortion among women increases with age: in women aged between 18 and 19 years, the abortion rate is 6%, whereas in women aged between 35 and 39 years, this rate increases to 22%. In addition to showing that voluntary termination of pregnancy is common in the reproductive life of Brazilian women, these data corroborate the statement that by 40 years of age, more than one in five women have undergone this procedure.[11] Unfortunately, even in situations that allow legal abortion, most women (approximately 95%) do not have knowledge of the services that are available in their defense in cases of sexual violence, and 48% of the population is unaware of the situations in which abortion is legally permitted.

Once again, the state's neglect is clear, given that there is no widely publicized official list of health facilities that perform these procedures,[12,13] which would enable a free, informed, and responsible choice regarding health issues. Women find difficulties when seeking a legal abortion because the health units that, in theory, should be prepared and equipped to perform legal abortions in cases of rape do not have the minimum necessary resources to perform a termination of pregnancy.[14]

Given this Brazilian and global reality, it becomes evident that, under the veil of discourse regarding the supposed protection of life, there is a hidden discourse of the moral punishment of women for their sexual enjoyment that implies that if a woman consented to a sexual relationship, then she should bear all the consequences of it, including an unwanted pregnancy. It is clear from the above that the greater the influence of vulnerability factors (such as economic situation, social situation, adolescence, childhood, unemployment, and lack of access to education), the greater the impact on women who seek voluntary termination of pregnancy or who continue their pregnancy.

The present chapter seeks to describe the abortion cases under review by the Federal Supreme Court (STF, for its initials in Portuguese) and seeks to defend a gender perspective in the court's most important case, which is still under review and which discusses the unconstitutionality of the criminal code with respect to the crime of abortion.

In this context, we will present the review of a case that discussed the possibility of therapeutic anticipation of delivery in the case of an anencephalic fetus and the lack of action by the Supreme Court regarding therapeutic anticipation of delivery for women diagnosed with Zika virus given the possibility of fetuses having microcephaly, a disease that leads to cerebral malformation. The aforementioned case was peculiar because it provided not only the possibility of abortion but also the possibility of defining public policies for protecting women and babies.

Then, the article will present the most important abortion case that is under review in the Brazilian Supreme Court. It is argued that this case must be reviewed from a perspective that promotes equality and equal freedom for women. This focus highlights the importance of argumentation, of feminist interpretive methods, and of the *woman question* as an important method for addressing the lack of neutrality of criminal legislation that criminalizes abortion and whether the impacts are proportional and equal for men and women.

Although the legal discourse often reproduces these prejudices—for example, in the case of punitive penal discourse or even in the biased reading of international human rights law—there are paths for female emancipation that also involve human rights law, as explained below.

THE PAST: THE CASE OF ANENCEPHALY

The issue of abortion in Brazil has seen significant advances in judicial interpretation in recent years. The first and most important of these precedents was case ADPF 54,[15] reviewed by the Federal Supreme Court, which allowed voluntary termination of pregnancies with anencephalic fetuses.

According to the decision signed by the Federal Supreme Court, the anencephalic fetus, even if biologically alive, is legally dead and does not enjoy legal protection, especially legal and penal protection. In the opinion of Minister Joaquim Barbosa, which was included in the vote on which he elaborated in Habeas Corpus No. 84,025/RJ,[16] it is unacceptable that the right to life of a fetus that has no chance of survival prevails at the expense of guarantees of the human dignity, sexual freedom, autonomy, privacy, health, and the physical, psychological, and moral integrity of the mother, all of which are provided for in the Constitution.

In a long vote based on information collected during a four-day public hearing held by the STF to discuss the topic, Minister Marco Aurélio concluded that the state's imposition on a woman to maintain a pregnancy, the final result of which will be the death of the fetus, goes against the basic principles of the constitutional system. For him, forcing a woman to carry this type of pregnancy places her in a kind of "private prison in her own body," leaving her deprived of the essential minimum of self-determination, which is similar to torture.

In the interpretation by this minister, the state has the duty to inform and provide medical and psychological support to the patient before and after the decision, regardless of what the decision is, a practice that is currently perfectly feasible in Brazil. With regard to the right to life, Minister Marco Aurélio argued that the decriminalization of abortion is not discussed in ADF 54 as there is a clear distinction between abortion and anticipation of delivery in the case of anencephaly. "Abortion is a crime against life. It protects potential life. In the case of an anencephalic fetus, I repeat, there is no possible life,"[17] he stressed. Anencephaly, which implies the partial or complete absence of the brain, is a lethal congenital disease for which there is no cure and no possibility of developing a brain mass at a later time.

Accordingly, in the rapporteur's view, one should not speak about the right to life or guarantees of the individual in the case of a stillborn being with an almost null chance of surviving for more than 24 hours, especially when the woman's rights are at stake. Data presented at the public hearing showed that the maintenance of pregnancy in these cases poses serious risks to the mother's health as well as severe and irreparable psychological consequences for the whole family.

Regarding the fact that there were no mentions in the penal code of cases of anencephaly as a situation that allows the termination of pregnancy, Minister Marco Aurélio argued that in the 1930s and 1940s, when the current penal code was published, medicine did not have the necessary technical resources to enable early identification of this type of fetal anomaly. "Even in the absence of an express provision in the Penal Code of 1940, it seems to me logical that the fetus without the possibility of life cannot be protected by the criminal law that protects life,"[18] he said. In addition, he recalled that at that time, the legislator, to protect the mental honor and health of women, established that abortion in cases of pregnancy resulting from rape, a situation in which the fetus is fully viable, would not be a crime.

For Minister Joaquim Barbosa, the subject should be seen through two lenses: the lens of the individual freedom of women, from which derives the self-determination of the pregnant woman, and the lens of the difference in degrees of protection of human life provided by the penal code. In cases where women are legally entitled to resort to abortion, the law is preserving the right to choose, not the (non)viability of the fetus, which is *pari passu* a matter of legal protection of the freedom and private autonomy of women. It recognizes that the reproductive rights of women cannot be dissociated from the fundamental right to freedom and the principle of self-determination.

In this sense, Minister Rosa Weber explains in her vote that it is the right of women to decide on the future of their pregnancy and that the termination of a pregnancy with a nonviable fetus is not abortion in a purely legal sense as it is not a fact within the sphere of "ought" on which law is grounded.

Minister Carmen Lúcia states that ADPF 54 addresses women's freedom of choice to continue or terminate their pregnancy and to choose the best route to take. It argues that women cannot be forced to birth a child and that their procreational function cannot be a burden to them. It emphasizes that there are international treaties signed by Brazil and that in these legal texts, it is provided that the signatory states will respect human rights, eradicate violence against women, and ensure the right to women's health. It cites *exempli gratia* the Declaration of Beijing; the Pact of San Jose, Costa Rica; and the Inter-American Convention on the Prevention, Punishment, and Eradication of Violence against Women.

The vote of Minister Celso de Mello is also of fundamental importance given that it states that forcing a woman to gestate is a way of subjugating her because her rights are suppressed and she is prevented from exercising the roles that modern society assigns to her by legitimate right of conquest. According to the illustrious minister, the role of the Federal Supreme Court is the concretization of civil liberties and fundamental rights; this highlights the court's counter-majoritarian function, essential in a Democratic State of Law, which should protect the most vulnerable from the excesses of the majority under the perspective of a material conception of constitutional democracy. Victims of prejudice, discrimination, and legal exclusion are not excluded, and the suppression, frustration, or annihilation of fundamental rights such as freedom, intimacy, and sexual and reproductive rights is not allowed.

The ministers who voted for the dismissal of ADPF 54 were Ricardo Lewandoski and Cezar Peluso. On a *pro forma* basis, they only claim that there is no expression in the law that allows for the voluntary termination of pregnancy.

As in the review of the Direct Action of Unconstitutionality (ADI, for its initials in Portuguese) 3510[19] on the possibility of conducting scientific research with embryonic stem cells, in which the STF emphasized the laity of the state within the scope of ADPF 54, minister Marco Aurélio indicated that moral and religious conceptions cannot guide the decisions of the state and should be limited to the private sphere.

In justifying his decision, Minister Marco Aurélio also rejected the premise used in defense of the anencephalic fetus that the infant's organs could be donated. According to the minister, in addition to law forbidding a pregnancy for the purpose of organ donation, organ donation is practically impossible in the case of anencephaly because the fetus will have other anomalies that preclude organ donation. Forcing a woman to maintain a pregnancy only for this purpose, in the rapporteur's view, is to regard her from a utilitarian perspective as an instrument for the generation of organs for donation, which also goes against the principle of the dignity of the human person.

INDICATIONS FOR THE FUTURE: NONACCEPTANCE OF THE PENAL CODE AND THE CASE OF THE PENAL CODE AND THE CASE OF THE ZIKA VIRUS

More recently, the First Chamber of the STF dismissed in HC 124306[20] the pretrial detention of E.S. and R.A.F., denounced by the Public Ministry of the State of Rio de Janeiro, for the alleged practice of the crime of abortion with the consent of the pregnant woman and conspiracy to commit a crime (articles 126 and 288 of the Criminal Code). According to the vote of the rapporteur Minister Luís Roberto Barroso,[21] which obtained the majority vote, in addition to the fact that the requirements authorizing pretrial detention were not met in this case, the criminalization of abortion is incompatible with several fundamental rights, including women's sexual and reproductive rights and autonomy, the physical and mental integrity of the pregnant woman and the principle of equality, which inform the essential core of women's fundamental rights as enshrined in the Constitution of the Republic.

According to the minister, the legal right being protected (the potential life of the fetus) is "obviously relevant," but the criminalization of abortion before the end of the first trimester of pregnancy violates several fundamental rights of women in addition to not sufficiently observing the principle of proportionality. Among the violated legal rights, the minister noted the autonomy of women, the right to physical and mental integrity, the sexual and reproductive rights of women and gender equality; she also referred to social discrimination and the disproportional impact of criminalization on poor women, emphasizing that in democratic and developed countries such as the United States, Germany, United Kingdom, Canada, France, Italy, Spain, Portugal, the Netherlands and Australia, *exempli gratia*, the voluntary termination of pregnancy during the first trimester is not a crime.

The rapporteur warned that it is not a matter of defending the dissemination of the procedure; *on the contrary, it is intended that it be rare and safe*,[22] he said. The vote maintained that the absolute criminalization of voluntary termination of pregnancy violates the principle of proportionality as well as its subprinciples of adequacy, necessity and, proportionality in the narrow sense. Regarding adequacy, this issue concerns the supposed protection of the fetus. Comparing data from countries where the procedure is allowed with those from countries where abortion is not allowed, it was found that the number of abortions in both groups is practically the same.[23] Regarding the subprinciple of necessity, it infers that the criminalization of abortion, in addition to not protecting the life of the unborn child, restricts women's enjoyment of their rights.

In the aforementioned decision, the religious freedom to reject the practice is ensured; however, it is emphasized that it is the state's role to support any side, and it should remain on the side of the most vulnerable party so as to allow a choice. In the same vein, the German Federal Court recognizes that the protection of the fetus will only be possible if it takes place in conjunction with the protection of the pregnant woman, and criminalization is a dubious measure for protecting the fetus.

As an alternative to the current criminalization, he argues that the state should ensure a network of protection and support that allows pregnant women to access childcare and social care and should ensure the availability of information about and access to contraceptive methods. In this sense, he reiterates the importance of promoting family planning programs with the free distribution of contraceptives and specialized care for pregnant women. Sex education, therefore, is of utmost importance in the fight against abortion.

For the rapporteur minister, it is necessary to provide interpretation in conformity with the articles 124–126 of the penal code, which criminalize abortion, to exclude from its scope of application the voluntary termination of pregnancy in the first trimester.

In the scope of the Supreme Court, important decisions on the subject that have unveiled the paths of punishment or emancipation, which are discussed below, are also pending evaluation.

It is worth highlighting the Direct Action of Unconstitutionality 5541, cumulated with the Claim of Non-compliance with a Fundamental Precept (ADPF, for its initials in Portuguese), with the request for a precautionary measure[24] that questions the provisions of Federal Law No. 13,301/2016, which addresses the adoption of health surveillance measures related to the dengue, chikungunya and Zika viruses. The main point questioned is article 18 of the aforementioned law, which addresses welfare and social security benefits for children with neurological sequelae and their mothers.

In this context, the penal code articles that address the issue of termination of pregnancy must be interpreted in conformity with the Constitution of the Republic. In the Claim of Non-compliance with a Fundamental Precept, the legitimized National Association of Public Defenders (ANADEP, for its initials in Portuguese) points to several omissions of the Public Power regarding access information, family planning and health services, in addition to the omission of the possibility of terminating a pregnancy, from state-level health policies for pregnant women infected with the Zika virus.

In this sense, the request is for the Public Power to adopt various public policies aimed at remedying such omissions, including ensuring the treatment of children with microcephaly in centers specializing in rehabilitation at a maximum distance of 50 km from their homes, the delivery of informational material and the distribution of long-term contraceptives to vulnerable women. ANADEP also requests the declaration of the unconstitutionality of the framework for termination of pregnancy for women infected by the Zika virus in article 124 of the penal code.

Alternatively, the request is for the termination in these cases to be considered constitutional, "as a function of the state of necessity with the current danger of damage to health caused by the Zika epidemic and aggravated by the neglect of the Brazilian State in the elimination of the vector," with the suspension of police investigations, arrests in flagrante delicto, and ongoing cases that involve the termination of pregnancy when there is proof of infection of the pregnant woman.

The merit of the case was not known since the preliminary hearing led to a decision not to hear the case. The virtual plenum of the STF decided in April of this year to reject the request of the ANADEP, according to the vote of the rapporteur, Minister Carmen Lúcia, which was supported by the majority. The rapporteur of the case voted to reject the action—not grant review of the action—without analyzing its merit, accepting the formal preliminary ruling of the illegitimacy of the association in bringing suit. In any case, at the time the case was reviewed in the virtual plenum, many ministers emphasized their support for the decriminalization of abortion, regardless of the insurmountable procedural issue that arose.

Thus, even if it is a negative precedent given that the merit of the issue was not considered, and in the face of the reservations of several judges, the future may bring about a more protective position of the court regarding the rights of women to voluntarily terminate a pregnancy.

WHAT WILL COME IN THE FUTURE? THE CASE UNDER REVIEW

At the same time, the most important discussion of the concentrated control of constitutionality on the subject, ADPF 442,[25] is under review. This case questions the acceptance by the Federal Constitution of 1988 of articles 124 and 126 of the penal code, which establishes the criminalization of voluntary termination of pregnancy according to the current normative order.

ADPF 442 states that the two articles of the penal code go against fundamental principles such as the dignity of the human person, citizenship, nondiscrimination, inviolability of life, freedom, equality, the prohibition of torture or inhuman and degrading treatment, women's health and family planning and sexual and reproductive rights[26].

The intention is that the STF exclude from the scope of application of the two articles the induced and voluntary termination of pregnancy in the first 12 weeks "to guarantee to women the constitutional right to interrupt pregnancy, according to their autonomy, without need for any form of specific permission from the State, as well as to guarantee to healthcare professionals the right to perform the procedure," given that "having a child is a central event in the lives of women; therefore, the conditions available for them to decide whether or how to do it concretizes fundamental principles of the dignity of the human person and citizenship, insofar as it configures their ability for self-determination, in order to accomplish the project of life" and given that regarding "the criminalization of abortion, the conditions are unfair: women are subjected to preventable risks of illness and death, as well as humiliating and degrading treatment at a time of intense vulnerability."

In November 2017, the rapporteur rejected a request for an urgent precautionary measure aimed at the suspension of arrests in flagrante delicto, of police investigations and ongoing legal proceedings or decisions based on the application of articles 124 and 126 of the penal code for cases of voluntary abortion performed in the first 12 weeks of pregnancy. To establish the constitutional debate and the configuration and scope of the legal problem, Minister Rosa Weber requested information from the Presidency of the Republic, the Federal Senate, the Chamber of Deputies, the Attorney General's Office (AGU, for its initials in Portuguese) and the Office of the Federal Attorney General (PGR, for its initials in Portuguese).

In addition, according to the minister, the issue of voluntary termination of pregnancy in the first 12 weeks involves different public values and fundamental rights. The discussion, in her view, is one of the most sensitive and delicate legal topics because it involves ethical, moral, religious and public health factors and the protection of individual fundamental rights.

In response to the request, the Presidency of the Republic maintains the existence of a "reasonable moral disagreement" on the issue in Brazilian society, given the absence of a minimal consensus on moral, philosophical, and even religious conceptions about the subject. For this reason, it argues that the appropriate space for politically discussing and deciding on the matter is the Legislative Branch, which is responsible "for protecting political pluralism, a premise for the legitimacy of the majority political decisions."

The Federal Senate, in turn, clarifies that the articles questioned in the ADPF were not the object of legislative reform undertaken in the penal code

(Law 7.209/1984) and notes that article 2 of the Civil Code of 2002 ensures rights to the viable fetus. It also states that the Parliament is promoting relevant discussions for the eventual modification of the legal parameter (petition 17722/2017).

Similarly, the Chamber of Deputies defends that decriminalization of this conduct, if it was to happen, should occur through the Legislative Branch and recalls that, when analyzing Bill 1,135/1991, the chamber considered the proposal "unconstitutional and ill-timed." It also reports that various proposals are under review in the chamber that proposes the protection of life starting at conception, in addition to projects that decriminalize abortion.

In March 2018, the minister rapporteur made a decision in which she convened a public hearing[27] to address the constitutional complexity *sub examine*. There was intense participation from society, including approximately 40 representatives from various sectors, including experts, institutions and national and international organizations, in hopes of effectively participating in establishing the public reason that will serve as the basis for the decision regarding this ADPF, which is still under review. Since November 9, 2019, the final reports have been assigned to Rapporteur Rosa Weber.

The decision regarding which path the Brazilian judiciary will take on the subject of decriminalization of abortion is still pending; however, the political moment is not favorable to the determination of the issue for review, which is why analysis indicates that we will have a deferral until the issue is defined.

ABORTION AND INTERPRETATION BASED ON FEMINIST CONSTITUTIONALISM: ASKING THE "WOMAN QUESTION"

It is important to emphasize that the STF, in addition to deciding on the nonacceptance of the penal code article that criminalizes abortion, must also take responsibility for setting abstract parameters that serve as precedents for subsequent cases involving issues of gender inequality.

In this sense, an interpretation of the case based on feminist constitutionalism is proposed to draw attention to the gender inequality in constitutional law, which has always been studied and applied with the assumption that it is neutral. Feminist constitutionalism also seeks to somehow rethink and reconstruct social democracy, but with the participation and voice of women in law and politics. It also seeks to examine the issues of constitutional law from the perspective of gender and proposes revisiting the classic themes of constitutionalism to advocate new ideas; in particular, it seeks to take on the responsibility of changing the focus of discussion and constitutional debate.

Constitutional law is foundational and fundamental to most legal systems in the contemporary world, which, in turn, implies that constitutions are designed with fundamental commitments related to citizenship, rights, and duties. In the literature on the problems and justifications of a binding judicial review in a democracy, one can expect the relatively obvious and unique problems of women to play at least a significant role.

Women were excluded from the judiciary for most of our history, and the judiciary operates within a system of precedents. It is necessary to change the interpretation filter so that new precedents with greater protection and promotion of the equality of women also serve to transform their protection. The legal mobilization of women's movements includes actions within the Supreme Court and the judicialization and framing of their demands through discursive frameworks that incorporate and interpret legal concepts;[28] within these frameworks, the jurisprudence of constitutional courts has a fundamental role in the interpretation of rights to ensure material gender equality.

In this sense, the aim is to present some possibilities for feminist constitutional interpretation as well as a constitutional interpretation that seeks to repair the disproportionality of the law that criminalizes abortion and restricts women's freedom regarding their bodies, their lives, and their future.

The feminist interpretation is a project that aims to rethink constitutional law and explore its relationship with feminism by examining, challenging, and redefining the very idea of constitutionalism from a feminist perspective.[29] Stereotypes and discriminatory approaches have left their mark on constitutional law and legal traditions. Feminism can play a role in the neutralization of these influences, and the feminist interpretation can be a very effective tool in the service of gradual jurisprudential change; in addition, it offers a new interpretive perspective for human knowledge, including the sphere of law. Some classic examples of the influence of stereotypes and discrimination on interpretation come from cases in which apparently neutral documents were interpreted in a manner that excluded women because of cultural biases.[30]

In general, women did not participate in the constituent processes or in the production of laws that disproportionately establish restrictions on their bodies and their choices and thus impose unjustifiable punishments on them. It is necessary to understand that the penal code, as well as all traditional law, contains sexist assumptions because it is produced in a patriarchal society that treats the female body as an instrument at the service of man or family. In addition, it is necessary to assume that there is no neutrality in a law conceived by men and for men.

It is necessary that the STF, when judging the voluntary termination of pregnancy, understands that it is possible to combat more than the public forms of injustice, which are supposedly neutral.

In this sense, one possibility is the use of the interpretative method proposed by Professor Katharine Bartlett,[31] "the woman question," to assess and expose the impact of legal norms on women. This method seeks to identify the implications of gender in legal norms and practices that seem to be neutral or objective. It can also be used in the case of abortion. For Professor Bartlett, this approach may provide interpretive alternatives that promote the more equitable and fair allocation of social outcomes.

"The woman question" seeks to assess the impact of norms on women through the following questions: "Have women been left out of consideration? If so, in what way, and how might that omission be corrected? What difference would it make to do so?"[32]

The method seeks to explore whether there is proportionality and, therefore, equality in the treatment and elaboration of a law and its impact on the lives of women. If the law only has restrictive impacts on the life, liberty, and body of women, it is not possible to talk about its neutrality or impartiality.

In the STF, "the woman question" can be used to ask and examine how the criminalization of abortion brings about normative standards that are disadvantageous for women. The question assumes that laws, especially those written in the beginning and middle of the last century, may not only not be neutral but may also be disadvantageous to women and sexist in a specific sense. The proposal of "the woman question" during case reviews can help to expose this disparity and disproportionality in the impact of the punitive norm on the life and on the body of women, suggesting the correction of the right by the STF to declare it unconstitutional.

It is necessary to address whether the issue affects only women, whether it affects only pregnant women, and whether this impact harms women. Additionally, it is necessary to consider whether the issue has a greater impact on poor women and on black women and whether the state acts to avoid termination of pregnancy in a way that is proportionate to economic and social incentives for women.

Does the state maintain specific social welfare policies for low-income mothers? Does the state maintain job stability policies for pregnant women? For pregnant women living under conditions of underemployment in the informal labor market, how does the state protect them? Are female executives guaranteed career advancements? Is there a gender concern surrounding the promotion of mothers in corporations? Does opting for the continuity of pregnancy and motherhood have an impact on the development of women? Does it negatively impact their professional development? Do female researchers have incentives and fair conditions to make motherhood a more equitable process? What inclusion and equity policies are implemented by governments? Do women who choose not to continue a pregnancy receive some type of punishment? These are the questions that we must answer to duly address the topic of abortion.

Similarly, Reva Siegel,[33] when studying restrictive policies related to abortion in the United States, proposed expanding the framework and analyzing abortion restrictions in a broader political context to ascertain whether there are integrity and proportionality in policies that criminalize or restrict abortion and whether the state is concerned with helping women avoid unwanted pregnancies and supporting pregnant women who want to raise their babies.

Other questions that could be asked, according to Siegel, are[34,35]

Click here to enter text.

> Is state interest in protecting new life consistent across contexts, or selective? Do states protect life in ways that enhance or restrict women's autonomy? Do states that restrict abortion also support new mothers and new life? Do schools teach sex education? Do states that restrict abortion help women who want to be mothers maintain their pregnancies?

According to the author, 49% of women or more cite financial reasons for interrupting a pregnancy: 49% are below the poverty level, and 75% are poor or low-income women. One cannot discuss policies that impose abortion restrictions if there are no policies to provide resources, health care, or employment protection for women.[35]

Asking "the woman question" may be an initial method for approaching debates on constitutional interpretation regarding abortion and the disproportionate effect that its criminalization has on women. The above questions can demonstrate with increased transparency whether there is indeed a concern about protecting the life of the fetus starting the moment after birth and whether there are policies in place to support women who wish to continue their pregnancy. If the law impacts only women and is the only existing policy that serves to restrict their freedom and treat them disproportionally, then the court must declare it is unconstitutional because it does not meet the parameters of material equality advocated in the Federal Constitution.

CONCLUSION: WHAT WILL THE FUTURE BRING?

For males, abortion already exists in Brazil: today, there are approximately 5.5 million children with no father listed on their birth certificates.[36] The prohibition of voluntary termination of pregnancy is, *ergo*, a question of equality because gender equality is harmed, insofar as women are subjugated to burdens that would not be imposed on men in any context, and their impacts are more pronounced for women in more socially disadvantaged groups.[37]

This approach of addressing the problem of inequality between men and women in terms of providing care for their offspring resulted in the legalization of the voluntary termination of pregnancy in France, for example, where this right was achieved due to failures of contraceptive methods[38] as well as the desire to achieve equality between men and women. In the United States, as in France, abortion is legally allowed, as recognized by the Supreme Court.

Since the *Roe* v. *Wade* case,[39] the voluntary termination of pregnancy has been a right of American women. Notwithstanding conservative viewpoints in that country, abortion is considered a form of expression of a right, a value, and a guiding principle of the entire American legal system: freedom. For Ruth Bader Ginsburg, the decision in the *Roe* v. *Wade* case, although it represented an advance in the defense of women's rights, failed by using biomedical arguments rather than a constitutional perspective of gender equality.[40]

We emphasize, however, that unfortunately, the issue of gender-based violence is not restricted to the exercise of women's sexual and reproductive rights: impediments in access to justice and health services, as well as professional and social life, are also harmful effects that women and girls experience as a result of this androcentric system. Therefore, male domination over the female condition is not only naturalized but hidden,[41] so that its effects are veiled. This widespread phenomenon affects a high number of women.[42]

Equality between men and women should be seen as an important interpretive key to the female condition in our society. The fight against violence against women and for gender equality forms the basis of social and economic development;[43] gender inequality is a real obstacle to progress[44] as it prevents the development of capable people who have much to contribute to society and the future of humanity.

Thus, the Brazilian Supreme Court, using a feminist interpretive method, asks "the woman question" to assess the impact and disproportionality of the existing criminal law on the life and body of women and to take an active position in favor of gender equality.

NOTES

1. Hungria, Nélson; Fragoso, Heleno Cláudio. *Comentários ao Código Penal.* Volume V, arts.121 a 136. 6th ed. Rio de Janeiro: Editora Forense, 1981, p. 271.

2. ADPF (Arguição de Descumprimento de Preceito Fundamental [Claim of non-compliance with a fundamental precept]) is a type of action of the abstract control of constitutionality that can be presented to the Brazilian Federal Supreme Court. Brasil. Supremo Tribunal Federal. ADPF 54. Rapporteur: Minister Marco Aurélio. DJ 12/04/2012. Disponível em <http://redir.stf.jus.br/paginadorpub/paginador.jsp?docTP=TP&docID=3707334>. Acesso em 18/11/2019.

3. Wapner, Ronald J. Diagnóstico pré-natal de desordens congênitas. In: Creasy, Robert K. Creasy e Resnik (eds.). *Medicina materno fetal: princípios e práticas*. 7th ed. Trad. Gabriella da Silva Mendes. Rio de Janeiro: Editora Elsevier, 2016, p. 419.

4. In addition to the concept of selective termination of pregnancy, the Federal Council of Medicine (CFM, for its initials in Portuguese) was in favor of the voluntary termination of pregnancy when it forwarded to the National Congress a favorable opinion on PLS 236 2012, advocating the end of the illegality of voluntary termination of pregnancy in the following cases: a) when "there is a risk to life or the health of the pregnant woman"; b) if the "pregnancy results from a violation of sexual dignity, or from the unauthorized use of assisted reproduction techniques"; c) if "anencephaly is confirmed or when the fetus suffers from serious and incurable anomalies that make independent life unfeasible, in both cases attested by two doctors"; and d) if "the pregnant woman wishes to do so until the 12th week of pregnancy". According to the then-president of the CFM, Roberto Luiz d'Avila, the autonomy of the woman's wishes must be respected (*CFM esclarece posição a favor da autonomia da mulher no caso de interrupção da gestação*. Conselho Federal de Medicina, 21 mar. 2013. Disponível em: <http://portal.cfm.org.br/index.php?option=com_content&view=article&id=23663:cfm-esclarece-posicao-a-favor-da-autonomia-da-mulher-no-caso-deinterrupcao-da-gestacao&catid=3>. Acesso em: 21 set. 2013).

5. Diniz, Débora; Vélez, Ana Cristina Gonzalez. *Aborto na suprema corte: o caso da anencefalia no Brasil. Revista Estudos Feministas, Florianópolis*, v. 16, n. 2, p. 647–652, mai./ago. 2008, p.648. Disponível em:<https://periodicos.ufsc.br/index.php/ref/article/view/S0104-026X2008000200019/8797>. Acesso em: 05 nov. 2016.

6. Gollop, Thomaz Rafael. Abortamento por anomalia fetal. In: Cavalcanti, Alcilene; Xavier, Dulce (Orgs.). *Em defesa da vida: aborto e direitos humanos*. São Paulo: Católicas pelo direito de decidir, 2006, p. 85.

7. Pimentel, Silvia; Pandjiarjian, Valéria. Aborto: descriminar para não discriminar. *Jornal da Rede saúde, São Paulo*, n. 21, set. 2000.

8. Williamson, Nancy. *Situação da população Mundial 2013*. Maternidade Precoce: Enfrentando desafios da gravidez na adolescência. Brasil, p.v. 2013.

9. Ob.cit.p.vi.

10. Barwinski, Sandra Lia Leda Bazzo. Não sou ninguém. In: Graciela Iurk Marins e Sandra Lia Leda Bazzo Barwinski (Org.). *A mulher e o direito*. Curitiba: OAB/PR, 2012, p. 182.

11. Diniz, Debora; Medeiros, Marcelo. Aborto no Brasil: uma pesquisa domiciliar com técnica de urna. *Ciênc. saúde coletiva* [online], Rio de Janeiro, v. 15, supl. 1, p. 959–966, jun. 2010. Disponível em: <http://dx.doi.org/10.1590/S1413-81232010000700002.>. Acesso em: 10 jul. 2015.

12. Breve panorama sobre o aborto legal e transparência no Brasil. Disponível em <http://catolicas.org.br/wp-content/uploads/2017/10/Pesquisa-de-Opini%C3%A3o-P%C3%BAblica-2017-CDD-e-IBOPE-Percep%C3%A7%C3%B5es-sobre-aborto-e-educa%C3%A7%C3%A3o-sexual_3-MB.pdf>. Acesso em: 18/09/2019.

13. On the other hand, in a survey conducted by Ibope and by Catholics for the Right to Decide, among the sample used, approximately 42% of the interviewees thought that public schools should teach sex education, a very positive fact if

interpreted in the current social context. In: Percepções sobre o aborto e educação sexual. Disponível em <http://catolicas.org.br/wp-content/uploads/2017/10/Pesquisa-de-Opini%C3%A3o-P%C3%BAblica-2017-CDD-e-IBOPE-Percep%C3%A7%C3%B5es-sobre-aborto-e-educa%C3%A7%C3%A3o-sexual_3-MB.pdf>. Acesso em 18/09/2019.

14. Abrantes, Talita. Hospitais barram aborto até em casos previstos por lei. Exame.com, 21 jun. 2016. Disponível em: <http://exame.abril.com.br/brasil/hospitais-barram-aborto-ate-em-casos-previstos-por-lei/>. Acesso em: 21 de outubro de 2016.

15. Brasil. Supremo Tribunal Federal. Arguição de Descumprimento de Preceito Fundamental 54. Relator Ministro Marco Aurélio. Dje 12/04/2012. Disponível em <http://redir.stf.jus.br/paginadorpub/paginador.jsp?docTP=TP&docID=3707334>. Acesso em 22/11/2019.

16. Brasil. Supremo Tribunal Federal. Habeas Corpus nº 84.025-6 – Rio de Janeiro. Relator Ministro Joaquim Barbosa. Dje 04/03/2004. Disponível em <http://redir.stf.jus.br/paginadorpub/paginador.jsp?docTP=AC&docID=384874>. Acesso em 22/11/2019.

17. Ibidem, p. 23.

18. Ibidem, p. 25.

19. Brasil. Supremo Tribunal Federal. Ação Indireta de Inconstitucionalidade n° 3510. Relator Ministro Ayres Britto. Brasília, Dje 29/05/2008. Disponível em <http://redir.stf.jus.br/paginadorpub/paginador.jsp?docTP=AC&docID=611723>. Acesso em 22/11/2019.

20. Brasil. Supremo Tribunal Federal. Habeas Corpus n° 124.306 – Rio de Janeiro. Relator Ministro Marco Aurélio. Brasília, Dje 09/08/2016. Disponível em <http://redir.stf.jus.br/paginadorpub/paginador.jsp?docTP=TP&docID=12580345>. Acesso em 22/11/2019.

21. Brasil. Supremo Tribunal Federal. Habeas Corpus n° 124.306—Rio de Janeiro. Ministro Relator Marco Aurélio. Disponível em <https://www.stf.jus.br/arquivo/cms/noticiaNoticiaStf/anexo/HC124306 LRB.pdf>. Acesso em 22/11/2019.

22. Brasil. Supremo Tribunal Federal. Habeas Corpus 124.306 Rio de Janeiro. Pacientes: Edilson dos Santos; Rosemere Aparecida Ferreira. Relator: Ministro Marco Aurélio. Brasília, 12 de abril de 2012. Disponível em <http://www.stf.jus.br/arquivo/cms/noticiaNoticiaStf/anexo/HC124306 LRB.pdf>. Acesso em 20/11/2019.

23. Sedgh, G. Abortion incidence between 1990 and 2014: global, regional, and subregional levels and trends. *The Lancet*, 2016. Disponível em: <https://www.guttmacher.org/infographic/2018/highly-restrictive-laws-do-not-eliminate-abortion>. Acesso em: 28/09/2019.

24. The petition, as well as other documents that support this action, are available at <http://redir.stf.jus.br/estfvisualizadorpub/jsp/consultarprocessoeletronico/ConsultarProcessoEletronico.jsf?seqobjetoincidente=5037704>. Accessed on 09/28/2019.

25. Brasil. Supremo Tribunal Federal. Arguição de Descumprimento de Preceito Fundamental 442. Requerente: Partido Socialismo e Liberdade. Relator: Ministra Rosa Weber. Brasília. Disponível em <https://portal.stf.jus.br/processos/detalhe.asp?incidente=5144865>. Acesso em 20/11/2019.

26. The initial petition is available at <https://www.conjur.com.br/dl/psol-stf-descriminalize-aborto-meses.pdf>. Accessed on 09/28/2019.

27. The initial petition is available at <https://www.conjur.com.br/dl/psol-stf-descriminalize-aborto-meses.pdf>. Accessed on 09/28/2019.

28. Freire, A. Interpretação constitucional comparativa: aproximação crítica e arcabouço metodológico. *Revista Publicum, Rio de Janeiro*, v. 2, p. 45–73, 2016.

29. Baines, Beverley; Barak-Erez, Daphne; Kahana, Tsvi. *Feminist Constitutionalism: Global Perspectives*. New York: Cambridge University Press, 2012, p. 1.

30. Barak-Erez, Daphne. Her-menutics: feminism and interpretation. In: Baines, Beverley; Barak-Erez, Daphne; Kahana, Tsvi (eds.). *Feminist Constitutionalism: Global Perspectives*. New York: Cambridge University Press, 2012, p. 85.

31. Bartlett, Katherine. Feminist Legal Methods. *Harvard Law Review*, v. 103, n. 4, p. 837, 1990.

32. Ibidem.

33. Siegel, Reva B., ProChoiceLife: asking who protects life and how—and why it matters in law and politics (September 10, 2017). *Indiana Law Journal*, Forthcoming; Yale Law School, Public Law Research Paper No. 613. Available at SSRN: https://ssrn.com/abstract=3035017, p. 5

34. Ibid, ibidem.

35. Ibid, p. 12.

36. Brasil tem 5,5 milhões de crianças sem pai no registro. UOL Notícias, 11 ago. 2013. Disponível em: <http://noticias.uol.com.br/ultimas-noticias/agencia-estado/2013/08/11/brasil-tem-55-milhoes-de-criancas-sem-pai-no-registro.htm>. Acesso em: 30 jul. 2015.

37. Sarmento, Daniel. Legalização do aborto e Constituição. Mundo Jurídico. Disponível em: <http://www.clam.org.br/bibliotecadigital/uploads/publicacoes/982_342_abortosarmentodaniel.pdf>. Acesso em: 03 jul. 2014.

38. Chatél, Marie Magdeleine. *Mal-estar na procriação: as Mulheres e a Medicina da Reprodução*. Rio de Janeiro: Editora Campo Matêmico, 1995.

39. The audio of the oral arguments in Roe v. Wade are available at <https://supreme.justia.com/cases/federal/us/410/113/>. Accessed on 11/2022/19.

40. Ginsburg, Ruth Bader. Some thoughts on autonomy and equality in relation to Roe v. Wade. *Hein Online*, n. 375, 1984–1985. Disponível em: <http://heinonline.org/HOL/LandingPage?collection=journals&handle=hein.journals/nclr63&div=20&id=&page=>. Acesso em: 20 mai. 2015.

41. Varikas, Eleni. Igualdade. In: Hirata, Helena; e outras. (Org.). *Dicionário Crítico do Feminismo*. São Paulo: Editora UNESP, 2009, p. 117.

42. Piovesan, Flavia; Pimentel, Silvia. *Conspiração contra a impunidade*. Folha de São Paulo, São Paulo, 25/11/2002. Opinião. Disponível em <https://www1.folha.uol.com.br/fsp/opiniao/fz2511200210.htm>. Acesso em 09/10/2019.

43. UNFPA. Annual Report 2018. One vision: Three zeros. Disponível em <https://www.unfpa.org/sites/default/files/pub-pdf/UNFPA_PUB_2018_EN_Annual_Report_3.pdf>. Acesso em: 03 de outubro de 2019.

44. Mill, John Stuart. *The Subjection of Women*. London: Kindle Edition, 1869.

REFERENCES

Abrantes, Talita. Hospitais barram aborto até em casos previstos por lei. Exame.co m, 21 Jun. 2016. Disponível em: <http://exame.abril.com.br/brasil/hospitais-ba rram-aborto-ate-em-casos-previstos-por-lei/>. Acesso em: 21 de outubro de 2016.

Alto Comissariado das Nações Unidas para os Refugiados. MC 114/13- B, El Salvador. p. 71. Disponível em <https://www.acnur.org/fileadmin/Documentos/BD L/2016/10488.pdf>. Acesso em 22/11/2019.

Baines, Beverley; Barak-Erez, Daphne; Kahana, Tsvi. *Feminist Constitutionalism: Global Perspectives.* New York: Cambridge University Press, 2012, p. 1.

Barak-Erez, Daphne. Her-menutics: feminism and interpretation. In: Baines, Beverley; Barak-Erez, Daphne; Kahana, Tsvi, eds. *Feminist Constitutionalism: Global Perspectives.* New York: Cambridge University Press, 2012, p. 85.

Bartlett, Katherine. Feminist legal methods. *Harvard Law Review*, v. 103, 1990, p. 829–888.

Barwinski, Sandra Lia Leda Bazzo. Não sou ninguém. In: Graciela Iurk Marins e Sandra Lia Leda Bazzo Barwinski (Org.). *A mulher e o direito.* Curitiba: OAB/PR, 2012.

Brasil tem 5,5 milhões de crianças sem pai no registro. UOL Notícias, 11 ago. 2013. Disponível em: <http://noticias.uol.com.br/ultimas noticias/agencia estado/2013/0 8/11/brasil-tem-55-milhoes-de-criancas-sem-pai-no-registro.htm>. Acesso em: 30 Jul. 2015.

Brasil. Supremo Tribunal Federal. Ação Indireta de Inconstitucionalidade nº 3510. Relator Ministro Ayres Britto. Brasília, Dje 29/05/2008. Disponível em <http:// redir.stf.jus.br/paginadorpub/paginador.jsp?docTP=AC&docID=611723>. Acesso em 22/11/2019.

Brasil. Supremo Tribunal Federal. ADPF 54. RELATOR: Ministro Marco Aurélio. DJ 12/04/2012. Disponível em <http://redir.stf.jus.br/paginadorpub/paginador.jsp ?docTP=TP&docID=3707334>. Acesso em 18/11/2019.

Brasil. Supremo Tribunal Federal. Arguição de Descumprimento de Preceito Fundamental 442. Requerente: Partido Socialismo e Liberdade. Relator: Ministra Rosa Weber. Brasília. Disponível em <https://portal.stf.jus.br/processos/detalhe.a sp?incidente=5144865 >. Acesso em 20/11/2019.

Brasil. Supremo Tribunal Federal. Habeas Corpus nº 124.306 – Rio de Janeiro. Relator Ministro Marco Aurélio. Brasília, Dje 09/08/2016. Disponível em <http: //redir.stf.jus.br/paginadorpub/paginador.jsp?docTP=TP&docID=12580345>. Acesso em 22/11/2019.

Brasil. Supremo Tribunal Federal. Habeas Corpus nº 84.025-6—Rio de Janeiro. Relator Ministro Joaquim Barbosa. Dje 04/03/2004. Disponível em <http://redir.stf.jus.br/p aginadorpub/paginador.jsp?docTP=AC&docID=384874 >. Acesso em 22/11/2019.

Breve panorama sobre o aborto legal e transparência no Brasil. Disponível em <http:// catolicas.org.br/wp-content/uploads/2017/10/Pesquisa-de-Opini%C3%A3o-P%C3 %BAblica-2017-CDD-e-IBOPE-Percep%C3%A7%C3%B5es-sobre aborto e edu ca%C3%A7%C3%A3o sexual_3-MB.pdf >. Acesso em 18/09/2019.

Chatél, Marie Magdeleine. *Mal-estar na procriação: as Mulheres e a Medicina da Reprodução.* Rio de Janeiro: Editora Campo Matêmico, 1995.

Colombo, Sylvia. *Em vez de aborto, médica faz cesárea em menina de 11 anos violentada na Argentina*. Folha de São Paulo, Buenos Aires, 27 de fevereiro de 2019. Disponível em <https://www1.folha.uol.com.br/mundo/2019/02/em-vez-de-aborto-medica-faz-cesarea-em-menina-de-11-anos-violentada-na-argentina.shtml>. Acesso em 19/09/2019.

Conselho Federal de Medicina, 21 mar. 2013. Disponível em: <http://portal.cfm.org.br/index.php?option=com_content&view=article&id=23663:cfm-esclarece-posicao-a-favor-da-autonomia-da-mulher-no-caso-de-interrupcao-da-gestacao&catid=3>. Acesso em: 21 set. 2013

Corte Interamericana de Direitos Humanos. *Caso Artavia Murillo y Otros ("Fecundación in vitro") vs. Costa Rica*. Sentença de 28 de novembro de 2012, p. 48. Disponível em: <http://www.corteidh.or.cr/docs/casos/articulos/seriec_257_esp.pdf>. Acesso em: 17 set. 2016.

Corte Interamericana de Direitos Humanos. *Caso Ximenes Lopes versus Brasil*. Sentença de 04 de julho de 2006. Disponível em: <http://www.corteidh.or.cr/docs/casos/articulos/seriec_149_por.pdf>. Acesso em: 10 set. 2016.

Diniz, Debora; Medeiros, Marcelo. Aborto no Brasil: uma pesquisa domiciliar com técnica de urna. *Ciênc. saúde coletiva [online], Rio de Janeiro*, v. 15, supl. 1, p. 959–966, jun. 2010. Disponível em: <http://dx.doi.org/10.1590/S1413-81232010000700002.>. Acesso em: 10 jul. 2015.

Diniz, Débora; Vélez, Ana Cristina Gonzalez. Aborto na suprema corte: o caso da anencefalia no Brasil. *Revista Estudos Feministas, Florianópolis*, v. 16, n. 2, p. 647–652, mai./ago. 2008, p.648. Disponível em:<https://periodicos.ufsc.br/index.php/ref/article/view/S0104-026X2008000200019/8797>. Acesso em: 05 nov. 2016.

É possível ouvir aos áudios das sustentações orais do caso Roe v. Wade em <https://supreme.justia.com/cases/federal/us/410/113/>. Acesso em: 22/11/2019.

Freire, A. Interpretação constitucional comparativa: aproximação crítica e arcabouço metodológico. *Revista Publicum, Rio de Janeiro*, v. 2, p. 45–73, 2016.

Ginsburg, Ruth Bader. Some thoughts on autonomy and equality in relation to Roe v. Wade. *Hein Online*, n. 375, 1984–1985. Disponível em: <http://heinonline.org/HOL/LandingPage?collection=journals&handle=hein.journals/nclr63&div=20&id=&page=>. Acesso em: 20 mai. 2015.

Gollop, Thomaz Rafael. Abortamento por anomalia fetal. In: Cavalcanti, Alcilene; Xavier, Dulce (Orgs.). *Em defesa da vida: aborto e direitos humanos*. São Paulo: Católicas pelo direito de decidir, 2006.

Hungria, Nélson; Fragoso, Heleno Cláudio. *Comentários ao Código Penal*. Volume V, arts.121 a 136. 6.ed. Rio de Janeiro: Editora Forense, 1981.

Mendonça, Alba Valéria. *Emoção e revolta marcam enterro de Jandira no Subúrbio do Rio*. G1, Rio de Janeiro, 28 set. 2014. Disponível em: <http://g1.globo.com/rio-de-janeiro/noticia/2014/09/emocao-e-revolta-marcam-enterro-de-jandira-no-suburbio-do-rio.html>. Acesso em: 15 set. 2016.

MENINA de 15 anos grávida de trigêmeos tem aborto em banheiro de colégio em Apucarana. TNOnline, Apucarana, 21 jun. 2016. Disponível em :<http://tnonline.uol.com.br/noticias/cotidiano/67,376978,21,06,menina-de-15-anos-gravida-de-tr

igemeos-tem-aborto-em-banheiro-de-colegio-em-apucarana.shtml>. Acesso em: 20 out. 2016.

Mill, John Stuart. *The Subjection of Women*. London: Kindle Edition, 1869.

Percepções sobre o aborto e educação sexual. Disponível em <http://catolicas.org.br/wp-content/uploads/2017/10/Pesquisa-de-Opini%C3%A3o-P%C3%BAblica-2017-CDD-e-IBOPE-Percep%C3%A7%C3%B5es-sobre-aborto-e-educa%C3%A7%C3%A3o-sexual_3-MB.pdf >. Acesso em 18/09/2019.

Pimentel, Silvia; Pandjiarjian, Valéria. Aborto: descriminar para não discriminar. *Jornal da Rede saúde, São Paulo*, v. 21, set. 2000, p. 5–9.

Piovesan, Flavia; Pimentel, Silvia. *Conspiração contra a impunidade*. Folha de São Paulo, São Paulo, 25/11/2002. Opinião. Disponível em <https://www1.folha.uol.com.br/fsp/opiniao/fz2511200210.htm >. Acesso em 09/10/2019.

Sarmento, Daniel. *Legalização do aborto e Constituição*. Mundo Jurídico. Disponível em: <http://www.clam.org.br/bibliotecadigital/uploads/publicacoes/982_342_abortosarmentodaniel.pdf>. Acesso em: 03 jul. 2014.

Sedgh, G. Abortion incidence between 1990 and 2014: global, regional, and subregional levels and trends. *The Lancet*, 2016. Disponível em: <https://www.guttmacher.org/infographic/2018/highly-restrictive-laws-do-not-eliminate-abortion>. Acesso em 28/09/2019.

Siegel, Reva B., ProChoiceLife: asking who protects life and how—and why it matters in law and politics (September 10, 2017). *Indiana Law Journal*, Forthcoming; Yale Law School, Public Law Research Paper No. 613. Available at SSRN: https://ssrn.com/abstract=3035017

UNFPA. Annual Report 2018. *One vision: Three zeros*. Disponível em <https://www.unfpa.org/sites/default/files/pub-pdf/UNFPA_PUB_2018_EN_Annual_Report_3.pdf >. Acesso em 03/10/2019.

Varikas, Eleni. Igualdade. In: Hirata, Helena; e outras. (org.). *Dicionário Crítico do Feminismo*. São Paulo: Editora UNESP, 2009.

Vitorelli, Edilson. *Manual de Direito Difusos*. Editora Jus Podivm, 2ª.ed.

Wapner, Ronald J. Diagnóstico pré-natal de desordens congênitas. In: Creasy, Robert K. Creasy e Resnik (ed.). *Medicina materno fetal: princípios e práticas*. 7. ed. Trad. Gabriella da Silva Mendes. Rio de Janeiro: Editora Elsevier, 2016.

Williamson, Nancy. *Situação da população Mundial 2013*. Maternidade Precoce: Enfrentando desafios da gravidez na adolescência. Brasil, p.v. 2013.

Women's link Worldwide. *Guía para poteger los derechos sexuales y reprodutivos de las mujeres ante el sistema interamericano*, p. 50–55. Disponível em <https://www.womenslinkworldwide.org/files/3041/guia-para-proteger-los-derechos-sexuales-ante-el-sistema-interamericano.pdf >. Acesso em 22/11/2019.

Chapter 5

Embryonic Stem-Cells Research at the Brazilian Supreme Court

Or How to Decide Not to Decide

Lucas de Laurentiis

INTRODUCTION

What is the value of life? Is an embryo a human being protected by constitutional norms? Is it possible for a Court to define precisely when life begins? These questions seem like the theoretical puzzles people usually find in philosophical books. Nevertheless, they were also the main themes of a quite controversial judicial decision: the judgment of the Direct Action of Unconstitutionality (ADI) 3510, decided by the Brazilian Supreme Court (STF). But this is not just a controversial decision since it deals with issues related to science regulation,[1] life protection, religion, and at last but not least judicial activism. It is also a very rich decision in theoretical terms, one in which Brazilian judges had to show their conceptions about their role as constitutional judges and how their decisions may change rules created by political actors. At the end of the day this is a fundamental decision one must know about in order to be familiar with the limits the right to live and die in the Brazilian constitutional law. It is a decision in which we can see the STF's true face: a Court divided by moral and philosophical visions, where judges are more likely to present their preconceptions in a most chaotic and rhetorical fashion than to give a precise and clear orientation about the juridical issue they face.[2] This chapter aims to explain how this issue arrived at STF and which were the arguments brought by the parties of this action (item two); what was the meaning of the decision those judges reached and why they did that (item three); at least some critical aspects of this decision will be presented, so that the foreigner reader may make their own mind not just on the issue of this judgment (what is life and when it begins?), but also about the way such themes are decided concerning the Brazilian law.

JUDGMENT CONTEXT

The problem began with the law 11.105 (Biosecurity Act) passed by the Congress in March 2005 and signed by the former President Luiz Inácio Lula da Silva in October of the same year.[3] Article 5 of this law authorizes the extraction of stem cells from human nonviable embryos created for assisted reproduction or which had been frozen for three or more years at the time the law was passed.[4] All that should be done with the genitor's expressed permission. In May 2005, the then General Attorney of Brazilian Republic, Claúdio Fonteles, a right-wing catholic Attorney, demanded the unconstitutionality of this rule before STF. His arguments were that this law negatively affected the right to life and human dignity, which were the foundation stones of Brazilian democratic rule of law. The central thesis of this claim sustained that "human life begins upon fertilization," an assumption that was based upon testimony, scientific articles, and a book published by the Brazilian National Bishops' Conference (CNBB). The conclusions of the plea are as simple as this: since a) the zygote is generated by the meeting of masculine and feminine chromosomes, human life begins at fertilization; therefore b) life is continuous because it develops by itself; finally and therefore, c) a zygote already consists of life and life can develop itself from a single cell to human proteins, enzymes, and body tissues. That reasoning ends up with one straight conclusion: every interruption of cell development or discard of embryos means an attempt to human life. In this sense, it was said at the lawsuit that:

> The embryo is a human being in the initial phase of his life. It is a human being due to its specific genetic constitution and for the fact that it was generated by a human couple through human gametes—sperm and egg. It comprises the development phase that goes from conception, with the formation of the zygote in the union of the gametes, until completing the eighth week of life.[5]

After accepting the suit, Justice Ayres Britto convoked the first public hearing. It is noteworthy that this procedure is grounded by Brazilian law (article 9, Federal Law 9.868/99), which authorizes rapporteurs—the one judge who conduces the suit—to convoke the "hearing testimonies from people with experience and authority in the matter."[6] Notwithstanding, at that time this procedure was yet to be completely regulated—nobody knew, for instance, how many people could take part in the hearing and for how long each presenter should speak. For that reason, the Court referred to the internal regiment of Brazilian federal Congress, where this procedure was thoroughly regulated.[7] This means that norms deemed to regulate political debates were used in a judicial procedure conducted by the STF, fact that raises several questions: First of all, because this importation was not expressly authorized by the Congress, who had created it for the sole purpose of regulating the legislative procedure; second because, following the US model, in Brazil, the Supreme Court is a judicial court, where political debates should be avoided and the use of this set of norms indicates that the debates conduced before the Brazilian Court was political in its nature.[8] Since nobody complained against that procedure, twenty-two specialists were invited to this public hearing, almost all of them professionals, researchers, and professors in the biomedical sphere. The sole exception was an anthropologist with a post-doctoral degree in bioethics. The testimony brought by them can be divided into two main blocks: one including those specialists chosen to testify for the aim of the General Attorney of the Republic and the CNBB and the other appointed by the authorities that defended the constitutionality of the law: the National Congress and the President, represented by the Union General Attorney (AGU). The hearing's goal was to seek "a jurisdictional concept for the word 'life' and for the expression 'human dignity,'" as the sponsor of this action said.

Examining the trajectories of both groups of specialists, one can see that most of those against the use of embryonic stem cells were involved with the institutions of the Catholic Church.[9] For this set of speakers, embryos life was understood to be a sacred right. This block surrounded itself with biological arguments, at the same time that they refuted other biology based arguments offered up by the one that favored research. This particular group made great usage of bioethical discourses, which at that time were not fully verified by scientific tests.[10] The arguments presented by them seem to take for granted that life and dignity are naturally absolute rights and, therefore, nor judges or the legislative should be able to limit them for any reason.[11] In this sense, they considered the human embryo to be a true human existence and thus establish it as a human person with all due legal rights. Therefore, the concept of life itself is here considered from a biological and sacralized point of view.

On the other hand, specialists that favored the usage of embryos in research argued that the search for a definition of life in its conceptualization was a "false problem," one that judges and the lawmaker were not able to answer.[12] In another vein, some specialists of this group proposed the establishment of the nervous system creation as the beginning point of human life, an argument that is grounded by Brazilian transplant law (Federal Law, 9.434/96). At his point, an analogy with cerebral death was sustained in order to invoke the establishment of the nervous system as the beginning of life. It was also sustained that embryo's viability should just be considered as a life in a situation where it is inside the mother's uterus since it is up from this point that they can be able to develop themselves.[13] Therefore, the elimination of nonviable embryos in scientific research was considered an affectless act in regard to the protection of human life. These arguments were supported by theatrical and normative fundamentals. The first holds that in the lack of a precise scientific definition concerning the exact points of beginning and ending of life, the legislative should be the one regulate it since representatives have a sort of democratic legitimation for doing it—and that was in fact done. At the normative level, the same conclusion was reached through the recourse of an old definition found at Brazilian Civil Code: "The person's civil personality starts from birth with life; but the law saves, from conception, the rights of the unborn" (article 2, of former Brazilian Civil Code). Finally, pro-research group's principal strategy was not just to avoid the question concerning the concept of life, but also to present a scientific, neutral, and secular side of the debate. In this sense it was sustained that "the argument against the use of stem cells in medical research and treatment is propelled, more often than not, by a religious feeling."[14]

In my point of view, both sides of this debate are in need of better arguments. In the case of the pro-life movement, it is not clear why it is necessary to consider the fecundation as the initial point of human life. Many places, including United States and Europe, do not think this way, so why should that conclusion be forbidden in Brazil?[15] This misconception is caused by a sort of naturalization of the right to life and human dignity, which is understood as something innate to humans as such and, therefore, something that cannot be touched by any political branch. That is not the way human rights, including the right to life, should be conceived since human rights are rights like any others and rights are not divine creations or something related to nature.[16] They are human creations, meant to solve human problems, most of them related to the abuse of power by the State. Further, the law as a whole, not just human rights law, is a system designed by humans who are in need of tools to solve their own social and political problems.[17] For this reason, the law has a changeable content and one cannot claim to have found the universal concept of the right to live or die, since these concepts are circumstantial. Furthermore, it is pointless to claim that any scientific research has found the most accurate concept of human life, since they usually have effects in a specific place and in a given moment, once its conclusions are adopted by lawmakers. Science cannot determine law, as law does not determine science.

In contrast, the opinions sustained by the defenders of the Biosecurity Act correctly consider that human life is a concept that must be designed by inland legislations, a fact that does not make this point of view less fragile, basically for two reasons. First of all, if it is true that scientists have not reached a comprehensive concept of human life, this fact must not imply that the law has not already achieved this goal. In other words, it is perfectly possible to achieve a juridical concept of life that is sufficiently determined, without the necessity of precise scientific basis. If that was not the case, the law would simply be affectless, since the scientific debate is continuous and never ends. Furthermore, it is soundless to say that there is scientific disagreement on the issue "life's beginning," since the main point of this lawsuit was not to know what science has told about life, but what Brazilian constitutional law says about the right to life. Second, the application of the Civil Code to solve this problem seems to be completely out of purpose. Not just because the question inquired was not about what this legislation has to say about human life, but about the constitutional concept of it.[18] Moreover, the problem concerning this argument seems to consider that the conception adopted by this Law (Brazilian Civil Code) cannot be changed or that it has a sort of canonical nature. Evidentially, that is not true, since this Code is a simple Bill like any other, able to be changed by other Bills. If that is true, any rule within the Brazilian Civil Code, including the one about life's beginning, could be changed by the Biosecurity Act. And that doesn't make any of these Bills invalid or unconstitutional. It is just a case of regular and simple abrogation. At the end of the day, this argument tries to use the Civil Code as if it was a constitutional norm, what is not just some way to avoid the problem, but also a way of giving a wrong answer to it.

JUDGMENT CONTENT

Judge Carlos Ayres Britto reported the case, and his vote was accepted by the majority of judges present on the trial day. First of all, this judge holds that the beginning of human life coincides with the moment of fertilization. However, he also points out that "the beginning of life is a reality that is set apart from those things that constitute a physical or natural person," a statement based on the Brazilian Civil Code.[19] For this reason, personality is thought to be an attribute of "a person in their biographical dimension and is thus more than simple biology." At this point in his vote, Britto mentions a passage of Ronald Dworkin's book *Live's Dominion*, where it is stated, "law protects in different ways each step of the biological development of the human being."[20] With these distinctions at hand, the vote continues in the sense of denying the arguments presented by the petitioner. Embryos are not fetuses, fetuses are not humans, and humans are neither embryos nor fetuses, he says. As strange it may sound, this circular conclusion was summarized by two statements of Judge Britto: "an embryonic human person doesn't exist, only embryos of human people do."[21] Through this word "puzzle" it is simply said that embryos are not human beings yet, what does not mean that embryos are not to be considered as living entities. Embryos exist and live, but they cannot be considered as humans.

Britto also proposed a differentiation between the use of embryos in research laboratories and the interruption of a pregnancy: in the first case, he states, there is no ongoing gestation, and so, Brazilian Bills that criminalizes abortion would not be applied in this case. Embryos conceived in a laboratory and confined in vitro are not subject to reproductive progression. Britto also emphasized the gestation importance for the continued life of a fetus, and traces a parallel between the criteria for establishing brain death and the embryos referred in Biosecurity Act: in embryo's case, it does not have a nervous system at all, unlike what happens with fetuses in gestation. Finally, this judge concluded that without a brain, there can be no human person, even potentially. In the context of the Biosecurity Act, then, an embryo is "a vegetative life that comes before the development of the brain."[22] As a result, in his vote it was considered that Brazilian Biosecurity Act is, in fact, constitutional. In terms of Britto's considerations, it is a "perfect set of rules," meaning that the Court should accept the law as it was created by legislative. His vote was fully followed by other five judges (Joaquim Barbosa, Carmen Lúcia, Celso de Mello, Marco Aurélio e Ellen Gracie).

In the opposite direction, Judge Menezes Direito was the first to raise a dissident vote. His reasoning was the longest among all the judges (it has more than eighty pages), and it covers issues related to religion, science, philosophy, history, and literature.[23] Law is an accidental theme in his vote. It seems that the goal of this myriad of references was to dwarf his image as a religion-oriented Judge.[24] This may sound paradoxical, but, at the end of this long speech, the key point of his vote was a quote of an Aristotle's book,[25] where this philosopher deals with the notions of potentiality and actuality. Based on these notions, it was concluded by the vote that "the embryo is not an entity that transmutes beyond its essence. It is the being itself in potency, and, above all, in essence, in continuous update that in its first stages, and, even in the culture, is represented by its successive divisions."[26] Putting it in simple words, this means that embryos must be considered as a living entity, because they are potentially humans. Menezes Direito also insisted that the Supreme Court had to explain its position regarding the beginning of life, once the right of embryos depends on that definition. Thus, he claimed that embryos are in themselves a potential being and would not only self-develop if prevented from doing so by outside circumstances. Embryos, in this sense, are viewed as holders of fundamental rights, including the right to life. Therefore, they deserved protection from the State, who should forbid any actions, whether they come from private actors or not, opposed to its self-development. At the end of this quite spectacular vote, the conclusion was that researches that causes embryos waste, be it for the sake of scientific development or human health, are forbidden. This sort of research was seen as an attempt to human life. With a few changes, this arguments and conclusions were followed by Judges Ricardo Lewandowsky and Eros Grau.

In the middle of the opposing sides, Judge Gilmar Mendes offered an alternative solution: to simply change the Law terms. Although he found it unnecessary to discuss the points where human life begins and ends in the sense of legal protection, his conclusion was that the Biosecurity Act was not in accordance with the Brazilian Constitution. This view was grounded on German conceptions, like the famous and obscure notion of deficient protection of human rights (*Untermassverbot*),[27] which means that as it was approved, Biosecurity Act gave not enough protection to embryos life. Based on that conclusion, this vote requires the creation of a new administrative organism that, once created, would have to integrate the structure of Health Federal Department: the Central Ethics and Research Committee, where all the researches related to human life should be submitted to authorization. This proposal was also adopted by Judge Cezar Peluzo, who, at the end of the trial, proposed that the organs mentioned in one federal Decree (n. 5,591/2005) should assume the task of regulating embryos researches and, for this very reason, all researches about this matter would have to be previously authorized by them. Inspired by Italian authors, these two Judges named this proposal a "declaration of constitutionality with adding effect," which means that their decision was meant to have the same effects as the creation of a new Act.

CRITICAL APPRAISAL

It is not hard to find the weaknesses in all of these opinions. First of all, no one reasonable enough would believe, like Judge Ayres Britto did, that an embryo lives without being human. If it lives, it is human, if it does not, then it is nothing at all. What is said in this vote is as trivial as wrong; it is in fact true that life cannot be reduced to biological terms, for the simple fact that once someone is living, he or she must do something with their life. But that was not the question posed at the trial and certainly do not change the simple fact that the Act at stake permitted the extinction, for the sake of science development, of frozen embryos. If these embryos were meant to be humans with lives and personal histories, we will never know due to the simple fact that their extinction was authorized by the Brazilian Supreme Court. At the end, it may sound beautiful to say that human life is social in its essence and even quote poets who wrote about that.[28] But that's not a proper way to judge nor to solve people's problems, who certainly would prefer to go to a theater to see someone reciting poems.

The other side of this trial does not have better arguments, either. To start with, as one should doubt about the seriousness of a paper where the author quotes as many articles and books as he could find on the internet, the same must be said about the opinion brought by Judge Menezes Direito: the sole quoting makes the argument not sound or better. In fact, the very opposite conclusion is true: who searches for an answer to their problems as something already expressed by someone else is the one that seems to be the least prepared to give any answer at all. This is just the case of Judge Menezes Direito. Things got worse when we see that the core argument of his vote is based on a quite controversial Aristotelic notion, which was not even problematized at the reasoning of the vote and was taken for granted by the judge as if something that could be true two thousand years ago is still the best answer to nowadays problems. Again, what this judge discusses at this point was not even the question posed at trial, which could be translated as: is it possible for a law to limit the process of scientific research based on the right to life? As we have seen, no vote stated at this trial has proposed an answer to the question. In the case of the vote of Judge Menezes Direito, the question was not even posed.

Finally, the proposal of Judge Gilmar Mendes may seem to be the most technical and elaborate one, but this perception is dissolved in a deeper analysis. Firstly, it is not even clear if there is a benefit in creating a new administrative organism to the protection of embryos life. Supposing that this organism really existed, one could not know what the effect of that would be to the protection of this right. The results would depend on the people who would work there, the procedure they follow, the structure they have, and finally, the amount of money they spend on it. Since no Judge can predict all these variables, maybe they should prevent themselves from proposing things they do not know how to implement. Summarizing the problem, one must see that Judges and Courts cannot create law, no matter the name they give or the idiom used to indicate it. That is the reason why the Germans do not accept the strange notion of defective protection anymore—no one knows how to determine the defectiveness of a law because of the simple fact that outside the law there is no right, and a right to be defective must, first of all, be a right.[29] Again, what has been done is a way of bypassing the real issue of the trial, besides what this is a way of creating a new power for the Court—the power to create laws—without coming any real benefit out of that.

FINAL REMARKS

What are the contributions of this decision? In practical terms they are very few, almost none. After all, the Brazilian Biosecurity Act was declared constitutional, without any change in its terms, as it was proposed by Judge Ayres Britto. In these circumstances one would expect to find in this judgment some clear answers about two simple questions: What is the concept of human life in the Brazilian law? And what are the limits of scientific researches that affect or pose a danger to human life? Instead of that, what is found at the votes is a sum of quotes, conjectures, and political proposals. Even the final holding of this decision (*Ementa*) is just an ensemble of statements of different Judges that don't even talk to each other. In this sense, one may categorically say that the practical effects of this decision are null, for the sole reason that it is indeed impossible to understand what its real meaning was. One must thus agree with the statement of Judge Cezar Peluso, who at the end of this judgment of more than 500 pages asked if "after all these hours of judging, all that we said was useless?".[30] Indeed it was, which is just a shame for Brazilian constitutional law.

NOTES

1. Defending that this matter was not enough discussed by the judges of this case: Martins, Leonardo. Lei de biossegurança e controle de sua constitucionalidade pelo STF na ADI 3510-DF, "Biosafety law and control of its constitutionality by the STF in ADI 3510-DF", in: Martins, Leonardo (ed.). *Bioética à luz da Liberdade científica: estudo de caso baseado na decisão do STF sobre a constitucionalidade da lei de Biossegurança e no direito comparado alemão*, São Paulo: Atlas, 2014.

2. In this sense it was already said that even judges that voted in the same direction (Britto and Gracie), "had different conceptions about the rights to live and dignity" (Rosler, Claudia Rosane; Betti, Gabriel Rübinger, O julgamento da ADI n. 3510 sob a perspectiva argumentative, "The judgment of case ADI 3510 of the Brazilian Supreme Court from an argumentative perspective", *Revista novos estudos jurídicos*, v. 19, n. 3, p. 663–694, 2014, p. 686).

3. For a reconstruction of the debated that occurred within Brazilian Senate see: Luna, Naara. O direito à vida no contexto do aborto e da pesquisa com células-tronco embrionárias: disputas de agentes e valores religiosos em um estado laico, *Religião e sociedade*, v. 33, no. 1, p. 71–94, Rio de Janeiro, 2013.

4. The entire text of this rule states that: For the purpose of research and therapy, the use of embryonic stem cells obtained from human embryos produced by in vitro fertilization and not used in the respective procedure is permitted, provided the following conditions are met: I—are non-viable embryos; or II—are embryos frozen for 3 (three) years or more, on the date of publication of this Law, or which, already frozen on the date of publication of this Law, after completing 3 (three) years, counted from the date of freezing. § 1 In any case, the consent of the parents is required. § 2 Research institutions and health services that carry out research or therapy with human embryonic stem cells must submit their projects to the appreciation and approval of the respective research ethics committees. § 3—The sale of biological

material referred to in this article is prohibited and its practice implies the crime typified in art. 15 of Law No. 9,434, of February 4, 1997.

5. See the complete petition at: Fonteles, Cláudio. Initial petition in ADI 3510-DF, original document available at: http://www.mpf.mp.br/pgr/copy_of_pdfs/ADIN_3510_Fonteles_inicial.pdf/view. In a matter of fact all this reasoning was not created by the petitioner, who simply sums up several statements of medicine and genetic experts.

6. Brazil, Federal Law 9,868, from 10 November 1999, original document available at: http://www.planalto.gov.br/ccivil_03/leis/l9868.htm

7. Articles 255 to 258 of such Internal Regiment regulate this procedure. This norm is available at: https://www2.camara.leg.br/atividade-legislativa/comissoes/comissoes-permanentes/cft/audiencias-publicas/Normas%20Regimentais.

8. In this same sense: Ramos, Elival da Silva. *Ativismo judicial: parâmetros dogmáticos*, "Judicial activism: judicial parameters", São Paulo: Saraiva, 2017.

9. To check the debates of this audience, see: Sales, Lilia. Em defesa da vida humana: Moralidades em disputa em duas audiências públicas no STF, "In defense of human life: Moralities in dispute at two public hearings at the Supreme Court", *Religião e sociedade*, v. 33, n. 1, Rio de Janeiro, p. 143–164, 2013.

10. One of the arguments sustained by this speakers take for granted, for instance, that "new methodologies for obtaining pluripotent cells from adult cells are patient-specific and similar, in expressive number, in their properties to human embryonic stem cells, which even led the researcher responsible for the creation of the Dolly sheep, Ian Wilmut, to publicly announce, in November 2007, his respective adherence to this option" (Martins, Ives Gandra da Silva; Rezek, Francisco; Souza, Fatima Fernandes de. Petição apresentada em nome de CCBB na ADI n. 3510 "Petition presented in the name of CCBB (Brazilian national confederation of Bishops) at the ADI n. 3510." Document is available at: https://www.conjur.com.br/dl/memorial_gandra_com_

11. An opposite view sustains that all fundamental rights are principles and, for this reason, none of them are to be considered as an absolute right. In this sense, holding that the notion of fundamental rights as "trumps" should be replaced by the less rigid notion of *prima facie* principle, see: Klatt, Matthias. Taking rights less seriously: a structural analysis of judicial discretion, *Ratio Juris*, v. 20, n. 4, 2007, p. 506–529, p. 520.

12. In this sense at the Brazilian literature: Dias, Roberto. *O Direito Fundamental à Morte Digna*. Uma Visão Constitucional da Eutanásia, "The Fundamental Right to Decent Death. A Constitutional Vision of Euthanasia," Belo horizonte: Forum, 2014. With similar view at US literature: Sunstein, Cass. *One Case at a Time*: Judicial Minimalism on the Supreme Court, Harvard University Press, 2001.

13. In this sense: Waldby, Catherine, Stem cells, tissue cultures and the production of biovalue. *Health*, v. 6, n. 3, p. 305–323, 2002.

14. This argument was brought by the to-be Minister of STF Luiz Roberto Barroso in his opinion for the Court. Document available at: https://www.migalhas.com.br/arquivo_artigo/art20060104.htm.

15. In this same sense, considering that "The point at which human life begins will always be seen differently by different individuals, groups, cultures, and religious

faiths. Embryonic and fetal life is a continuum, but there are points and processes within the continuum—birth of the new-born, viability, neuromaturation, implantation, and conception—that may be considered as the beginning of human life" (Beller, F.K., Zlatnik, G.P. The beginning of human life. *Journal of Assisted Reproduction and Genetics*, v. 12, p. 477–483, 1995).

16. See in this same vein: Dembour, Marie-Bénédicte. What are human rights? Four schools of thought, *Human Rights Quarterly*, v. 32, n. 1, pp. 1–20, February 2010.

17. For further developments of this argument, see: Poscher R. The hand of Midas: when concepts turn legal, or deflating the Hart-Dworkin debate, in: Hage, J.C., von der Pfordten, D. (eds.), *Concepts in Law*. Law and Philosophy Library, v. 88, Springer, 2009.

18. In a matter of fact the Brazilian Civil Code does not talk about the concept of life too. It simply states that a every living person has a personality, what is very different from defining when or why life begins.

19. See Brazil, STF, *Ação direta de inconstitucionalidade* 3510—inteiro teor, "Direct action of unconstitutionality 3510—entire content", p. 163.

20. The decision does not identifies where Dworkin said that, but it seems that it refers to the page 89 of the first edition of the oeuvre, where the author said that he "just described a natural course of human life—beginning in conception, extending through birth and childhood, culminating in successful and engaged adulthood in which the natural biological investment and the personal human investment in that live are realized, and finally ending in a natural death after a normal span of years" (Dworkin, Ronald, *Live's Dominion*, New York: Alfred Knopf, 1993, p. 89). This quote is surprising since: Dworkin does not deal with the question discussed at this process—researches conduced with frozen embryos—nor this passage reflects the author's thinking, for here he is just introducing the subject of the chapter, not presenting his own view.

21. See Brazil, STF, *Ação direta de inconstitucionalidade* 3510—inteiro teor, "Direct action of unconstitutionality 3510—entire content", p. 172.

22. See Brazil, STF, *Ação direta de inconstitucionalidade* 3510—inteiro teor, "Direct action of unconstitutionality 3510—entire content", p. 198.

23. Between other references this opinion quoted names like: Arthur Schopenhauer, Emmanuel Kant, Francis Fukuiama, David Hume, Ludwig Wittgenstein, Tomas de Aquino, Jurgen Habermas, and Umberto Eco.

24. At the time of his appointment Menezes Direito had to answer questions about his neutrality in questions related to religious issues. This sort of questioning can be found in several interviews, likewise: https://www.conjur.com.br/2007-set-02/minha_fe_nunca_interferiu_julgamentos_direito.

25. The book here quoted was Aristotle's *Methafisics* in a quite popular Brazilian edition (Aristoteles, *Metafísica*, Bauru: Edipro, 2006). One may wonder why this specific edition was used, since there are other translations more sophisticates and up to date in Brazilian market, like the bilingual edition published by the Loyola Publisher (Aristoteles, *Metafísica*, São Paulo: Loyola, 2014).

26. See Brazil, STF, *Ação direta de inconstitucionalidade* 3510—inteiro teor, "Direct action of unconstitutionality 3510—entire content", p. 271.

27. See Brazil, STF, *Ação direta de inconstitucionalidade* 3510—inteiro teor, "Direct action of unconstitutionality 3510—entire content", p. 630.

28. At the end of his vote Judge Ayres Britto recite a famous poem named "Tabacaria" from Portuguese Poet Fernando Pessoa.

29. In a similar sense: Kingreen, Thorsten; Poscher, Ralf. *Grundrechte—Staatsrecht II*, 34. ed. Heidelberg: C.F. Müller, 2018, p. 48.

30. See Brazil, STF, *Ação direta de inconstitucionalidade* 3510—inteiro teor, "Direct action of unconstitutionality 3510—entire content", p. 643.

REFERENCES

Beller, F.K., Zlatnik, G.P. The beginning of human life. *Journal of Assisted Reproduction and Genetics*, v. 12, p. 477–483, 1995.

Brazil, STF. *Ação direta de inconstitucionalidade* 3510—inteiro teor, "Direct action of unconstitutionality 3510—entire content", p. 271.

Dias, Roberto. O Direito Fundamental à Morte Digna. Uma Visão Constitucional da Eutanásia, "The Fundamental Right to Decent Death. A Constitutional Vision of Euthanasia", Belo horizonte: Forum, 2014.

Dembour, Marie-Bénédicte. What Are Human Rights? Four Schools of Thought, *Human Rights Quarterly*, v. 32, n. 1, pp. 1–20, February 2010

Dworkin, Ronald. *Live's Dominion*. New York: Alfred Knopf, 1993.

Fonteles, Cláudio. *Initial petition in ADI 3510-DF*, original document available at: http://www.mpf.mp.br/pgr/copy_of_pdfs/ADIN_3510_Fonteles_inicial.pdf/view, accessed at the 10th April 2020.

Kingreen, Thorsten; Poscher, Ralf. *Grundrechte—Staatsrecht II*, 34. ed. Heidelberg: C.F. Müller, 2018.

Klatt, Matthias. Taking rights less seriously: a structural analysis of judicial discretion. *Ratio Juris*, v. 20, n. 4, 2007, p. 506–529, p. 520.

Luna, Naara. O direito à vida no contexto do aborto e da pesquisa com células-tronco embrionárias: disputas de agentes e valores religiosos em um estado laico. *Religião e sociedade*, v. 33, no. 1, p. 71–94, Rio de Janeiro, 2013.

Martins, Ives Gandra da Silva; Rezek, Francisco; Souza, Fatima Fernandes de. Petição pela CCBB na ADI n. 3510 "Petition presented in the name of CCBB (Brazilian national confederation of Bishops) at the ADI n. 3510". Document is available at: https://www.conjur.com.br/dl/memorial_gandra_com_resumo_manifesto_20080221.pdf

Poscher R. The hand of midas: when concepts turn legal, or deflating the Hart-Dworkin debate. In: Hage, J.C.; von der Pfordten D. (eds.), *Concepts in Law*. Law and Philosophy Library, v. 88, Springer, 2009.

Ramos, Elival da Silva. *Ativismo judicial*: parâmetros dogmáticos, "Judicial activism: judicial parameters", São Paulo: Saraiva, 2017.

Sales, Lilia. Em defesa da vida humana: Moralidades em disputa em duas audiências públicas no STF, "In defense of human life: Moralities in dispute at two public

hearings at the Supreme Court", *Religião e sociedade*, v. 33, n. 1, Rio de Janeiro, p. 143–164, 2013.
Sunstein, Cass. *One Case at a Time*: Judicial Minimalism on the Supreme Court, Harvard University Press, 2001.
Sunstein, Cass; Vermeulle, Adrian. Interpretation and institutions. *Michigan Law Review*, v. 101, n. 4, p. 885–951, 2003.
Waldby, Catherine. Stem cells, tissue cultures and the production of biovalue. *Health*, v. 6, n. 3, p. 305–323, 2002.

Chapter 6

Affirmative Action at the Federal Supreme Court

The Difficult Promotion of Racial Equity in Brazil

Maria Paula Bucci Dallari

THE FORMATION OF BRAZIL AS A SLAVE COUNTRY: OFFICIAL SLAVERY AND THE DEFEATS OF THE FOUNDING FATHERS JOSÉ BONIFÁCIO, JOAQUIM NABUCO, AND RUI BARBOSA

Racial equity in Brazil has always been a stormy issue, given the country's formation as a slave nation since its colonization. In the nineteenth century, when it became independent from Portugal, the matter of slavery was an important social dispute, which occupied the entire period between the Proclamation of Independence in 1822 and the Republic in 1889. In that period, the Brazilian Empire was governed by descendants of the Portuguese crown, D. Pedro I (1822–1831) and D. Pedro II (1840–1889), who maintained the institution of slavery.

Three of the Brazilian founding fathers struggled in the fight against this institution: José Bonifácio, Joaquim Nabuco, and Rui Barbosa. Despite having moved important forces towards abolitionism, they did not achieve full victory. On the contrary, this position cost them political rise in their lifetime.[1]

Joaquim Nabuco, a liberal parliamentarian, defined slavery as a unifying element of the political, legal, and social system of the Brazilian Empire. Its "structuring character" imposed abolitionism as a "primordial political reform" (NABUCO, 2000, p. 14).

Brazil's first constitution, approved in 1824, marks the first defeat of abolitionism in the newly created country.[2] José Bonifácio, who had been the main strategist in the independence process, defended a liberal constitution, with a regime of constitutional monarchy. The "Patriarch of Independence" asked himself: "How can there be a liberal and lasting Constitution in a country continually inhabited by an immense multitude of brutal and enemy slaves?" (ANDRADA E SILVA, pp. 46–47). In the Constituent Assembly, Bonifácio presented the *Representation to the General Constituent Assembly and Legislature of the Brazilian Empire on Slavery*,[3] a seminal text that proposes the gradual but effective emancipation of the enslaved over four or five years, and their integration into the life of the country, through education and work. This document was accompanied by a proposal for a *new regulation to promote the general civilization of the native Indians of Brazil, which will make slaves useless over time*. The Representation's vision is quite advanced, defining the slavery regime not only as legally unsustainable ("it is not, therefore, the right of property that you want to defend, but the right of force," ANDRADA E SILVA, p. 60) but also as a factor of economic and moral loss: "*Luxury and corruption were born among us before civilization and industry. ... The man who has slaves lives in indolence and indolence brings all addictions behind itself. ... The masters who own slaves live, for the most part, in inertia, as they are not needed by hunger or poverty to perfect their industry or improve their crops*" (ANDRADA E SILVA, pp. 54, 57).

The Representation foresees the delivery of land to the freemen, who will later unsuccessfully inspire the abolitionist movement: "Article X: All freemen of colour who do not have a trade or a certain way of life will receive from the State a small amount of land to cultivate, and they will also receive the necessary aid to establish themselves, the value of which they will pay over time" (ANDRADA E SILVA, p. 69).

This idea comes with the proposal to create a Mercy Fund, which would raise funds to finance initiatives related to emancipation. As in France and England, the "savings trusts" would receive certain public rents and allow slaves "to yield the pecuniary products of their labour and industry" (ANDRADA E SILVA, p. 76). The master's obligation to grant freedom to an old or incurably sick slave to support them, dress them, and treat them during their life was also provided.

These proposals precipitated the fall of Bonifácio in the Constituent Assembly (ANDRADA E SILVA, p. 41). Together with defending the idea of establishing boundaries and counterbalances against the monarch's action and being against the concentration of powers, it cost Bonifácio's exile. For Nabuco, this anti-slavery role would have blocked Bonifácio's political career. After laying the foundations for Independence, "there was never a place for the creator of the Empire" (NABUCO, 2000, p. 39, note 3). The Constituent Assembly was dissolved, and the Constitution granted by Emperor Pedro I in 1824 was silent about slavery.

In 1826, Brazil signed a treaty with the British, with a commitment to stop the slave trade in exchange for supporting the recognition of Independence. This commitment is materialized in the Law of 1831,[4] edited in the regency period, after the abdication of D. Pedro I. Despite the clarity of article 1 ("All slaves that entered the territory or ports of Brazil, coming from outside, are free."), its effectiveness was reduced.[5] Nabuco sums up this and the succession of laws that are followed as a big institutional lie, unfulfilled promises, "commitments formulated in such a way as to never be demandable" (NABUCO, 2000, p. 31).

The constant pressure from the British, with the addition of the Aberdeen Bill, in 1845, results in the edition of the Eusébio de Queiroz Law, Law No. 581,[6] from 1850, which finally prohibits the international slave trade to the country. Internal trafficking would remain.

From then on, the abolition strategy followed the gradualism adopted in the slave countries of Hispanic America, such as Cuba (ALONSO, p. 31). The phased model aimed to prevent the undesirable revolutionary outcome of Haiti in 1791. Prohibiting the slavery of those born after a certain date (*libertad de vientres*), slavery would end "naturally," when the last enslaved person disappeared.

Along these lines, in 1871 the *Rio Branco Law*, Law No. 2.040, which is in progress for five years, with many mishaps, even causing the fall of the cabinet of Ministers of Emperor Pedro II. This law is emblematic of the ambiguity with which the theme was treated, since at the same time that it defined that "no one is born a slave," it postponed the definitive extinction of this figure for about fifty years. Furthermore, on practical concrete provisions, such as maintaining captivity until the age of 21 and the right to compensation to the master for the child, frustrated the abolitionist spirit. Nabuco considered this shameful disposition, characteristic of a law made "without love" and 'without humanity,' even more if compared to José Bonifácio's project, which showed "victims of social injustice the deepest interest, actual affection" (NABUCO, 2000, p. 37).

In 1885, the *Sexagenários* Law, Law No. 3.270,[7] that would free slaves who were sixty years old or older. There was resistance from the rural landowners and the Dantas project, which provided for the freedom of the sexagenarians without compensation, written by Rui Barbosa, caused the dissolution of the Chamber in 1884, and was rejected (BARBOSA, p. 13). The approved law provided for the payment of indemnity by the freeman, through the provision of services to their master for another three years or until they were 65 years old.

Finally, on May 13, 1888, the *Áurea* Law was proclaimed, signed by Princess Isabel, heir to the throne. The very brief text of the law excludes land guarantees and education for ex-slaves, which had been proposed by the progressive side. At the same time, it blocks the indemnity claim, defended by the conservative side (ALONSO, p. 354). Of course, the losses on both sides are nowhere near equivalent. The omission of the law in relation to the future of freedmen takes its toll today, both for their descendants and for the whole of Brazilian society.

After the law, there is a reflux of the forces of abolitionism (MATTOS; NABUCO, 1998). Its supporters are dispersed and the measures that would be necessary for the integration of freed blacks into society do not take place. Without work, education, and even minimal guarantees of existence, such as housing, they are thrown into complete abandonment. As Rui Barbosa would say, years later, "Executed in this way, abolition was an atrocious irony. Giving freedom to the black, being disinterested as they were absolutely disinterested in their luck, was nothing more than releasing the masters" (BARBOSA, p. 14).

The proclamation of the Republic, in 1889, ended the monarchical period and the aspirations for government of Princess Isabel, who went into exile with the Emperor and her family. The side of the ex-masters quickly recovered, to demand compensation for the losses, just eleven days after the proclamation of the Áurea Law (ALONSO, p. 362). Having their request rejected in the legislative process, the allies insist, now through administrative means. The answer was the incineration of documents, starting in 1890, to suppress the registration of the facts that could support the compensation claims, with the festive support of the former abolitionists. "Rui Barbosa, then Minister of Finance, ordered the collection, in Rio de Janeiro, of 'all the existing papers, books and documents within the Ministry of Finance's offices, regarding the servile element, registration of slaves, naive, slaved women's free children and sexagenarian freemen' to be incinerated.

Barbosa justified the initiative as a humanitarian act towards ex-slaves, new Brazilian citizens. In fact, the historic abolitionist militancy not only supported the measure but also celebrated the burning of documents, which began a few days later, still in December 1890, and was repeated a few times in the following years. ... It was as if the historical abolitionists were sealing with the ex-slaves, in the name of Brazilian society, a pact to forget slavery and as if burning the documentation guaranteed the minimum—that is, that the past would not return." (MAMIGONIAN, pp. 454–455)

The final period of abolitionism was one of accelerating economic development, with new perspectives linked to the beginning of industrialization, construction of railways, and the expansion of coffee growing to the west. The need for labor was debated in the Legislature of São Paulo between the decades of 1870 and 1880, regarding bills that foresaw the use of freemen, advancing the adoption of incentives, and advantages. The option for immigration prevailed, financed with public funds, openly racist, in the opinion of Mário Theodoro. It was justified by an alleged "indolence" of the black workforce and "cultural superiority" of European workers, which would result in advantages of the "whitening" (THEODORO, pp. 40–41).

At the beginning of the twentieth century, there was a history of incomplete or ineffective worker protection laws, such as those dealing with occupational accidents excluding quarry workers, miners, and agricultural workers, which prohibited child labor, or which provided housing for workers, without regulation, among many others (BARBOSA). Giving a speech in his second presidential campaign, from which he left, as in the previous one, defeated, Rui Barbosa in 1919 demonstrates how Nabuco's prediction continued: "Ending slavery is not enough for us; it is necessary to destroy the work slavery has left behind" (NABUCO, 2005, p. 58).

Throughout the twentieth century, "racial ideology" developed. From the governments of Getúlio Vargas (1930–1945 and 1950–1954), when the social state was inaugurated in Brazil, with the enactment of labor protection laws and the creation of unions, the myth of "racial democracy" was installed, based on the denial of racism and on the "naturalization of racial inequalities," which remained and deepened during the military government (1964–1985).

In re-democratization, from 1985 onward, the racial equity agenda emerges with the articulation of the black movement. In 1996, after the Zumbi dos Palmares March against Racism, which brought together 30,000 people (JACCOUD et al., p. 272), for the first time there is a public recognition by a Brazilian government (Fernando Henrique Cardoso) about the existence of discrimination and racial inequality against blacks (JACCOUD, p. 274, note 28). Not only does it combat violent racism, but also structural prejudice, based on covert and repeated forms of discrimination, becoming officially accepted guidelines. An important impulse to generalize this matter came from the Third World Conference against Racism, Racial Discrimination, Xenophobia, and Related Intolerance, held in Durban, South Africa, in 2001, preceded by intense mobilization in preparatory meetings (JACCOUD, p. 274). After the Conference, affirmative action became a unified agenda of the black movement in the world (AMARAL E MELLO; ALVES). The lead on this agenda in Brazil is taken by the Lula government in 2003, who creates the Secretariat for the Promotion of Racial Equality.

PERFORMANCE BY CONGRESS AND THE EXECUTIVE BRANCH FOR AFFIRMATIVE ACTION

The historical panorama demonstrates the difficult evolution of the racial equity agenda in the process of creating laws and especially in its implementation during the nineteenth and twentieth centuries.

But the definitive solution of the controversy, due to the action of the Federal Supreme Court, as late as the twenty-first century, would not have been possible had it not been for some changes in its institutional role, which anticipated a new political and social disposition in the country to face the problem. It should be noted, in particular, the widening of the possibilities of action of the court defined by the 1988 Constitution, which increased the number of legitimate entities to propose actions in defense of constitutionality and expanded the ways of direct access to the court. This more active role of the Judiciary, not only at the top, but also at lower levels, gave rights an enhanced set of guarantees.

The role of the National Congress and the Executive Branch,[8] that in Brazil has relevant participation in the legislative process (e.g., exercising the legislative initiative in matters that involve public budget or the creation of public services), it was important in producing the context for the structural changes necessary to overcome racism. Over the years between 2000 and 2010 several laws were passed, with respect to racial equity, creating the institutional environment in which affirmative actions started to be accepted and confirmed. What these laws show is that there was a political and social convergence to support a transformation movement, as it had occurred in the final moments of the abolitionist struggle in the nineteenth century (ALENCASTRO).

Some of these laws are referred to in the ADPF 186 decision (commented below), not as reasons for deciding, but as elements of strengthening constitutional interpretation based on the right to material equality. Law No. 10.172 of 2001 is mentioned, which approves the National Education Plan from 2001 to 2011,[9] establishing among the objectives and goals for higher education "to create policies that facilitate minorities, victims of discrimination, access to higher education, through programs to compensate for deficiencies in their previous school education, thus enabling them to compete under equal conditions in the selection and admission processes at this level of education" (item 19); Law No. 10.558, of 2002, which creates the Diversity Program at the University, defining as its purpose "to implement and evaluate strategies for promoting access to higher education for people belonging to socially disadvantaged groups, especially Afro-descendants and Brazilian native Indians" (article 1); Law No. 10.678, of 2003, which created the Special Secretariat for Policies for the Promotion of Racial Equality, referred to above, linked to the Presidency of the Republic, which is responsible for coordinating the National Policy for the Promotion of Racial Equality (Decree No. 4,886 / 03), encompassing affirmative actions aimed at "eliminating any source of direct or indirect racial discrimination and inequality, through the generation of opportunities" (Annex: Specific objectives), and Law No. 12.228, of 2010, which instituted the Racial Equality Statute, stipulating that, for the black population's right to education, "the public power will adopt affirmative action programs" (article 14), among others.

But to complete the legislative framework of the movement that leads to the approval of affirmative action, it is necessary to examine the first Brazilian federal law to provide for quotas based on racial criteria, even in private higher education.

PROUNI LAW

In 2004, Provisional Measure 213 was issued, later converted into Law 11.09,[10] 2005, which created the University for All-PROUNI Program. The program provides for the granting of scholarships in private higher education institutions, in exchange for tax incentives. In fact, these benefits were already provided for in the Constitution (articles 150, IV, c, and 195, § 7); what the program does is to regulate the counterpart of the institutions, now established in a defined number of scholarships (HADDAD, 2009). This is important, given the relative weight of private education in Brazil, which accounts for about 75% of the approximately 8.5 million enrolments in higher education.[11]

> Art. 1° The University for All Program—PROUNI, under the management of the Ministry of Education, is instituted, for the granting of full scholarships and partial scholarships of 50% (fifty percent) ... for students of undergraduate courses ..., in private institutions of higher education, with or without profit.
>
> § 1° The full scholarship will be awarded to Brazilians who do not hold a college degree, whose monthly family income per capita does not exceed the value of up to 1 (one) minimum wage and 1/2 (half).
>
> ...
>
> Art. 7° The obligations to be fulfilled by the higher education institution ...:
>
> ...
>
> II—percentage of scholarships for the implementation *of affirmative policies for access to higher education for people with disabilities or self-declared indigenous and black people.* (my emphasis)

§ 1º The percentage referred to in item II of the caput of this article must be at least equal to the percentage of self-declared indigenous, brown or black citizens, in the respective Federation unit, according to the last census of the Brazilian Institute of Geography and Statistics—IBGE.

This law is the first to have its constitutionality questioned before the STF, by the Democrats political party, in Direct Action of Unconstitutionality 3.330, commented on in part 3, below.

QUOTA LAW

In August 2012, the so-called Quota Law, Law No. 12.711,[12] which provides for the reservation of vacancies in federal institutions of higher education based on ethnoracial criteria. Its structuring elements are the reservation of places for public school students, combined with a minimum proportion of blacks, browns, and indigenous people corresponding to the population of the State, according to the last census of the Brazilian statistical authority, the Brazilian Institute of Geography and Statistics (IBGE).

But in fact, before the enactment of the federal law, several public universities already adopted some form of affirmative action, making use of university autonomy, provided for in article 207 of the Federal Constitution:[13] *article 207. Universities relish didactic-scientific, administrative, and financial and patrimonial management autonomy and will obey the principle of inseparability between teaching, research, and extension.*

The pioneering experience took place in the state of Rio de Janeiro, with the state law 3.524, of 2000, which reserved 50% of the places for students from public schools, and the state law 3.708,[14] 2001, which reserved 40% of vacancies for students who declared themselves to be black or brown. The admission according to these criteria in the public universities of the State, State University of Rio de Janeiro (UERJ), and State University Norte Fluminense (UENF) took place from 2003 (AMARAL E MELLO). At the federal level, the University of Brasília was the first to adopt the reserve of places, starting in 2004 (ALMEIDA and others), followed later by other federal universities.

The processing of Law 12.711 begins with a project proposal presented in 1999. In 2004, a new text is brought to Congress. For more than ten years, intense debates have taken place, including the mobilization of intellectuals and liberal university professors who opposed affirmative actions, which saw risks of "racialization" of society (MAGGIE, 2008).

The Manifesto of One Hundred Thirteen Anti-Racist Citizens Against Racial Laws,[15] of 2008, invoked the "Brazilian tradition, which for exactly

120 years since the abolition of slavery, has not been supporting racial laws and policies." In other words, they understood that the enactment of yet another law could be a new reason for social frustration, as demonstrated by the history presented in part 1. They defended the "identity supported by the anti-racist idea of miscegenation and ... laws that criminalized racism" as the most appropriate tools to remedy the lasting effects of racial discrimination. Mestizaje, it is worth remembering, was defended by José Bonifácio, a geologist by training, who saw the future of Brazil as an amalgam between the various heterogeneous parts, in which miscegenation would be a way of "perfecting the existing races" (ANDRADA E SILVA, p. 82), "So that we can form in a few generations a homogeneous nation ..., that does not crumble under the small touch of any new political upheaval" (ANDRADA E SILVA, pp. 48–49).

But this thesis did not prevail. The proposal for a false "mixed-race democracy" was rejected. As we saw in the previous topic, miscegenation, the central argument of the "racial democracy" thesis that prevailed throughout the twentieth century, came to be combated after the emergence of the black movement shortly before the 1988 Constituent, as it was considered an expedient for denying racism (JACCOUD, p. 298). In short, there would be no risk of "racializing" Brazilian society, as racialization was already in place.

The Congress understood, with open support from the Executive Branch, that affirmative actions were crucial to guarantee the supply of opportunities. And Law No. 12.711, of 2012, was enacted, which provides:

> Art. 1° The federal institutions of higher education linked to the Ministry of Education will reserve, in each selective competition for admission to undergraduate courses, by course and shift, at least 50% (fifty percent) of their places for students who have completed high school in public schools.
>
> Single paragraph. When filling the vacancies mentioned in the caput of this article, 50% (fifty percent) must be reserved for students from families with an income equal to or less than 1.5 minimum wages (one and a half minimum wages) per capita. ...
>
> Art. 3° In each federal institution of higher education, the vacancies referred to in art. 1° of this law will be filled, by course and shift, by self-declared blacks, browns and indigenous people and people with disabilities, under the terms of the legislation, in proportion to the total number of vacancies at least equal to the respective proportion of blacks, browns, indigenous people and people with disabilities in the population of the Federation unit where the institution is installed, according to the last census of the Brazilian Institute of Geography and Statistics—IBGE. (Given by Law No 13.409, de 2016)

In articles 4° and 5° of the law the same system of affirmative action is applied to federal institutions of high school technical education.

AFFIRMATIVE ACTION AT THE FEDERAL SUPREME COURT

In this legislative environment that favored quotas, the opponents of affirmative action sought the Judiciary to try to contain their use. The leading case on the subject is the Fundamental Precept Failure Statement (ADPF) n. 186, proposed by the Democrats Party, located on the right side of the Brazilian political spectrum, against the University of Brasília, which was ultimately decided in favor of the constitutionality of affirmative action.[16]

The case of Prouni (Direct Action of Unconstitutionality 3.330), whose constitutionality was also questioned, started to be judged before ADPF 186, in April 2008, although the final decision was only published in May 2012 after it. Unanimously, following the vote of Justice Ayres Britto, the Plenary decided that the University for All Program—PROUNI, through affirmative actions by the State, gave "compliance with the constitutional principle of isonomy."

The Federal Supreme Court had its composition renewed by several appointments of Ministers by the Lula government (2003–2010), and this contributed to a more favorable environment for affirmative action. Illustrative of this is the fact that two of the eleven Ministers of the Court had academic work defending the constitutionality of affirmative action in higher education as a mechanism to minimize inequality of opportunities in Brazil.[17]

The processing of ADPF 186 had some procedural peculiarities. Among them, the holding of a public hearing on March 3, 4, and 5, 2010, with the participation of public authorities and experts invited to bring information and clarifications on the subject. In addition, a large number of entities have been admitted as *amici curiae* both in defense of affirmative actions and contrary to them. There were non-governmental entities (Educafro—Education and Citizenship of Needy Afro-Descendants, Unified Black Movement, Brazilian Pardo-Mestizo Movement, Racial and Environmental Advocacy Institute, Movement against the Misrepresentation of the Spirit of Affirmative Action Policy at Federal Universities, Institute of Public Law and Popular Community Defense, National Association of Afro-Descendent Lawyers, Conectas Human Rights) and government entities (Palmares Cultural Foundation, National Foundation of Indio-Funai), in addition to other organizations, such as the Public Defender of the Union and the Federal Council of the Order of Lawyers from Brazil.

The final decision of the Plenary, on April 26, 2012, was to unanimously reject the action as groundless, under the vote of Justice Lewandowski, summarized as follows:

> Summary: claim of fundamental requirements. Acts that installed a vacancy reserving system based on ethnicracial criteria (quotas) in the selection process for entry in a public institution of higher education.
>
> Alleged offense to arts. 1º, caput, III, 3º, IV, 4º, VIII, 5º, I, II, XXXIII, XLI, LIV, 37, caput, 205, 206, caput, I, 207, caput, and 208, V, all of the federal constitution. Action dismissed.
>
> I—It does not contradict—on the contrary, it honors—the principle of material equality, provided in the caput of article 5 of the Constitution, the possibility for the State to use either universalist policies, which cover an undetermined number of individuals, through structural actions, or affirmative actions, which reach specific social groups, in a punctual manner, attributing certain advantages, for a limited time, in order to allow them to overcome inequalities arising from particular historical situations.
>
> II—The Brazilian constitutional model incorporated several institutional mechanisms to correct the distortions resulting from a purely formal application of the principle of equality.
>
> III—This Court, in several precedents, established the constitutionality of affirmative action policies.
>
> IV—Measures that seek to reverse, at the university level, the historical picture of inequality that characterizes ethnic-racial and social relations in our country, cannot be examined only from the perspective of their compatibility with certain constitutional precepts, considered in isolation, or from the perspective of possible advantage of certain criteria over others, which, on the other hand, must be analyzed in the light of the framework of principles on which the Brazilian State itself is based.
>
> V—Differentiated selection methodology can perfectly take into account ethnic racial, or socioeconomic criteria, in order to ensure that the academic community and society itself are benefited by the pluralism of ideas, besides, one of the foundations of the Brazilian State, as provided in article 1º, V, of the Constitution.
>
> VI—Today, social justice, more than simply redistributing wealth created by collective effort, means distinguishing, recognizing and incorporating diverse

cultural values into society as a whole, often considered inferior to those considered dominant.

VII—However, affirmative action policies based on reverse discrimination are only legitimate if their maintenance is conditional on the persistence, over time, of the framework of social exclusion that gave rise to them. Otherwise, such policies could become permanent benefits, instituted in favor of a specific social group, but to the detriment of the collective as a whole, a situation—needless to say—incompatible with the spirit of any Constitution that is intended to be democratic, and should, moreover, respect the proportionality between the means employed and the ends pursued.

VIII—Claims of non-compliance with a fundamental precept judged groundless.

The reason for deciding is the principle of material equality, provided for in article 5º of the Federal Constitution: "Everyone is equal before the law, without distinction of any kind." In the perspective of the constituent process that led to the writing of this provision, the Constitution did not limit itself to proclaiming formal equality, but "sought to lend the utmost concreteness to this important postulate, in order to ensure material equality for all Brazilians and foreigners who live in the country, taking into account—of course—the difference that distinguishes them for natural, cultural, social, economic or even accidental reasons, in addition to paying special attention to the imbalance in the world of facts between different social groups."[18]

Reinforcing this argument, the decision makes reference to John Rawls' distributive justice (*A Theory of Justice*). As for affirmative action being a good way of doing this, the vote quotes Michel Rosenfeld (*Affirmative Action, justice, and equalities: a philosophical and constitutional appraisal*): "the adoption of a new principle of distributive justice will possibly create conflicts between claims based on the old and the new principles."

Among the arguments against the constitutionality of affirmative actions, brought in the initial petition, in public hearings or in the *amici curiae* demonstrations and referred to in the decision, there was the fear that a "racialized state or institutionalized racism would be created, in the same way as practiced in United States, South Africa or Rwanda," which would be inappropriate for Brazil. The creation of a "state race conscience" would promote an arbitrary offence to the principle of equality, favoring only the black middle classes. And that would cause segregation between the different social groups, creating a true "social apartheid." Furthermore, affirmative action would not be necessary for Brazil, since "no one is excluded for the simple fact of being black."

Comparisons with the United States were rejected by the decision, initially because it considered the manifestations of racism in the two countries to be different, in Brazil more disguised than in the United States, according to a report by the Brazilianist Thomas Skidmore, referred to in the vote:

> it was not possible to claim that Brazil had escaped racial discrimination, although it has never been made official, since the colonial period [it was] a type of discrimination much more complex than that existing in American biracial society. ... Florestan Fernandes accused his compatriots of 'having the prejudice of not having prejudice' and of clinging to the 'myth of racial democracy'. By believing that skin colour was never a barrier to the social and economic rise of non-whites [and that it could not] be attributed to anything other than the relative underdevelopment of society or the lack of individual initiative.

The thesis of the denial of racism is also rejected, demonstrating how it is present in Brazilian society, in general in a veiled way.

Regarding affirmative actions in the American reality, the decision cites Ronald Dworkin's rejection (*The sovereign virtue: the theory and practice of equality*) to the thesis of racial hostility, based on the study he mentioned (*The Shape of the River*, by William Bowen and Derek Bok, former Rectors of Princeton and Harvard Universities), which demonstrates the "impressive success" of affirmative actions in training "more black leaders in the industry, professions, community and community services, as well as a more lasting interaction and friendship between races than would otherwise have been possible."

The Brazilian decision devotes an entire topic to analyzing the jurisprudence of the American Supreme Court and its differences in relation to Brazil, highlighting the fact that in Brazil, unlike the United States, equality is expressly stated in the Constitution, central argument of ADPF 186, as saw.

> The Brazilian Constitution—it is important to note—allows for a much more comprehensive approach to affirmative policies than that made by the United States Supreme Court. In the three main precedents of that Court—Bakke v. Regents of the University of California, *Gratz v. Bollinger* and *Grutter v. Bollinger*—it was understood that the use of ethno-racial criteria would be constitutional provided that (i) it did not configure reservation of vacancies or the establishment of quotas; and (ii) were used in conjunction with other factors to assess merit.

The difference in the student admission process at the American and Brazilian universities is relevant to understand the specificities of the two Courts' approach. In Brazil, the selection is made through an objective test, the "vestibular exam,"[19] to which all candidates uniformly submit. There is no practice of interviewing or analyzing candidates' résumés and documents to differentiate them according to subjective characteristics. In fact, this individual differentiation is considered discriminatory and illegal in the Brazilian system, as it could give rise to unjustified preferences, according to nonaccountable criteria.

That is why, in Brazil, talking about affirmative actions in this context has been equivalent to talking about quotas and both presuppose objective selection. In practice, two student rankings are prepared based on the exam scores, in decreasing order. There is a list of candidates in "wide competition" and a separate list of those who postulate some differentiation according to the affirmative action criteria, for a specific quota of vacancies, as specified in the selection notice for each institution. The increase in diversity is achieved as an effect of the selection of shareholders and is not directly sought. Thus, the requirement of a strict criterion (*narrowly tailored*, according to the case of Grutter, of American jurisprudence) for positive discrimination would be more difficult in Brazil, as the selection notices deal with the differentiation that grants the right to quotas with a reasonable degree of generalization (blacks, browns, indigenous people, graduates of public schools. or low-income students).

The admission system based on objective evidence also rejected criticism of affirmative actions for allegedly denying the merit criteria of the selection in favor of factors such as skin color, hair type, and ethnic origin. As all students take the same tests, the decision understood that descendants of Africans are not barred from accessing higher education because they are black, but because of a deficiency in their previous school education. The selection exam "does not measure capacity, but investment."[20]

Another argument by the authors of ADPF 186 said that the policies adopted in other countries would have brought more pain than relief, "there would be no shortcuts to social justice." The decision rejects the argument, stating that affirmative action contributes to "a drastic transformation in the very understanding of the concept of social justice." Quoting Nancy Fraser and Axel Honneth (*Redistribution on Recognition? A Political Philosophical Exchange*), redistributive policies would be insufficient when examining the problem of recognizing and incorporating diverse cultural values into society.

Another reference to the jurisprudence of the American Supreme Court, regarding the transience of affirmative actions as a condition for its constitutionality, was recognized in the same way in the decision of ADPF 186, based on the forecast of a 10-year period for reevaluating the program, as provided for in the rules of the University of Brasília. This deadline is usually set out in university notices based on the constitutional provision of university autonomy. And it was also adopted in the Quota Law (article 7º[23]).

The decision also faces the debate on the concept of race. In view of the claim of the authors of the lawsuit that there is no race as a biological concept, the vote accepts the argument but reiterates that racism exists as a historical-social phenomenon. This is illustrated with the information that blacks corresponded, at the time of the decision, to 2% of university students in the country, despite representing 45% of the population. In addition, even observing a general increase in the school enrolment rate in Brazil, a study by the federal government's Institute for Applied Economic Research (IPEA) (*Portrait of Gender and Race Inequalities, 1995–2015*) of 2017 points out that the improvement overall educational indicators did not lead to "equalization, maintaining the distances between racial and gender groups, especially at the highest levels of education." The persistence of distance between racial groups invalidates the common sense that the passage of time tends to reduce differences between them.

In the understanding of the decision, this implies "reproduction and perpetuation of the same ruling elite, ... concentration of privileges [which] affects the distribution of public resources." In addition, "if the race was used to build hierarchies, it should also be used to deconstruct them."

> Thus, students from private middle schools, with more economic and cultural resources, are better prepared for the selection tests.

> Article 7° within a period of ten years from the date of publication of this Law, the revision of the special program for access to higher education institutions for black, brown and indigenous students and persons with disabilities, as well as those who have completed high school in public schools.

The race would oppose, still according to the opponents of the affirmative actions of racial bias, the social criterion (poverty, accomplishment of the elementary and high school in the public school[21]), that would be more fair and comprehensive. By privileging the access of poor students and graduates of public high school, this would automatically favor blacks as well. This thesis was not supported by the decision, which rejected the equivalence between class and race prejudice. Racial discrimination is an additional element: public school places do not necessarily include blacks. "Nonwhites suffer increasing disadvantages when trying to move up the social ladder, at all stages of the transition from one social status to another."

Finally, opponents of the quotas point out that a "racial tribunal" would be needed to define who is black and who is not, which would be especially difficult in Brazil due to miscegenation. This would mean "the political and ideological elimination of the Brazilian mestizo identity." The Brazilian reality is multiracial, with a large number of browns, representing different ethnic combinations. Instead of talking about people of African descent, it would be more correct to speak of Afro, indigenous, and Euro-descendants. The decision rejects the racial court's thesis, stating that in practice each university has adopted its own procedures to hinder fraud in the use of the benefit, such as conducting interviews, presenting photos, and others. But this is undoubtedly a difficult aspect to implement in the decision.

FINAL CONSIDERATIONS

The decision records a change in trend in the Brazilian census data, with a significant increase in the self-declared black or brown population, from 5.4% to 6.9% (blacks) and from 40% to 44.2% (browns), between 1999 and 2009, which was probably due to the "recovery of racial identity," according to the Brazilian Institute of Geography and Statistics (IBGE).

This new social visibility can be identified in the emergence of a new generation of black leaders. Although a causal relationship cannot be established between this and affirmative actions, it is reasonable to admit the correlation between them. The time to evaluate the effects of these laws and decisions is still not enough, considering that it is just over ten years after the formation of the first classes of new entrants under affirmative actions. But the recognition of its constitutionality and the stabilization of the rules of this form of access pacified the understandings about the direction to follow for racial equalization in Brazil.

The renewal of speeches and the strengthening of the black movement are highlighted by Marielle Franco. Young black leader, sociologist graduated from the Pontifical Catholic University (PUC) of Rio de Janeiro, as a Prouni fellow, with a master's degree from the Federal Fluminense University, elected councilor in the Municipality of Rio de Janeiro, was murdered in March 2018 and became a symbol of resistance in the social emancipation of blacks, the poor, women, and gays in Brazil. Like several of this new generation of black leaders admitted to the university, usually the first of their families, thanks to affirmative actions, Marielle represented the breaking of innumerable social barriers, both symbolic and concrete, that have historically been imposed on this population. She was defined as "child of Maré,"[22] speaking of the reality of the favela and its formation as elements from which it made its intervention in reality. Marielle is just one of many cases that demonstrate the importance of affirmative action in Brazil, not only for the members of this flourishing movement but for the whole of Brazilian society, so unfair and unequal.

NOTES

1. This chapter uses and develops arguments from previous work published by the author in Brazil on the topic (BUCCI).

2. The first initiative to ban the slave trade in Brazil dates back to 1810, still in the colonial period, shortly after the arrival of the royal family in Brazil, who had been escorted by the British to escape the Napoleonic Continental Blockade, when Portugal and England signed an alliance treaty and friendship. In 1815, in Vienna, a new treaty was signed with England, prohibiting Portugal, its nationals, from "buying slaves or trafficking them anywhere in the coast of Africa north of the equator" (Comparato, pp. 198–199).

3. *José Bonifácio de Andrada e Silva. Representation to the Constituent and Legislative General Assembly of the Empire of Brazil on Slavery.* (Andrada E. Silva, pp. 45 ff.)

4. Also known as *Lei Feijó,* due its author, the Minister of Justice Diogo Feijó. Text available: http://www.planalto.gov.br/ccivil_03/leis/lim/LIM-7-11-1831.htm.

5. Although Nabuco criticizes the fact that half of the slaves remained illegally in captivity (Nabuco, 2000, p. 41), Jorge Caldeira brings figures to the contrary, stating that "between 1831 and 1835, the slave trade had been virtually extinct in Brazil; in 1836, with the beginning of the affirmation of the *Regresso* (the Conservative Return was a shift through a backlash orientation brought by the new conservative regency, in 1836), 5,000 Africans were brought; in 1837, first with the government paralyzed and then with the regressionists in power, 35,000 slaves came, a number that would grow in the coming years." In Caldeira's interpretation, this confrontation of Diogo Feijó, author of the 1831 Law, against trafficking would be among the reasons for his fall as Regent, in 1836. After that, the period of the Conservative Return begins, led by Bernardo Pereira de Vasconcelos, whose program would be "a parliament at the service of the slave trade and of the slave owners" (Caldeira, pp. 37–38).

6. Text available: http://www.planalto.gov.br/ccivil_03/leis/lim/LIM581.htm.

7. Text available: http://www.planalto.gov.br/ccivil_03/leis/lim/LIM3270.htm.

8. The period refers to the governments of Fernando Henrique Cardoso (1995–2002), Luis Inácio Lula da Silva (2003–2010) and Dilma Rousseff (2011–2016).

9. The National Education Plan for the following period, approved by Law No. 13,005, 2014, is even more explicit as to racial equity: "Goal 8: increase the average schooling of the population from 18 (eighteen) to 29 (twenty-nine) years, in order to … match the average schooling among blacks and non-blacks declared to the Brazilian Institute of Geography and Statistics—IBGE" (my emphasis). IBGE data referred to in the decision (2009) inform that the white population had an average of 8.4 years of study, while blacks and browns have 6.7 years.

10. Text available: http://www.planalto.gov.br/ccivil_03/_ato2004-2006/2005/lei/l11096.htm.

11. According to the 2018 Higher Education Census, available at http://download.inep.gov.br/educacao_superior/censo_superior/documentos/2019/censo_da_educacao_su perior_2018-notas_estatisticas.pdf.

12. Available from http://www.planalto.gov.br/ccivil_03/_ato2011-2014/2012/lei/l12711.htm.

13. Available from http://www.planalto.gov.br/ccivil_03/constituicao/constituicao.htm. There is an English version of Brazilian Constitution (not fully updated) available from https://www2.senado.leg.br/bdsf/item/id/243334.

14. State laws 3.524 e 3.708 were revoked, with their provisions consolidated in state law 4.151 of 2003.

15. http://www.schwartzman.org.br/sitesimon/?p=195&lang=pt-br.

16. http://redir.stf.jus.br/paginadorpub/paginador.jsp?docTP=TP&docID=6984693. Another relevant decision on the topic is that of extraordinary appeal 597.285, also reported by Minister Lewandowski and decided along the same lines, in 2012.

17. One of these Ministers was Joaquim Barbosa, the first black man to join the STF, appointed in 2003, whose academic training was done exactly on the study of affirmative actions in the USA. The other was Minister Carmen Lúcia, appointed in 2006, only the second woman to be a member of the Court, which to date has only had three women. The works of the two Ministers are referred to in the ADPF 186 decision.

18. This and all the following transcripts, when different sources are not specified, were extracted from the decision of the ADPF 186.

19. Since 2010, admission to most public institutions of higher education has also been based on the National High School Exam (ENEM), which evaluates, in theory, the aptitude achieved at the end of high school, differently from the traditional entrance exam, explicitly focused on the "selection of the best," according to the criteria of each university. Despite the differences, for the purposes of admission the forms are equivalent, insofar as each institution uses exclusively the results of tests applied uniformly to all students.

20. In Brazil, high-quality secondary education is private, in contrast to higher education, in which public institutions in general occupy the top positions in the national and international evaluation rankings.

21. In Brazil, social segregation in education is manifested by the elite's attendance at primary and private middle schools, while the mass of students attend public schools, as mentioned in note 22.

22. Allusion to the Maré favela, a poor community in Rio de Janeiro.

REFERENCES

Alencastro, Luiz Felipe. (2018). Abolição da escravidão em 1888 foi votada pela elite evitando a reforma agrária, diz historiador. Interview given to Amanda Rossi, BBC Brasil, 13/05/2018, http://www.bbc.com/portuguese/brasil-44091474.

Almeida Filho, Naomar de; Marinho, Maerbal Bittencourt; Carvalho, Manoel José de, Santos Jocélio Teles dos. (2005). Ações afirmativas na universidade pública: o caso da UFBA. Centro de Estudos Afro-Orientais da UFBA. Salvador, Bahia. http://flacso.redelivre.org.br/files/2013/03/1090.pdf.

Alves, J.A. Lindgren. (2002). A Conferência de Durban contra o Racismo e a responsabilidade de todos. *Revista Brasileira de Política Internacional*, 45(2), 198–223. Edição 22, volume 1, artigo no 2, julho/setembro 2012. http://www.scielo.br/pdf/rbpi/v45n2/a09v45n2.pdf.

Amaral, Shirlena Campos de Souza; Mello, Marcelo Pereira de. (2012). Cotas para negros e carentes na educação pública superior: análise do caso UENF, de 2004 a 2010. *Revista Científica Internacional*, ed. 22, v. 1, art. n. 2, julho/setembro.

Andrada E. Silva, José Bonifácio. (1998). *Projetos para o Brasil. Organização de Miriam Dohlnikoff.* São Paulo: Companhia das Letras.

Alonso, Angela. (2016). *Flores, votos e balas. O movimento abolicionista brasileiro (1868–1888).* São Paulo: Companhia das Letras.

Barbosa, Rui. (1983). *A questão social e política no Brasil. Conferência pronunciada no Teatro Lírico, do Rio de Janeiro, a 20/3/1919.* São Paulo: LTr/Rio de Janeiro: Fundação Casa de Rui Barbosa.

Brasil. (2017). *Retrato das Desigualdades de Gênero e Raça (1995–2015).* Brasília: Instituto de Pesquisas Econômicas Aplicadas (IPEA), http://www.ipea.gov.br/portal/images/stories/PDFs/170306_retrato_das_desigualdades_ de_genero_raca.pdf.

Bucci, Maria Paula Dallari. (2019). Estratégias e embates jurídicos nas políticas públicas para a superação da ordem escravista. In *Trinta Anos de Constituição e 130 Anos de Lei Áurea. Avanços e Retrocessos.* (Álvaro Ricardo de Souza Cruz e Poliana Lino Rodrigues, editores). Rio de Janeiro: Lumen Juris, pp. 705–736.

Caldeira, Jorge. (1999). *Diogo Antonio Feijó (organização e introdução).* São Paulo: Editora 34.

Comparato, Fabio Konder. (2003). *A Afirmação Histórica dos Direitos Humanos.* 3a. ed. São Paulo: Saraiva.

Domingues, Petrônio. (2018) "Em Defesa da Humanidade": A Associação Cultural do Negro. *Dados*, 61(1), 171–211.

Feres Jr., João; Daflon, Verônica Toste. (2015). Ação afirmativa na Índia e no Brasil: um estudo sobre a retórica acadêmica. *Sociologias*, 17(40), 92–123.

Ferreira, Ligia Fonseca. (2010). Um retrato: Luiz Gama, defensor dos escravos e do Direito. In *Os juristas na formação do Estado-Nação brasileiro (1850–1930).* Carlos Guilherme Mota e Gabriela Nunes Ferreira (coords.). São Paulo: Saraiva, pp. 219–244.

Haddad, Fernando. (2009). O Plano Nacional de Educação: Razões, Princípios e Programas. In *Direitos Humanos, Democracia e República. Homenagem a Fábio Konder Comparato* (Maria Victoria de Mesquita Benevides, Gilberto Bercovici e Claudineu de Melo, orgs.). São Paulo: Quartier Latin, pp. 429–458.

Jaccoud, Luciana; Silva, Adailton; Rosa; Waldemir; Luiz, Cristiana. (2008). Entre o racismo e a desigualdade: da Constituição à promoção de uma política de igualdade racial (1998–2008). In: IPEA (Ed.). *Políticas sociais: acompanhamento e análise*, n. 17, vol. 3. Brasília: IPEA, pp. 261–328.

Maggie, Yvonne. (2008). Pela igualdade. *Revista Estudos Feministas*, 16(3), 897–912.

Mamigonian, Beatriz. (2017). *Africanos livres: a abolição do tráfico de escravos no Brasil.* São Paulo, Companhia das Letras.

Mattos, Hebe. (2013). André Rebouças e o Pós-abolição: entre a África e o Brasil (1888–1898). XXVII Simpósio Nacional de História, ANPUH, Natal, http://www.snh2013.anpuh.org/resources/anais/27/1364674765_ARQUIVO_HebeMattos_anpuh.pdf.

Nabuco, Joaquim. (1998). *Minha formação.* Brasília: Senado Federal. (1a ed. 1900).

Nabuco, Joaquim. (2000). *O abolicionismo.* Rio de Janeiro: Nova Fronteira/São Paulo: Publifolha (Grandes Nomes do Pensamento Brasileiro) (1a ed. 1883).

Nabuco, Joaquim. (2005). *Campanha abolicionista no Recife. Eleições de 1884.* Brasília: Senado Federal.

Nogueira, Marco Aurélio. (2010). *O encontro de Joaquim Nabuco com a política. As desventuras do liberalismo.* 2a ed. São Paulo: Paz e Terra.

Ribeiro, Djamila. (2017). *O que é lugar de fala?* Belo Horizonte: Letramento/ Justificando.

Theodoro, Mário (org.). (2008). *As políticas públicas e a desigualdade racial no Brasil 120 anos após a abolição.* 2a edição. Brasília: IPEA.

The accesses to the sources available from the internet were verified in April and May 2020.

Maria Paula Dallari Bucci. Professor at the Faculty of Law of the University of São Paulo. mariapaula@usp.br

Largo São Francisco, 95, 11° floor of the attached building. 01005-010. São Paulo—SP. Brazil

Chapter 7

Gay Marriage

The Role of the Brazilian Supreme Court in Recognizing the Right to Same-Sex Civil Unions

Fernando de Brito Alves

INTRODUCTION

The objective of this chapter is to examine the Brazilian judiciary's role in the legal recognition of gay marriage by analyzing the decision of the STF (*Supremo Tribunal Federal—STF*)—the highest court in the Brazilian judiciary—in the combined ruling in early May 2011 on the Claim of Noncompliance with a Fundamental Precept (*Arguição de Descumprimento de Preceito Fundamental—ADPF*) no. 132 (which was filed in the state of Rio de Janeiro) and Declaratory Action of Unconstitutionality (*Ação Declaratória de Inconstitucionalidade—ADI*) no. 4277 (which was filed in the Federal District [*Distrito Federal—DF*]).

This chapter presents the legal context of the debate, beginning in the mid-1990s, on same-sex marriage in the Brazilian political landscape and describes how the debate was being carried out in the Brazilian National Congress, particularly in the Chamber of Deputies, where most of the bills were concentrated. This chapter also specifies the main regulatory changes promoted by the executive branch, which facilitated the recognition of homoaffective civil unions for tax and social security purposes. Then, to conclude the characterization of the context, this chapter mentions the first judicial decisions on the issue.

Regarding gay marriage, after analyzing the legal precedent set by the STF, which has jurisdiction over constitutional review in Brazil, this chapter examines the decision of the Superior Court of Justice (*Superior Tribunal de Justiça—STJ*), one of the most important courts in the country. The main function of this court is to standardize the interpretation of infraconstitutional legislation (which declared that there were no impediments to same-sex marriage) and the Resolution of the National Council of Justice (*Conselho Nacional de Justiça—CNJ*). This resolution forbade officials in the justice system—which is responsible for converting stable unions into marriages and performing marriage ceremonies—from refusing to carry out these procedures in the case of same-sex couples.

In addition, we describe the main reactions of the legislative branch to the judicial decisions that recognized the right to gay marriage in Brazil. The method used in this article is analytical-descriptive.

THE LEGAL CONTEXT OF THE DEBATE IN THE LEGISLATIVE BRANCH AND THE JUDICIARY WHEN THE MOST IMPORTANT LEGAL PRECEDENT ON GAY MARRIAGE WAS ESTABLISHED.

Despite evidence to the contrary, Brazil is often seen as a sexually permissive country with excessively liberal customs, as its external image is still closely associated with nudity on the beaches and during Carnival.

This stigma of permissive customs was created as a result of the advertising strategy employed by the Brazilian Tourist Board (*Empresa Brasileira de Turismo—Embratur*), which used the image of women—usually wearing little clothing—as the focal point of materials for promoting domestic tourism in a range of official publications from the 1970s until the mid-1990s.

This liberality is invariably restricted to heterosexual men, whereas women are almost always stereotyped as objects that are being denied rights and populations whose sexuality diverges from the heteronormative are simply ignored.

Compared to the United States and some European countries, the lesbian, gay, bisexual, and transgender (LGBT) movement in Brazil began organizing more consistently and significantly relatively late—in the late 1970s—and arose during the end of the military dictatorship and the beginning of the democratic transition in Brazil. Within this context, the first newspapers and associations began to emerge and gradually started to articulate the demands of the population, monitor violent situations, and pressure the government to develop public policies.

To understand how gay marriage was legalized by the STF on May 5, 2011, it is essential to contextualize the debate in both Congress and the judiciary on gay marriage when the precedents were being set.

One of the first bills that sought to legalize same-sex civil unions was presented by Deputy Marta Suplicy (PT/SP [Workers' Party (*Partido dos*

Trabalhadores—PT)/São Paulo]): Bill no. 1151/1995. According to journalist João Silvério Trevisan,[1] when the proposal was read on the floor of the Chamber of Federal Deputies, several members made obscene gestures, booed, shouted, made rude remarks to members who supported the proposal, and categorically stated that same-sex civil unions were an aberration of nature.

Subsequently, Deputy Roberto Jefferson (PTB/RJ [Brazilian Labor Party (*Partido Trabalhista Brasileiro—PTB*)/Rio de Janeiro]) presented a replacement to Bill no. 1151/1995. Later that year, Deputy Marta Suplicy also spearheaded a Proposed Amendment to the Constitution (*Proposta de Emenda à Constituição—PEC* no. 139/1995), which amended articles 3 and 7 of the Constitution to broaden the fundamental objectives of the Republic to include promoting the good of all without prejudice, promoting freedom of sexual orientation, prohibiting wage discrimination, and prohibiting sexual orientation discrimination in the performance of duties and in admissions criteria. The proposed amendment was shelved in 1999.

In 2003, the content of PEC no. 139/1995 was retrieved for PEC no. 66/2003. This new proposal was shelved on January 31, 2001, and revived on February 16, 2011, at the request of Deputy Paulo Pimenta (PT/RS [Rio Grande do Sul]). Later in 2003, Sérgio Cabral, who was a Senator of the Republic, presented PEC no. 70 to modify the wording of article 226, §3 of the Constitution to include the possibility of recognizing stable unions between homosexual couples as a family unit. In 2006, he requested that the proposal be shelved.

Beginning in 2003, there was a progressive increase in bills that sought to regulate same-sex civil unions, establish a gay marriage, or simply regulate issues and conflicts (related to social security, property, inheritance, and child custody, among others) that could arise from these relationships.

A main example is Bill No. 2383/2003, presented by Deputy Maria José da Conceição—better known as Maninha. This bill sought to extend private health care plans and insurance to people in homoaffective unions. Additionally, Bill No. 6297/2005, authored by Deputy Maurício Rands (PT/PE [Pernambuco]), sought to authorize—for social security purposes—the inclusion of homosexual partners as the dependents of insured persons and the inclusion of the partners of federal civil servants in the National Institute of Social Security (*Instituto Nacional de Seguridade Social—INSS*).

In 2007, Deputy Sérgio Barradas Carneiro presented Bill no. 2285/2007 (PT/BA [Bahia]), which would have recognized homoaffective unions as family units and ensured the partners' rights regarding child custody and relationships, the adoption of children, social security, and inheritance. This bill was under consideration, together with Bill no. 674/2007, which was proposed by Deputy Cândido Vaccarezza (PT/SP). Bill no. 674/2007 was the object of a replacement bill from Deputy Eliseu Padilha (PMDB/RS [Brazilian Democratic Movement Party (*Partido do Movimento Democrático Brasileiro—PT*)]). Additionally, Bill no. 674/2007 received numerous amendments and was the subject of debates within committees of the Chamber of Deputies.

Meanwhile, as the legal recognition of gay marriage—or the regulation of the consequences of such recognition for inheritance, social security, and family law—became a possibility, there were also conservative reactions in the National Congress. An example of these reactions was Bill no. 4508/2008, presented by Deputy Olavo Calheiros (PMDB/AL [Alagoas]). This bill sought to prohibit the adoption of children by homosexuals. Moreover, this bill was not the only one to address the subject: in 2010, Bill no. 7018/2010, which was presented by Deputy Zequinha Marinho (PSC/PA [Social Christian Party (*Partido Social Cristão—PSC*)/Pará]), sought to amend the Child and Adolescent Statute (*Estatuto da Criança e do Adolescente—ECA*) to prohibit the adoption of children by same-sex couples.

In 2003, a new Civil Code regarding civil unions came into effect. The code kept the issue of homoaffective families unchanged and equated only civil unions between men and women to marriage.

In response, Bill no. 4914/2009 was presented in 2009. Except for converting homoaffective unions into marriage, the bill, which was jointly authored by several deputies (including José Genoíno, Fernando Gabeira, and Solange Amaral), would have applied the rules for ordinary stable unions to homoaffective unions by adding article 1727-A to the Civil Code. The bill was attached to Bill no. 580/2007, which was presented by Deputy Clodovil Hernandes (PTC/SP [Christian Labor Party (*Partido Trabalhista Cristão—PTC*)]), the first openly gay federal deputy; both bills were revived on February 16, 2011, and were processed routinely until they were shelved.

From the presentation of the first bill to legalize same-sex civil unions to the STF's decision in 2011 to legalize gay marriage, the different bills presented during this period were generally not well-received by Congress and were shelved, processed atypically, or simply forgotten. This refusal to properly guide the debate in Congress to deliberation on gay marriage resulted in the executive branch taking a few isolated initiatives, member states legislating on the matter and several judicial decisions on the subject being made.

In that context, which is what precedes the STF's decision on the leading case, the Federal Prosecutor's Office (*Ministério Público Federal—MPF*) filed a class action (Public Civil Action [*Ação Civil Pública—ACP*] no. 200.71.00.009347-0) against the INSS in the Federal Court of Rio Grande do Sul. This class action led to Normative Instruction INSS/DC no. 25 (published 06.07.2000), which extended death pension and imprisonment allowance benefits to homoaffective partners. This subject was also addressed in

Normative Instruction INSS/DC no. 50 of 05.08.2001 until Instruction no. 25 was revoked in 2010.

On December 9, 2010, the Ministry of Social Security (*Ministério da Previdência Social—MPS*) issued MPS Ordinance no. 513, which established that, within the General Regime of Social Security (*Geral de Previdência Social—RGPS*), the provisions of Law No. 8213 (enacted July 24, 1991), which deal with dependents for social security purposes, must be interpreted in such a way as to encompass stable unions between same-sex persons.

In 2010, it also became possible to include same-sex partners as dependents on income tax returns (National Treasury Attorney's Office/General Coordination of Tax Affairs [*Procuradoria Geral da Fazenda Nacional/ Coordenação-Geral de Assuntos Tributários—PGFN/CAT*] Opinion no. 1503 of July 19, 2010).

Beginning in 2005, state legislation recognizing the rights of homoaffective families also began to emerge. In the State of Rio de Janeiro, Law No. 5034 (the origin of ADPF 132, a leading case that we will analyze in the following section) was enacted May 29, 2007; this law allowed state public servants to register same-sex partners for social security purposes, as long as the partners maintained a permanent civil relationship—duly proven—to which would be applied the same legal precepts as those applied to stable unions between different-sex partners.

Initiatives to recognize the rights of homosexual couples occurred in other states: for example, Law No. 5260 of June 11, 2008; Supplementary Law No. 1012 (enacted July 5, 2007, in the State of São Paulo), which altered article 147 of Supplementary Law No. 180/78; Supplementary Law No. 412 (enacted June 26, 2008, in the state of Santa Catarina); Law No. 7517 (enacted December 30, 2003, in the State of Paraíba); and Supplementary Law No. 308 (enacted October 25, 2005, in the State of Rio Grande do Norte). In 2010, with Decree 55,839, the State of São Paulo instituted the State Plan to Combat Homophobia and Promote LGBT Citizenship, among other measures, with different actions to protect and develop the rights of those who are lesbian, gay, bisexual, transvestite, or transsexual.

Within the judiciary, isolated cases began to be tried. In ADI 3299/DF, the São Paulo Education and Health Incentive Association filed an ADI against article 235 of the Military Penal Code (*Código Penal Militar—CPM*)[2] to determine the unconstitutionality of the article, considering its highly prejudiced nature. In this case, the rapporteur, Minister Carlos Velloso, stated that the legislation predated the Constitution and would be incompatible with it, and thus, the case could not be processed as an ADI.[3]

We also found Petition 1984 of Rio Grande do Sul. In this petition, which was decided by the then-president of the STF, Minister Marco Aurélio de Mello, the INSS requested the suspension of a preliminary injunction that made homosexual partners dependents. The minister rejected the suspension,[4] determining that there was no reason to discriminate against family units due to the type of affection. The decision was widely cited by other STF decisions in similar cases.

The STJ, which is a Superior Court, has jurisdiction to unify the interpretation of federal legislation to standardize the determinations of the different bodies in the judiciary. Many decisions by the STJ concern homosexuality, if only incidentally. In Special Appeal (*Recurso Especial—REsp*) no. 758905—SC (Santa Catarina), Minister Gilson Dipp stated that interpreting "stable union" as excluding homosexuals—because of the notion that such a union can only occur between a man and a woman—would mean excluding the recognition of relationships among homosexuals, and this notion would evidently be divorced from reality and at odds with constitutional precepts.

In another monocratic decision by the STJ, Minister Paulo Galloti[5] determined that de facto partnerships between homosexuals deserve a treatment that is equal to the treatment of heterosexual unions; this determination stems from the constitutional principles of equality, the dignity of the human person, and the promotion of the good of all without prejudice or discrimination. The absence of a rule contemplating the possibility of a deceased civil servant's homosexual partner claiming a death pension benefit cannot be considered an obstacle to recognizing the existence of the union when the legal requirements for the recognition of stable unions have been met.

The judicial focus, in a concentrated constitutional review, on same-sex unions was the result of the legislative branch's reluctance to legislate on the topic and the increasing demand for the judiciary to rule on conflicts arising from family arrangements. Homoaffective families affected by such conflicts, formerly on the margins of the law, now sought judgment on claims governed by family law and specific regulatory innovations promoted by states and some institutions in the federal executive branch.

In particular, the changes that were increasingly declared by the judiciary[6] to the concept of family paved the way for the STF to recognize the right to gay marriage.

THE LEADING CASE

The Brazilian system of constitutional review is one of the most complex reviews in the world, as this system mixes a set of techniques typical of *principaliter* review (carried out by the STF and, in specific cases, by the state Courts of Justice), *incidenter tantum* review (the jurisdiction to carry out this type of review is distributed among all the institutions in the judiciary) and judicial review carried out by institutions in the judiciary and by the legislative branch (or by auxiliary institutions in the legislative branch, such as the Courts of Accounts); additionally, the constitutional review can be preventive or repressive.

The cases analyzed in this text are related to two constitutional actions that were brought together and judged concurrently by the STF: ADPF no. 132 (filed in the State of Rio de Janeiro) and ADI no. 4277 (filed in the DF).

The ADPF is provided for in the Brazilian Federal Constitution of 1988 but was regulated by Law 9882/99 to serve as a means of integrating main constitutional review and incidental constitutional review, thereby enabling state acts, such as preconstitutional norms or even judicial decisions that violate fundamental clauses of the constitutional order—previously unable to be directly considered by the STF—to be included as an object of review in an objective process. Despite expanding the main constitutional review carried out by the STF, the regulation of this new constitutional act, Law 9882/99, required that acts contested through it encapsulate a type of qualified constitutional grievance due to their (a) relevance (because they directly contravene a constitutional paradigm of fundamental importance) and (b) difficult reversibility (because there was no subsidiary procedural technique capable of ending the alleged grievance with equal effectiveness).[7]

In contrast, the objective of an ADI is to declare that a federal or state law or normative act, or part thereof, is unconstitutional. An ADI is also a main constitutional review action, and the entities that have the legitimacy to propose an ADI to the Brazilian STF are the same entities that can propose an ADPF (which has a certain subsidiary relationship to an ADI); consequently, the STF itself came to recognize that the two actions are fungible; thus, the STF declared that it is lawful to hear an ADI as an ADPF when all the admissibility requirements of the latter coexist, in the event of the inadmissibility of the former.[8]

ADPF 132 was proposed by the Attorney General's Office against the Governor of Rio de Janeiro for allegedly violating fundamental precepts by interpreting items II and V of article 191 and items I to X of Art. 332 of Decree-Law 220/1975 (Statute of Civil Servants of the State of Rio de Janeiro) as being in violation of the Federal Constitution (insofar as such an interpretation implies an effective reduction of rights for persons with a homosexual preference or concrete orientation) and judicial decisions rendered in the State of Rio de Janeiro and in other federal units in the country, thus denying stable homoaffective unions the list of rights peacefully recognized as being enjoyed by those whose sexual preference is defined as "heterosexual."

As an alternative, in the event that this ADPF was inappropriate, the plaintiff requested that the ADPF be received as an ADI to render an interpretation of items II and V of article 19 and article 33 of Decree-Law No. 220/75

(Statute of Civil Servants of the State of Rio de Janeiro) and article 1723 of the Civil Code "in accordance with the Constitution," an interpretation that, similarly, would result in the nonprohibition of the legal regime for stable unions between persons of a different sex for same-sex unions.

Article 19 of Decree-Law No. 220/75 recognizes that public servants in the State of Rio de Janeiro are able to take a leave of absence from their position due to an illness in the family or to accompany their spouse under certain specific circumstances; article 33 of that rule governs social security and assistance for public servants and their families. In both cases, the Governor of Rio de Janeiro interpreted the concept of a family strictly, thereby recognizing the rights provided for in the rule solely for heterosexual unions.

In contrast, article 1723 of the Civil Code established that "a stable union between a man and a woman is recognized as a family unit, configured in a public, continuous and lasting relationship established with the objective of creating a family." The expression "stable union between a man and a woman" was also used by the Constitution; this expression is why part of the doctrine and the judiciary determined that other forms of stable unions could not be recognized as family units.

ADI 4277 was initially filed with the STF as ADPF 178. The action sought a declaration of the recognition of same-sex unions as family units. The action also requested that the same rights and duties of partners in stable unions be extended to partners in same-sex unions. The rapporteur for the action decided that the action would be reclassified as an ADI because there was no evidence at the time that there was a lack of a specific object related to the violation of a fundamental precept resulting from an act of public power.

As an ADI is a type of action that can be filed without meeting the more restrictive requirements of the ADPF and considering the subsidiary nature of this type of action, the STF determined that it was acceptable to judge the actions together, thus recognizing that ADI no. 4277-DF expropriated the fundamentals of ADPF no. 132-RJ.

In its ruling, the STF determined that unless there is an explicit or implied constitutional provision to the contrary, a person's sex does not justify legal inequality. In certain situations, the 1988 Constitution of the Federative Republic of Brazil promotes affirmative actions based on biological sex or gender, as in the case of the protection of the labor market for women through specific incentives provided for by law (article 7, XX), the minimum age for retirement for working women (article 40, §1, III and article 201, §7, I, II) and the exemption of women from mandatory military service (article 143, §2.).

However, the Brazilian Constitution has no rule that authorizes discrimination due to sexual orientation (this absence implies a "negative general rule," according to which anything that is not explicitly prohibited or required is permitted for private individuals); on the contrary, the Constitution itself prohibits any kind of prejudice, as article 3, item IV of the Federal Constitution instituted a fundamental objective of "promoting the good of all."

The decision of the STF established that imposing a heteronormative family model would violate concrete individual rights, particularly freedom of conscience, the right to pursue happiness and the constitutionally protected rights of intimacy, privacy, and autonomy of will.

One of the impasses found in the ruling concerns the assertion in article 226, §3 of the Brazilian Constitution that "for purposes of protection by the State, the stable union between a man and a woman is recognized as a family unit, and the law must facilitate its conversion into marriage." Consequently, for a time, part of Brazilian doctrine held that it would be impossible for the judiciary's action to lead to the legal construction of a new concept of family distinct from a "union between a man and a woman."

The STF recognized that the Brazilian Constitution does not assign any specific meaning to the noun family and that the normative text emphasizes the family institution, rather than a specific form of a family's composition. The STF affirmed that the rule did not limit family even to formal unions, thereby recognizing the family as a private institution formed voluntarily by adults. Interpreting the concept of a family unit as a "stable union between a man and a woman" thus implies unconstitutionally reducing the concept of a family, which is the *locus* where several fundamental rights—particularly the rights of intimacy and privacy—provided for in the Brazilian Constitution become concrete.

The structural analysis of the judicial decision indicates that the STF struggled to try to identify the intention of the constituent (*mens legislatoris*) to oppose it to any attempt at a reductionist and literal interpretation of the text. This is quite evident in certain votes, such as in the case of Minister Joaquim Barbosa (ADPF no. 132-RJ, pp. 117), who rhetorically wonders "should the silence of the Constitution be interpreted as indifference, contempt or hostility?" and continues, "Did the constituent of 1988 want to ostracize, maintain in a kind of legal limbo, legally banned, the affective choices made by an appreciable number of citizens, with the legal and material consequences that result?" to finally conclude that "because I believe that this was not the intention of the constituent legislator, I understand that it is the duty of this Court to search through the rich axiological palette that informs the entire constitutional framework created in 1988."

This phenomenon is also evident in the vote of Minister Gilmar Mendes, although he attempts to mischaracterize the pursuit of the *legislator's intention*, stating that it is the application of techniques of interpretation according to the Constitution (ADPF No. 132-RJ, pp. 148); this statement implies that eliminating or fixing meanings in the normative text actually modifies certain original meanings of the text. In decisions like this, the STF is, therefore, not a mere negative legislator (position of self-restraint); rather, in the exercise of constitutional jurisdiction, the STF can correct the law through its decision.[9]

The STF thus determined that the constitutional reference to the "union between a man and a woman," present in Art. 226, §3 of the Brazilian Constitution, was intended only to favor horizontal or hierarchical legal relationships within families, thus favoring the reduction of any form of discrimination that could occur between documented families and informal families. The decision of the constituent would be related to the need to create normative reinforcements to *combat the patriarchal reluctance of Brazilian customs* (ADPF no. 132-RJ, pp. 4). To leave no doubt, the constituent uses the phrase "family unit" as a synonym for family, thereby indicating that there is no hierarchy among the different possible forms of family, thereby opening up the possibility of other forms, then unimagined.

In addition to enshrining cultural-political-social pluralism, the Brazilian Constitution does not prevent the formation of families by people of the same sex. Furthermore, the STF stated that there is no reason to distinguish between different forms of family, as there is no right *by heteroaffective individuals to their legal nonequivalence with homoaffective individuals.*

The STF thus decided that, due to the possibility that the Civil Code (Art. 1723) could be interpreted in a prejudiced or discriminatory sense and because this problem cannot be resolved in the code itself, it is necessary to interpret the rule in accordance with the Constitution to exclude from the rule any meaning that prevents the recognition of the continuous, public and lasting union between people of the same sex as a family. The recognition of same-sex unions as family units—when the legal requirements are met—have the same legal consequences as stable unions between men and women.

The three ministers (Ricardo Lewandowski, Gilmar Mendes, and Cezar Peluso) reluctantly admitted that despite the unconstitutionality of discrimination between homoaffective and heteroaffective unions, it would be impossible to call the family unit formed by same-sex unions a family, as the Constitution would have reserved the concept of a family for heterosexual unions. This caveat, based on specific techniques of constitutional hermeneutics, is, in fact, a symptom of the heteronormativity and cultural centrality of patriarchy in discussions involving topics in family law; heteronormativity and patriarchy are strongly present in Brazilian culture, which on this point is quite conservative.

Finally, the STF's decision demonstrated an openness to comparative law and the solutions found by different foreign legal systems. Both in the ministers' debate and in the grounds for the votes, there was no lack of references to Portuguese, Argentine, Dutch, Belgian, and South African legislation, among others.

The STF's decision equated same-sex civil unions to marriage, and such civil unions are quite different from other forms of protection for homoaffective families, such as "civil partnerships" (England), "registered partnerships" (Scandinavian countries), and "domestic partnerships" (the United States and some European countries).

In general, the ministers were very attentive to decisions by the US Supreme Court and European Courts, which are usually more progressive and take a *pro homine* position in discussions involving a conflict of rights, interpretation of rules, and constitutional review.

When Minister Celso de Mello justified one of the foundations used in his vote—the right to pursue happiness—as an important hermeneutic vector in the interpretation of fundamental rights, he cited several precedents by the US Supreme Court, such as the Slaughter-House Cases (83 U.S. 36, 1872), *Butchers' Union Co.* v. *Crescent City Co.* (111 U.S. 746, 1884), *Yick Wo* v. *Hopkins* (118 U.S. 356, 1886), *Meyer* v. *Nebraska* (262 U.S. 390, 1923), *Pierce* v. *Society of Sisters* (268 U.S. 510, 1925), *Griswold* v. *Connecticut* (381 U.S. 479, 1965), *Loving* v. *Virginia* (388 U.S. 1, 1967) and *Zablocki* v. *Redhail* (434 U.S. 374, 1978), cases in which the concept of the "pursuit of happiness" was significantly expanded and was extended to issues involving the protection of intimacy, the guarantee of marriage between different ethnicities, custody of minors, learning foreign languages, remarriage and the use of contraceptives, among others.

Before Minister Celso de Mello, Minister Gilmar Mendes had already made references to the fact that although the European Court of Human Rights had not recognized any kind of right for same-sex couples, the court had indicated parameters for the acceptance of such right in European states. Although no decision was cited, there is an indirect reference to cases such as *E.B.* v. *France* (no. 43546/02, January 22, 2008), in which the applicant's request to adopt a child was refused based on the fact that there was no male figure in her family arrangement. The national law permitted the adoption of children by unmarried parents, and the European Court of Human Rights concluded, after review, that the authorities' decision was primarily based on the fact that the applicant maintained a relationship and lived with another woman. The court thus considered the refusal of the request to adopt to be discrimination based on the applicant's sexual orientation.

Another case is *Vallianatos and Others* v. *Greece* (Applications no. 29381/09 and no. 32684/09, November 7, 2013), in which the European Court of Human Rights condemned Greece for excluding homoaffective couples from their right to a civil union. The subject matter addressed unjustified discrimination in civil union contracts in which civil unions (recognized by Law No. 3719/2008, titled "Reforms concerning the family, children and society") included only unions between people of different sexes. The decision highlighted that many European Union countries recognize the possibility for some form of union (between people of different sexes or not) to be registered. The decision describes the resistance of the Church of Greece, which considered civil unions to be "prostitution," and the Minister of Justice, who argued that homoaffective unions should not be contemplated by the legislation. The decision reinforces the flexible concept of the family present in international treaties and stresses that domestic laws must be adapted to treaties and conventions; the decision even stated that national constitutions may have to be amended for that purpose.

There is also the case of *Frédéric Hay* v. *Crédit agricole mutuel de Charente Maritime et des Deux Sèvres*, where the plaintiff entered into a stable union agreement (a PACS) with a person of the same sex. Hay requested the benefits (special license and marriage premium) that are granted to workers who marry, as provided for in the collective agreement of Crédit agricole. The benefits were denied to him because there was no marriage, which, notably, is not provided for by law in the case of same-sex unions. This restriction eventually creates indirect discrimination due to sexual orientation, as stated in article 2, No. 2, Paragraph b) of Directive 2000/78. The case law of the Court of Justice recognizes that the provision creates direct discrimination based on sexual orientation for homosexual workers with a PACS. The ruling also observes that because marriage is reserved for people of a different sex, homosexual workers are, by logical conclusion, unable to fulfill the requisite requirement to obtain the claimed benefit. The Fifth Chamber of the Court of Justice declared that article 2, No. 2, Paragraph b) of Council Directive 2000/78 of November 27, 2000, establishes a general framework for equal treatment in employment and occupation and that this framework also applies to the provisions of collective agreements.

Finally, the caveat established by the court in the case of *Oliari and Others* v. *Italy* (decision of July 21, 2015) is based on article 8 of the European Convention on Human Rights (respect for private and family life—The court decision states that countries do not have an obligation to permit gay marriage, but they are required to guarantee the same protection.

All this indicates that when the Brazilian STF ruled on gay marriage, the court intended to, among other things, a) encapsulate the intentions of the 1988 Constituent by committing to the elimination of all forms of discrimination and establishing human dignity, in addition to citizenship and pluralism, as the foundation of the Federative Republic of Brazil; b) declare the unconstitutionality of prejudiced interpretations of the concept of family, stable union or family unit; such a declaration may eventually prefigure infra-constitutional legislation (specifically, article 19, items II and V and article 33 of Decree-Law No. 220/75 (Statute of Civil Servants of the State of Rio de Janeiro) and article 1723 of the Civil Code); c) recognize that the Federal

Constitution of 1988 is progressive in its customs and that when Congress, either under pressure from conservative groups or to avoid discussions about complex moral dissent, the judiciary has the legitimacy to correctly interpret the rules, declaring the unconstitutionality of prejudiced or restrictive interpretations of rights that lack any foundation in the Constitution; and d) signal an openness to international and foreign law by examining how the issue was resolved in different systems.

CONSENSUS AND DISSENT FOLLOWING THE DECISION

Although the leading case was established on May 4, 2011, the Brazilian justice system took a certain amount of time to create instruments for implementing the STF's decision. Consequently, at the end of 2011, another important court in the country would rule on gay marriage.

Unlike the STF, the STJ ultimately has jurisdiction over all nonspecialized infraconstitutional matters (which do not fall under the jurisdiction of the Labor, Electoral and Military Courts and are not addressed in the Federal Constitution) and rules on issues related to the application of federal law or divergence of jurisprudential interpretation.

In the exercise of its appellate jurisdiction, the STJ had to rule on REsp No. 1183378, which originated in a lawsuit filed in the State of Rio Grande do Sul concerning how Art. 1514, 1521, 1523, 1535, and 1565 of the Brazilian Civil Code should be interpreted, particularly to verify whether there was any impediment to marriage for same-sex couples.

Considering the previous ruling by the STF, this court found that the Federal Constitution of 1988 began a new phase in Brazilian family law and, consequently, in the concept of marriage, which started to be conceptualized based on a polymorphic conception of the family, in which multifaceted arrangements are equally appropriate for composing the domestic nucleus called a "family"; according to the court, all such arrangements receive "special protection by the State." The Brazilian Constitution of 1988 rejected the historical concept of marriage, which was always considered the only path for creating a family and was often an environment for subverting the principles of equality and human dignity enshrined in the current Constitution. The current constitutional conception of marriage is that *it must be necessarily plural, as families are also plural and, moreover, marriage is not the ultimate recipient of protection by the State but only the intermediary of a greater purpose, which is the protection of the human person in their inalienable dignity.*

In the end, the STJ considered that "articles 1514, 1521, 1523, 1535 and 1565, all in the Civil Code of 2002, do not expressly prohibit same-sex marriage, and there is no way to envisage an implicit prohibition on homoaffective marriage without an affront to cherished constitutional principles." The court goes on to state that "while the National Congress, in the Brazilian case, does not explicitly assume its coparticipation in this constitutional process of defending and protecting the socially vulnerable, the judiciary cannot resign from this task, under penalty of a tacit acceptance of a State that is only formally 'democratic,' without that predicative resisting a minimum investigation regarding the universalization of civil rights."

Despite the favorable decisions of the country's highest courts affirming the unconstitutionality of any interpretation of laws preventing the conversion of same-sex civil unions into marriage and that homoaffective couples (just like heterosexual couples) can qualify for marriage, in many parts of the country, there were refusals by some of the institutions in the justice system to perform gay marriage ceremonies or recognize the rights of married homoaffective couples.

These refusals led the CNJ, which is the external supervisory body of the Brazilian judiciary, to issue Resolution 175 (published in May 14, 2013), which prohibited competent authorities from refusing to issue a license, perform a marriage ceremony or convert a civil union into a marriage for same-sex couples.

The same year that the CNJ Resolution was published, there were legislative and judicial reactions. The first significant legislative reaction was Draft Legislative Decree 106/2013, which intended to halt Resolution 175/2013—CNJ, stating that the CNJ had exceeded the limits of its power to regulate and clarify the law by illegally acting as a positive legislator. The second significant legislative reaction was the presentation of Bill 6583/2013, which would have created the "Family Statute." This bill would have restricted stable unions and marriage to unions between men and women. Additionally, the PSC filed an ADI (ADI 4966) against the resolution. To date, none of the reactions has produced any regressive effect, as the normative proposals were not deliberated by Congress and the action presented was not heard.

Although same-sex marriage still raises occasional debates, the number of same-sex marriages in the country has increased. According to the 2010 Census conducted by the Brazilian Institute of Geography and Statistics (*Instituto Brasileiro de Geografia e Estatística—IBGE*), at the time of the STF's decision, there were approximately 60,000 homoaffective couples. In 2013, approximately 4,000 homoaffective couples made their unions official (either by requesting the conversion of a stable union into marriage or by qualifying for marriage); in general, the number of couples interested in recognition of their unions has increased every year, with 9,520 gay marriages in 2018.

Finally, in the ruling on Extraordinary Appeal no. 846102 in March 2015, the STF recognized the right of a homosexual couple to adopt, although there was strong opposition from the Public Ministry of the State of Paraná. The court recognized that, in adoption, obstacles not provided by law cannot be created and that if homosexual couples can create a family, their right to adopt (right to filiation) cannot be restricted in situations where heterosexual couples have that right.

CONCLUSION

The STF's recognition of gay marriage signified a profound advance in protecting the rights of the LGBT population and was an important step in protecting the rights of subjects with sexualities diverging from the heteronormative. This recognition enabled homoaffective families to emerge from invisibility and have some measure of confidence that their relationships would produce valid legal consequences with respect to finances, sharing of assets and inheritance, custody of children, and all aspects involving family law, including the protection of affection.

The STF's decision and the judicial recognition of gay marriage is also the affirmation of an absence. We Brazilians are not liberal! Kindness, cordiality, and liberality only distort and mask our vulgarity. It is not that there is a Brazilianness and that it is vulgar—that is not the case. However, conservatism is revealed in our customs daily and is increasingly evident in the forms of violence against women, black people, the LGBT population, minorities, and vulnerable groups, in general.

A wide range of empirical evidence indicates that although inequality in Brazil has significantly decreased in recent years, conservatism has also, paradoxically, increased. This conservative regression is often supported by the false idea that the recognition of rights for minority or vulnerable groups arises not from the practical implications of the principle of equality but from a kind of privilege, which these groups evidently do not have.

This context may indicate that the next decade will deepen the crisis of democracy, hasten the antipolitical return to the private, increase the exhaustion of politics as a means of resolving the fundamental differences and divergences regarding the distribution of resources (rights and positions), increase the growth of conservative and reactionary discourse and deepen differences, at least in Brazil.

Hopefully, conservative reactions to the recognition of the right to gay marriage do not lead to the reduction of rights and the reestablishment of an orthodox and monolithic model of the family.

NOTES

1. Trevisan, João Silvério. *Devassos no Paraíso*. 3 ed. Rio de Janeiro: Record, 2002.

2. Decree-law 1001 (CPM), of 10.21.1969. "Child abuse or another act of lewdness Art 235. Practicing, or allowing the practice of lewd acts, homosexual or not, in a location subject to military administration: Penalty—from six months to one year of detention."

3. Monocratic Decision published in the Court Gazette (*Diário da Justiça—DJ*) 09/29/2004 P—00016.

4. Pet 1984, Min. Rap. MARCO AURÉLIO, j. 02.10.2003.

5. RESP No. 717525—RN (Rio Grande do Norte) (2005/0006760-7) Published in the DJ on 04/07/2005.

6. "As long as civil law remains inert, the new social structures that are knocking on the doors of the Courts must have their jurisdictional protection based on the existing laws and humanitarian parameters that guide not only constitutional law but most of the legal systems in the world. Specifically, with regard to subject at hand, a normativity identical to that of a stable union should be attributed to the same-sex affective relationship, with the legal effects derived therefrom, preventing the fundamental rights of the people involved from being suppressed due to prejudice" (STJ, REsp 1026981, Rap. Nancy Andrighi, Electronic Court Gazette (*Diário da Justiça Eletrônico—DJe* 02.23.2010); and others, such as STJ, REsp 395904, Min. Rap. Hélio Quaglia Barbosa, DJ 02.06.2006; TRF-3, AC 2004.61.83.000175-5, Fed. Jud. Rap. Nelson Bernardes, DJe 04.14.2008; TJMG, AC/RN 1.0024.05.750258-5/002, Jud. Rap. Belizário de Lacerda, DJ/MG 11.23.2007.

7. ADPF 127, Min. Rap. Teori Zavascki, monocratic decision, ruling on 2-25-2014, DJE of 2-28-2014.

8. ADI 4180-REF-MC, min. rap. Cezar Peluso, ruling on 3-10-2010, Plenary, DJE of 8-27-2010. See also ADPF 178, min. rap. President Gilmar Mendes, monocratic decision, ruling on 7-21-2009, DJE of 8-5-2009; ADPF 72-QO, min. rap. Ellen Gracie, ruling on 6-1-2005, Plenary, DJ of 12-2-2005.

9. ADI 3324, ADI 3046, ADI 2652, ADI 1946, ADI 2209, ADI 2596, ADI 2332, ADI 2084, ADI 1797, ADI 2087, ADI 1668, ADI 1344, ADI 2405, ADI 1105, ADI 1127, ADIN 1105-DF, ADIN 1127-DF, DI 3324, ADI 3046, ADI 2652, ADI 1946, ADI 2209, ADI 2596, ADI 2332, ADI 2084, ADI 1797, ADI 2087, ADI 1668, ADI 1344, ADI 2405, ADI 1105, ADI 112.

REFERENCES

Alves, F. B.; Nascimento, A. R. Retrato das uniões homoafetivas no contexto normativo decisório da União Européia: Democracia e Direitos Fundamentais. In: Tomaz Esposito Neto; Henrique Sartori de Almeida Prado (Org.). *União Européia: Visões Brasileiras*. 1 ed. Curitiba: Appris/Cátedra Jean Monnet, 2019, v. 1, p. 15–32.

Alves, F. B.; Turatti Junior, M. A. Não há padrões! Abordagens sobre identidade a partir da Teoria Queer e da Teoria do Reconhecimento de Axel Honneth. In: Nilson

Tadeu Reis Campos Silva (Org.). *Fractais dos direitos de minorias*. 1 ed. Rio de Janeiro: Lumens Juris, 2018, p. 93–119.
Trevisan, João Silvério. *Devassos no Paraíso*. 3 ed. Rio de Janeiro: Record, 2002.

I would like to thank the Araucária Foundation for the Support of Scientific and Technological Development in the State of Paraná (Fundação Araucária de Apoio ao Desenvolvimento Científico e Tecnológico do Estado do Paraná—FAPPR).

Chapter 8

Criminalization of Homophobia—Trial at the Brazilian Supreme Court

Simone Cristine Araújo Lopes

INTRODUCTION

This chapter describes, in a succinct way, the general lines of legal discussion and the facts that marked the result of the trial responsible for settling the criminalization of homophobia in Brazil, at the Brazilian Supreme Court.

In only one year (2019), the Supreme Court delivered its judgment on two lawsuits—Direct Action of Unconstitutionality by Omission No. 26 and Writ of Injunction No. 4733—which aimed to criminalize discriminatory practices towards people due to their sexual orientation or individual gender identification, points that have been traditionally defended by the Brazilian LGBTTQIA + (lesbians, gays, bisexuals, transvestites, transsexuals, homosexuals, intersexuals, asexuals) civil society organizations.

The methodology employed in the present chapter consists in analyzing the case considering the description and explanation of legal aspects of the normative and jurisdictional Brazilian organization, especially regarding the foreign readers. Interdisciplinary content will be approached, especially in respect to the observation of the historical and evolutionary bias regarding the defense of the rights of minorities in a Democratic Constitutional State, as advocated by the Constitution of the Federative Republic of Brazil of 1988.[1] The correlation of this aspect and the result of the 2019 trial, 30 years later than the enactment of the Brazilian Supreme Law (October 5, 1988), will also be analyzed.

The starting point of this research is Law No. 7716, which was passed on 5, 1989, three months after the approval of the new Constitution by the National Constituent Assembly. This law dealt with the criminalization of acts of prejudice regarding race or color in the whole country. Therefore, it is readily apparent that the study about the criminalization of homophobia is a study, which pertains to the field of Brazilian Criminal Law, in the shade of the Supreme Law—the Constitution. It is in this context that the following lines will be written.

THE CONTEXT OF LAW NO. 7716/1989 AND SOME ASPECTS OF CRIMINAL LAW REGARDING HOMOPHOBIA

The Brazilian Constitution of 1988 introduced an innovation never seen in the previous documents since the independence of the country in 1922: the inclusion of the word "racism" in two prominent places on the body of the fundamental rules of the Republic.

The first mention appears in article 4, VII, which deals with the principles that rule the relationship between Brazil and foreign countries, affirming the "repudiation of terrorism and racism." The norm curiously condemns both terrorism and racism as if they were equivalents, deserving to be fought in a global level.

The second mention can be found in article 5, XLII, which refers to the fundamental rights and guarantees. A fundamental clause, it cannot be mitigated or suppressed by means of an ulterior Constitutional amendment.[2] According to it, "the practice of racism is a non-bailable crime, with no limitation, subject to the penalty of confinement, under the terms of the law."[3]

It should be noted that although disposed in the Constitution that racism is a crime, the action itself was not considered a criminal act immediately after the promulgation of the diploma, due to the reservation found in the sentence "under the terms of the law." This means that the Brazilian Constitution of 1988 led to an ulterior law the task of defining the offense, that is to say, to define which elements of an action characterize it as a racist offense. This is the reason why the Law No.7716/1989,[4] which brings the specific elements of the offense, was enacted: to comply with the requisitions of Brazilian Criminal Law.

This need of a law which defines the offense elements stems from article 1º of the Brazilian Criminal Code (1940), according to which "there is no crime without a previous law defining it. There is no sentence without previous legal provision."

It is one of the classic tenets of modern criminal law since Cesare Beccaria who, in the work "On Crimes and Punishments," already pointed out the need for previous knowledge of what is to be considered a crime within a society and its related punishment, so that every person can adjust his or her behavior to the standards of the social body to which he or she belongs to. Indeed:

No magistrate then, (as he is one of the society) can, with justice, inflict on any other member of the same society, punishment that is not ordained by the laws. But as a punishment, increased beyond the degree fixed by the law, is the just punishment, with the addition of another; it follows, that no magistrate, even under a pretence of zeal, or the public good, should increase the punishment already determined by the laws.

The sovereign, who represents the society itself, can only make general laws to bind the members; but it belongs not to him to judge whether any individual has violated the social compact, or incurred the punishment in consequence.[5]

That is the reason why Carlos Alberto Cao Oliveira dos Santos,[6] a historic figure of the black social movement and a journalist, who, at the time, was a federal representative, submitted, speedier as he could, the draft bill criminalizing racism, which culminated in the Law No. 7716/1989. According to this law, the sentence of imprisonment can vary from one to five years, and the punishment includes fines and a few administrative penalties.

Before the law that criminalized racist behavior in Brazil and settled imprisonment as a punishment there was Law No. 1390/1951, elaborated by the federal representative Afonso Arinos de Melo Franco,[7] which settled the "practice of acts resulting from prejudices of race or color" as a criminal misdemeanor. This law punished the criminal with imprisonment that could last from 15 days to one year and other consequences as loss of public post or role or suspension of activities of private educational institutes for three months, as well as fines.

In the years of 1997 and 2010, Law No. 7716/1989 underwent some adjustments and alterations to increase the possibility of also criminalizing conducts of discrimination or prejudice against ethnicity, religion, or national origin. It also included the criminalization of acts related to prejudice practiced in the web environment.

Notwithstanding all this normative evolution in Brazil, there was no innovation to criminalize prejudicial conducts regarding sex, gender identification, or homophobia. For this reason, and as a result of the Principle of the Separation of Powers,[8] several legislative bills have been proposed to the members of the Legislative to include these spheres of protection of minority rights, but none of them has, until today, been approved by the Brazilian National Congress, which comprises the Chamber of Deputies, representing the most varied lines of thought and social class defense, and the Federal Senate, which represents the States in the federalist form of State, as it is into force in the country. A bicameral federal legislative system is, therefore, similar to that of the United States of America.

However, there was a change in the role of the Supreme Court after the 1988 Constitution that culminated in the criminalization of homophobia by the court, as it shall be seen in the following topic.

THE PERFORMANCE OF THE SUPREME COURT AFTER THE PROMULGATION OF THE CONSTITUTION OF THE FEDERATIVE REPUBLIC OF BRAZIL (1988)

Brazil became independent of Portugal in 1822, and, in 1824, the Constitution of the Empire of Brazil was imposed by the first ruler, Dom Pedro I, son of the Portuguese king, Dom João VI. It was a monarchy. The first Brazilian Constitution embodied the Judiciary, Executive, and Legislative branches, but it also included the so-called Moderating Power, which was exclusive of the reigning Emperor, who could interfere in the other powers. Moderating power was influenced by the French political scientist Henri-Benjamin Constant de Rebecque (1767–7830), with some characteristics specific to the largest country of South America. Therefore, it is not possible to consider a Judiciary similar to that endorsed by the United States of America, especially after the precedent set in the famous case *Marbury* v. *Madison*. The Brazilian judicial organization was inspired by the French one, which means constitutional control over laws was given to parliamentary bodies during the legislative process. The largest judicial body at that time was the Supreme Court of Justice, based in Rio de Janeiro, at the time the capital of the Brazilian empire. The function of the court, though, was not to control the constitutionality of laws, but to review the ones applied.

With the proclamation of the Republic, in 1889, care was taken to ensure the adherence to the *common law* system and, specially, to North American law. This was made even before the enactment of the Republican Constitution of 1981, by the Decree 848/1890, as displayed in article 386:

> Article 386. The omitted cases shall have as subsidiary legislation the former laws of criminal, civil and commercial process, since not contrary to the spirit and the displayed in the present decree. The statutes of educated peoples, especially those ruling legal relations in the Republic of the United States of America, the cases of common law and equity, will also be subsidiary to the jurisprudence and federal process.[9]

This decree also created the Brazilian Supreme Court as an entity of Federal Justice and as a final instance of appeal on the Brazilian judiciary system. The French tradition was abandoned in order to get closer to the North American model of justice and Constitutional Law. However, over the nearly one hundred years between the creation of the Supreme Court and the promulgation of the Brazilian Constitution of 1988, currently valid, the court faced many comings and goings in this role concerning not only constitutionality review, but also review of the acts performed by public authorities or other branches of the trinity "Judiciary, Legislative, and Executive."[10] So that the reader can have a clear picture of the situation, the role of the Supreme Court as the "guardian of the Constitution" was expressed only in the Brazilian Constitution of 1988. This has never been mentioned in the previous diplomas in such an eloquent way as it is now in article 102, the main section.[11]

For this reason, to simplify the debate, it can be said that the Supreme Court achieved *a more active role*[12] in judging issues solved in the light of constitutional rules after the promulgation of the current Constitution. Moreover, it can interfere in the sphere of other powers of the Brazilian State if there is an understanding, duly motivated and reasoned by the plenary composed of its eleven ministers in the assessment of the merits of the case, that there is an unconstitutional legislative omission on the part of the legislative bodies, as occurred at the judgment of the criminalization of homophobia dealt with in the present work.

Interestingly enough, when it concerns trials by omission, the Brazilian Constitution of 1988, in article 103, § 2º, states that "When unconstitutionality is declared on account of lack of a measure to render a constitutional provision effective, the competent power shall be notified for the adoption of the necessary actions and, in the case of an administrative body, to do so within thirty days." This is the reason why, for a long time after the promulgation of the Brazilian Constitution of 1988, jurisprudence, as employed by the Supreme Court, was understood in the sense that it could not decide with concrete effects and in general, for everyone, or for individual concrete cases and of immediate effect to the plaintiffs. The Supreme Court was limited to summon the competent legislative body to provide the legal diploma without setting a deadline. However, what happened frequently was that the delay of the Legislative persisted, the reason that the Supreme Court started to indicate the legal rule to be applied so that the plaintiff of the lawsuit—and eventual third parties also benefited by the judicial decision when it had an *erga omnes* effect–could have, regarding some harmed right or a right in danger of being harmed as a result of the inexistence of the legal diploma, the right materialized.[13]

Important to bear in mind that when the current body of constitutional rules came into force, in October 1988, the President of the Supreme Court was Rafael Mayer, and among the members were Ministers Djaci Falcão, Moreira Alves, Néri da Silveira, Oscar Corrêa, Aldir Passarinho, Francisco Rezek, Sydney Sanches, Octávio Gallotti, Carlos Madeira, and Célio Borja, only two of the latter being nominated by the President of the Republic, the first elected civilian, during the period of redemocratization (albeit in an indirect manner and figuring on the list headed by Tancredo Neves) since the military dictatorship established on March 31, 1964.

Of that composition contemporary to the Brazilian Constitution of 1988, the last one to retire was Minister Sydney Sanches, on April 27, 2003. In 1990, there were already five new ministers in the Supreme Court: Paulo Brossard, Sepúlveda Pertence, Carlos Velloso, Celso de Mello, and Marco Aurélio, being the latter two members of the Court until today. Ellen Gracie, now retired, was the first woman to be appointed, in October 2000. In 2003, between the end of April and the beginning of May, three ministers were compulsorily retired because they reached the maximum age of 70 years allowed for the exercise of public office, bringing to an end the period of activity of all the ministers who composed the higher body of Brazilian judiciary in October 1988: Ilmar Galvão, Sydney Sanches, and Moreira Alves. That was when the new members joined: Cezar Pelluso, Ayres Britto, and Joaquim Barbosa, the first black member of the Court, who took office on June 25, 2003. In Brazil, slavery was abolished on May 13, 1888—it was the last country in America to do so.[14]

In the opinion of the author, the period concerning the government of President Luís Inácio Lula da Silva (Worker's Party—PT), elected with a mandate from January 1, 2003, to January 1, 2011, with the rise of Nelson Jobim (June 3, 2004, to March 28, 2006) to the position of President of the Supreme Court[15], was one of a significant change in the way of solving processes within the competence of the Brazilian Supreme Court after the 1988 Constitution. This is, of course, a topic prone to academic debate. The aforementioned change was deepened during the period known as "court Mendes," which refers not only to the presidency of Minister Gilmar Mendes between April 23, 2008, and April 22, 2010, but also to the role of this minister since he joined the Attorney General's Office with opinions considered brilliant by Minister Moreira Alves, presented in cases where he was the rapporteur and the themes concerned constitutional matters.[16] Conventionally, this performance by the Supreme Court in favor of the implementation and guarantee of fundamental or social rights advocated by the Brazilian Constitution of 1988 is called "judicial activism" by the Brazilian legal doctrine.

In fact, some members of the Court began a more active movement concerning the judicial answer given to demands. The author highlights the case in which Minister Celso de Mello was the rapporteur, in November 2005,[17] when he not only declared the right of children between zero and six years of age to attend daycare facilities in the cities they lived, facilities that should be built by order of the mayor, according to article 208, IV of the present Constitution, but also determined the implementation of this social right by the rulers. In other words: the previous jurisprudence of the Court was limited to declare the right, but not to implement it, because this would be an interference in the power sphere of another branch, hurting, therefore, the Principle of Separation of Powers. The new approach of the Court, more activist, began to understand that to merely declare the right was not enough; the Supreme Court, in the role of guardian of the Constitution, should demand from members of other powers (Executive or Legislative), by the judicial commandment, the real fulfillment.

It is according to this new layout, which started and evolved especially after 1988, that the decision regarding "criminalization of homophobia" can be analyzed, since the Writ of Injunction was turned effective by application of the law as mentioned by the Supreme Court, in order to avoid the indefinite delay of the legislative concerning the elaboration of judicial norms. It is in this context that the following topics—dedicated to the trial of the case here studied—will be analyzed.

THE CONTEXT OF THE TRIAL CONCERNING THE CRIMINALIZATION OF HOMOPHOBIA AT THE SUPREME COURT

Two lawsuits were submitted before the Supreme Court with the same intention: criminalize behaviors that are homophobic or transphobic: Writ of Injunction No. 4733[18] and Direct Action of Unconstitutionality by Omission No. 26.[19] Both the lawsuits had the same lawyer, Paulo Roberto Iotti Vecchiatti, and were submitted to trial together, during the same six plenary sessions of the Brazilian Supreme Court. The reason that there were two lawsuits with the same intention is, probably, due to a procedural strategy in order to avoid the frustration of the procedural success, since the Writ of Injunction could be denied for inadmissibility of the way and, therefore, never even have its merit analyzed. Such concern turned out to be pointless, since only one minister—Marco Aurélio de Mello—made an option for the inadmissibility of the way of choice. All the others admitted the lawsuit and moved forward to the merit; two votes that were against the criminalization of homophobia were defeated (Ricardo Lewandowski and Dias Toffoli, President of the Supreme Court at the time). Concerning the Direct Action of Unconstitutionality by Omission, the admissibility was unanimous, with a partial divergence only regarding the merit.[20]

Another innovative feature of the performance of the Supreme Court after the 1988 Constitution was the granting of procedural assistance from entities or bodies representing the *sub judice* matter under constitutionality control that may result in a judicial decision *erga omnes*. This procedural performance was guaranteed in the actions judged jointly through the *amicus curiae* institute. In fact, in both cases there were a total of twelve *amici curiae*[21] with antagonistic strands as to the merits of the cause, which can be exemplified by the Gay Group of Bahia, in favor of the criminalization of homophobia and the "Mixed" Parliamentary Front of the Family and Support to Life, contrary to the criminalization. These assistants have the procedural right to present opinions, studies and allegations in the case file, as well as to exercise the right of oral argument before the Supreme Court plenary when causes are being judged, which in fact occurred, with uniform times of oral presentation to each of the lawyers appointed by each *amicus curiae*. This required a session of approximately three hours in the first of the six sessions that make up the total of the trial.[22]

Many points were debated at the trial. However, the author, with regard to the debate concerning the merits of the case, opted to explore the argumentative development on the following points: 1) possible delay, by the Legislative, concerning criminal and the possibility of action by means of the judiciary in the face of the principle that reserves criminal law to parliament and 2) freedom of expression and religion *versus* racism or discrimination.

On the first point, which will be briefly summarized, the Senate, in its defense, claimed that it was not in delay, since there were several procedural protocols in progress in the chamber of elected representatives and that the possible delay was due to intense debates on the theme, which is natural in a democracy and for the performance of the most varied parliamentary fronts for the defense of LGBTTQIA + rights as well as those who defend the family and rights related to religiosity.

Similarly, the Attorney General, in his oral presentation, pointed out that the Supreme Court could not legislate on criminal law in view of the Principle of Legal Reserve (only the parliament can legislate on this matter), so much so that the current Constitution denies the President to provide on this matter even through a Temporary Measure.[23] Therefore, if the Executive is prohibited from doing it, the judiciary is much more indeed.

In contrast, the plaintiffs' lawyer argued that the legislative procedures of the aforementioned bills had been dragging on for almost two decades, leaving the population in a situation of vulnerability and permanent danger to their honor, physical integrity, life, and other juridical assets which are guaranteed to other people. This argument that was recognized by the rapporteur, Minister Celso de Mello, based on statistical data[24] that points to hate speeches and hate crimes against minority groups represented in the cause.

Minister Celso de Mello stated that the Judiciary was not going beyond its competence to legislate in substitution to the competent power, but that it only indicated an analogous norm, applicable to "social racism"—that goes beyond the reductionist concept of racism by color or by ethnic origin or nationality—to protect vulnerable groups of any kind, which includes the LGBT group, until a legal norm enacted by the Legislative comes. Thus, the legislative delay will be eliminated, and the legal diploma will prevail over the judgment, within its constitutional competence. In this case, the analogous law—which was promulgated by the Legislative—applicable to the crime of homophobia would be the law against racism, Law No. 7716/89. In fact, in the extract of the result of the final judgment it appears that

> until autonomous legislation supervenes, edited by the National Congress, either because it is considered, under the terms of this vote, that homotransphobic practices qualify as species of the racism genre, in the dimension of social racism accepted by the Supreme Federal Court in the plenary judgment of HC 82.424/RS (Ellwanger case), inasmuch as such behaviors matter in acts of segregation that undermine members of the LGBT community, due to their sexual orientation or gender identity, that is, also, because such homotransphobia behaviors are based on the concept of acts of discrimination and offense to fundamental rights and freedom of those who make up the vulnerable group in question (BRASIL. Supremo Tribunal Federal. Direct Action of Unconstitutionality by Omission No. 26. Minute of Judgment No. 22 published. Electronic Justice Journal, June 28, 2019, Brasilia, June 13, 2019.)

Regarding the second point, it is interesting to note that the plaintiffs' lawyer sustained that the criminalization of homophobia would not prevent any religious leader from pointing out sodomy as a sinful practice, since "ignorance is also a fundamental right." So that the action did not violate freedom of expression or religion, but would only curtail any eventual abuse of the right to expression that could lead to hate speech or incitement to violence against minority groups by anyone, religious or not. And he gave an example: the sermon of a religious leader who says homosexuality as a sin, based on a sacred book, does not constitute a crime, but it constitutes a crime if that same leader encourages his followers to embarrass, expel from the temple or public spaces, or even deny fundamental rights of anyone just for the reason of his or her sexual orientation, restraining the person from the right to be what he or she is or wants to be[25]. He went further, saying that defending heterosexuality is discriminatory by group; it goes beyond race because it aims to show that heterosexuality is "normal." Race prejudice or prejudice against a person's sexuality is always based on power relations or privileges of a dominant group in relation to another, much more vulnerable and, therefore, dominated, quoting Djamila Ribeiro, black feminist, philosopher and academic. And that this type of situation and its acceptance by the State violated the principle of legal equality between people due to illegitimate issues in the light of the national legal order.

In opposition to this line of argument, the Attorney General pointed out that there is not, as for racism, a determination expressed in the 1988 Constitution to criminalize homophobia by law. He added that the discriminatory conduct is already punishable by law in several spheres in addition to the criminal one, including for religious reasons that protect ministers of religious denominations, for example. Thus, it is not necessary to create a specific norm for the LGBT group, which is already protected by the general rule, valid for each and every Brazilian.

The views of the antagonistic parties converged, in a way, in the oral support given by the lawyer Luigi Mateus Braga who, arguing in favor of the *amicus curiae* "National Association of Evangelical Jurists" thanked the plaintiff's lawyer for the words that recognized the pastor's right to preach, on a biblical basis, against homosexual practice, respecting the homosexual person who is also created by God and, therefore, every Christian has the duty to be against violence in all its aspects. However, it does not recognize this clarity in the procedural requests presented, requesting the balance between religious freedom and freedom of gender identification, recognizing both situations as social facts which are imposed.

The rapporteur, Minister Celso de Mello, when presenting his winning vote on the case, justified the decision by saying that there is a constitutional determination regarding the duty to legislate against discrimination not only by the content of item XLII (referring to racism and already explained on item 2 of this article), but it is also present on item XLI of the same article—the 5th—of the 1988 Constitution, *ipsis literis*: "—the law shall punish any discrimination which may attempt against fundamental rights and liberties." On the other hand, the minister brought up the memorable debate held on the occasion of the "Ellwanger case."[26] Then, the penal concept of "social racism" is pointed out for segregationist situations that tend to deny rights and liberties to vulnerable groups as it is the case of the LGBT community. In this sense, see the extract from the minutes of the trial, with the thesis established by the Supreme Court for the actions that where decided:

> The concept of racism, understood in its social dimension, projects itself beyond strictly biological or phenotypic aspects, as it results, as a manifestation of power, from a construction of a historical-cultural nature motivated by the objective of justifying inequality and destined to ideological control, political domination, social subjugation and denial of otherness, dignity and humanity of those who, because they belong to a vulnerable group (LGBTI +) and do not belong to the stratum which holds a position of hegemony in a given social structure, are considered stranger and different, degraded to the condition of marginals of the legal system, exposed, as a result of odious inferiority and perverse stigmatization, to an unfair and harmful situation of exclusion from

the general system of protection of the law (BRAZIL. Supreme Federal Court Direct UnConstitutionality Action for Failure No. 26. Proceedings No. 22 publicada … Electronic Justice Diary, June 28 2019, Brasilia, j. Jun 13 2019).

On the other hand, the vote of the rapporteur recalled that, due to the constitutional provision, international treaties related to Human Rights, because they converge with the principles and norms of the democratic regime of law, have receptivity in the Brazilian legal system. And the protection of minority rights is part of the list of guarantees of the legal treaties on Human Rights, applicable in Brazil.

Minister Ricardo Lewandowski started partial divergence when recognizing the legislative delay and the duty of legislating on the part of Brazilian parliamentarians due to the sensitivity of the subject of protective bias to a social group that, in fact, has historically suffered violence based on prejudice or hatred. However, unlike the majority of the plenary, Minister Lewandowski denied the request for the criminalization of homophobia to be upheld on the grounds of the Principle of Absolute Legal Reserve to the Legislative as the only one capable of legislating on criminal matters. The minister's dissenting vote was accompanied, in its entirety, by the President of the Supreme Court during the trial sessions, Minister Dias Toffoli. In order to be more practical, the next topic will be addressed, together with the analysis of Brazilian doctrine regarding the majority decision of the Supreme Court in favor of criminalizing homophobia, which had conflicting opinions, many of them according to the divergent vote of the minister.

DOCTRINAL STANDPOINTS ABOUT THE CRIMINALIZATION OF HOMOPHOBIA BY THE JUDICIARY

It is interesting to note that the two unsuccessful votes of Minister Ricardo Lewandowski—who wrote the content and basis—and Minister Dias Toffolli had no disagreement about the importance of criminalizing homophobia, making considerations that coincided with the primary request of the plaintiffs and the winning votes in the trial. For this reason, they decided favorably to summon the National Congress regarding the legislative delay and, therefore, pointing out the need for a legal diploma of a protective nature to the LGBT category, in fact a group constantly subject to violence in its most varied forms in Brazilian society.

The partial point of disagreement is about the competence of the Supreme Court to legislate on criminal matters, something that, in this judgment, was, in fact, unprecedented in the entire history of the court. The overdue judges based their arguments on more than the secular criminal garantist[27] norm of western criminal law, explicitly since 1940 in the Brazilian Code, as already mentioned in item 1 of this paper—or in the Principle of the Absolute Legal Reserve of parliament for criminalizing conducts. Next, part of the vote of eminent Minister Lewandowski:

> Much more could be done to protect these minority groups and criminalizing the conduct would be an important step. It seems to me indisputable that the legislative delay in this case must be recognized. However, in addition to recognizing the legislative delay, there is little that this Court can do, since it is not feasible to invoke the precedents established in the Writs of Injunction 670, 708 and 712, due to a fundamental distinction to be applied in this case: this process concerns criminal matters, subject to the absolute legal reserve. Notwithstanding the disgust caused by a prejudicial conduct of any kind, it is certain that only the Legislative can criminalize a conduct, being absolutely essential that a formal law is enacted. Effectively, the principle of legal reserve, inscribed in the Constitution in art. 5th, XXXIX, "there is no crime without a previous law to define it, nor a punishment without a previous legal commination." The Supreme Law is clear: only the law, in a formal sense, can criminalize a conduct. (BRAZIL. Supreme Federal Court. Direct Action of Unconstitutionality by Default No. 26. Vote by Minister Ricardo Lewandowski. Available at: http://www.stf.jus.br/arquivo/cms/noticiaNoticiaStf/anexo/ADO26votoRL.pdf Access: May 11, 2020)

Diverging from the other votes, the Minister recalled that the Supreme Court did not even admit criminalization by means of International Treaties, even though they deal with matters related to the legal receptivity set in the Constitution in force in some cases, as occurred with the Palermo Convention, rejected by the Supreme Court on a previous trial. On the contrary, the plenary decided that it is mandatory the existence of a law made by the parliament, ratifying international standards.

Since the ministers diverged, the following question remains: why the Supreme Court decided to criminalize homophobia? Minister Lewandowski seems to point out, in specific assertions in his vote, the reason: the invasion of the political sphere in the jurisdictional one. Quoting Ran Hirschl, the divergent judge points out that recognized constitutional supremacy has brought constitutional courts to the center of political conflicts, once they are demanded by minorities to protect their rights and liberties since politicians exempt themselves from this responsibility in view of the unpopularity of the decision. This observation by Ricardo Lewandowski (also a professor at Universidade de São Paulo) has its confirmation in the light of the facts after the praetorian decision, since it provoked a series of criticisms and praise for the judicial decision in favor of criminalizing homophobic and transphobic acts, as soon as the result was announced by the plenary of the Supreme Court.

The highest authority of the Brazilian Executive, President Jair Bolsonaro, is quoted as saying that "the verdict was totally wrong, and the Supreme Court is legislating, what is an attribution of Congress." According to Bolsonaro, the decision may even hinder homosexuals from getting a job, because employers, he said, will be afraid that the former employee could make a false accusation of homophobia. Once more, the President defended that the Supreme Court ought to have a religious minister (an evangelical Christian) and said that this is not mixing justice with religion.[28] Note that the current Brazilian representative was a Federal Deputy for twenty-eight years, always with a conservative agenda in matters of morals and religion. He is famous for statements such as: "if defending the family and children, etc., etc. is to be homophobic, I am homophobic with pleasure," or that "people should take homosexuality from their children by means of a beating "or that if a child starts hanging out with gays "he may find this normal" and that "he prefers a dead son to a gay son."[29] A President who denies that there is homophobia in Brazil and says that eventual deaths of LGBT people occur for reasons unrelated to prejudice and hate speech.[30] In fact, this statement by the current head of the Executive presents a paradox because, if there was no homophobia in Brazil, the Supreme Court criminalized a conduct that is not practiced and, therefore, there is no reason for anyone, much less the President of the Republic, to be concerned with the positioning of the Supreme Court. But no. There are many who criticize and fear its application for, perhaps, meta-legal reasons, that is, to be free to be intolerant. After all, the current Brazilian representative obtained almost 58 million votes in the second round in a universe of approximately 147 million voters.

It is important to say that the elections of 2018 generated fierce academic debate about the normality of the process, a point that will not be explored here due to space available and limitations on the theme. However, something evident can be extracted from the electoral result, not only for the major position, but the fact that the new composition of the National Congress is expressively conservative and, therefore, tends to align with the presidential thought concerning the LGBT theme, as can be seen in the data collected by DIAP, already mentioned in footnote n. 20. Therefore, to pretend that the current deputies and senators deliberate favorably on topics of interest to the LGBT community is a chimera.

Perhaps it was for this very reason that the Supreme Court decided to judge the lawsuits that, as already noted, were waiting for approximately eight years for a final judicial decision, much of that time in a period in which the heads of the Executive were of liberal or left tendency which coincides with the bills without a conclusion in Parliament, mentioned in the praetorian ruling in favor of the criminalization of homophobia. The fact is that, even when Brazil was ruled by a President linked to a party considered to be a leftwing one, Dilma Roussef,[31] the National Congress and—why not recognize it?—a good part of the Brazilian society was against the LGBT agenda for reasons that are difficult to explain and that demand in-depth studies, suitable for future research and essays.

Therefore, the Supreme Court, in view of the conservative dominance in the federal Executive and Legislative, chose to put this matter on the agenda for trial, probably as a way of exercising the counter-majoritarian function, consisting of restraining and counterbalancing the political powers. It was a way of signaling to society its role in constitutional control according to the Principle of Division of Powers, which is harmonic and independent. It should be noted that the trial took place in the first months of the mandate of the new President of the Republic and the conservative composition of Brazilian National Congress, which will last until January 1, 2022.[32]

In addition to this political aspect pointed out in the vote of the eminent Minister Lewandowski, there are other aspects that could be mulled over, demonstrating the impossibility of criminalizing homophobia through the judicial system. This is so especially if one takes into account aspects of Criminology that, lately, in its more progressive bias, has recommended penal minimalism[33]. However, for the purposes of this article, this and other points could well be better addressed in studies that are left for the future.

FINAL CONSIDERATIONS

Thus, the present chapter is concluded, fulfilling the objective of presenting and analyzing the vote and the context in which, by a majority of the Supreme Court plenary, homophobia was criminalized in Brazil, since June 13, 2019.

Brazilian public opinion, be it from a layman or law specialists, can make the most varied remarks about the success or failure of the decision of the Brazilian Supreme Court. However, in the opinion of the author, it is a fact that, even in the face of this decision that aimed to strengthen the Supreme Court in this position for the benefit of minorities and as a balance point to avoid a setback for the achievement of human rights and respect for the dignity of the human person in present times, the National Congress, more than a year after the conclusion of the trial, has not taken a single step forward to deliberate on the bill against homophobia.[34] The very thesis of the conclusion of the trial is absolutely clear in saying that the praetorian decision will be valid "until a law emanating from the National Congress comes to implement the criminalization warrants defined in items XLI and XLII of article 5 of the Constitution of the Republic."[35] Thus, if the National Congress wants to legislate differently from what was defined by the Supreme Court when determining the application of Law No. 7716/89, it would be enough to do it in order to satisfy its most conservative voter, which has not been done so far and, as we can see, may not be done in view of the unpopularity of the matter, which would attract an electoral cost difficult to be measured, especially in post-truth times and when fake news can demolish reputations based on a misplaced word spoken during parliamentary debates.

It matters little whether the Supreme Court decided politically or not. A determining factor was—and still is—the absence of the exercise of politics in the National Congress on the matter, leaving the latent opportunity to occupy spaces of power, perhaps intentionally left in a vacuum.

NOTES

1. All the remarks on articles of the Brazilian Constitution can be checked on the English version, available at the website of the Senate, updated with Constitutional amendments until 2013: https://www2.senado.leg.br/bdsf/bitstream/handle/id/243334/Constitution_2013.pdf?sequence=11&isAllowed=y

Brasil. Constituição da República Federativa do Brasil. Diário Oficial da União, Brasília, 5 out. 1988. Available at: http://www.planalto.gov.br/ccivil_03/constituicao/constitui%C3%A7ao.htm. Access: April 13 2020.

2. The Brazilian Constitution of 1988 devoted special care to some topics which cannot be even the object of a proposal of Constitutional amendment, for example one that would "abolish individual rights and guarantees" (article 60, §4°, IV). This is exactly the nomenclature of title II, which begins in article 5th: Fundamental Rights and Guarantees (Brasil. Constituição da República Federativa do Brasil. Diário Oficial da União, Brasília, 5 out. 1988. Available at: http://www.planalto.gov.br/ccivil_03/constituicao/constitui%C3%A7ao.htm. Access: April 13 2020).

3. According to José Afonso da Silva, Brazilian scholar, this type of Constitutional norm is termed "non self-executioning," since it depends on an ulterior law to render it applicable. This is exactly the case of article 5th, XLII. (Afonso da Silva, José. *Aplicabilidade das Normas Constitucionais*. 3 ed. São Paulo: Malheiros, 1998).

4. Brasil. Lei n° 7716, de 05 de janeiro de 1989. Define os crimes resultantes de preconceito de raça ou de cor. Diário Oficial da União, Brasília, 09 jan. 1989. Available at: https://www.planalto.gov.br/ccivil_03/leis/l7716.htm. Access: April 13 2020.

5. Beccaria, Cesare. Dos Delitos e das Penas. Ed. eletrônica ridendo castigant mores, p. 10–11. Available at: http://www.dominiopublico.gov.br/download/texto/eb000015.pdf Access in April 13 2020. English version available at: http://files.libertyfund.org/files/2193/Beccaria_1476_EBk_v6.0.pdf. Access: May 14 2020.

6. Lima, Eneida. Carlos Alberto Cao Oliveira dos Santos. In FGV-CPDOC. Rio de Janeiro. Available at: http://www.fgv.br/cpdoc/acervo/dicionarios/verbete-biografico/carlos-alberto-cao-oliveira-dos-santos Access: April 13 2020.

7. Brasil. Lei nº 1390, de 03 de julho de 1951. Inclui entre as contravenções penais a prática de atos resultantes de preconceitos de raça ou de côr. Diário Oficial da União, Rio de Janeiro, 10 jul. 1951. Available at: http://www.planalto.gov.br/ccivil_03/LEIS/L1390.htm#art9 Access: April 13 2020.

8. The principle is explicit in article 2nd of the Brazilian Constitution of 1988 and the branches are three: the Legislative, the Executive and the Judiciary.

9. Brasil. Decreto n.º 848, de 11 de outubro de 1890. Organiza a Justiça Federal. Coleção das Leis do Brasil, Rio de Janeiro, 1890. Available at: https://www.planalto.gov.br/ccivil_03/decreto/1851-1899/d848.htm. Access: April 13 2020. English version by the author.

10. A detailed description of the legal, circumstantial and political reasons is beyond the scope of the present chapter which, besides, has a limit of written characters. Nevertheless, by reading the doctoral thesis of the author, one can have an idea of the Brazilian juridical organization history with the references used: Lopes, Simone Cristine Araújo. Jurisdição Popular: Evolução histórica. O caso equatoriano. 2017. 320f. Tese (Doutorado em Direito) – Faculdade de Direito, Universidade de São Paulo, São Paulo, 2017.

11. Brasil. Constituição da República Federativa do Brasil. Diário Oficial da União, Brasília, 5 out. 1988. Available at: http://www.planalto.gov.br/ccivil_03/constituicao/constitui%C3%A7ao.htm. Access: April 13 2020.

12. This matter shall not be argued, but the fact is that most Brazilian Constitutionalists understand that the Supreme Court adopted an activist bias only after the 1988 Constitution, which the author, with due tribute to these brilliant scholars, disagrees with. This is because there were historical moments—albeit occasional—of more active performance by the Supreme Court, especially when Minister Pedro Lessa and his peers were in action. They had, at the beginning of the 20th century, outstanding activity in favor of the construction of the Habeas Corpus doctrine, to remain in just one example.

13. In this regard, see: Novelino, Marcelo. *Direito Constitucional.* 4 ed. São Paulo: Método, 2010. Also: Lenza, Pedro. *Direito constitucional esquematizado.* 14 ed. rev. atual. e ampl. São Paulo: Saraiva, 2010. Other one: Lunardi, Soraya. *Teoria do Processo Constitucional – análise de sua autonomia, natureza e elementos.* São Paulo: Atlas, 2013.

14. All data on the composition of the Supreme Court such as presidencies, mandates and others can be checked out at the website http://www.stf.jus.br/portal/composicaoPlenaria/composicaoPlenariaAnterior.asp. Access: April 13 2020.

15. The President of the Court is elected among the peers of the jurisdictional body and the term of office is limited to two years, in the manner of a turnover between the members and an internal agreement according to which the vice-president assumes the presidency in the immediately following period. As a result of this gentlemen's agreement, the next President of the current composition of the Court should be Minister Luiz Fux, now Vice-President. The term of President Dias Toffoli is due in September 2020.

16. See: Ferreira, Siddharta Legale; Fernandes, Eric Baracho Dore. O STF nas "Cortes" Victor Nunes Leal, Moreira Alves e Gilmar Mendes. *Revista Direito GV,*

v. 9, n. 1, São Paulo, jan./jun. 2013. Available at: http://www.scielo.br/scielo.php?script=sci_arttext&pid=S1808-24322013000100002&lng=pt&tlng=pt. Access: April 15 2020.

17. Brasil. Supremo Tribunal Federal. Recurso Extraordinário n.º 436.996 AgR. Criança de até seis anos de idade … Diário de Justiça, 07 nov. 2005, Brasília, j. 26 out. 2005. Available at: http://redir.stf.jus.br/paginadorpub/paginador.jsp?docTP=AC&docID=343060 Access: April 15 abr. 2020.

18. The Writ of Injunction was proposed on May 10, 2012, by the Brazilian Association of Gays, Lesbians eand Transgenders (Associação Brasileira de Gays, Lésbicas e Transgêneros—ABGLT), in face of the Brazilian National Congress. Differently from its cognate in the English Language, the Brazilian Constitution of 1998, in article 5th LXXI, *ipsis literis,* conceptualizes this type o action as: "a writ of injunction shall be granted whenever the absence of a regulatory provision disables the exercise of Constitutional rights and liberties, as well as the prerogatives inherent to nationality, sovereignty and citizenship." This point was already made in the item 3 of the present work. This sort of constitutional remedy which, before, aimed only to intimidate the Legislative in relation to the delay in the elaboration of a law in order to materialize rights, now, with judicial activism, received the effects of a general concrete proposition by means of which the Judiciary – integrated by the Supreme Court, being its maximum instance – can determine the application of an analogous legal rule while there is no law able to meet the legislator's omission, with an *erga omnes* effect, biding all the powers in Brazil in all its levels. Brasil. Supremo Tribunal Federal. Mandado de Injunção n. 4733. Supremo Tribunal Federal. Disponível em: http://portal.stf.jus.br/processos/detalhe.asp?incidente=4239576. Acesso em: 26 abr. 2020.

19. The Direct Action of UnConstitutionality by Omission was filed in December 19 2013, by the Popular Socialist Party in the face of the President of the Senate ando f the Brazilian National Congress. This action is described in article 103, §2º, aforementioned. Brasil. Supremo Tribunal Federal. Ação Direta de Inconstitucionalidade por Omissão n. 26. Supremo Tribunal Federal. Available at: http://portal.stf.jus.br/processos/detalhe.asp?incidente=4515053. Access in: April 26 2020.

20. One of the peculiarities of the Brazilian Constitutionality control system is a certain ease of access to the Constitutional court, guaranteed by the Constitution in its article 103 which legitimizes various bodies and entities to promote lawsuits, as well as other applicable laws in addition to Constitutional rules such as national laws n. 9868 (November 10, 1999) and n. 12063 (October 27, 2009). Although the LGBTTQIA + individual could not directly plead for the criminalization of homophobia, he or she could, for example, ask associations related to their cause to do so, or even ask the Attorney General of the Republic, any of the State or Federal District governors or any political party with representation in the National Congress (the latter being the case of ADO n. 26, proposed by the Popular Socialist Party—PPS). In a country like Brazil where there are approximately 30 parties with representation in the Chamber of Deputies and 22 parties with representatives in the Federal Senate for the term between 2019 and 2023, it is enough that only one of them embraces a case defended by a group that points to a violation of Constitutional rights to demand

jurisdictional control of Constitutionality before the Supreme Court. See: BRASIL. Departamento Intersindical de Assessoria Parlamentar—DIAP. Novo Congresso Nacional em Números—2019–2023. Brasília, 2019. Available at: https://static.poder360.com.br/2018/10/Novo-Congresso-Nacional-em-Numeros-2019-2023.pdf. Access on 26 abr. 2020.

21. A historical fact at the trial was the oral statement made by the lawyer Maria Eduarda Aguiar, a transsexual with a license issued by the Order of Lawyers of Brazil, section of Rio de Janeiro, with a social name, that is, the name by which the person chooses to be called and not that gave to his or her by the parents. The person has the right to register in his or her identity documents the name of her choice for not identifying with his or her own gender that the birth name designates. The lawyer represented the National Association of Transvestites and Transsexuals.

22. It should be noted that only the records with the extract of the judgment have been published until today, while the judgment with the full judicial decision has not yet been published, which is why the author supports her considerations on the videos made available by the Supreme Court channel on YouTube for the trial sessions, whose links are as follows: Supremo Federal Court. Full trial started on criminalizing homophobia. 2019. (3h06m01s). Available at: https://www.youtube.com/watch?v=EmDZ_-lueJs&t=176s. Accessed on April 27 2020. Supreme Federal Court. Full—Dean declares legislative omission on homophobia (1/2). 2019. (1h34m04s). Available at: https://www.youtube.com/watch?v=H0crBs4Gqc4. Accessed on April 30. 2020. Supreme Federal Court. Full—Dean declares legislative omission on homophobia (2/2). 2019 (1h40m50s). https://www.youtube.com/watch?v=fgqcnP4CCLY. Accessed on May 01 2020. Supreme Federal Court. Full—Suspended Judgment on legislative failure to criminalize homophobia (1/2). 2019. (2h01m29s). Available at: https://www.youtube.com/watch?v=o_0dl0ZxZjE. Accessed on May 01 2020. Supreme Federal Court. Full—Suspended Judgment on legislative omission to criminalize homophobia (2/2). 2019. (1h26m22s). Available at: https://www.youtube.com/watch?v=zZBpYwxcmcE. Accessed on May 01 2020. Supreme Federal Court. Full—criminalization of homophobia. 2019. (47m49s). Available at: https://www.youtube.com/watch?v=UFUa1EJeDMo. Accessed on May 02 2020. Supreme federal court. Full—criminalization of homophobia. 2019. (2h23m00s). Available at: https://www.youtube.com/watch?v=qZUGC_l_0GY&t=367s. Accessed on May 02 2020.

23. This measure is a type of law of initiative of the President of the Republic for urgent and exceptional cases, with a fixed term. To become valid indefinitely, it has to be ratified by the Legislative in up to 60 days, which can be extended for another 60, under penalty of loss of validity and effectiveness of the law beyond that time. Provided in art. 62 of the 1988 Constitution.

24. In this sense, the Gay Group of Bahia presented data from a report based on a research by Prof. Dr. Luiz Roberto de Barros Mott (Federal University of Bahia), who is also founder of the group and a LGBT activist since the 1980s, with decorations by the Brazilian federal government for his decades of work in the academic field, including studies on gender. One of the reports, from 2012, had excerpts presented and read during the oral arguments of the lawyers, in which it is concluded that there is "one murder every 26 hours" in Brazil for reasons of hatred of people of

different sexual orientation. The survey raised data collected from newspaper articles, as high underreporting of crimes motivated by intolerance to LGBTTQIA + groups was identified in police investigations that might even mention the crime, but never the detail of prejudice resulting from acts or speeches of hate or intolerance, which is why the research includes cases of deception by the offender as was the fact that two heterosexual brothers were attacked for being hugged on the streets, mistaken for a gay couple. For this reason, the groups that defend the theses against the criminalization of homophobia, linked to religious movements, in particular, refuted the research data because they did not stick to the group and did not consider the official statistics, obtained through police records, which nevertheless, it is precisely the point of criticism of the research for placing the vulnerable minority in a situation of social invisibility over the violence suffered. For details: Gay da Bahia Group. Report 2012—Murder of homosexuals (LGBT) in Brazil. Available at: https://grupogaydabahia.files.wordpress.com/2013/06/relatorio-20126.pdf. Accessed on May 03 2020.

25. Minister Luiz Fux showed similar examples in his vote, which followed the vote of the rapporteur, Minister Celso de Mello.

26. It refers to Habeas Corpus n. 82424, filed by Siegfried Ellwander, who alleged a lack of legal classification and the consequent absence of crime in view of the fact that he edited and published books in which he denied the Jewish holocaust. The competent Prosecution Ministry, on the other hand, for envisioning, in the works, an anti-Semitic nature, filed a criminal action with a condemnatory request for the crime of racism, which is incurred in Law No. 7716/89. The key point of this trial by the Supreme Court referred to the fact that the law which defines the crime of racism was designed and based on racism for reasons of color, and not for reasons of people or ethnic groups. Minister Moreira Alves, who was the rapporteur, and Minister Marco Aurélio granted security in favor of the defendant for recognizing that the criminal practice was of discrimination, and not racism, being only the latter only an imprescriptible crime. As the statute of limitations for the crime of discrimination had passed, they recognized this fact in favor of Siegfried Ellwander, while Minister Ayres Brito acquitted him due to the fact that his conduct did not fit any configuration of a crime. However, most of the ministers who participated in the trial diverged to recognize that the crime of racism, as it appears in the 1988 Constitution, was not limited to issues of color, let alone race, since there is only one race: the human race, as already pointed out by genetic studies to demonstrate that, practically, we all carry genes of various ethnicities, places and variables of the human race, to a greater or lesser degree, to demonstrate the practical irrationality of prejudices of this nature. Racism, therefore, for the Supreme Court, since that judgment, is related to attitudes towards segregation and the reduction of human groups at lower levels or the denial of rights for unethical reasons, not accepted in contemporary society. And that, finally, freedom of expression is not an absolute right to the point of authorizing the violation of the principle of human dignity.

27. Expression coined by Luigi Ferrajoli, author of Diritto e Raggione (Law and Reason). He constructed the thesis of *garantismo penale, garantismo* being a term that does not translate to English smoothly. It's about the defense and promotion of fundamental rights, entailing the rights of the vulnerable against the rights of the

powerful. For more information, see: Ruggiero, V. (1994). Book Reviews: Luigi Ferrajoli, *Diritto e ragione: Teona del garantismo penale*. Bari-Roma: Laterza, 1990, 1034p. *Social & Legal Studies*, 3(1), 185–187. https://doi.org/10.1177/09646639940 0300110

28. Band Jornalismo. Bolsonaro critica decisão do STF sobre homofobia. 2019. (00m36s). Available at: https://www.youtube.com/watch?v=pqDEcSng0aQ. Accessed on May 11, 2020.

29. Jefthe Collins. Ellen Page confronta Jair Bolsonaro sobre homofobia no Rio de Janeiro. 2016. (03m31s). Available at: https://www.youtube.com/watch?v=wbm Bp8WLhjI. Accessed on May 11, 2020.

30. Pedro Surreaux. Stephen Fry entrevista Jair Bolsonaro – Out There. 2014 (04m59s). Dis Available at: https://www.youtube.com/watch?v=o3ZBeX9uC8s. Accessed on May 11, 2020.

31. It is suffice to mention the setback of the public policy implemented by the Ministry of Education and Culture under the Presidency of Dilma Roussef, who, because of the strong manifesto and opposition of parliamentarians linked to conservative and religious groups, stopped distributing educational material for the promotion of gender tolerance, the so-called anti-homophobia kit, which, on the contrary, was called by evangelical parliamentary fronts "gay kit" as if it were a way of "stimulating homosexuality" of school-age children and youth. These facts occurred in May 2011. In this sense, see: https://veja.abril.com.br/blog/reinaldo/dilma-suspende-8220-kit-gay-8221-apos-protesto-da-bancada -evangelica. Accessed on 12 May. 2020.

32. In this sense, a recently book published in Brazil on the profile of the Supreme Court ministers and the role of the Brazilian Supreme Court from 2005 to early 2019 drew attention from the public. The book demonstrates several moments of friction between members of the Legislative and Executive when facing the highest body of the Judiciary in Brazil. There were manifestos of some officers of the Armed Forces, and a Colonel even used strong and very offensive words to Minister Rosa Weber, due to disagreement with judicial decisions, demanding more severe legal measures from the competent bodies. All of this because, inevitably, some decisions of the Supreme Court dissatisfies sometimes Greeks, sometimes Trojans, being rare any judicial decision taken by any judge on the planet that is unanimous before the nationals of his country. And the Supreme Court was urged, in recent years, to decide on very sensitive points, which divided national public opinion, such as procedural acts of the so-called Lava Jato Operation, the validity and legitimacy of acts of the impeachment process of the former President Dilma Roussef, the possibility of a second instance arrest and not just in the unappealable sentence of a condemnatory criminal sentence, which resulted in the imprisonment, for 580 days, of former President Lula and which prevented him from running for the 2018 elections, etc. See: "The Supreme did indeed seem ready to do battle. On another front, it took a stand on the manifestations of members of the government and its parliamentary support base that indicated setbacks in the protection of minority rights. Celso de Mello was rapporteur of one of the lawsuits that questioned the delay of the Congress in passing a law criminalizing homophobia. And he insisted with Toffoli that the topic be put on the agenda. In the trial started on February 20, 2019, Mello led the Supreme Court and

guaranteed support for the criminalization, through judicial means, of homophobia. The process was interrupted by decision of the president of the court, with no date for resumption, but another schism was created. Congress was determined to confront the Supreme Court—some deputies, especially novices, called for the impeachment of the four ministers who had already voted in favor" (Recondo, Felipe; Weber, Luiz. Os Onze—o STF, seus bastidores e suas crises. São Paulo: Companhia das Letras, 2019, p. 16–17).

33. In short, this is a trend of Criminology that defends a minimum list of crimes punishable by incarceration because it considers innocuous the punishment by incarceration, being it not an effective means of preventing and reducing the practice of crimes. It relates to the principle of minimum criminal intervention. Some important names of this approach are the Italians Alessandro Baratta and Luigi Ferrajoli and the Argentine Raul Zaffaroni.

34. Both draft bill no. 860, 2019, attached to drafted bill no. 4240, 2019 are underway in legislative houses.

35. Brasil. Supremo Tribunal Federal. Ação Direta de Inconstitucionalidade por Omissão n. 26. Ata de julgamento n. 22 publicada ... Diário de Justiça Eletrônica, 28 jun. 2019, Brasília, j. 13 jun. 2019.

REFERENCES

Afonso da Silva, José. *Aplicabilidade das Normas Constitucionais*. 3 ed. São Paulo: Malheiros, 1998.

Brasil. Constituição da República Federativa do Brasil. Diário Oficial da União, Brasília, 5 out. 1988. Available at: http://www.planalto.gov.br/ccivil_03/constituicao/constitui%C3%A7ao.htm

Brasil. Departamento Intersindical de Assessoria Parlamentar—DIAP. Novo Congresso Nacional em Números—2019-2023. Brasília, 2019. Available at: https://static.poder360.com.br/2018/10/Novo-Congresso-Nacional-em-Numeros-2019-2023.pdf Access in: 26 abr. 2020.

Brasil. Decreto n.º 848, de 11 de outubro de 1890. Organiza a Justiça Federal. Coleção das Leis do Brasil, Rio de Janeiro, 1890. Available at: https://www.planalto.gov.br/ccivil_03/decreto/1851-1899/d848.htm. Access: April 13 2020.

Brasil. Lei nº 7716, de 05 de janeiro de 1989. Define os crimes resultantes de preconceito de raça ou de cor. Diário Oficial da União, Brasília, 09 jan. 1989. Available at: https://www.planalto.gov.br/ccivil_03/leis/l7716.htm. Access: April 13 2020.

Brasil. Lei nº 1390, de 03 de julho de 1951. Inclui entre as contravenções penais a prática de atos resultantes de preconceitos de raça ou de côr. Diário Oficial da União, Rio de Janeiro, 10 jul. 1951. Available at: http://www.planalto.gov.br/ccivil_03/LEIS/L1390.htm#art9 Access: April 13 2020.

Brasil. Supremo Tribunal Federal. Recurso Extraordinário n.º 436.996 AgR. Criança de até seis anos de idade ... Diário de Justiça, 07 nov. 2005, Brasília, j. 26 out. 2005. Available at: http://redir.stf.jus.br/paginadorpub/paginador.jsp?docTP=AC&docID=343060. Access: April 15 abr. 2020.

Brasil. Supremo Tribunal Federal. Mandado de Injunção n. 4733. Supremo Tribunal Federal. Disponível em: http://portal.stf.jus.br/processos/detalhe.asp?incidente=4239576. Acesso em: 26 abr. 2020.

Brasil. Supremo Tribunal Federal. Ação Direta de Inconstitucionalidade por Omissão n. 26. Supremo Tribunal Federal. Available at: http://portal.stf.jus.br/processos/detalhe.asp?incidente=4515053. Access in: April 26 2020.

Brasil. Supremo Tribunal Federal. Ação Direta de Inconstitucionalidade por Omissão n. 26. Ata de julgamento n. 22 publicada … Diário de Justiça Eletrônica, 28 jun. 2019, Brasília, j. 13 jun. 2019.

Beccaria, Cesare. Dos Delitos e das Penas. Ed. eletrônica ridendo castigant mores. p. 10–11. Available at: http://www.dominiopublico.gov.br/download/texto/eb000015.pdf. Access in April 13 2020. English version available at: http://files.libertyfund.org/files/2193/Beccaria_1476_EBk_v6.0.pdf. Access: May 14 2020.

Ferreira, Siddharta Legale; Fernandes, Eric Baracho Dore. O STF nas "Cortes" Victor Nunes Leal, Moreira Alves e Gilmar Mendes. *Revista Direito GV*, v. 9, n. 1, São Paulo, jan./jun. 2013.

Gay da Bahia Group. Report 2012—Murder of homosexuals (LGBT) in Brazil. Available at: https://grupogaydabahia.files.wordpress.com/2013/06/relatorio-20126.pdf. Access: May 03 2020.

Lenza, Pedro. Direito constitucional esquematizado. 14. ed. rev. atual. e ampl. São Paulo: Saraiva, 2010.

Lima, Eneida. Carlos Alberto Cao Oliveira dos Santos. *In*: FGV-CPDOC. Rio de Janeiro. Available at: http://www.fgv.br/cpdoc/acervo/dicionarios/verbete-biografico/carlos-alberto-cao-oliveira-dos-santos. Access: April 13 2020.

Lopes, Simone Cristine Araújo. Jurisdição Popular: Evolução histórica. O caso equatoriano. 2017. 320f. Tese (Doutorado em Direito)—Faculdade de Direito, Universidade de São Paulo, São Paulo, 2017.

Lunardi, Soraya. *Teoria do Processo Constitucional—análise de sua autonomia, natureza e elementos*. São Paulo: Atlas, 2013.

Novelino, Marcelo. *Direito Constitucional*. 4 ed. São Paulo: Método, 2010.

Recondo, Felipe; Weber, Luiz. *Os Onze—o STF, seus bastidores e suas crises*. São Paulo: Companhia das Letras, 2019.

Ruggiero, Vincenzo. Book review: Luigi Ferrajoli, Diritto e ragione: Teoria del garantismo penale. Bari-Roma: Laterza, 1990, 1034p. *Social & Legal Studies*, 3(1), 185–187.

Chapter 9

Political Citizenship

Constitutional Commitments and Limits in the Exercise of Brazilian Party Democracy

Orides Mezzaroba

INTRODUCTION

The 1988 Constitution of the Federative Republic of Brazil establishes the institute of political representation as a resource in the process of forming the political will of the people. From this point of view, at least two of the requirements necessary for the foundation of the Democratic State of Brazilian Law are directly related to the constitutional political-representative notion: sovereignty and political pluralism. The idea of a Democratic State of Law based on sovereignty refers directly to the concept of national sovereignty, a fundamental constitutional principle of contemporary democratic experience. In addition, it comprises two dimensions: one internal to the State, in relation to the very foundation of the exercise of sovereign power, and an external one, relevant to the independence of the State before the other States of the international community. Thus, while political representation is a way of exercising sovereignty, it also has a fundamental commitment to respect and defense. The idea of political pluralism has a clear internal dimension, related to the democratic form of political self-organization adopted by the State. In its article 1, the Federal Constitution ensures for Brazil a rule of law of a markedly democratic character, constituting itself in a representative state of a pluralist character. The democratic principle underlying the political requirement of pluralism makes it possible to state that, from the 1988 Constitution, a representative party democracy was formally established in the country.

With the adoption of the proportional system (article 45 of the Federal Constitution), the fidelity of representation to that plurality of ideas within Brazilian society is constitutionally guaranteed, especially in the Legislative. In addition, voters' votes are numerically equated with parliamentary representation, since one of the characteristics of the proportional system is to ensure the highest possible degree of correspondence between the votes received by a party and the number of seats it will occupy in a legislature. In the same direction, the caput of article 14 determines the exercise of popular sovereignty by universal suffrage, with a direct and secret vote of equal value for all citizens. Therefore, by an equal vote, citizens will be represented before the Legislative and Executive branches. The Brazilian Constitution of 1988 establishes that party affiliation is mandatory for candidacy to electoral elections (article 14, § 3, V). Based on this requirement, political parties had a prominent role in political engineering in Brazil.

After the promulgation of the Constitution of the Federative Republic of Brazil, on October 5, 1988, the chapter that started to deal with political parties was subsumed in only one article, although comprehensive. It provides for the creation of parties, at the same time that it imposes on it the observance of certain constitutional principles and some mandatory procedures, in addition to two express prohibitions. The caput of article 17 of the 1988 Constitution guarantees the right to free creation, merger, incorporation, and extinction of political parties. The party's freedom of creation and self-determination with regard to possible mergers, incorporations, and its own extinction—added to the constitutional guarantees of party organization and functioning (article 17, § 1) enshrined one of the most liberalizing texts in all history of Brazilian party politics. The freedom to create parties, however, is not absolute; it was limited to the protection of four constitutional principles: a) national sovereignty, b) democratic regime, c) multiparty system, and d) Fundamental Rights of the Human Person (caput of article 17).

In addition to these limitations, political parties, due to constitutional requirements, must also observe the national character (article 17, I); render accounts to the Electoral Justice (article 17, III); and to have the parliamentary functioning adequate to the pertinent, infraconstitutional legislation (article 17, IV). The Constitution also imposes two prohibitions: it prohibits the use of paramilitary organizations (article 17, § 4) and to receive resources and subordination to foreign organizations (article 17, II). On the other hand, the parties now enjoy the following constitutional guarantees: a) autonomy to define their internal structure, organization, and functioning, and their statutes must establish rules of fidelity and party discipline (article 17, § 1); b) legal personality according to the civil law (article 17, § 2); and c) the right to receive resources from the party fund and free access to radio and television, in accordance to the law (article 17, § 3).

This article aims to analyze the constitutional context and limits of the performance of Brazilian political parties enshrined in the 1988 constitutional text. Fundamentally analyzing what is the role reserved for political parties in articulating and implementing the principles of political pluralism, exercising citizenship, democratic rule of law, and the defense of human rights?

CONSTITUTIONALIZATION OF BRAZILIAN POLITICAL PARTIES

Article 17 was approved in its entirety with the promulgation of the Federal Constitution on October 5, 1988. Paragraph 1 of article 17 were voted by 417 (four hundred and seventeen) constituents, 134 (one hundred and thirty-four) voted *yes*, 272 (two hundred and seven and two) voted *no* and 11 (eleven) abstained from voting. In the vote, the amendment that included in the original text of the first paragraph the party's previous draft for the selection of candidates was rejected.

Constitutional Amendment no. 52/2006 included in the first paragraph of article 17 the following wording: *[. . .functioning] and to adopt the selection criteria and the regime of its electoral coalitions, without obligatory binding between candidacies at national, state, district or municipal level [should . . .].*

The caput of article 17, items I, II, III, IV, and §§ 2, 3, and 4 were approved by 360 (three hundred and sixty) favorable votes, 59 (fifty-nine) votes against and 4 (four) abstentions. Constitutional Amendment No. 91, of February 18, 2016, established in its article 1 that:

> *The holder of an elective mandate is allowed to withdraw from the party for which he was elected within thirty days after the promulgation of this Constitutional Amendment, without prejudice to the mandate, and this disillusionment is not considered for the purpose of distributing the resources of the Party Fund and free access to the radio and television time.*

The approval of Constitutional Amendment No. 91 received 61(sixty-one) favorable votes among the 81 (eighty-one) Senators.

With Constitutional Amendment No. 97, of October 4, 2017, the following wording was included in § 1 of article 17 the following wording:

> *and establish rules on the choice, formation and duration of its permanent and provisional bodies and on its majority [... electoral organization], its celebration in proportional elections being prohibited.*

In paragraph 3 of article 17 it was included as follows:

> Only political parties that alternatively:
>
> *I—obtain, in the elections for the Chamber of Deputies, at least 3% (three percent) of the valid votes, distributed in at least one third of the Federation units, with a minimum of 2% (two percent) of the valid votes in each of them; or*
>
> *II—have elected at least fifteen Federal Deputies distributed in at least one third of the Federation units.*

Still in §3 of article 17 the 5th was fully included with the following wording:

> *The elected by party that does not fulfill the requirements foreseen in §3 of this article is guaranteed the mandate and allowed the affiliation, without losing the mandate, to another party that reached them, this affiliation not being considered for the purpose of distributing the party fund's resources and free access to radio and television time.*

Article 2 of Constitutional Amendment nº97, of October 4, 2017, determined that: *The prohibition on the establishment of coalitions in proportional elections, provided for in §1 of art. 17 of the Federal Constitution will apply from the 2020 elections.*

In turn, the article 3 of Constitutional Amendment 97, of October 4, 2017, established the following rules for future elections:

> *The provisions of § 3 of art. 17 of the Federal Constitution regarding the access of political parties to the resources of the party fund and free advertising on radio and television will apply from the 2030 elections onwards.*
>
> *Single paragraph.*
>
> *Political parties will have access to the resources of the party fund and to free advertising on radio and television that:*
>
> *I—in the legislature following the 2018 elections:*
>
> *a) obtain, in the elections for the Chamber of Deputies, at least 1.5% of the valid votes, distributed in at least one third of the units of the Federation, with a minimum of 1% of the valid votes in each of them; or*
>
> *b) have elected at least nine Federal Deputies distributed in at least one third of the Federation units;*
>
> *II—in the legislature following the 2022 elections:*
>
> *a) obtain, in the elections for the Chamber of Deputies, at least 2% of the valid votes, distributed in at least one third of the units of the Federation, with a minimum of 1% of the valid votes in each of them; or*
>
> *b) have elected at least eleven Federal Deputies distributed in at least one third of the Federation units;*

III—in the legislature following the 2026 elections:

a) obtain, in the elections for the Chamber of Deputies, at least 2.5% of the valid votes, distributed in at least one third of the Federation units, with a minimum of 1.5% of the valid votes in each of them; or

b) have elected at least thirteen Federal Deputies distributed in at least one third of the Federation units.

Constitutional Amendment No. 97/2017 was unanimously approved by the Federal Senate.

GUIDING CONSTITUTIONAL PRINCIPLES FOR THE CREATION OF POLITICAL PARTIES IN BRAZIL

In the first part of the caput of article 17, the Constitution establishes party freedoms such as freedom of creation, merger, incorporation, and extinction of political parties. Thus, the life of the party may not suffer any external interference from the State aimed at its control or, even, its extinction. In order to preserve the democratic regime, the Constitution imposes, however, on the parties the following ideological limitations:

a) National sovereignty: this precept appears in the 1988 Constitution as one of the fundamental principles of the Federative Republic of Brazil and the Democratic State of Law (article 1, I). In the caput of article 17, however, respect for national sovereignty takes on the proportions of a guiding principle in the process of creating party organizations. It is understood, therefore, that, in their programs, political parties cannot defend ideas that endanger the fullness of national sovereignty. Party statutes are prevented from adopting programmatic principles that propose the submission of the Brazilian State to any other State or international body. Brazilian political parties must safeguard, in their constitutive acts, as well as in the execution of their political and parliamentary activities, the commitment to the defense of national sovereignty as one of the fundamental principles of the Federative Republic of Brazil;

b) democratic regime: according to the caput of article 1 of the Federal Constitution, the Brazilian political regime is based on the democratic principle, which constitutes it in a Democratic State of Law. This is equivalent to affirming that the State and the Brazilian parties must respect the dignity of the human person (article 1, III), guarantee the inviolability of citizenship (article 1, II), life, freedom, equality, and security citizens (caput of article 5) and, fundamentally, to strive for the construction of a free, just, solidary society and without any prejudice (article 3, II and IV). In addition to their commitment to the preservation of democracy in the Brazilian political system, political parties are responsible for ensuring that democratic principles are properly respected in their structure and functioning. The commitment that is imposed on the constituted Brazilian political parties is respect for the democratic regime in all its dimensions, both in its internal and external actions. Finally, by adopting the regime of democratic government (article 1), based on the principle of popular sovereignty (article 14), the Democratic State under Brazilian Law is now conceived as that regime in which all power emanates from the people, and this exercise it directly, through plebiscites, referenda or popular initiatives (article 14, I, II, and III), or indirectly, through representatives elected by the intermediation of political parties (article 14, § 3, V);

c) pluripartisanship: provided for in the caput of article 17, this principle is directly related to another principiological device, constitutionally enshrined, namely political pluralism (article 1, V), which imposes itself as one of the foundations of the Federative Republic of Brazil. The principle of political pluralism is characterized by the opposition to any monopoly artifact, be it social, political, cultural, educational, economic, or communication. The principle of pluripartisanship, in turn, is based on the commitment of the Brazilian State to institutionalize a political system that is based on the existence of several socially representative parties, and all with a certain equality to reach power through the free and democratic electoral process. When establishing the principle of pluripartisanship, the will of the State, therefore, ceases to coincide with the will of a single group, and starts to guarantee that the different political groups can express themselves and compete with each other, without any kind of political limitation. Thus, from the moment that the Constitution recognizes the principle of party pluralism, it must recognize it without any reducing device, without imposing, for example, the clauses of barrier or exclusion. Such requirements, without any doubt, allow a reasonable limitation to the right of representation of minorities in the Legislative, consequently violating the constitutional pluripartisan principle and, consequently, the political pluralism itself;

d) fundamental human rights: this principle is directly related to the commitments that political parties must assume in defense and preservation of the dignity, equality, and freedom of the human person (article 1, III and caput of article 5). Following the process of historical consolidation of the fundamental rights of the human person, political parties are also committed to safeguarding and respecting the principles established in a) individual rights and guarantees (article 5), b) social rights (arts. 6 and 193 et seq.), c) rights to nationality (article 12), and d) political rights (articles 14 and 17). In addition to others that the constituent power may establish; the protection of the fundamental rights of the human person, provided for in the caput of article 17 of the Constitution, obliges political parties to adopt two complementary positions: first, to exclude from their programmatic principles guidelines that do not accept them, which would characterize an affront to the principle of the Democratic Rule of Law. On the other hand, due to the improvement of the democratic regime, it is permissible for parties to have different interpretations of certain fundamental rights and to have the freedom to defend broader and more democratic interpretations of such principles. And second, the political parties are committed to upholding the principles of fundamental rights, which obliges them to link them and make them effective in their own structures.

CONSTITUTIONAL REQUIREMENTS FOR THE CREATION OF POLITICAL PARTIES IN BRAZIL

In addition to making a commitment to uphold the principles set out in the item above, political parties must respect the following precepts: a) national character (article 17, I), b) rendering of accounts to the Electoral Justice (article 17, III), and c) parliamentary functioning according to the law (article 17, IV).

a) national character: the constituent legislator did not refer to the regulation of this provision to ordinary legislation, so it is not clear how this precept would be applied in practice. In fact, with the imposition of the principle of national character, it was sought, fundamentally, to prevent the formation of parties with regional or local programs, as were, for example, the political organizations of the First Brazilian Republic (1889-1930). Indeed, those regional republican parties identified themselves much more with factions than with the contemporary spirit of political parties. The meaning of including the expression "national character" in the constitutional text is to guarantee the federative principle of national unity. To guarantee that the parties, in their programs, establish proposals of national scope and not only focused on regional specificities. The important fact in this precept is in the definition of the term "character," which should not be confused with the expression scope. While the term "character" has the meaning of particular traits, specificities, and ideological qualities, the term "scope" means the zone of activities, the field of action. The sense of the national character of the party is linked to the demand for a political party program that contains proposals aimed more at the whole of Brazilian territory than at the obligation to build a party structure that contains organizational ramifications in some units of the Federation. The spirit of the national character requires that the parties have commitments aimed, above all, at the construction of political projects that involve the whole country, and not the interests of small groups or local factions. However, as much as the 1988 Constitution failed to establish the parameters that would characterize the meaning of the national expression character of the parties, the fact is that ordinary legislation cannot restrict constitutional principles.

However, this was not the understanding of the ordinary legislator when Law No. 9,096, of September 19, 1995, (Law on Political Parties) and, later, modified by Law No. 92,259, of January 9, 1996, Law No. 9,504, of September 30, 1997, Law No. 9,693, of July 27, 1998, Law No. 12,034, of September 29, 2009, Law No. 12,875, of October 30, 2013, Law No. 12,891, of December 11, 2013, Law No. 13,107, of March 24, 2015, Law No. 13,165, of September 29, 2015, Law No. 13,487, of October 6, 2017, and Law No. 13,488, of October 6, 2017. By article 17, I, of the 1988 Constitution, it was established that, when a party is created, its national character must be taken into account. However, as previously seen, the Constitution is silent on the meaning or scope of such an expression. In view of this incompleteness, the ordinary legislator ended up claiming for himself and, of course, for his own political conveniences, the right to establish his understanding of the party's sense of national character. Thus, replacing the meaning of the term character for the term scope, the configuration of the national character was strictly defined by proving the "support" of a certain number of voters, distributed by a certain number of States, when creating political parties.

As established in article 7 of Law No. 9,096/1995, modified by Law No. 13,165/2015, after acquiring legal personality under civil law, the political party must register its status in the Superior Electoral Court. However, according to § 1 of the same article, the registration of the statute in the Superior Electoral Court will only be admitted to that "political party that has a national character (sic), considering as such the one that proves, in the period of two years, the support of voters not affiliated to a political party, corresponding to at least five-tenths of the votes in the last general election for the Chamber of Deputies, white and null votes not counted, distributed by one third, or more, of the States, with a minimum of one-tenth percent of the electorate that has voted for each one of them ." That is, in practice, if a given social movement intends to become a party, in order to act in the sphere of political representation of the State, it must first demonstrate its "national character" (sic), when it should be "national scope," for only after acquiring the privilege of political action. Naturally, in this specific case, the ordinary legislator ended up imposing a restrictive mechanism for the creation of parties, in this case, when registering the party statute.

However, the biggest doubt that remains is whether or not the Superior Electoral Court has the power to deny the registration of party status that does not quantitatively comply with that number of supporters, since § 2 of article 17 of the 1988 Constitution is incisive in stating: "after political parties acquire legal personality, in the form of civil law, they will register their statutes in the Superior Electoral Court." As seen in the Constitution, it does not establish at any time that the registration of the party's statute must comply with any type of procedure or requirement, referring to the usual jargon: according to the law. Thus, the jurisdiction of the Superior Electoral Court would be restricted to statutory registration, and it would not have any control over the number of people who subscribe to the founding of parties, much less their ideological or organizational control.

Thus, if the misinterpretation of the term "national character" by the ordinary legislator were not enough, in fact, a principle that, as seen, did not need any kind of regulation, as it is a programmatic commitment by the parties, the conclusion reached is that the wording of § 1 of article 7 of Law No. 9.096/1995 deeply violates the constitutional principle provided for in the caput of article 17 of the 1988 Constitution, which guarantees full freedom of party creation;

b) accountability to the Electoral Justice: this precept seeks, above all, to establish mechanisms that can prevent the abuse of economic power in electoral processes. Due to this constitutional requirement, political parties are obliged to account for financial donations received and for all expenses incurred in electoral processes. In practice, however, this requirement ends up being impaired as a result of two basic problems: a) the lack of logistical structure of the Electoral Justice, which despite all efforts made, does not yet have adequate mechanisms to inspect the accounting tangled presented by the political parties and b) the diversity of contributions, many of which do not even end up appearing in the accounts presented by the parties.

In any electoral process, the legislation must give priority to the right of equal competition between political parties. So, when the party receives direct or indirect contributions from individuals or legal entities, according to the law, even if this procedure is lawful, is it not a privilege, considering that the other parties did not have the same opportunity? And under what parameters will the Electoral Justice be able to assess whether or not there has been an abuse of economic power? Did the donations fulfill all legal formalities? However, in practice, what is verified is that the control over the abuse of economic power in electoral processes ends up being carried out by the opposing parties and that only after very well-founded and documented complaints does the Electoral Justice come into action.

In addition to the fact that the Electoral Justice is not adequately equipped to supervise all the complexity and intricate accountability, as a way of guaranteeing equality of dispute between the political parties, it also ended up definitively losing its function of protecting and controlling the political parties internally and externally. With the new Constitutional Charter of 1988, the powers of the Electoral Justice, as an organ of the judiciary, are restricted to the control of electoral processes (articles 118 to 121). Finally, the Electoral Justice has a long way to go until it definitively detaches itself from the interventionist legacy of the laws of past times;

c) parliamentary functioning: according to the provisions of article 17, IV, of the 1988 Constitution, political parties must have parliamentary functioning in accordance with the law. However, here again the constitutional definition is not clear about the scope of that expression. The current understanding is that, in order to function, the parties must have representation in the Legislative, in order to enjoy the right to the leadership structure and participate in the proportional division of the composition of the tables and commissions in accordance with the Internal Regulations of each Legislative House. Through parliamentary action or functioning, political parties are present in the legislature, constituting benches and leaders through their elected representatives (article 12 of Law No. 9,096/1995). Participating with representations in Commissions, analyzing and discussing matters of social relevance, presenting and voting on draft laws, the legislator will be developing the party's parliamentary action (article 25 of Law No. 9,096/1995).

By article 12 of Law No. 9,096/1995, it is defined that "the political party functions, in the Legislative Houses, through a bench, which must constitute its leaders in accordance with the party's statute, with the regulations of the respective Houses" and in accordance with the determinations contained in the Party Law itself. However, then, in the same law, article 13 points out that only "is entitled to parliamentary functioning, in all Legislative Houses for which representatives have been elected, the party that, in each election to the Chamber of Deputies, obtains the support of at least five percent of the votes cast, null and blank ones are not accounted for, distributed in at least one third of the States, with a minimum of 2% of the total of each of them."

Regarding the regulation of the constitutional provision that deals with the precept of parliamentary functioning of political parties, the following question remains: the ordinary legislator could or could not establish limitations for the parliamentary functioning of political parties through barrier clauses without violating the principle contained in the caput of article 17 of the Constitution, which ensures that the creation of political parties in Brazil is "free"? Wouldn't the requirement to comply with the barriers clause by itself already represent a violation of this constitutional precept? For, as it has been seen, when talking about parliamentary functioning, it is understood that the political party must, in addition to having life and social representativeness, be present and act through its representatives within the Legislative Branch.

Article 45 of the 1988 Constitution establishes that the Chamber of Deputies is composed of representatives of the people, proportionally elected in the States, Territories, and the Federal District. The Constitution itself thus established the proportional election for the choice of representatives in the different units of the Federation, taking into account the number of votes obtained (nominal or captions) by the political parties (article 45,

§§ 1 and 2). The regulation by the ordinary legislator could not, therefore, establish a new formula, unequaling the mandates won by party legends. Under the proportional system, the criterion that guarantees the effective representation of each party would be the proportionality of votes obtained by the parties, converted into mandates (legislative seats). Therefore, the constitutional limitation imposed by the ordinary legislator should be restricted to the establishment of this proportionality criterion, and not around clauses of barriers quantified by the number of votes to be obtained in proportional elections. To the extent that political representation is restricted, the democratic space of the decision is automatically reduced and violating the fundamental principle of the Republic, set forth in article 1º, V (political pluralism), as well as the principle contained in the caput of article 17 (multi-party system). Finally, it should be noted that the only democratic mechanism that can determine the existence or not of political parties is the vote, and only it is that which can express the most sacred spirit of representative democracy and its absolute holder, which is the people, no one else. This, however, was not the case in article 13 of Law No. 9,096/1995, which, using a daring mechanism in the democratic game, such as the barrier clause, ended up linking the parliamentary functioning of political parties to the achievement of minimum support for votes to be obtained in elections to the Chamber of Deputies.

In this same direction, the Brazilian STF's decision followed when, unanimously, through ADIn n. 1,351 and 1,354/2007, declared the full text of article 13 of Law No. 9.096/1995, as he understood that this violated, among others, the constitutional principles of political pluralism (article 1) and the wide freedom of creation of political parties (caput of article 17). In the same resolution, the STF declared those provisions of Law No. 9.096/1995 that were directly related to the provisions of the text of article 13; they are: a) the expression "obeying the following criteria" in the caput of article 41, as well as the full texts of items I and II, which were part of his article; b) the full text of article 48; c) of the caput of article 49 the part "that meets the provisions of article 13"; d) the temporal limitations contained in the caput of article 56 and in the caput of article 57 and the expression "in article 13"of item II of this last article.

CONSTITUTIONAL PROHIBITIONS APPLIED TO BRAZILIAN POLITICAL PARTIES

Item II and § 4 of article 17 of the 1988 Constitution establish two express prohibitions for political parties: a) prohibition on receiving financial resources from or subordination to foreign entities or government b) prohibiting the use of paramilitary organizations:

a) prohibition on receiving financial resources and subordination to foreign bodies: the caput of article 17 establishes that, in the statutes and procedures for the creation of political parties, the principle of national sovereignty must be duly respected. Thus, the prohibition on receiving funds from foreign entities, in order to avoid any kind of subordination to them, would be a natural consequence. It should be noted, however, that approximations by ideological affinities of national parties with foreign institutions or parties do not necessarily characterize any type of subordination, but rather the internationalization of certain political principles, which, due to their scope or greatness, often end up surpassing geographical or cultural boundaries. Therefore, the possibility for Brazilian political parties to establish contacts or partnerships with foreign institutions is fully legal and legitimate. This is what article 5, XVII when it guarantees that the "freedom of association is full, provided that for lawful purposes, only the paramilitary character is prohibited." Such understanding is reinforced by article 5, VI, of the same constitutional text, when it ensures full "freedom of conscience." Finally, it is concluded that the Brazilian political parties enjoy full freedom to join international ideological currents that correspond with their programmatic principles and lines of thought, as long as the precepts established by the Constitution itself are respected;

b) prohibition on the use of paramilitary organizations: as from the imposition of this precept, political parties are prohibited from constituting any form of uniformed or armed corporation in their structure and political activities. This prohibition, due to the associative nature of political parties, only reinforces the prohibition contained in the provision of article 5, XVII, of the 1988 Constitution, which provides for "full freedom of association for lawful purposes, with paramilitary character prohibited." Based on a more rigorous interpretation of this provision, it can be concluded that party organizations under no circumstances can be characterized as organs of a military character. Thus, at the internal level, the parties must ensure that they do not establish any rigid hierarchical structure that sets up a relationship of command and obedience, within the perspective of the "iron law," designed by Robert Michels. On the other hand, externally, political parties are prohibited from using uniforms or nomenclatures that characterize any type of patent or command insignia. Considering, however, that it is up to the parties to safeguard the principles of national sovereignty, the democratic regime, pluripartisanship, and the Fundamental Rights of the Human Person (caput of article 17), both internally and externally, concluded. It is understood that the inclusion of this precept in the Constitutional text represents only a rhetorical figure, without any meaning at the point where it is inserted if the democratic spirit of the 1988 Constitution is taken into account. Unless it is there, perhaps, only to reinforce such a ban.

LEGAL NATURE OF BRAZILIAN POLITICAL PARTIES

The innovation introduced by the 1988 Constitution is in the device that establishes the *legal nature of the parties*. According to § 2 of article 17, the party only acquires legal personality after registration in the form of civil law. That is, from the 1988 Charter, parties started to be considered legal persons under private law. Thus, they must first be registered in the Registry of Titles and Documents and only after that the registration of the statute will occur in the Superior Electoral Court. This procedure significantly changed what was established in the previous legislation. Under the revoked legislation, party institutions were treated as legal entities under domestic public law. According to article 4 of Law No. 5,682/1971 (Organic Law of Political Parties), in force at the time, only the registration of the political party with the Superior Electoral Court occurred, with no need for prior registration in the form of civil law. Thus, in establishing that political parties acquire legal personality in the form of civil law, the 1988 Constitution incorporated the principle that they are legal entities under private law. As a result, Brazil began to treat political parties no longer as organs of the State, but as private associations with constitutional functions. Associations that began to assume the commitment to express the political will of their militants, supporters, and voters. Following the principle established by the 1988 Constitution, Law No. 9.096/1995 reaffirms, right in its article 1, that the political party is a legal entity under private law, which is intended "to ensure, in the interests of the democratic regime, the authenticity of the representative system and to defend the fundamental rights defined in the Federal Constitution." In turn, the sole paragraph of Law No. 13.488/2017, determined that "The political party does not match parastatal entities."

With the new legal provision, after acquiring legal personality under civil law, the political party is in a position to submit or register its statute with the TSE (Superior Electoral Court). Before, however, according to article 8 of Law No. 9.096/1995, the registration request of the political party, addressed to the competent registry office of the Civil Registry of Legal Entities, of the Federal Capital, must be signed by its founders, in a number never lower than 101, with electoral domicile distributed in, at least, one third of the states. Proof of support for party registration must be made, in accordance with article 9, § 1, of Law No. 9,096/1995, "by means of signatures, mentioning the number of the respective electoral title, in lists organized for each Zone, with the veracity of the respective signatures and the number of titles attested by the Electoral Registrar." Once this first stage is completed, the political party will be able to request its registration with the Superior Electoral Court. In the absence of any need to carry out any diligence, the Superior Electoral Court will have a period of thirty days to register the statute of the political party (Paragraph 4 of Article 9 of Law No. 9,096/1995).

In determining that the legal nature of political parties occurs in the form of civil law, the 1988 Constitution, regulated by Law No. 9.096/1995, sought to guarantee political freedom and, fundamentally, to prevent the interference of the Electoral Justice in the process of creation, organization, and functioning of the political parties. In the party registration process, the function of the Electoral Justice is to only receive the registration and check whether the necessary formalities have been completed or not. Any discussion involving party programmatic issues must be dealt with in a judicial forum other than the electoral one.

The most attentive comparative analysis between the provisions of the text of the Constitution and the Law on Political Parties (Law No. 9,096/1995) shows a contradiction. While, on the one hand, § 2 of article 17 establishes that the political party acquires legal personality in the form of civil law, on the other, article 8 of Law No. 9,096/1995 determines that, in order to be required to register the political party in the competent Registry, a number of founders must never subscribe to less than 101, with an electoral domicile in at least one third of the states. In this case, the ordinary legislator ended up creating restrictive mechanisms to create political parties, which confronts the principle contained in the caput of article 17 of the Federal Constitution, which establishes that the creation of parties is free. Firstly, the ordinary legislator could not have determined a mandatory minimum number of founding members for the creation of a party, and secondly, there could be no requirement that the party's founding members have an electoral domicile in at least one third of the States of the Federation. With the requirement to comply with these requirements, the ordinary legislator ended up reproducing the interpretative mistake between the national "character" and "scope" precept. Due to the requirement, we are talking about the "scope" of the party's geographical scope and not of the programmatic "character" or quality of the party. As seen, the two terms are distinct; in this case the ordinary legislator could not have used the word "character" to impose any type of restrictive device for the creation of political parties.

CONSTITUTIONAL GUARANTEES OF BRAZILIAN POLITICAL PARTIES

In addition to recognizing the political party as a private legal entity, the 1988 Constitution innovated by guaranteeing autonomy so that it can define its internal structure, form of organization and functioning, and its statutes are responsible for establishing the rules of fidelity and party discipline (article 17, § 1). The other important constitutional guarantee granted to the political party was the right to the resources of the party fund and free access to radio and television, with its regulation on the form of distribution of resources being in charge of ordinary legislation (article 17, § 3). Constitutional guarantees are as follows:

a) party autonomy: on the one hand, if the constitutional text did not make very clear the scope of some precepts, such as national character and parliamentary functioning, on the other hand, in § 1 of article 17, the right to self-regulation by political parties was expressly determined. With this, for the first time in Brazilian political history, a Constitution delegates responsibility to the party itself so that it can regulate internal corporis issues, such as the form of structure, organization, and functioning. Within the scope of each statute, it is also up to the party to establish its own guidelines for party loyalty and discipline, always in compliance with the principles contained in constitutional rights and guarantees.

The prediction of party autonomy by the 1988 Constitution enabled a complete redefinition of the legal-political relationship that until then existed between parties and the Electoral Justice. From the new constitutional text, the control of the Electoral Justice over the parties was restricted to the verification of the fulfillment or not of the formal requirements and demands in electoral processes. In matters dealing with internal corporate issues, the competence to assess and judge will be that of the Common Justice, no longer that of the Electoral Justice. Always prevailing the principle that "the law will not exclude from the Judiciary's assessment, injury or threat of rights" (article 5, XXXV, of the 1988 Constitution). Judgment n. 13,750 (Special Electoral Appeal), dated November 12, 1996, from the Superior Electoral Court, irrefutably summarized the relationship that started to be established, from the 1988 Constitution, between Electoral Justice and political parties. According to the Judgment,

> the autonomy referred to in the constitutional precept concerns the establishment of norms whose scope is to outline the structure of its staff, the establishment of party bodies and their functioning. ... however, once these rules are established, subjective rights will arise from them, which, once violated, can be supported by the Judiciary, according to the art. 5, XXXV, of the Federal Constitution. And in that there will be no vilification for the principle of party autonomy, on the contrary, it will take care to reveal the exact meaning of the rules defined by the party itself [because, it would not be possible], to characterize the political party as a true enclave, in which the only remedy left at the disposal of affiliates disrespected in their rights would be to abandon the association .

Finally, the vote concludes that "because it is a fundamental cell in the democratic system, the party cannot become an organization whose life is governed" outside the law. In the party organization there must also "prevail the rule of law, which, once violated, must be reinstated by the action of Justice."

By recognizing the political party as an institution of private law, endowed with internal corporis autonomy, the 1988 Constitution, even though it delegated the task of political representation, began to guarantee the insubstance of any act that is characterized as an intervention to the party organization. That said, it can be concluded that the Electoral Justice lacks the competence to analyze and judge issues involving the organization and functioning of political parties, as these are not matters of an electoral nature, but, fundamentally, because they are internal issues corporis, which concern each party. Such autonomy, however, does not guarantee the party legal immunity in the event of an offense against any constitutional principle. If there is a violation of the constitutional principles, the competence to assess and judge the matter will not be of the Electoral Justice, but of the Common Justice. In view of this new context, the Electoral Justice has the competence to only manifest itself in matters that involve only and exclusively electoral processes after this period the internal demands of the parties, if any, must be dealt with by the common justice. On the other hand, under no circumstances does the constitutional guarantee of party autonomy exclude the party from exercising its rights and respecting its duties in the legal world;

b) internal democracy: the 1988 Constitution does not manifest itself in relation to internal or intra-party democracy. When it determines the parties' autonomy in defining their own internal organization and functioning, the constitutional text only requires that, in its statutes, the political party regulates party fidelity and discipline. Law No. 9,096/1995 is silent on this subject. In addition, currently the understanding of the courts is based on non-external interference in so-called internal corporate matters. Intra-party democracy stands out as a minimum assumption for maintaining the rationality of the formation of the will of the State, translating a type of radically democratic political representation. That democracy that is consistent with the rational organization of the mechanisms for measuring the collective will, here understanding rationality as a democratic principle of the formation of the will of the State. The intraparty structures with a profile not compromised with democratic dictates exclude the possibility of fully realizing the political potential of the party. Such a party model is reminiscent of Robert Michels 'famous "Iron Law of the Oligarchy," in which the parties' steep internal verticality stifles any possibility of free expression by their non-governing members;

c) party loyalty: this institute can be defined as the commitment that the political representative assumes to respect the democratically approved deliberations of his party and to remain faithful to the party while in office, both in the sphere of the Executive Branch and in that of the Legislative power. The party loyalty institute was introduced in the Brazilian legal system by article 152 of Constitutional Amendment no. 1/1969 and later regulated by Law No. 5,682/1971. But it lost its effectiveness with Constitutional Amendment no. 25/1985. Received by the 1988 Constitution, its regulation was sent to the statutory sphere of political parties.

The inclusion of the party loyalty institute in the 1988 Constitution made it possible to reinvigorate the discussion around the theory of party mandate, as opposed to the mandatory mandate or the representative mandate since the parliamentarian would no longer represent the set of voters indistinctly to only represent the will established by their party. In accordance with the spirit of party loyalty, the representative must give an account of his actions, solely and exclusively, to the party, under penalty of being replaced in the exercise of political representation. This would be one of the basic assumptions that underlie what is called the State of parties in opposition to the model of liberal political representation, which works with the idea of the disconnection of control of the mandate by the political party. In the liberal conception, the mandate presents itself as something that concerns only the representative and the impersonality of that group that has elected him. In this case, the political party would have no control over the mandate, and accountability for the acts of the representative would be with its voters. Although the 1988 Constitution referred not to the law, but to the statutes of each organization, to the possibility of establishing sanctions for acts that constitute party infidelity, the most drastic action that the party can take is to exclude the infidel from its caption. However, in the case of a member of the legislature, such exclusion will only reflect the loss of any positions held at the board of directors in the house to which he is attached, due to the fact that these nominations are partisan. Following this reasoning, there is no mention of term protection for unfaithful representatives, who often incorporate political mandates as if they were personal property, often disregarding the importance that the caption votes represented in the totality of the votes won by the party political.

The loss of mandate due to an act of party infidelity is not foreseen in the 1988 Constitution. Article 55 of the 1988 Constitution lists a number of possibilities that could cause the legislative representative to lose his mandate; however, under no circumstances is the loss due to infidelity to the party foreseen. According to the aforementioned article, anyone who: a) violates any provision provided for in article 54 (cases of incompatibilities); b) for lack of parliamentary decorum; c) fail to attend a certain number of legislative sessions; d) lose or have political rights suspended; e) decree the Electoral Justice, in the cases provided for in article 15; or, who suffer criminal conviction in a final and unappealable sentence. Although the 1988 Constitution does not provide for the loss of the mandate of the parliamentarian for the act of party infidelity, this does not mean that the representative cannot be punished by the party. The characterization of party infidelity by Law No. 9.096/1995 refers to the confluence of three basic requirements, namely: a) that the party has established its party guidelines, b) that this establishment of the guidelines has been carried out legitimately, and c) that the decision has been taken by the competent bodies of each party. As a result of constitutional omission, the mandate remains linked to the representative, and, therefore, control over the mandate can only be exercised by the parties to a limited extent, since the representative can only be punished with, at most, the expulsion of the association, without, however, causing any damage to the mandate's ownership.

With regard to Brazilian jurisprudence, it appears that the Courts tend to accept the thesis of the inapplicability of the principle of party fidelity, on the grounds that the 1988 Constitution did not link the loss of the legislative or executive mandate to party infidelity. On the matter, the Full Court of the STF understood by the majority, when analyzing the Writ of Mandamus no. 20.927-5, which does not apply "the principle of party fidelity to sworn parliamentarians." In justifying the vote, the Rapporteur of the process argued that, under the constitutional system in force, "although the Constitution gives a strong value to party representation (article 5, LXX, a; article 58, § 4; article 103, VIII), did not want to preserve it with the adoption of the legal sanction for the loss of the mandate," a basic requirement that would prevent the reduction of the initial representation of parties in parliament. If the Constitution "so wished, it would be enough to have placed this hypothesis among the causes of loss of mandate." The understanding of the Superior Electoral Court moved in the direction adopted by the STF, when, through Judgment n. 11.075, considered that the 1988 Constitution did not establish any "sanction of loss of mandate for party infidelity, being revoked or ineffective any infraconstitutional rules that provide otherwise. … loss of mandate is a matter of Public Electoral Law, object of private legislation of the Federal Union, and the rules of party statutes that provide for it are inoperative."

More recently, by Resolution no. 22,526/2007, in response to Consultation request (CTA) no. 398/2007, formulated by the political party, which questioned whether "parties and coalitions have the right to preserve the vacancy obtained by the proportional electoral system, when there is a request to cancel membership or transfer the candidate elected by the party to another party," the Superior Electoral Court, by a majority of its members, decided "yes." That is, that the political party can apply for the vacancy. The Superior Electoral Court based its response on the understanding that in proportional elections, the winning of mandates is practically determined by the electoral quotient, composed of the nominal votes, of captions and remainders (votes of unelected candidates). In the Brazilian case, mostly, the filling of vacancies ends up being determined by the caption votes and the surplus. Thus, the mandate ceases to be a personal achievement of the elected to be a party victory. As a result, the cancellation of membership or change of title of the mandate holder gives the political party the right to claim the respective mandate, so that a new representative can be appointed, according to the list of alternates. The Superior Electoral Court took this decision on March 27, 2007.

On October 16, 2007, in response to another request for Consultation (CTA), n. 1407/2007, which questioned whether "Political parties and coalitions have the right to preserve the vacancy obtained by the majority electoral system, when there is a request to cancel membership or transfer the elected candidate by one party to another party," the Court, the Electoral Superior, unanimously by its members, decided to extend the imposition of party loyalty also to the mandate holders elected by the majority system (senators, mayors, governors, and president of the Republic). According to the understanding deliberated by the Superior Electoral Court, the mandate of all positions held through the majority system belongs to the political party that granted its caption for the electoral dispute.

Following the same line of understanding, with the vote of the majority of its ministers, the STF, on the occasion of the judgment of the Writ of Mandamus No. 26,602, 26,603, and 26,604/2007, considered the interpretation of the Superior Electoral Court regarding the application of the rule of party loyalty to be constitutional. According to the decision, political parties that feel harmed by the change of party of their representatives may request the Electoral Justice to control the mandate and the consequent designation of the alternate to fill the vacancy. The timeframe established by the STF was the date of March 27, 2007, the date on which the Superior Electoral Court approved the response to Consultation No. 1,398. In other words, all mandate holders elected by the proportional system who changed captions as of that date are subject to losing their right of representation. The resumption of the mandate must be requested by the aggrieved party before the Electoral Justice, which must judge the request, guaranteeing the right of ample defense. Regarding the application of the rule of party loyalty to those elected by the majority system, the STF did not manifest.

It is worth mentioning that the party fidelity institute is closely linked to a political conception in which the state political organization is not only based on a state with parties but, fundamentally, on a state of parties. In the perspective of the State of Parties, the general state will would be built within the political parties, with the representative body; in this case, the Legislative, being relegated to a plan to harmonize party wills. Within this reasoning, of course, one cannot demand party loyalty to a political system that is based around individual leaders or political factions at the expense of institutional wills. In this context, loyalty would not be to the party, but to the leaders or to the oligarchies or party factions. This understanding is of fundamental importance when discussing the application of party loyalty in Brazil. It is not enough to recognize its application; above all it must be ensured that its existence produces the desired effects, the strengthening of the Political Party Institution and not of the top that has control over the organization. Did the judiciary bodies take these questions into account in their response to the Consultation on Mandate Ownership? The thesis defended is correct; however, in practice, the question remains: who will benefit from such a decision? The people, as pointed out by some ministers, or the "caciques," who in practice control the parties with *the iron law?* What are the parameters that the Electoral Justice will adopt to judge if the termination of a certain mandate holder occurred due to unilateral will or due to internal policy issues?

Constitutional Amendment No. 91, of February 18, 2016, did not change any constitutional provision; its objective was to guarantee the exceptional possibility for a determined period, of party affiliation, without any loss of mandate loss. In practice, what was created was a constitutional "window" that would allow captions to be exchanged by representatives without losing their mandate due to party infidelity. The referred Constitutional Amendment is composed of only one article which establishes that "It is allowed for the holder of an elective mandate to disconnect from the party for which he was elected within thirty days after the promulgation of this Constitutional Amendment, without prejudice to the mandate, this disillusion being considered for the purpose of distributing party fund resources and free access to radio and television time." Constitutional Amendment No. 91 established the maximum term for the holder of an elective mandate to leave the party for which he was elected and did not determine the obligation of a new affiliation. According to the Constitutional Amendment the holder of an elective mandate could leave the party without losing the mandate due to party infidelity if it occurred in the period from February 19, 2016, to March 19, 2016. The rule provided for by Constitutional Amendment No. 91 generated two conflicting situations with the basic principles of representative party democracy: first, by allowing the representative of the party for which he was elected to leave without prejudice to the loss of his mandate, and, second, by allowing the existence of elected representatives in representative bodies without any party affiliation. Due to its validity of only thirty days, in practice, Constitutional Amendment No. 91/2016 sought to accommodate short-term political interests and with previously determined recipients. Such casuistic and inopportune behavior only corroborates the argument that the commitments of the majority of elected political representatives are more focused on meeting their personal and immediate interests than on social, institutional, and long-term interests.

d) party discipline: for this institute, affiliates of political parties are required to respect the principles, the program, and the political aims of the organization. To the extent that the individual joins a political party, he is committed to respecting, defending the program, and the objectives defined democratically by the political organization in which he joined. In addition to respecting the determinations provided for in the party statutes, the affiliate must exercise his duties with dignity and, when summoned, exercise party functions or mandates with integrity. In its internal scope, in case of indiscipline to the statutory precepts, the party may apply penalties of warning, suspension, removal of internal functions, or even the expulsion of the affiliate from the organization. In the case of internal corporate matters, naturally, in all situations that involve punitive acts, it is up to the party organization to observe the principles of individual rights and guarantees, contained in article 5 of the 1988 Constitution. Mainly the principle of contradictory and broad defense (item LV of article 5). Even so, the final decision of the party does not exclude the right of the party involved to seek protection in the common Justice, as guaranteed by the constitutional principle that the law will not exclude from the judiciary's assessment, injury, or threat to the right (item XXXV of article 5). Regarding the competent judicial forum for examining electoral matters or internal *corporis* of the party, see the item on party autonomy;

e) party fund and access to the media: the legal provision of the party fund was introduced for the first time through Law No. 4,740/1965, being maintained by Law No. 5,682/1971. The 1988 Constitution innovated by providing, in its own text, the right to the party fund and the right of access to the media for political parties (§ 3 of article 17). Faced with this constitutional guarantee, party organizations started to use resources from this fund for the functioning and dissemination of their programs. In addition to providing transparency to the resources received by the parties, the constitutionalization of the right to the party fund allows each party organization to finance its own activities, without having to rely on donations from private legal entities or individuals, whose political pressure often ends up occurring.

Thus, both the right to the party fund and the right to free access to radio and television impose the necessary conditions for parties to freely disseminate and promote the democratic debate of ideas. At the same time, these constitutional guarantees make it possible for the parties to act to seek to shape the will of their militants and supporters for the structure of the State and not the other way around. By virtue of article 7, § 2, of Law 9,096/1995, all political parties that register their statutes with the TSE (Superior Electoral Court) are entitled to the party fund and free access to radio and television.

With the declaration of unconstitutionality of article 41 and its items I and II of Law 9,096/1995, by the Federal Supreme Court, through Direct Action of Unconstitutionality n. 1.351-3/2006, the ordinary legislator was responsible for regulating the constitutional provision provided for in § 3 of article 17 from new parameters. With the approval of article 41-A, through Law No. 11,459/2007, which was integrated into the body of Law No. 9,096/1995 (Law of Political Parties), the distribution of the resources of the party fund started to be carried out through two mechanisms: (a) 5% (five percent) of the total of the party fund started to be distributed in equal parts to all parties that have statutes registered with the Superior Electoral Court and (b) the remaining percentage, 95% (ninety-five percent), is now distributed among all parties, respecting the proportionality of votes obtained in the last general election for the Chamber of Deputies.

Likewise, with the declaration of unconstitutionality of the full text of article 48 and part of the caput of article 49 "that meets the provisions of art. 13" ... of Law No. 9,096/1995, by the STF, through Direct Action of Unconstitutionality n. 1.351-3/2006, the new regulation, § 3 of article 17, guaranteed political parties the right to carry out a national chain program and a state chain program each semester, lasting twenty minutes each (article 49, I, of Law No. 9,096/1995) and, also, the use of the total time of forty minutes, per semester, for insertions of thirty seconds or one minute, in the national networks, and of equal time in the state broadcasters (article 49, II, of Law No. 9,096/1995). According to the sole paragraph of article 52 of Law No. 9,096/1995, "radio and television broadcasters will be entitled to tax compensation for providing the free hours provided by law."

As stated in article 17, § 3, of the 1988 Constitution, political parties "are entitled to resources from the party fund and free access to radio and television, as provided by law." Therefore, it fell to the Federal Supreme Court, through Direct Action of Unconstitutionality No. 1.351-3/2006, to guarantee among all parties the possibility of participation in receiving the resources of the party fund and access to radio and television, without any type of constraint limited by compliance with barrier clauses. The criteria for accessing the party fund cannot be exclusive, since the constitutional text is very clear in stating that political parties are entitled. Thus, any party that has its statutes registered with the Superior Electoral Court is now entitled to the resources of the party fund and free access to radio and television. Thus, to avoid inequalities between parties, the STF ended up reestablishing the principle of free competition between political parties, based on the republican principle of political pluralism (V of article 1) and pluripartisan democracy (caput of article 17). These guarantees were not materialized in the previous wording of articles 41, 48, and 49 of Law No. 9,096/ 1995; with this the greatest beneficiaries were the great captions, which greatly hampered the growth and consolidation of the small party captions.

However, disregarding the principle of equal electoral competition between political parties, Constitutional Amendment No. 97/2017 profoundly modifying the original text of the 1988 Constitution by establishing two alternative conditions for political parties to be entitled to the resources of the party fund and free access to radio and television. By the first condition (I, 3§, of article17) the political party must obtain, in the elections for the Chamber of Deputies, at least 3% of the valid votes, distributed in at least one third of the units of the Federation, with a minimum 2% of the valid votes in each one; or, second condition (II, 3§, of article 17), the political party must have elected at least fifteen Federal Deputies distributed in at least one third of the Federation units. According to article 3 of Constitutional Amendment 97/2017, the above conditions will only apply as of the 2030 elections.

Until the 2030 election, Constitutional Amendment 97/2017 imposes conditions for political parties to have access to the resources of the party fund and to free radio and television advertising:

In the legislature following the 2018 elections, will have access to the resources of the party fund and to free radio and television advertising only political parties who obtain, in the elections to the Chamber of Deputies, at least 1.5% of the valid votes, distributed in at least one third of the Federation units, with a minimum of 1% of the valid votes in each of them; or, who have elected at least nine Federal Deputies distributed in at least one third of the Federation units; for the legislature following the elections of 2022 to those who obtain, in the elections to the Chamber of Deputies, at least 2% of the valid votes, distributed in at least one third of the Federation units, with a minimum of 1% of the valid votes in each one of them; or, they have elected at least eleven Federal Deputies distributed in at least one third of the Federation units; and, for the legislature following the 2026 elections, only those who obtain, in elections to the Chamber of Deputies, at least 2.5% of the valid votes, distributed in at least one third of the Federation units, with a minimum of 1.5% of the valid votes in each of them; or, to those who have elected at least thirteen Federal Deputies distributed in at least one third of the Federation units.

CONCLUSION

In essence, the Constitutional Amendment 97/2017 aimed to establish constitutional and legal interpretative limits hitherto applied by the STF and TSE on the distribution of the party fund and free access to radio and television, as seen above. Constitutional Amendment No. 97/2017 §1 reinforces the understanding of party autonomy to establish rules on, formation and duration of its permanent and provisional bodies and on their organization and functioning, prohibiting coalitions in proportional elections from the 2020 elections onwards. However, at the same time that the amendment in its paragraph 5 reinforces the idea of party autonomy, it demonstrates a total disregard for the strengthening of party organizations by establishing that the "elected by a party that does not meet the requirements of paragraph 3" of the Constitutional Amendment 97/2017 "the mandate is guaranteed and affiliation is granted, without loss of mandate, to another party that has reached them, and this affiliation is not considered for the purpose of distributing the resources of the party fund and free access to radio and television time." The conclusion reached is that with the Constitutional Amendment 97/2017, what was sought to establish was an even greater concentration of the resources of the party fund and free access in the media for some little political parties. By making it possible for the elected party to migrate to other parties than the one for which the ordinary legislator was elected, in the exercise of his constitutional prerogatives, he completely changed the original will of the constituent legislator who sought to guarantee the republican principles of freedom among all parties, equality, political plurality and pluripartisanship.

The conclusion reached is that the decision of the STF in 2006 corrected an anti-democratic reality that made equality of opportunity between party organizations unfeasible. Naturally, the legislation must, necessarily, establish proportional criteria for the distribution of the resources of the party fund, as well as for the access of the parties to the free time in the media. In this case, however, what must be taken into account is the structure and the political projection of each party group, which is reflected by its political representativeness. What cannot happen is the legislation to institute mechanisms that, in practice, end up discriminating and preventing captions that are in the process of consolidation, as provided for in the provisions deemed unconstitutional in Law No. 9,096/1995. Finally, Constitutional Amendment 97/2017, by imposing certain conditions so that political parties may be entitled to resources from the party fund and free access to radio and television, and to enable those elected by political parties that have not met such requirements to maintain their mandate or affiliate with another party association, materializes the assumption that political parties are mere structures administered by a few with the sole and exclusive purpose of guaranteeing the privileges and power of their own controllers.

Perhaps the ordinary legislator has forgotten that democracy is a project in permanent construction. As a consequence, today's small parties could become tomorrow's big parties or vice versa. As well as the new social movements that are articulating today, they will have a commitment tomorrow, perhaps as new parties, to continue carrying out their projects. In short, the political party cannot be seen as an end in itself: it is part of a larger project that must be inserted in social practice, committed to collective demands, never to personal interests. This is the basic condition for a party state to cease to be a state of *some* parties.

REFERENCES

Acquaviva, Marcus Cláudio. *Nova lei dos partidos políticos anotada:* Lei n. 9.096/1995 e legislação correlata. Brasília: Editora Jurídica, 1996.

Bispo Sobrinho, José. *Comentários à lei orgânica dos partidos políticos.* Brasília: Editora Jurídica, 1996.

Bonavides, Paulo. A decadência dos partidos políticos e o caminho para a democracia direta. *Revista da OAB*, Rio de Janeiro: Conselho Federal da OAB, v. 62, pp. 57–67, jan. /jun. 1996.

Canotilho, J. J. Gomes. *Direito constitucional e Teoria da Constituição.* 7 ed. Coimbra: Almedina.

Cunha, Sérgio Sérvulo da. A lei dos partidos políticos. In: Rocha, Cármen Lúcia Antunes; Veloso, Carlos Mário da (eds.). *Direito eleitoral.* Belo Horizonte: Del Rey, pp. 139–156, 1996.

Jardim, Torquato. *Direito eleitoral positivo.* Brasília: Editora Jurídica, 1998.

Mezzaroba, Orides. Verbete Dos Partidos Políticos. In J.J. Gomes Canotilho; Gilmar F. Mendes; Ingo W. Sarlet; Lenio L. Streck (eds.). *Comentários à Constituição do Brasil.* 2 ed. São Paulo/Coimbra: Saraiva/Almedina, pp. 753–765, 2018.

Mezzaroba, Orides. *Introdução ao direito partidário brasileiro.* Florianópolis: Qualis, 2019.

Ribeiro, Fávila. *Direito eleitoral.* Rio de Janeiro: Forense, 2000.

Silva, José Afonso da. *Curso de direito constitucional positivo.* São Paulo: Malheiros, 2014.

Chapter 10

Corporate Campaign Donations

João Andrade Neto

INTRODUCTION

Corporate donations to the financing of electoral campaigns or political parties were until very recently accepted in Brazil. The Federal Constitution (FC) does not expressly prohibit legal entities, for-profit or not, to make political donations. And in fact, both the Political Parties Act (Law 9,096/1995) and the Elections Act (Law 9,504/1997) expressly allowed for corporate contributions, given certain limits and conditions. In virtue of such statutory rules, this type of campaign finance or political party funding was rarely discussed in courts. Debates about the influence of money on politics and its social implications usually took place in academic spheres or the National Congress and were encouraged by the press. Corporate political donations were regarded as an essentially political matter, to be discussed and decided by legislators, economists, and political scientists, outside the forensic environment. There was no significant case law against the practice. However, to the surprise of some in the academy[1] and the political class, on September 17, 2015, the STF judged a direct action of unconstitutionality (ADI 4650) and banned political donations from legal entities to either candidates or political parties, ruling that the laws that allowed them violated the Constitution. In this chapter, I analyze the *Legal Entity's Political Donation Case*,[2] as the decision has been known, and the circumstances leading up to and the consequences following the judgment.

At the outset, I shall clarify that I call political donations both donations for the maintenance of political parties beyond the electoral period as well as donations for electoral campaigns, whether directed to the parties themselves or specific candidates. Brazilian law admits all three forms of political financing by natural persons—and it also admitted them by legal entities. Each form gives rise to a specific type of reporting before the Electoral Justice: annual reports of financial activity, for the political parties; campaign reports of these parties, handled only in election years, after the elections; and reports of elected or unelected candidates, also handled only in an election year, after the end of the elections.

Having established this, another disambiguation is necessary concerning the expression "corporate donations." In Brazilian law, "corporations" are just one type of private legal entity. There are also different companies (distinguished according to their type of liability), societies, cooperatives, enterprises, associations, and foundations. Not all of them are for-profit—as in the case of associations, which are nonprofit. And even corporations differ in for-profit and not-for-profit corporations. Besides, amongst for-profit companies, there is a wide range of structures, from micro- and small businesses to large companies and business corporations. Nonetheless, unlike what happened in other countries,[3] in Brazil, the ban on political donations went beyond corporations and reached all public and private legal entities. Therefore, in this chapter, I differentiate between the expressions "*legal entities' political donations*" and "*corporate political donations*"; I will normally refer to the former, using the latter for the cases in which it does apply.

This chapter is organized as follows. In the next section, I will offer an overview of the Brazilian political funding system and its evolution since the 1970s, when the country adopted exclusively public financing, until the 1990s, when an electoral reform changed the legislation to also admit private fundraising by parties and candidates, establishing a mixed model. In the following topic, I analyze the *Legal Entity's Political Donation Case*, from the context that preceded the petition and the petitioner's arguments, to the STF's opinion written by Justice Luiz Fux and the dissenting opinion by Justice Teori Zavascki, followed by the minority. Finally, I gather the main criticisms against the decision into two categories: de facto (or empirical) claims and legal (or normative) claims. In the end, I intend to demonstrate that, by abruptly restricting the contribution to parties and campaigns, without an equivalent reduction in spending, the STF's decision forced political agents to pursue new sources of public and private financing, with disastrous consequences for the political financing system as a whole. Furthermore, it remains highly debatable whether the STF's decision in the *Legal Entity's Political Donation Case* was in fact based on the Constitution.

AN OVERVIEW OF THE BRAZILIAN POLITICAL FINANCING SYSTEM

Since before the re-democratization, which occurred in the 1980s, Brazil adopted public funding of political parties and elections, with exclusivity, following articles 91 and 92 of the Organic Law on Political Parties (Law 5,682/1971), then in force. Exclusively public funding continued to be practiced even after the Federal Constitution was enacted in 1988. The FC did not expressly impose a form of financing for campaigns or political parties; it only prohibited donations from foreign sources, and if on the one hand, it charged political parties with the duty of reporting their fundraising and spending, on the other, it granted them the right to receive resources from the party fund and free access to radio and television.[4] Only in the 1990s, a legislative reform would turn political financing into a mixed system, allowing donations from corporations and other private legal entities. The alleged goal of this reform was to increase control over the private resources that effectively moved the campaigns in order to fight against the corruption associated with the political financing model then in place, considered unreal.

FROM EXCLUSIVELY PUBLIC FINANCING TO MIXED FINANCING

The first election of the democratic period was held in 1989, under the previous legislation from the period of military dictatorship, which provided for exclusively public political financing. In 1992, former President Fernando Collor de Melo's involvement in corruption scandals related to the funding of his campaign triggered a discussion about the Brazilian system and its subsequent reform. As explained by Lara Ferreira, "the activities of [Mr. de Melo's] campaign treasurer, illegal donations, and the influence-peddling between financiers and government" were "at the core of the investigations of the Parliamentary Commission of Inquiry (PCI) that led to the impeachment of the first president of the Republic elected after the military regime."[5] In fact, as Ferreira highlights, "the PCI report contains a chapter that analyzes the issue [of election funding], as well as proposals aimed at regulating the fundraising and the inspection of these financial resources."[6]

The commission instituted by the National Congress found that, although prohibited, private financing was a reality and met the need imposed by increasing electoral spending, which was not a Brazilian idiosyncrasy, but a worldwide phenomenon. As a result, the commission recommended the legalization of private funding, accompanied by the intensification of regulation and inspection by the Electoral Justice, and not by the inter-party commissions that still existed. "As a conclusion, the report presented a law proposal for the adoption of a mixed financing system for electoral campaigns, with the contribution of public and private resources," observes Ferreira.[7]

The proposal was embodied in two temporary laws that governed the 1994 and 1996 elections until the Political Parties Act was promulgated in 1995 (Law 9,096/1995), and the Elections Act in 1997 (Law 9,504/1997). The latter two, still in force, regulate the mixed system of political financing and the supervision of political parties' and candidates' fundraising and spending, performed by the Electoral Justice. The claims of unconstitutionality that were the subject of the *Legal Entity's Political Donation Case* fell on both statutes.

DONATIONS AUTHORIZED BY THE CONSTITUTION AND LEGISLATION

The system of political financing in Brazil, as designed in electoral and party legislation from the 1990s, was therefore mixed. Political parties were supplied by the party fund, to which both public and private resources converged. These resources could be used both in election campaigns as well as in maintaining the parties' functioning. Another source of indirect public funding was granted by means of free radio and TV hours for political party and electoral propaganda.[8] With regard to private sources, up to the limits established by law, legal entities and natural persons could make donations to specific candidates and also to political parties, whether for their maintenance or electoral campaigns. In the latter case, the parties could pass on the resources to their candidates also according to some contribution limits. Exceptional prohibitions of donation were imposed on specific entities only, such as foreign companies, for instance. Other forms of private financing were candidates' donations for their own campaigns (self-financing), also subject to the limits provided for by law, and the fundraising from the sale of goods and services and the holding of events.[9]

Article 24 of the Elections Act prohibited parties and candidates from receiving direct or indirect campaign donations from some categories of legal entities: unions and other class bodies, charitable and religious organizations, civil society organizations of public interest, and others that receive resources from abroad or public money. Concerning companies, to donate, they could not have received money from abroad, nor could they be foreign, public service concessionaires, or permit holders, nor direct beneficiaries of mandatory contributions provided by law or of other public resources.

For companies that were authorized to donate, article 81 of the Elections Act determined that donations and contributions to election campaigns were to be limited to 2% of the gross revenue for the year preceding the election.

If the amount donated exceeded this limit, the company donating was subject to the payment of a fine equivalent to five or ten times the amount in excess. Furthermore, it could be prohibited from participating in public tenders and entering into contracts with the government for a period of five years, as determined by the Electoral Justice, following a due process.

With regard to the Political Parties Act, it prohibited political parties from receiving, "directly or indirectly, under any form or pretext, contribution or financial aid or aid estimated in cash, including through advertising of any kind, coming from: … public companies or public service concessionaires" and other entities "whose resources come from government agencies or entities." Except for this, any political party could receive donations from private legal entities, including national corporations, for constituting its funds, as long as it reported to the Electoral Justice. This was expressly provided for in articles 38 and 39 of the Political Parties Act.

THE LEGAL ENTITY'S POLITICAL DONATION CASE

As seen in Section 2, the adoption of the mixed system of political financing in the mid-1990s was preceded by a corruption scandal that led the National Congress to abandon the previous model, which was exclusively public. Such an option seemed to meet public opinion. However, a decade later, criticism against the newly created mixed system was already abundant. As Portugal and Bugarin recall, "in November 2000, the newspaper Folha de S. Paulo published a report on parallel accounts of President Fernando Henrique Cardoso, re-elected in 1998."[10] Once again, at the center of the scandal were undeclared electoral donations. The case showed that the adoption of mixed financing was not enough to overcome the problems of the previous model. As a result, bills defending the return to exclusively public financing began to be considered by the National Congress.[11] The growing social dissatisfaction as what appeared to be one of the main problems of the Brazilian political system culminated with the filing of the *Legal Entity's Political Donation Case* in 2011 and its judgment in 2015.

THE CONTEXT BEFORE THE FILING

A decade after the adoption of the mixed financing system, there was significant literature in applied social sciences pointing out the flaws of the Brazilian model, with several suggestions for improvement, in view of the growing correlation identified between campaign costs and the number of votes obtained by a party or candidate.[12] Not all critics were in favor of restoring the exclusively public system of political funding. But, in general, there was a perception that the maintenance of private financing, unaccompanied by instruments that would give effectiveness to the control and inspection bodies, would accentuate the influence of economic power on the results of electoral dispute.

Political scientist David Samuels, for instance, claimed that money had become excessively important in Brazilian elections, which "[made] the balance weigh in favor of the candidate who had wealthy taxpayers on her side."[13] In his opinion, "money accentuated the viability of the candidacies and its lack limited enormously the competitiveness of the candidates."[14] Besides, "the 'closed' nature of campaign financing in Brazil," when compared to the US, would suggest that it was, to a large extent, "'service-oriented,' rather than 'oriented towards politics,'" meaning that "taxpayers expect a specific 'service,' which only a public office may offer in return for their investment," concludes the author.[15]

The influence of economic power on Brazilian elections also concerned jurists. Velloso and Agra, for instance, drew attention to the problems arising from the "predominance of the private financing system" in Brazilian elections, which would have given notable advantages to the "holders of economic power" and made electoral disputes extremely unequal, by "privileging the citizens who counted on sources of finance to the detriment of those who did not have sufficient financial conditions."[16] Similarly, Sarmento and Osório argued that the pathologies of the country's political system were "enhanced by the Brazilian legislation in force regarding the private financing of electoral campaigns."[17] And Sanseverino affirmed that "private financing, in the least, put at risk the freedom of organization and functioning of political parties as institutions of public interest, in the face of dependence on pressure groups, with greater economic capacity."[18]

Although the political financing system adopted since the 1990s was mixed, private resources prevailed and, among them, donations from corporations and other legal entities. According to Denise Schlickmann, figures obtained from official data reported to the Superior Electoral Court revealed that more than 40% of the revenues that financed parties and candidates during the 2014 elections came from private legal entities.[19] The analysis of donations received by candidates running for President confirmed that political funding involved "many resources donated by few funders, while the largest part of the electorate was completely absent from the campaign financing system."[20]

THE FILING

Criticisms on the influence of economic power in Brazilian elections were growing along with the cost of campaigns. The emergence of new corruption scandals from 2005 onward, involving electoral donations not accounted by the campaigns of the parties that formed the coalition governments of Lula da Silva and his successor's, Dilma Rousseff, reinforced before part of the public opinion the idea that political financing was "the snake's egg" of corruption in the country.[21] In this context, the Federal Council of the Brazilian Bar Association (OAB) filed the *Legal Entity's Political Donation Case* (ADI 4650) before the STF, on September 5, 2011. The petitioner argued for the unconstitutionality of provisions of the Elections Act and the Political Parties Act that, explicitly or implicitly, authorized the financing of political parties and electoral campaigns through donations from legal entities.

In some cases, as in the sole paragraph of article 24 and the first paragraph of article 81 of the Elections Act, the petitioner required that the article or paragraph of that law be declared null and void; in others, as in the case of articles 38 and 39 of the Political Parties Act, demanded the declaration of partial unconstitutionality with reduction of the text, to declare the references to "legal entities" contained therein invalid. Finally, in cases such as the *caput* of article 24 of the Elections Act, the petitioner sought the declaration of partial unconstitutionality without reduction of the text, to render invalid the reading of these rules that resulted in the authorization for legal entities to donate to political parties or electoral campaigns.

The petitioner's main arguments were as follows:

(a) the democratic and republican principles, as well as the constitutional principle of equality bind the legislator to the duty to impose limits on the private financing of electoral campaigns to avoid some damaging consequences;
(b) the fact that political financing is dependent on economic power is harmful to democracy because it increases the influence of the wealthiest on the outcome of the elections and, consequently, on the State itself;
(c) the legislation then in force was insufficient to preserve democracy from the detrimental influence of economic power because it allowed corporations and other types of legal entities to make political donations directly or indirectly;
(d) "while class entities, unions and most of the institutions that make up the so-called 3rd sector cannot make such donations, these contributions are possible to the absolute majority of private companies that pursue profit";
(e) the constitutional principles of political pluralism and equality of chances among candidates are severely compromised by the possibility that for-profit corporations may finance the campaign of candidates who defend hegemonic economic interests, to the detriment of candidates who defend equally legitimate social interests;

(f) the republican principle is threatened by the fact that a small number of corporations can make large donations, which tends to privilege them in their relationship with the government and with elected public officials;
(g) the right to finance politics is in itself a political right, and legal entities do not have political rights, as they do not vote nor can they be voted—therefore, they have no legitimate claim to participate in the political-electoral process, not even through donations;
(h) all things considered, the current legislation would be disproportionate, and therefore unconstitutional because it promoted the democratic, republican, and equality principles beneath the minimum required by the Constitution.[22]

Furthermore, the petitioner compared its arguments to those of the U.S. Supreme Court, which, in *Citizens United* v. *Federal Election Commission*, declared the unconstitutionality of a Federal law that prohibited "corporations and unions from using their general treasury funds to make independent expenditures for speech defined as an 'electioneering communication' or for speech expressly advocating the election or defeat of a candidate."[23] According to the Brazilian Bar Association, the U.S. Supreme Court's equation of political donations to the exercise of freedom of expression, a constitutionally assured right, was not convincing.

First, in Brazil, it was not uncommon for a company to donate "simultaneously to rival candidates, with a greater chance [of winning]," which weakened the argument that the donation was the expression of a legitimate political preference. Quoting Ronald Dworkin's assertion that, "companies are legal fictions. They have no opinions of their own to contribute and rights to participate with the same voice and vote in politics," the petitioner maintained that "freedom of expression … was simply not in question" in the *Legal Entity's Political Donation Case*.[24]

Second, and more importantly, for the petitioner the right to make political donations was inherent to citizenship, and therefore legal entities should not have the right to donate. And concerning the possible objection that a ban on corporate political donations could correspond to an undue intrusion on the economic freedom of which the companies are entitled, the petitioner claimed that, in situations of collision with this right, the Constitution privileged the citizens' right to equal participation in politics.

While defending the unconstitutionality of donations, the petitioner acknowledged that political funding by legal entities had been a reality for some time, so that its sudden ban by the court could cause inconvenience and bring irremediable problems. Based on these considerations, the Brazilian Bar Association demanded the declaration of unconstitutionality to only be effective for the future, in order to exempt from responsibility donors and beneficiaries who had made or received donations in the past, provided that they had been made following the law then in force. The petitioner also considered the possibility that legal articles would remain effective for a period after the declaration of nullity, suggesting 24 months, to avoid a legislative gap. In the period, the National Congress could issue other laws to provide for and regulate new forms of political financing that conformed with the Constitution. In case the legislator did not act within the deadline, it would be up to the Superior Electoral Court to issue rules to fill the gap.

The STF received the initial petition and, recognizing the relevance and social repercussion of the matter, set a date for holding public hearings. On the designated day, lawyers, political scientists, federal congresspersons, professors of law from prestigious universities, former ministers of the Superior Electoral Court, retired Justices of the STF, and representatives of political parties, of the National Confederation of Bishops of Brazil (CNBB), of the São Paulo Lawyers Institute (IASP), among others, attended the hearing and spoke against or in favor of the declaration of unconstitutionality. The public hearings took place on June 17 and 24, 2013. The action, however, would only be judged on September 17, 2015, in the wake of new corruption scandals investigated by the *Operation Car Wash*.[25]

THE OPINION OF THE STF

The rapporteur's vote begins by answering three questions: (a) whether the judiciary and particularly the STF are the legitimate bodies "to appreciate issues that reach the core of the democratic process, such as the financing of election campaigns," or whether such a political decision falls to the National Congress; (b) if there is such a possibility of intervention, what is the legitimate extent of judicial review "in order not to be characterized as undue (and, therefore, unconstitutional) judicial interference within the scope of powers conferred primarily to the political powers," and finally, (c) "if an eventual pronouncement by the Court is in itself definitive, forbidding a new discussion of the matter in political instances and society in general."

Regarding the first question, Justice Luiz Fux concluded that, because they are directly interested in issues concerning political funding, political spheres are not the best place to discuss the matter. The decision then rests with the judiciary not because judges are experts in Constitutional and Electoral Law, but because they are sufficiently distant from the problem to assess the issue more neutrally and impartially. As for the second question, he understood that the absence of rules in the Constitution that directly impose or prohibit a given campaign financing model should not be read as the granting of "a blank check to the legislator, which would enable her to adopt the financing criteria that best suits her." He explained that the Constitution "provided a framework that draws limits to legislative discretion" and that "the Court's approach *in casu* is precisely to define whether the legislator acted within this constitutional framework, not having the intention of replacing her." Finally, as for the third question, he stated that it is up to the Court "to open channels of dialogue with other political actors, notably the Legislative Branch, to formulate a constitutionally adequate model for campaign financing," not suffocating, as a result, the activity of the legislator.

Concerning the question of financing itself, the rapporteur understood that the claim of legal entities to participate in political life similarly to citizens would be contrary to the essence of the democratic regime. For him, although legal entities had some fundamental rights, such as freedom of expression, they had no political rights, as they could not vote in elections, plebiscites, or referendums, nor run for office or draft a law; the rights inherent to citizenship would be guaranteed by the Constitution to citizens, exclusively. This would already have been implicitly recognized by the STF and it would be the rationale behind STF Precedent no. 365, according to which, "legal entities do not have the legitimacy to file a popular lawsuit," since the right to file this type of action is also inherent to the condition of citizen in the strict sense, that is, being a voter.

Also, for him, "there was a correlation of almost 100% (one hundred percent) between the amount of money spent on the election campaign and the votes obtained by the candidates." For this reason, the fact that companies were the main financiers of electoral campaigns would increase the relative cost of candidacies, excluding candidates that would otherwise be competitive. Using the 2010 elections as an example, he highlighted that, in that year, "only 1% of donors, equivalent to 191 companies, were responsible for 61% of the amount donated. As if that weren't enough, the top ten financiers—generally construction companies, banks, and industry—contributed to approximately 22% of the total raised." Regarding the evolution of expenses, he stressed that "in the 2002 elections, candidates spent a total of R$798 million, whereas in 2012, ten years later, the amounts raised exceeded R$4.5 billion, an increase of 471%. ... In the same period, Brazilian GDP grew 41%, accumulated inflation was 78%." He concluded that "There is no reasonable justification for this massive expansion of campaign spending."

As we can see, a major concern for the rapporteur was the numbers involved in Brazilian election campaigns, which he considered excessive. He stated that in Brazil, per capita spending in campaigns "reaches $10.93, while in France it is $0.45, in the United Kingdom $0.77, and in Germany 2.21. When compared proportionally to the GDP, Brazil is also at the top in the ranking of countries that spend the most on election campaigns: 0.89% of all the wealth generated in the country is used to finance candidacies for representative positions. Here, we even surpass the United States, where only 0.38% of the GDP goes to electoral campaigns." Justice Fux believed that "the option to exclude financing by legal entities would not give rise to systemic consequences on fundraising, either because access to party fund resources and free electoral propaganda is maintained, or because financing by natural persons would continue."

In the end, he voted for the partial validity of the request, to declare: "the partial unconstitutionality without change of the text of article 24 of Law No. 9,504/97, in the part that authorizes, *contrario sensu*, the donation by legal entities to electoral campaigns;" the "unconstitutionality of article 24, sole paragraph, and article 81, *caput*, and first paragraph, of Law No. 9,507/94"; "partial unconstitutionality without change of the text of article 31 of Law No. 9,096/95, insofar as it authorizes, *contrario sensu*, the making of donations by legal entities to political parties"; the "declaration of unconstitutionality of the expressions 'or legal entity,' contained in article 38, III, and 'and legal entities,' in article 39, *caput* and paragraph 5, all of Law No. 9,096/95." As a final result, a majority of justices followed him and rejected modulating the effects of the declaration of unconstitutionality, defining that the decision would apply to the 2016 and subsequent elections, starting from the Judgment Session, regardless of the publication of the judgment.

THE DISSENT

The rapporteur was followed by Justices Joaquim Barbosa, Dias Toffoli, Roberto Barroso, Marco Aurélio, Ricardo Lewandoswski, Cármen Lúcia, and Rosa Weber, forming a majority. Justices Celso de Mello and Gilmar Mendes followed Justice Teori Zavaski's dissenting opinion. For the minority, private campaign financing was an "unavoidable contingency" of contemporary democracies, because if, on the one hand, "economic power can negatively interfere in the democratic system, favoring electoral corruption and other forms of abuse, it is also certain that a quality democratic system cannot be envisaged without strong and active political parties, … which, of course, presupposes the availability of significant financial resources."

Concerning the normative aspect of the matter, Justice Zavaski underscored that "what was at issue is not whether the Brazilian normative model is convenient, or not, … whether or not it represents the best way to face the troubles produced by the interference of money in the political arena."

According to him, what was in dispute was whether the rules indicated by the petitioner were constitutional or not. Justice Zavaski pointed out that the Constitution does not prohibit private campaign donations, as it does not combat mere economic influence, but the abuse of economic power. According to paragraph 9 of article 14 of the FC, illicit is only "the abusive economic influence, that is, the one that compromises the normality and legitimacy of elections." He explained that it was up to the Legislative Branch to implement the political financing system and that the judiciary branch could not, based on principles that say little about the case, impose "biased interpretations that impose an artificial and permanent obstacle on the alternatives that ... the Constitution offers to the legislator."

In response to the argument that the right to make political donations is in itself a political right owned exclusively by citizens, Justice Zavaski replied that "the Constitution does not make, not even implicitly, this necessary connection between the capability to vote and the ability to contribute, also because there are many natural people who are not qualified to vote and yet are not prohibited from contributing financially to parties and campaigns." Regarding the accusation that legal entities only finance politics to assert their interest, he replied that the same could be said about natural persons, and added that it is not possible, beforehand, to define such a posture and the interests it aims to satisfy as constitutionally illegitimate.

Furthermore, Justice Zavaski regarded as unfounded the belief that the Brazilian political system's troubles were due to the private financing of campaigns by legal entities. He recalled that Brazil adopted the mixed political financing system in the 1990s, permitting for private donations precisely in response to cases of corruption involving the campaign of the former President Collor de Melo. At that time, the financing system adopted in the country was exclusively public, and the distancing of this model from the social practices actually in place was pointed out as one of the major defects of the Brazilian model. The possibility of private financing was then introduced by the legislature as an answer to correct the problem, in an attempt to "discipline, limit, and make legal entities' contributions transparent."

As a conclusion, Justice Zavaski initially voted for the direct action of unconstitutionality to be considered groundless, deeming as constitutional all the laws it attacked. However, after hearing opposing opinions, he modified his vote to judge the action as partially grounded, recognizing that the following forms of political donation violated the Constitution: "(i) from legal entities or from their subsidiaries and affiliates that maintain onerous contracts with the Public Administration, regardless of their form and object; (ii) from legal entities to different parties (or their candidates) that compete with each other." He also acknowledged that there is an implicit principle in the Federal Constitution prohibiting legal entities that have made contributions to parties or campaigns from contracting with the Public Administration, since the date of their donation to the end of the subsequent legislature.

CRITICISM OF THE DECISION

Criticisms against the STF's decision are numerous and range from (1) factual (or empirical) claims that it has brought adverse and harmful consequences to the Brazilian financing system as a whole, to (2) legal (normative) claims on insufficient legal grounds and absence of reasons to justify the ban on legal entities' political donations. In the first case, empirical criticisms of the decision's effects in general stem from the fact that it imposed an abrupt restriction on fundraising without an equivalent reduction in electoral spending. As a consequence, it generated real incentives for the use of hidden, unregistered donations, and other types of private financing, especially self-financing, to reveal that there remains a strong influence of economic power on the elections. Besides, under pressure, political agents were able to approve a reform that created a new fund for campaigns, using public resources to fill the space left empty by the ban on corporate financing.[26] As for the legal arguments, the criticism falls on the absence of constitutional grounds to support the judgment.

A BAD DECISION FOR THE POLITICAL FINANCING SYSTEM AS A WHOLE

The STF's decision, issued in 2015, had an immediate impact on the 2016 elections. As explained by Schlickmann, the Brazilian political financing model remained mixed after the trial. The resources destined for parties and candidates remained both public, coming from the party fund, as well as private, from donations of natural persons, campaign self-financing, events, and the sale of products and services. However, considering the amounts effectively declared to the Electoral Justice, the percentage participation of public resources increased considerably, to the detriment of the private ones. The ban on donations from legal entities reduced the private portion of resources because donations from natural persons could not match up the loss resulting from the end of the financing from large corporations.[27]

The National Congress reacted immediately to the STF's decision by approving a Mini Electoral Reform based on Law 13,165/2015, which expressly provided for the possibility of donations from legal entities, but imposed more rigid limits and severe additional restrictions. The statute clauses that dealt with the matter were, however, vetoed by the Presidency of the Republic, being considered unconstitutional, and did not compose the final text of the enacted law.[28] In response, in 2017, the National Congress approved another electoral reform, in this case, to encourage donations from natural persons, through crowdfunding, and expand the public means of political financing by creating the Special Campaign Financing Fund (FEFC).[29]

This consequence, of increased public spending on politics, may be considered an undesired effect of the STF's decision, as several justices who voted to ban donations from legal entities expressed concern about the high cost of electoral campaigns in Brazil and did not seem to have in mind that the losses resulting from the reduction in private fundraising could be partially offset by the increase in public expenditures. Another unwanted effect concerns the increase in the participation of candidates' self-donations. Jorge and Soares demonstrate that the resources allocated by candidates to their own campaigns corresponded to about 16% of the total raised in the 2012 elections and were the fourth largest source of contribution; in the 2016 elections, they accounted for approximately 32% of the total and were the second-largest source of funds.[30]

A powerful argument against the STF's decision was thus the fact that it only shifted the influence of economic power from corporate donations to self-financing candidates, with their own resources. Before the ban, even though a small number of companies were responsible for large donations, the resources were destined to several candidates and parties from different positions in the political spectrum. Self-financing, in turn, increases the advantage of the wealthiest candidates and makes the dispute even more unequal. This became clear after the 2016 elections, in which some candidates who were victorious in big cities were notorious millionaires.[31] For authors like Decomain, even after the ban on legal entities' donations, the harmful influence of economic power on Brazilian elections persists through the use of candidates' own resources, which, in his point of view, would be contrary to the Constitution.[32]

Even more serious than the two effects mentioned, a third adverse effect may have been the increase in political resources not accounted for. Political donations from legal entities remain prohibited in Brazil; however, the problem that the ban was supposed to solve remains unresolved. The STF made a bet that, by reducing the sources of financing for corruption, the illicit use of money in elections would cease to exist. However, nothing demonstrates that it is so. On the contrary, the decision may actually have favored undeclared forms of contributions. As Schlickmann observes, the ban on legal entities' political donations did not automatically impose an end to this type of financing, "instead, it put [private fundraising] on the margins of the most modern mechanisms of inspection and control that the Electoral Justice currently has."[33]

A DECISION NOT BASED ON THE CONSTITUTION

In addition to the factual objections to the STF's decision in the *Legal Entity's Political Donation Case*, there is also a powerful legal argument against it. As stated, there is no clause in the FC that expressly authorizes private entities and corporations to make political donations; however, since before the legislative reform of the 1990s, it was widely understood that such express authorization was not required. First, as neither clause in the Constitution prohibited private financing, the issue was regarded as a matter of legislative competence of the National Congress. Second, item II of article 5 of the FC allows individuals and private legal entities to do everything that the law does not prohibit—which includes the right to make cash donations to third parties. Thus, in the case of private donors, whether persons or entities, such legal authorization was unimportant. Relevant was the fact that there was no legal clause in Brazilian law that completely banned their donations.

Regarding the beneficiary parties and candidates, there were only legal provisions establishing limits and conditions for such donations to occur. Since the adoption of the mixed system of political financing, no law prohibited them from receiving such donations. Vis-à-vis the political parties, receiving private financing was justified by the same reasons discussed earlier about the right of corporations to make donations, since political parties are private legal entities in Brazil. The second paragraph of article 17 of the FC provides for political parties to acquire legal personality "following the civil law." And item V of article 44 of the Civil Code is clear in stipulating that they are included amongst the "private legal entities."

Qualifying political parties as private, not public, legal entities reverberates broadly on the rules applicable to them. As said before, item II of article 5 of the FC states that private persons and entities can do everything the law does not prohibit; conversely, public legal entities can only do what the law authorizes. Therefore, the fact that there is no explicit constitutional authorization for candidates and parties to receive electoral donations from private corporations should be irrelevant. What mattered was the fact that neither the constitution nor the law expressly prohibited such a source of financing. On the contrary, the authorization of political finance by legal entities derived from both the Elections Act and the Political Parties Act, which only deemed to be illegal donations that exceeded certain limits.

CONCLUDING REMARKS

All things considered, the STF's decision in the *Legal Entity's Political Donation Case* allows us to question whether it was based rather on political arguments than on arguments of principle, to quote Dworkin again.[34] The majority that voted to ban donations from legal entities appeared to believe they were doing so in the benefit of improving the Brazilian political system. It would not be the first time the STF adopted a loose reading of the constitutional text, allegedly to increase the effectiveness of the Constitution itself. And it comes as no surprise to closer observers that the court has done it to obtain a result that only seemed desirable because justices deliberately minimized or neglected the difficult prognosis issues involved in this type of rationale.[35]

In reality, however, almost five years after the final decision of the case, none of the fundamental problems that were believed to be resolved with the judgment were indeed settled, and several unwanted effects unexpectedly came about, as demonstrated in this essay. Particularly the fight against corruption, which since the 1990s, has justified the successive reforms promoted in the Brazilian political financing system, both by the National Congress and the judiciary, may have been actually weakened after the trial. There is strong evidence that campaign costs have not decreased significantly, although the resources officially admitted to financing them have. This raises suspicions that unofficial or unaccounted sources continue to irrigate Brazilian political life, now further than before from the media spotlight and the control of the Electoral Justice.

NOTES

1. For example, the decision was considered "abrupt" by Santano, Ana Claudia. Como sobreviver na selva: fontes alternativas de financiamento de campanhas eleitorais. In: Pereira, Rodolfo Viana; Santano, Ana Claudia (Orgs.). *Conexões Eleitoralistas*. Belo Horizonte: Abradep, 2016, p. 59.
2. Brazil. STF. ADI 4650/DF, judgment of Sep. 17, 2015 ('Legal Entity's Political Donation Case'). Rapporteur: Justice Luiz Fux. D.J.e. 34, Feb. 24, 2016 (Brazil, 2016).
3. About the US, see, for example, *Federal Election Comm'n v. Beaumont*, 539 U.S. 146 (2003).
4. *Cf* Ferreira, Lara Marina. O financiamento de partidos políticos e de campanhas eleitorais no contexto da reforma política brasileira. *Estudos Eleitorais*, v. 6, no. 1, pp. 91–110, 2011, p. 92 ff.
5. Ibid., p. 95.
6. Ibid.
7. Ibid., p. 97.

8. Ibid., p. 98.

9. Schlickmann, Denise Goulart. O fim das doações empresariais: o impacto do julgamento da ADI 4.650 pelo Supremo Tribunal Federal sobre o financiamento das campanhas eleitorais no Brasil. In: Fux, Luiz; Pereira, Luiz Fernando Casagrande; Agra, Walber de Moura (Coord.); Peccinin, Luiz Eduardo (Org.). *Financiamento e prestação de contas*. Belo Horizonte: Fórum, 2018, p. 58.

10. Portugal, Adriana Cuoco; Bugarin, Maurício. Financiamento público e privado de campanhas eleitorais: efeitos sobre bem-estar social e representação partidária no Legislativo. *Economia Aplicada*, v. 7, no. 3, pp. 1–36, 2003, p. 4.

11. Ferreira, 2011, p. 99 ff.

12. *Cf*, for example, Portugal, Adriana Cuoco. *Lobby pré-eleitoral e financiamento público de campanhas eleitorais: uma exploração em economia política positiva*. Thesis (doctorate—Department of Economics). Brasília: Universidade de Brasília, 2006; Speck, Bruno Wilhelm. O financiamento de campanhas eleitorais. In: Avritzer, Leonardo; Anastasia, Fátima (Orgs.). *Reforma Política no Brasil*. Belo Horizonte: UFMG, 2006, pp. 153–158.

13. Samuels, David. Financiamento de campanhas no Brasil e propostas de reforma. In: Soares, Gláucio Ary Dillon; Rennó, Lúcio R. (Orgs.). *Reforma Política:* Lições da História Recente. Rio de Janeiro: FGV, 2006, p. 148.

14. Ibid.

15. Ibid., p. 147.

16. Velloso, Carlos Mário da Silva; Agra, Walber de Moura. *Elementos de Direito Eleitoral*. São Paulo: Saraiva, 2009, p. 223.

17. Sarmento, Daniel; Osório, Aline. Eleições, dinheiro e democracia. *Revista Brasileira de Direitos Fundamentais & Justiça*, v. 8, n. 26, pp. 15–38, 2014, p. 21.

18. Sanseverino, Francisco de Assis Vieira. Financiamento de campanha eleitoral—entre o público e o privado. In: Ramos, André de Carvalho. *Temas de direito eleitoral no século XXI*. Brasília: ESMPU, 2012, p. 269.

19. Schlickmann, 2018, pp. 59–60.

20. Cervi, Emerson Urizzi. Doadores, partidos e estratégias para o financiamento de campanhas eleitorais no Brasil: uma análise sobre o reduzido número de doadores e os elevados valores doados para os candidatos a presidente em 2014. *Política & Sociedade*, v. 15, n. 32, pp. 65–101, 2016, p. 95.

21. Villar, João Heliofar de Jesus. Corrupção: o ovo da serpente. Folha de S. Paulo, Jan. 4, 2010. Available at: https://www1.folha.uol.com.br/fsp/opiniao/fz0401201009.htm.

22. For an analysis of the application of proportionality by the STF in the *Legal Entity's Political Donation Case*, see Andrade Neto, João. *Borrowing Justification for Proportionality: On the Influence of the Principles Theory in Brazil*. Springer, 2018, p. 219.

23. *Citizens United v. Federal Election Commission*, 558 US_ (2010).

24. Dworkin, Ronald. The "devastating" decision. *The New York Times Review of Books*, v. 25, no. 3, v. 57, Feb. 25, 2010.

25. Jorge, André Guilherme Lemos; Soares, Michel Bertoni. Financiamento eleitoral por pessoas jurídicas: a influência do poder econômico sobre a democracia. *Revista de informação legislativa: RIL*, v. 54, n. 216, pp. 87–104, out./dez. 2017, p. 90.

26. Jorge; Soares, 2017, p. 91.

27. Schlickmann, 2018, pp. 59–65.

28. Souza, Bruno Cezar Andrade de. *Financiamento das campanhas eleitorais por pessoas jurídicas*: a ADI 4.650 à luz da Crítica Hermenêutica do Direito. Rio de Janeiro: Universidade Estácio de Sá, 2018.

29. Barcelos, Júlia Rocha de. Financiamento de campanha e participação: o financiamento coletivo na internet. In: Fux, Luiz; Pereira, Luiz Fernando Casagrande; Agra, Walber de Moura (Coord.); Peccinin, Luiz Eduardo (Org.). *Financiamento e prestação de contas*. Belo Horizonte: Fórum, 2018, p. 84 ff.

30. Jorge; Soares, 2017, p. 91.

31. Ibid., p. 92 ff.; Pitombo, João Pedro. Com restrições de campanha, partidos buscam peixes grandes para disputa. *Folha de S. Paulo*, Jul. 4 2016. Available at: https://www1.folha.uol.com.br/poder/2016/07/1788200-com-restricoes-de-campanha-partidos-buscam-peixes-grandes-para-disputa.shtml.

32. Decomain, Pedro. Influência do poder econômico e financiamento público de campanhas eleitorais. *Resenha Eleitoral*, v. 13, pp. 11–28, 2006, pp. 24–25.

33. Schlickmann, 2018, p. 65.

34. Dworkin, Ronald. *Taking Rights Seriously*. Cambridge, MA: Harvard University Press, 1978.

35. See other cases in Andrade Neto, 2018, p. 319 ff.

REFERENCES

Andrade Neto, João. *Borrowing Justification for Proportionality: On the Influence of the Principles Theory in Brazil*. Springer, 2018.

Barcelos, Júlia Rocha de. Financiamento de campanha e participação: o financiamento coletivo na internet. In: Fux, Luiz; Pereira, Luiz Fernando Casagrande; Agra, Walber de Moura (Coord.); Peccinin, Luiz Eduardo (Org.). *Financiamento e prestação de contas*. Belo Horizonte: Fórum, 2018.

Cervi, Emerson Urizzi. Doadores, partidos e estratégias para o financiamento de campanhas eleitorais no Brasil: uma análise sobre o reduzido número de doadores e os elevados valores doados para os candidatos a presidente em 2014. *Política & Sociedade*, v. 15, n. 32, pp. 65–101, 2016.

Decomain, Pedro. Influência do poder econômico e financiamento público de campanhas eleitorais. *Resenha Eleitoral*, v. 13, pp. 11–28, 2006.

Dworkin, Ronald. The "devastating" decision. *The New York Times Review of Books*, v. 25, no. 3, v. 57, February 25, 2010.

Ferreira, Lara Marina. O financiamento de partidos políticos e de campanhas eleitorais no contexto da reforma política brasileira. *Estudos Eleitorais*, v. 6, no. 1, pp. 91–110, 2011.

Jorge, André Guilherme Lemos; Soares, Michel Bertoni. Financiamento eleitoral por pessoas jurídicas: a influência do poder econômico sobre a democracia. *Revista de informação legislativa: RIL*, v. 54, n. 216, pp. 87–104, out./dez. 2017.

Portugal, Adriana Cuoco; Bugarin, Maurício. Financiamento público e privado de campanhas eleitorais: efeitos sobre bem-estar social e representação partidária no Legislativo. *Economia Aplicada*, v. 7, no. 3, pp. 1–36, 2003.

Portugal, Adriana Cuoco. *Lobby pré-eleitoral e financiamento público de campanhas eleitorais*: uma exploração em economia política positiva. Thesis (doctorate—Department of Economics). Brasília: Universidade de Brasília, 2006.

Samuels, David. Financiamento de campanhas no Brasil e propostas de reforma. In: Soares, Gláucio Ary Dillon; Rennó, Lúcio R. (Orgs.). *Reforma Política:* Lições da História Recente. Rio de Janeiro: FGV, 2006.

Sanseverino, Francisco de Assis Vieira. Financiamento de campanha eleitoral—entre o público e o privado. In: Ramos, André de Carvalho. *Temas de direito eleitoral no século XXI*. Brasília: ESMPU, 2012.

Santano, Ana Claudia. Como sobreviver na selva: fontes alternativas de financiamento de campanhas eleitorais. In: Pereira, Rodolfo Viana; Santano, Ana Claudia (Orgs.). *Conexões Eleitoralistas*. Belo Horizonte: Abradep, 2016.

Sarmento, Daniel; Osório, Aline. Eleições, dinheiro e democracia. *Revista Brasileira de Direitos Fundamentais & Justiça*, v. 8, n. 26, pp. 15–38, 2014.

Schlickmann, Denise Goulart. O fim das doações empresariais: o impacto do julgamento da ADI 4.650 pelo Supremo Tribunal Federal sobre o financiamento das campanhas eleitorais no Brasil. In: Fux, Luiz; Pereira, Luiz Fernando Casagrande; Agra, Walber de Moura (Coord.); Peccinin, Luiz Eduardo (Org.). *Financiamento e prestação de contas*. Belo Horizonte: Fórum, 2018.

Souza, Bruno Cezar Andrade de. *Financiamento das campanhas eleitorais por pessoas jurídicas*: a ADI 4.650 à luz da Crítica Hermenêutica do Direito. Rio de Janeiro: Universidade Estácio de Sá, 2018.

Speck, Bruno Wilhelm. O financiamento de campanhas eleitorais. In: Avritzer, Leonardo; Anastasia, Fátima (Orgs.). *Reforma Política no Brasil*. Belo Horizonte: UFMG, 2006.

Velloso, Carlos Mário da Silva; Agra, Walber de Moura. *Elementos de Direito Eleitoral*. São Paulo: Saraiva, 2009.

Villar, João Heliofar de Jesus. Corrupção: o ovo da serpente. *Folha de S. Paulo*, January 4, 2010. Available at: https://www1.folha.uol.com.br/fsp/opiniao/fz0401201009.htm.

Chapter 11

Home-Schooling and Religious Education in Brazil

Nina Beatriz Stocco Ranieri

INTRODUCTION

The regulation of religious education and home-schooling is not an unprecedented or recent topic in the history of education in Brazil. Since the proclamation of the Republic in 1889, legal debates on religion, freedom of education, and subsidiarity of the State's activities in the educational field have included, under different perspectives, discussions on secularism, home-schooling, compulsory school enrolment and public funding of confessional educational institutions under the strong influence of the Catholic Church.

The adoption of Catholicism as the religion of the Brazilian Empire and the consequent catechization promoted by the State apparatus, through public primary education, until the first Republican Constitution of 1891, are striking examples of the relations between Church and State. Even in Republican Brazil, the provision of religious education for optional enrolment in public schools was a constant in the Constitutions of 1931, 1946, 1967, and 1988. Along this route, from the end of the nineteenth century to the twenty-first century, draws attention to the fact that religious education was included in the curriculum of public schools by pressure from groups outside the educational field (the Catholic Church, religious entities, conservative wings), based on political-ideological arguments.[1] On the other hand, from the Constituent Assembly from 1823 to 1987/1988, debates on freedom of education have always had in the Catholic Church a traditional defender of the family's priority in the choice of the educational regime.

The current *Federal Constitution of 1988 [BR]* provides for religious education, with optional enrolment, during the normal hours of public elementary schools. Its offer must respect the cultural and religious diversity of Brazil, prohibiting any forms of proselytizing, as determined by the *National Education Act of 1996—NEA [BR]* (Law 9,396). With reference to home-schooling, there is no constitutional or legal permissive Brazilian legal system recognizing the lawfulness of its offer by the family as a way of meeting the duty to provide education and compulsory school enrolment. Nevertheless, several families have opted for this type of education, raising the role of the Judiciary.

The main national sources of Brazilian Education Law are the *Federal Constitution of 1988*, the *NEA of 1996,* and the *National Education Plan of 2014—NEP [BR]*. The Brazilian schooling system is decentralized and complex at each level; as a Federal State, Brazil's educational system comprises all the 26 states and 5.561 municipal systems in addition to those of the Union and of the Federal District. According to the *Federal Constitution of 1988*, education is a social and an individual right. In this light, education is a duty of the State and will be provided by all the federate entities, as set forth in article 205: "Education, which is the right of all and duty of the State and of the family, shall be promoted and fostered with the cooperation of society, with a view to the full development of the person, their preparation to exercise citizenship and their qualification for work." In relation to children and adolescents, the right to education has absolute priority. Not for other reasons, unlike other social rights, the right to basic education is compulsory, from 4 to 17 years old (*Federal Constitution of 1988*, article 208, I), and individuals at this stage are not given the option to exercise it or not; therefore it is free and must be universalized. This educational level includes early childhood education, primary education, and secondary school. Hence the correlated obligations of the other taxable subjects of the right to education: the State (which must promote, protect, and guarantee it), the family (who is responsible for promoting access to education) and society (which finances it), translated into fundamental duties.

In view of this situation, from 2017 and 2018, the history of Brazilian education gained new chapters on religious and home education, written by the STF, due to the decisions of the Court in two cases that aimed at an abstentionist attitude on the part of the State in educational matters: (a) Direct Action of Unconstitutionality *(Ação Direta de Inconstitucionalidade—ADI)* no. 4439, regarding the provision of religious confessional education in public schools, and (b) Extraordinary Appeal *(Recurso Extraordinário—RE)* no. 888815, related to home-schooling. In the first, the Court understood the constitutionality of the offer. In the second, the Court decided that, in the absence of a law that regulates the practice of home-schooling, there is, at the moment, no way to recognize it sufficient to supply the duty of parents with the education of their children.

In the case of religious education, what was at stake was the constitutionality of the provision of optional, confessional, religious education in public schools in the light of the secularity of the State and freedom of religion. In the case of home-schooling, the aim was to ensure that it was offered by the family, without the student attending public- or private school. The arguments against religious education in public schools were based on the principle of secularism (*Federal Constitution of 1988*, article 19, I); in home-schooling, in the principle of freedom of education and pedagogical conceptions (*Federal Constitution of 1988,* article 206, II and III), both of which requires the neutrality of the State in relation to religion and its participation, directly or indirectly, in the formation of citizens, through education (*Federal Constitution of 1988*, article 205). Both cases dealt with so-called educational rights, that is, with the right of the instruments that cover the range of state abstentions, with the use of the regime of freedoms and guarantees, of full effectiveness and immediate applicability. In a nutshell, consider the right to education as the gender of which the other educational rights are consequences. The right to education (gender) is fundamentally a right to promotion and protection, performed using positive actions. Now, educational rights (developments) have the function of defending liberties in the field of education, such as the freedom to learn, teach, use and disseminate thinking, the art and knowledge; the pluralism of pedagogical ideas and concepts, and the coexistence of public and private educational institutions; the democratic management of public education; optional religious education; university autonomy, and so on. This chapter aims to analyze the respective decisions, from which effects and impacts have not been clearly dimensioned yet.

THE CASE OF RELIGIOUS EDUCATION—ADI 4,439: SECULARITY AND FREEDOM OF EDUCATION

The main point discussed here was the role of the State in the religious education of children in public schools. The action started with the questioning, by the Attorney General's Office *(Procurador Geral da República—PGR)*, of the constitutionality of paragraph 1°, of article 11 of

Decree no. 7,107/2010, which expresses the ratification, by the National Congress, of the Concordat celebrated between Brazil and the Holy See in 2008. Its article 11, paragraph 1° provides: "§1°. Religious, Catholic and other religious denominations, with optional enrolment, constitute a discipline in the normal hours of public elementary schools, ensuring respect for the religious cultural diversity of Brazil, in accordance with the Constitution and other current laws, without any form of discrimination." As an education specialist notes, the article expresses what had never happened, not even during the Empire, when Catholicism was an official religion, and had seemed impossible since, in 1889, the Republican regime had abolished the State/Church relationship: "the worldwide leadership of the Catholic Church managed for the Brazilian State to sign a treaty with it that guarantees it special privileges, in political, fiscal, labour, educational and other terms."[2]

According to the PGR, it is forbidden for the public school to become a space for catechesis and religious proselytizing, Catholic or of any other denomination. Thus, secularism imposes on the State a neutral stance in relation to the different religious conceptions present in society, being forbidden to take sides in matters of faith, favor, or embracing of any belief, or group of beliefs. For this reason, according to the PGR, the only way to make the State's secularity viable with religious education in public schools viable would be through a non-denominational model, which included doctrines and social dimensions of different religions. Eighteen entities were admitted as *amici curiae* in the lawsuit, and among them, only seven spoke out against the PGR's request.[3] Due to the repercussion of the issue, before the trial, in June 2015 a public hearing was held in which about thirty religious and civil society entities participated; of these, twenty-three spoke out against religious confessional education in the public school system and eight in favor.[4] In September 2017, the Court, by a majority of 6 to 5 votes, judged the action, deciding on the constitutionality of confessional religious education. The arguments for and against used by the members of the Court were based on the same articles of the *Federal Constitution of 1988*, namely: 5, VI and VIII; 19, I and 210, paragraph 1, involving the harmonization of constitutional norms related to religious education, freedom of religion, and the principle of secularity of the State.

The Constitution determines that the Union, the States, the Federal District, and the Municipalities should not "establish religious cults or churches, subsidise them, hinder their functioning or maintain relations of dependency or alliance with them, except in the form the law, collaboration in the public interest" (*Federal Constitution of 1988*, article 19, I). The secular state is one in which government action is legitimized by popular sovereignty and not by religious power; its foundation is the secular, not sacred, conception of political power. Its corollaries are the formal separation between Church and State, state neutrality in religious matters, and the guarantee of religious freedom. The Constitution of the Federative Republic of Brazil of 1891 made the State secular (article 72, § 6), a principle maintained in all other Constitutions from 1934, 1937, 1946, 1967–1988 (article 19, I). In the field of education, the secularity of the State had, as an immediate consequence, the suppression of religious education in public schools, despite the strong pressure from political and Catholic sectors. In the 1934 Constitution, these sectors managed to include the provision of religious education provision in public schools, which now appears in all subsequent constitutional texts, always on an optional basis (note that this is the only mention made of a particular discipline in the Brazilian Constitutions).

The principles of religious freedom, the dignity of the human person, and the rejection of any form of discrimination also permeated all Brazilian Constitutions. The optional offer of religious education, in turn, is restricted to elementary education, during normal class hours (*Federal Constitution of 1988*, § 1°, art. 210).[5] The *NEA of 1996* (article 33, I) prohibits, according to the constitutional guideline of secularism, any form of proselytizing in the offering of religious[6] education and attributes to the state and municipal education systems the competence to definition of content, as well as for the qualification and admission of teachers. Coupled with these provisions to the principle of secularism of the State, the interpretation of unsuccessful votes, unlike that of the majority, was that religious education in public establishments cannot be confessional given the secular republican tradition. In support of this thesis, they argued that in the *Federal Constitution of 1988*, the principle of equality, freedom of religion, and freedom of worship are guaranteed among fundamental rights (article 5, VI and VIII).

According to the minority current, therefore, the request for unconstitutionality should prevail given that (i) in view of the secularity of the State, public spaces cannot be appropriated by religious entities; (ii) there is a breach of the principle of isonomy given that the confessional nature of teaching is related to the legal and ideological link between teachers and religious institutions, creating differences between lay and religious teachers in the public network; (iii) fostering tolerance and respect for differences requires plural religious training, in which the student has access not only to his own, but to the most diverse religious manifestations. Therefore, religious education in public schools could only be of a nondenominational nature, and it cannot be attached to any religion, nor intend to convey dogmas and beliefs of a specific religion. In the view of the majority current, the same articles guarantee the compatibility of the secularity of the State with religious freedom. First, because religious education is an individual subjective right and not a duty imposed by the State; secondly, because the constitutional text guarantees voluntary enrolment for religious education, which guarantees freedom of religion, and prevents the government from creating its own religious education, with a specific content for the discipline. Thirdly, it remains clear that the State is not only obliged to abstain and not interfere in the teaching of a certain belief, but also to guarantee the necessary means for religious education in public schools, in the broadest way, without discrimination, due to the freedom of each student to receive, if he/she wishes, religious education.

In the winning votes, the interpretation prevailed that the principle of secularism in Brazil is related to the view of invoking God in the preamble to the *Federal Constitution of 1988* ("God be praised"), and of several constitutional provisions, such as article 210, §1°, which would effectively allow religious proselytizing; article 226, §2, which provides for religious marriage with civil effects; article 5, VII, which provides for religious assistance in official entities. Another point worth noting in the foundation of this current is the conclusion that neutrality in the offer of religious education is not possible, since the dogmas of faith constitute its core, with its own structuring dogmas, postulates, methods, and conclusions. This core is fully protected by the freedom of belief, of each one of the diverse religious denominations; hence, according to this view, in respect to the uniqueness of each religion, there is no way to confuse religious teaching with the study of history, philosophy, or science of religions. The winning decision concludes that "It is in this context that the prediction of religious education must be understood: it is about taking advantage of the physical structure of public schools—as is widely available in the public space of hospitals and prisons, which are already used in partnerships—to ensure the free dissemination of beliefs and ideals of a religious nature to those who profess the same faith and voluntarily adhere to the discipline, maintaining the neutrality of the State in this matter." In short, according to the winning thesis: (i) religious education in public schools as an elementary school subject (for students aged 9 to 14) must be strictly optional and offered during normal school hours and (ii) the education systems may hire representatives of religions to teach the classes.

The STF's (Brazilian Supreme Court) decision creates several practical problems for the implementation of religious confessional teaching in state and municipal education systems. Until 2017, the year in which the Common National Curriculum Base (*Base Nacional Comum Curricular—BNCC*) was approved by the National Education Council (*Conselho Nacional de Educação—CNE*) in compliance with article 26 of the *NEA of*

1996,[7] religious education was regulated by the education systems (CNE Resolutions CEB nº 04/2010 and nº 07/2010). With BNCC, religious education began to apply curriculum requirements, initial and continuing training courses, and didactic-pedagogical materials that contributed to the construction of the area, without confessional content. According to BNCC,[8] "an intercultural and ethical change of theoretical and pedagogical foundations of religious education, because it favors or recognizes and respects the histories, memories, beliefs, convictions and values of different cultures, religious traditions, and philosophies of life." Evidently, a decision by the STF alters the view of a common national basis for the discipline, given its confessional character; on the other hand, although it is not mandatory, religious education is a specific discipline of elementary education, being certain that there is no curricular component without defined content and without permission for teachers. Other problems have been foreseen by experts for a while now: religious propaganda during classes, the secondary treatment given to minority religions, such as the Afro-Brazilian ones, the growth of religious intolerance in schools, the lack of teachers' ability to teach the discipline.[9] Even more serious is the intertwining of religious confessional teaching with other curricular content, whether in the area of science, for example, in attempts to impose creationism to the detriment of evolution, or in attempts to prohibit the presence of sex education in basic education, as proposed at BNCC, or in other topics related to scientific research, as in the case of stem cell research, or even in discussions about the concepts of family, marriage, procreation, among other topics.

As a conclusion, one cannot fail to consider, as does Cunha[10] that the instrumentalization of the public school for the imposition of religious and political-ideological contents was a constant in our history, resulting from the weak autonomy of the educational field. This was also evident when the Legislative Decree that approved the *Brazil–Vatican Concordat* in 2010 was approved by the Chamber of Deputies, with a 66% vote of its members, including evangelical deputies. The fact that the Catholic Church was privileged was compensated by the future approval of the project of the General Law of Religions (*Bill of the House No. 160/2009 [BR]*), in which the mention of the Catholic Church was replaced by the expression "religious institutions." As a result of the tense correlation of forces, the Chamber of Deputies adopted a contradictory procedure: it approved the concordat, benefiting the Catholic Church, and the General Law of Religions, benefiting the Evangelical Churches; in the first, it approved confessional religious education, in the second, interfaith religious education. However, unlike the Concordat, which passed the legislative decree at an accelerated pace, the bill that would give Evangelical Churches the same political status as the Catholic

Church was abandoned to the vicissitudes of ordinary procedure, being filed by the Senate, without appreciation, at the end December 2018. It is another victory for the Catholic Church.

THE CASE OF HOME-SCHOOLING. RE 888,815: FREEDOM OF TEACHING AND PEDAGOGICAL CONCEPTS AND EDUCATION FOR THE TRAINING OF CITIZENS

In RE no. 888,815 the problem concerns the freedom of teaching and pedagogical concepts, with the legal possibility of a child being educated at home being at stake. By a majority of 8 to 2 votes, the STF, ruled in plenary, for the failure of the appeal; that is, the request made by the family that intended to offer home education to their daughter was not granted because although the practice is not prohibited by the Constitution, there is no law regulating its practice.

According to the votes of the winning chain, it was established that: "Home schooling is not a subjective public right of the student or his family, but its creation is not constitutionally prohibited by federal law, edited by the National Congress, in the modality "utilitarian" or "for circumstantial convenience," as long as the obligation is fulfilled, from 4 to 17 years old, and the family/State solidarity duty, the basic nucleus of academic subjects, is respected, supervision, although the practical evaluation and inspection by the Public Power; as well as other provisions imposed directly by the constitutional text, including with regard to the purposes and objectives of education; in particular, to avoid school dropout and guarantee the socialization of the individual, through extensive family and community coexistence (*Federal Constitution of 1988*, art. 227). The winner—the need for a specific law to implement the practice in Brazil, was achieved by a tiebreak. Of the ten ministers present at the trial, two of them manifested themselves through the appeal process (current overdue); four understand it to be an unconstitutional practice (current expired) and the others believe it is possible to offer home education, using the law. The tiebreaking vote was given by the President of the Court.

The appeal assessed by the STF originated in a writ of mandamus, dismissed both in the first instance and by the Court of Justice of the State of Rio Grande do Sul *(Tribunal de Justiça do Rio Grande do Sul TJ-RS)*, on the same grounds: there is no legal provision for teaching in this modality, there is no net and certain right to be protected. The family that appealed against the decision of the TJ-RS "understands that living with students of various ages does not reflect an ideal criterion of coexistence and socialization, whether for social or moral aspects, or for religious and even sexual aspects."[11] They maintain that "they are economically able to study at home, with the hiring of teachers for the various subjects and propose to take tests regularly, but they understand that they have the right not to attend the School because they disagree with the conventional and public education system."[12]

In Brazilian law, from the Empire to the Republic, home-schooling was never expressly prohibited. In the *National Education Act of 1961—NEA [BR]* (Law 4,024), the first law of national education, provided, in its article 2º, that "education is everyone's right and will be given at home and at school." The *Federal Constitution of 1988* transformed this scenario by instituting free and compulsory basic education (article 208, I). In addition, economic and financial changes that made it possible to control inflation, social policies that reduced poverty, and ensured satisfactory levels of income and employment for populations that traditionally walked on the margins of the country's development. In this set, in the specific case of education, new ways financing of compulsory education, the consolidation of large-scale evaluation policies, among other measures, were initiatives of undeniable scope.[13]

The term "basic education" is recent and innovative in Brazilian educational law. Introduced in the educational system by the *NEA of 1996,* it designates the group formed by early childhood education (for children from 0 to 5 years old), elementary education (from 6 years of age, lasting nine years) and high school (duration of three years), aiming "to develop the student, to ensure the common formation that is indispensable for the exercise of citizenship and to provide him with the means to progress in his work and in further studies" (article 22). The concept is unprecedented in Brazilian educational law and in the history of education since it articulates and organizes, in an organic and sequential way, the development of education at different times in the life of children and adolescents. The fact is extremely relevant, given that, in Brazil, the trajectory of basic education as a right—lagging behind the most developed countries and Latin America as a whole—was marked by the dominant features of our Catholic, agricultural, and slave culture, reflected in an elitist and selective education system, which suffered from a lack of organization.[14] To give an idea, the country became independent in 1822 with practically the entire population illiterate. In 1900, the literacy rate was 35%; in 1959, 49%; in 1990, 80%, with the percentage growth following the population growth (Coelho de Souza, 1999). In 2018, compared to about 208.5 million inhabitants, the illiteracy rate was 6.8%.[15]

Among basic education modalities, elementary education deserved greater protection when it was qualified by the constitutional legislator as a subjective public right and surrounded by specific requirements and guarantees (*Federal Constitution of 1988*, article 208, I).[16] With a duration of nine years, it starts, compulsorily, at the age of six, which does not remove the possibility of being offered even to those who did not have access to it at their own age (*Federal Constitution of 1988*, article 208, I).[17] Any citizen, group of citizens, community association, union organization, class entity, or other legally constituted and even the Public Prosecutor's Office, can call on the Public Power to demand it, and the corresponding judicial action (*NEA of 1996*, article 5; *The Child and Adolescent Statute of 1990—ECA [BR]* (Law 8,069) articles 54 and 208). If social and individual interests are unavailable, their defense may also be the subject of a writ of mandamus or injunction, in any court, instance or court, with the Public Prosecutor's Office legitimized to do so (*ECA of 1990*, arts. 98, I and 201, IX).

For the State, the specific nature of elementary education determines the primacy and priority of its attendance, in relation to the set of basic education (*NEA of 1996*, article 5, § 2). The omission or negligence in its attendance implies the responsibility of the competent authority (*Federal Constitution of 1988*, article 208, § 2; articles 98, I and 208, I). If the negligence is proven, the competent authority may be charged with a crime of liability. Courts have also determined the State's civil liability for the omission or neglect in the provision of compulsory education, in the latter case even in situations of harmful acts caused to the student under school custody, surveillance and protection. In order to ensure that no child fails to attend compulsory education, the constitutional legislator also determined that the Public Authority should register the students and ensure, with their parents and those responsible for attending school. The registration obligation extends to young people and adults (*NEA of 1996*, article 5, § 1, I; *ECA of 1990*, article 98, I). In order to guarantee the fulfillment of the compulsory education, the Public Power must create alternative ways of accessing the different levels of education, regardless of previous schooling (*NEA of 1996*, article 5, § 5). Public civil action against the Public Treasury is necessary to ensure educational conditions (*Federal Constitution of 1988*, article 129, III; *The Public Civil Action Law of 1985 [BR]*—Law 7,347, of 7/24/85 arts. 11 and §2nd, and 54, §1).

For the family, the specific legal nature of elementary education implies the obligation to enroll minors, from six years of age onward (*Federal Constitution of 1988*, articles 208, § 3 and 227; *NEA of 1996*, article 6, *ECA of 1990*, articles 4, 22, and 98). Public civil action is possible against the parents or guardians themselves (*Federal Constitution of 1988*, article 129, III; *The Public Civil Action Law of 1985*, articles 129, 155, and 156), in case of noncompliance with the constitutional norm, as well as the actions own private institutions, either in the face of noncompliance with the obligations inherent to parental power (*Civil Code [BR],* Law 10406 of 10/01/2002, article 1.634), or due to economic issues (prohibition of the private school to shut the student down in case of default of school fees). The *Penal Code [BR]* (Decree-Law 2,848/1940) in turn, defines, in article 246, as a crime against family assistance "failing, without just cause, to provide primary education for a school-age child." committing the penalty of "detention from fifteen days to one month, or fine, from twenty cents to fifty cents."

In this context, the issue related to home-schooling was brought to the STF covered three questions: (i) whether or not there is a constitutional prohibition on home-schooling; (ii) if there is no such absolute prohibition, what types of home education would be allowed; (iii) if there is no prohibition, if home-schooling is self-applicable or if it needs regulation by the National Congress. The first question was resolved by the Court based on articles 226, 227, and 229 of the *Federal Constitution of 1988*, which deal with the family, child, adolescent, and youth, and in articles 205, 206, and 208, which discipline education, concluding that there is no absolute prohibition on home education. For the Court, the Constitution requires the family and the State to show solidarity in the formation of the individual and the citizen; in addition, regardless of whether it is public or private education, the same constitutional principles and norms related to education will be applied to its offer, including the plurality of pedagogical concepts and the observance of the common national curriculum base, with authorization and inspection by the Public Power. Therefore, the *Federal Constitution of 1988* only authorizes home-schooling that meets those requirements. In response to the second question, therefore, it remained fixed that "the species of radical unschooling, moderate unschooling and pure home-schooling, in any of its variations, will be unconstitutional, as they deny the possibility of solidary state participation, including the establishment of a basic inspection and evaluation nucleus."[18]

According to the STF's decision, the expression "radical unschooling" refers to the practice of home education totally free from State interference. In moderate unschooling, there is no prohibition on the provision of education by the State, but it is up to the parents, exclusively, to choose school education or home education with full freedom of content and method, without any state interference, and even state-owned supervision is prohibited. Finally, in pure home-schooling, it is understood that education is the primary task of the family and only subsidiary to the State.

The *Federal Constitution of 1988*, therefore, allows only "utilitarian" home-schooling, that is, one that aims to face religious situations, bullying, drugs in schools, violence, as long as it follows the same basic contents of public school and private school education, that allows supervision, inspection, and periodic evaluations, that is, that accompanies and fulfills the solidarity duty of the Family and State in educating children, adolescents, and young people, in constitutional terms. At this point, the STF's emphasis on solidarity between the family and the State in its duty to education is noteworthy:

> The fact that the family is also solidary in the duty to participate in education does not allow it to alienate the State, as well as the State you can never drive it away. This is not an option, because this solidarity … was a clear decision of the constituent legislator and it is for the benefit of the child, the youth, the adolescent. Neither State nor family can give up this coexistence, as it is a duty of both. Therefore, only the possibility of "utilitarian home-schooling" is allowed by the Federal Constitution, based on the Family /State solidarity duty, with legal regulation, with inspection, with periodic evaluations and observance of the constitutional purposes and objectives.

The family, therefore, in a situation of utilitarian home-schooling, assumes the direction and responsibility for the formal education of the child, without delegating it to public or private educational institutions.

Several problems emerge from this situation. What is the capacity of parents or teachers hired by them to achieve the broad objectives of education? According to article 1° of the *NEA of 1996*, "Education encompasses the formative processes that develop in family life, in human coexistence, at work, in education and research institutions, in social movements and civil society organizations and in cultural events." Furthermore, according to §2°, of the same article 1°: "school education must be linked to the world of work and social practice." Education, therefore, under the terms of the law, has a specific formative *iter* and content; would home-schooling have the capacity to encompass the countless factors that make up the long, complex, and arduous educational path of individuals? The answers to these and other questions will only be considered as home-schooling is implemented in the country.

One aspect little explored in the vote of the Ministers of the Court was, precisely, the right of minors to attend school. The point was raised in just one vote, without further elaboration.[19] From this perspective, the STF's decision did not take into account the prevalence of the principle of the primacy of the child over parental power, due to the ratification of the United Nations Convention on the Rights of the Child promulgated in Brazil by Decree No. 99.710/90.[20] In short, even if recognized, would the parents' ability to provide a good education be enough to deprive the child of the right to school? At this point, they are opposed (i) the right to attend school—the right of citizenship that materializes, in its entirety, in the public space, where the plurality resulting from human relations is expressed and, consequently, where the solidarity and *res publica* and (ii) the prevalence of the family over the State, under the invocation of article 226 of the Federal Constitution and article 26.3 of the Universal Declaration of Human Rights—UDHR, which states that the right to choose the type of education to be given to children belongs to parents, a winning argument in the light of freedom of education and pedagogical guidance (*Federal Constitution of 1988* article 206, I and II).

Finally, in relation to the third question, it was decided that home education will only exist if created and regulated by the National Congress, by means of federal law "as long as the requirement is met, from 4 to 17 years old, and the Family/State solidarity duty, the basic core of academic subjects, the supervision, evaluation, and inspection by the Government are respected; as well as other provisions imposed directly by the constitutional text, including with regard to the purposes and objectives of teaching; in particular, to avoid dropping out of school and guarantee the individual's socialization, through extensive family and community coexistence (*Federal Constitution of 1988*, article 227)."[21] It remains to be seen how the law will regulate practical issues of authorization and inspection of the activity, monitoring the BNCC, conducting exams and certification. On the other hand, it cannot be ignored that the *NEA of 1996* admits students to enter any grade or stage, except for the first year of elementary school, regardless of previous schooling, through an assessment made by the school, according to the regulations of the respective education system (article 24, II, c). This means that, at any time, the student may enter the regular school, as long as the knowledge acquired in home-schooling is admitted as valid, according to the results of the assessment.

In summary, home-schooling in Brazil is not prohibited by the *Federal Constitution of 1988*, but will only be recognized as sufficient to compulsory schooling after the enactment of a specific law. The process on going in the parliament of number 2401/2019, authored by the federal government, is aiming to regulate the offer of home-schooling.[22] According to the project, which affirms the parents' right to decide on the type of instruction that will be given to their children (article 2º), all registration, monitoring, evaluation, and certification of students will be the responsibility of the Ministry of Education. Thus, an exception is made to the federative teaching model, organized according to the creation and maintenance of schools by States and Municipalities. If the project is approved, the federal government, although not offering it directly, becomes responsible for basic education.

CONCLUSION

Confessional religious education and home-schooling are controversial and recurring themes. Considering the history of education in Brazil, both from the Empire to the Republic, consisted of regular, habitual practices, only restricted after the 1980s, in different ways and for different reasons. Under the *Federal Constitution of 1988* and *NEA of 1996*, the STF is currently considering: confessional religious education can be offered in public schools, without affront to the secularity of the State (ADI 4439); home-schooling, as long as regulated by law, may be accepted as a sufficient modality to attend mandatory education (RE 888,815).

Several problems have emerged in these cases. What is the scope of the freedoms questioned in view of the State's actions? If, in the case of religious education, the objective of the Brazilian government, when celebrating the Concordat, was to expand the State's participation in an area reserved for the private sphere that of the PGR was to prevent such an expansion. On the other hand, in the case of home education, the parents' objective was to expand the family's area of activity, by intending to directly offer elementary education to their daughter, while that of the State was to prevent such expansion. Furthermore, in guaranteeing social, generic, or instrumental rights, collisions of principles or norms are frequent, as is the case with secularism and teaching freedom, or between the freedom of pedagogical conceptions and education for training of the citizen. Which should prevail? Even more serious is the problem of the primacy of the right of the child or adolescent, in relation to religious or home-schooling.

HOW TO EVALUATE IT?

The answers to these questions are not simple and the issue has assumed special relevance because it involves constitutional matters. Not for other reasons, in both trials, the narrow winning margins standout—2 votes in the case of religious education and 4 votes in the case of home education, which confirms its complexity. Another point to be emphasized is the use of the same articles of the Constitution to justify, in the defeated and winning votes, the unconstitutionality and constitutionality of religious confessional and home education, respectively, which demonstrates that the debate developed mainly on the ideological level. From this point of view, we are facing *hard cases*, that is, lawsuits that cannot be subject to a clear rule of law and, therefore, allow greater discretion for the judge to indicate the legal solution of the social problem presented.

The STF's jurisprudence on the right to education took shape from the 2000s onward. Until then, there were very few cases brought before the Court that, directly, demanded protection for the individual or collective exercise of the right to education, except in cases related to payment of enrolment fees. After 2010, issues related to the financing and expansion of fundamental education by the States and Municipalities (Judicial Appeal in Extraordinary Appeal 410,715—5) were judged. Subsequently, the Court influenced the issuing of federal legislation (*The Federal Universities' Quotas Law [BR]*

Law 12,711/2012) governing the adoption of affirmative actions by federal universities, after the judgment of the Fundamental Precept Failure Statement (*Ação de Descumprimento de Preceito Fundamental*—ADPF) no. 186/DF and Extraordinary Appeal (*Recurso Extraordinário*—RE) no. 597.285/RS. As previously pointed out (RANIERI, 2008; 2009a; 2009b), some hypotheses may explain the phenomenon of this significant increase in actions: the strengthening of the protection of the right to education, with legal instruments appropriate to its implementation and characterization of elementary education as a public subjective right; the expansion of the activity of the Public Ministry by the *Federal Constitution of 1988* (articles 127 and 129), highlighting the defense of unavailable social and individual interests; and the consolidation of public civil action to defend collective interests.

The examples above are expressive. They demonstrate, in the first place, that the constitutional interpretation points to new ways of ensuring fundamental rights, in addition to promoting their strengthening and influencing the Legislative. Second, they reveal that, after the year 2000, the participation of the STF in the realization of the right to education was more efficient than that of the Legislative, a fact also proven by thematic researches related to educational legislative production between 1995 and 2010. But, if until then, in the STF, judicial demands related to the right to education prevailed, that is, demands related to positive material benefits to be guaranteed by the State, such as equal conditions for access and permanence in school, among others provided for in Brazilian legislation, the circumstances regarding religious confessional teaching and home teaching were entirely different. In those cases, it was about demands concerning rights in education, basically involving controversies related to the scope and limits of the relationship between State and individual freedom in education. With the respective decisions, the limits of private autonomy *vis-à-vis* the State were expanded in the field of education and, as a result, a new level in educational jurisprudence was reached.

Judicial decision is not discussed, it is fulfilled. In this minefield of religion and home-schooling, it will not be easy for public education systems to regulate the activities of public schools. The solution of the Ministry of Education to call for itself home education control does not seem to be satisfactory either, given its lack of action at the level of basic education, an area of exclusive competence of States and Municipalities. The effects of both STF decisions are yet to be assessed.

NOTES

1. CUNHA, LUIZ ANTÔNIO (2007) – *Sintonia oscilante: religião, moral e civismo no Brasil.* 1931/1997. Cadernos de Pesquisa, v. 37, n. 131, maio/ago. 2007. CURY, Carlos Roberto Jamil (2004). *Ensino religioso na escola pública: o retorno*

de uma polêmica recorrente. Revista Brasileira de Educação Set /Out /Nov/Dez 2004 No 27; pp. 183/191.

2. CUNHA, Luiz Antonio (2014) – *A laicidade em disputa: Religião, moral e civismo na educação brasileira*. Revista Teias v. 15, n. 36, 5–25 (2014), p. 17.

3. BRAZILIAN SUPREME COURT (2017) – The ADI 4,439's contests of decision.

4. BRAZILIAN SUPREME COURT (2017). Cf. the contents of the Public Hearing.

5. 'Art. 210—... § 1° Religious education, with optional enrolment, will be the discipline of the normal hours of public elementary schools.'

6. 'Art. 33—Religious education, with optional enrolment, is an integral part of the basic education of the citizen and constitutes a discipline in regular school hours of public primary schools, guaranteeing respect for Brazil's religious diversity, rejecting any form of proselytizing.'

7. "Art. 26. The curriculum of kindergarten, primary and secondary education should have a national base, to be complemented, in each teaching system and each school establishment, in part diversified, required by the regional and local characteristics of the society, culture, economy and of learners."

8. CONSELHO NACIONAL DE EDUCAÇÃO – CNE (2018). *Common National Curricular Base. Religious Education Area.*

9. FISCHMANN, Roseli (2012) – *Inconstitucional: o ensino religioso em escolas públicas em questão*. Notandum 28 jan-abr. CEMOrOC-Feusp / IJI-Universidade do Porto.

10. CUNHA, Luiz Antonio (2014) – *A laicidade em disputa: Religião, moral e civismo na educação brasileira*. Revista Teias v. 15, n. 36, 5–25 (2014): Estado, Educação Pública e Laicidade.

11. BRAZILIAN SUPREME COURT (2018) SUPREME COURT (2018) – The RE 888,815's contents of decision, p. 3–4.

12. BRAZILIAN SUPREME COURT (2018) SUPREME COURT (2018) – The RE 888,815's contents of decision.

13. RANIERI, Nina (2009a) – "The democratic state of law and the need to prepare the person for the exercise of citizenship, though education," Habilitation presented at the Faculty of Law of the University of São Paulo.

14. CURY, Carlos Roberto Jamil (2004). *Ensino religioso na escola pública: o retorno de uma polêmica recorrente*. Revista Brasileira de Educação Set /Out /Nov/ Dez 2004 No 27.

15. INSTITUTO BRASILEIRO DE GEOGRAFIA E ESTATÍSTICA – IBGE (2018).

16. "Art. 26. The curriculum of kindergarten, primary and secondary education should have a national base, to be complemented, in each teaching system and each school establishment, in part diversified, required by the regional and local characteristics of the society, culture, economy and of learners."

17. Two judicial processes in course in the STF question the beginning of elementary education at 6 years old: Direct Action of Constitutionality (ADC) (ADC) no. 17 and Action of Non-compliance of Basic Principle (ADPF) no. 272.

18. BRAZILIAN SUPREME COURT (2018) SUPREME COURT (2018) – The RE 888,815's contents of decision.

19. BRAZILIAN SUPREME COURT (2018) SUPREME COURT (2018) – The RE 888,815's contents of decision, p. 141.

20. "All actions related to children brought to the attention of administrative authorities or legislative organs should consider, primarily, the best interest of the child."

21. BRAZILIAN SUPREME COURT (2018) SUPREME COURT (2018) – The RE 888,815's contents of decision, p. 3–4.

22. Cf. Proposed Law no. 2401/2019. https://www.camara.leg.br/proposicoesWeb/prop_mostrarintegra?codteor=1734553&filename=PL+2401/2019

REFERENCES

Brazil-Vatican Concordat of 2010 (Decree no. 7,107/2010). Retrieved from http://www.planalto.gov.br/ccivil_03/_Ato2007-2010/2010/Decreto/D7107.htm

Brazilian Civil Code of 2002. Law 10406 of 10/01/2002. Retrieved from http://www.planalto.gov.br/ccivil_03/LEIS/2002/L10406.htm

Brazilian Penal Code of 1940 (Decree-Law 2,848/1940). Retrieved from https://presrepublica.jusbrasil.com.br/legislacao/91614/codigo-penal-decreto-lei-2848-40

Brazilian Federal Constitution of 1891. Retrieved from http://www.planalto.gov.br/ccivil_03/constituicao/Constituicao91.htm

Brazilian Federal Constitution of 1988. Retrieved from http://www.stf.jus.br/arquivo/cms/legislacaoConstituicao/anexo/Brazil_federal_constitution.pdf

Brazilian Supreme Court (2017). The ADI 4,439's contests of decision. Retrieved from http://redir.stf.jus.br/paginadorpub/paginador.jsp?docTP=TP&docID=15085915redir.stf.jus.br

Brazilian Supreme Court (2017). Cf. the contents of the Public Hearing. Retrieved from http://www.stf.jus.br/portal/cms/verNoticiaDetalhe.asp?idConteudo=293563

Brazilian Supreme Court (2018) Supreme Court (2018).—The RE 888,815's contents of decision. Retrieved from http://redir.stf.jus.br/paginadorpub/paginador.jsp?docTP=TP&docID=749412204

Child and Adolescent Act of 1990 (Law No. 8,069).—ECA. Brazil. Retrieved from https://presrepublica.jusbrasil.com.br/legislacao/91764/estatuto-da-crianca-e-do-adolescente-lei-8069-90

Conselho Nacional de Educação—CNE (2010). Decisions CNE/CEB nº 04/2010 and 07/2010. Brazilian Ministry of Education. Retrieved from: http://portal.mec.gov.br/dmdocuments/rceb004_10.pdf

Conselho Nacional de Educação—CNE (2018). *Common National Curricular Base. Religious Education Area.* Retrieved from http://basenacionalcomum.mec.gov.br/abase/#fundamental/a-area-de-ensino-religioso

Coelho de Souza, Marcelo.—*The Illiteracy in Brazil under Demographic Focus.* O Analfabetismo no Brasil sob enfoque demográfico. Julho, 1999. Retrieved from http://www.scielo.br/pdf/cp/n107/n107a07.pdf

Cunha, Luiz Antônio (2007). *Sintonia oscilante: religião, moral e civismo no Brasil.* 1931/1997. Cadernos de Pesquisa, v. 37, n. 131, maio/ago. 2007. Retrieved from http://www.scielo.br/pdf/cp/v37n131/a0437131.pdf

Cunha, Luiz Antonio (2014). A laicidade em disputa: Religião, moral e civismo na educação brasileira. *Revista Teias* v. 15, n. 36, 05–25 (2014): Estado, Educação Pública e Laicidade. Retrieved from https://www.e-publicacoes.uerj.br/index.php/revistateias/article/view/24381/17359

Cury, Carlos Roberto Jamil (2004). *Ensino religioso na escola pública: o retorno de uma polêmica recorrente.* Revista Brasileira de Educação Set /Out /Nov /Dez 2004 No 27; pp. 183/191. Retrieved from http://www.scielo.br/pdf/rbedu/n27/n27a12.pdf

Fischmann, Roseli (2012). *Inconstitucional: o ensino religioso em escolas públicas em questão.* Notandum 28 jan-abr. CEMOrOC-Feusp / IJI-Universidade do Porto. Retrieved from http://www.hottopos.com/notand28/05-16Roseli.pdf

Instituto Brasileiro de Geografia e Estatística—IBGE (2018). Indicadores. Retrieved from https://www.ibge.gov.br/indicadores

National Education Act of 1996 (Law 9,396). NEA. Brazil. Retrieved from https://www.planalto.gov.br/ccivil_03/Leis/L9394.htm

Public Civil Action Law of 1985—Law 7,347, of 7/24/85. Retrieved from http://www.planalto.gov.br/ccivil_03/LEIS/L7347orig.htm

Ranieri, Nina (2008). The states and the right to education in the constitution of 1988—Comments on jurisprudence in the Federal Supreme Court by Alexandre de Moraes, *Os 20 Anos da Constituição da República Federativa do Brasil*, São Paulo: Atlas, 2008, p.183.

Ranieri, Nina (2009a). The democratic state of law and the need to prepare the person for the exercise of citizenship, though education, Habilitation presented at the Faculty of Law of the University of São Paulo.

Ranieri, Nina (2009b). The Federal Supreme Court and international education law. In: Alberto do Amaral Junior e Liliana Jubilut (orgs.), *O STF e o Direito Internacional dos Direitos Humanos.* São Paulo: Quartier Latin.

Ranieri, Nina (2019). Brazil. In: *Handbook of Comparative Education Law: Selected Nations from Africa and the Americas.* Russo, Charles J. (ed.). Lanham, MD: Rowman & Littlefield Education, vol. 4, 2019, pp. 07–30.

United Nations (1989). Convention on the rights of the child. Retrieved from https://downloads.unicef.org.uk/wp-content/uploads/2010/05/UNCRC_united_nations_convention_on_the_rights_of_the_child.pdf?_ga=2.34130849.1407683776.1588699470-875580650.1588699470

Chapter 12

High Cost Medicines and Medical Treatments in the Supremo Tribunal Federal (Brazilian Supreme Court)

Fernanda Duarte and Rafael Mário Iório Filho

INTRODUCTION

The goal of this chapter is to explain and understand and how the Brazilian Supreme[1] Court (STF) has been deciding cases concerning the right to health—provided for in articles 6 and 196 of the 1988 Brazilian Constitution[2]—especially when dealing with the right to the population's access to high-cost treatments and/or medicines. The timeline considered is the post-Constitutional Amendment no. 45, promulgated on December 8, 2004, which established the institute of general repercussion[3] in article 102 paragraph 3º[4] in the Brazilian Constitution of 1988. The reason for choosing the timeframe from the emergence of general repercussion is therefore justified since the themes that emerge from the use of this procedural legal institute guide the decisions of the Brazilian Supreme Court on cases related to the right to health.

To accomplish this goal, we will move through three steps. First, we will present very briefly the legal design of the right of health in Brazil which works as the normative background of the judicial debates. Then we will showcase the Brazilian Supreme Court describing some procedural aspects necessary to understand the way the cases reach the court and that have impact in the extent of the decisions taken by the court. And finally we will present the most important cases dealing with this subject as well as the so called themes that were picked by the Brazilian Supreme Court as the legal controversies surrounding the issue.

RIGHT TO HEALTH IN BRAZILIAN CONSTITUTIONAL LAW (THE NORMATIVE FRAMEWORK)

In the Brazilian legal system, the right to health is enshrined in the constitutional text and it has a double aspect: according to articles 6 and 196–200,[5] it is considered as a fundamental social right of all the people and it is also seen as a duty of the State. And it is in line with the definition of health established in the Constitution of the World Health Organization—WHO.

> Health is a state of complete physical, mental and social well-being and not merely the absence of disease or infirmity. The enjoyment of the highest attainable standard of health is one of the fundamental rights of every human being without distinction of race, religion, politic al belief, economic or social condition. The health of all peoples is fundamental to the attainment of peace and security and is dependent on the fullest co-operation of individuals and States. The achievement of any State in the promotion and protection of health is of value to all. Unequal development in different countries in the promotion of health and control of diseases, especially communicable disease, is a common danger. Healthy development of the child is of basic importance; the ability to live harmoniously in a changing total environment is essential to such development. The extension to all peoples of the benefits of medical, psychological and related knowledge is essential to the fullest attainment of health. Informed opinion and active co-operation on the part of the public are of the utmost importance in the improvement of the health of the people. Governments have a responsibility for the health of their peoples which can be fulfilled only by the provision of adequate health and social measures.

This right reveals a very important complexity in the Brazilian constitutional dynamics because, as informed by Sarlet (2018, p. 676), it safeguards the effectiveness, as a *conditio sine qua non,* of the fundamental rights to life, to the dignity of the person, to physical integrity and mental health, to the environment, to education, to food, to housing, to privacy, to work, and so on.

The legal nature of the right to health is a social right (article 6º) or a second generation right[6] which means that it requires the State to act positively offering services in broad terms. It is an animus of effective protection in the pursuit of that right to the prevention and treatment of diseases, as well as an integrated right to protection from social risks and social security (Section II of Chapter II of Title VIII of the Brazilian Constitution).

The health benefits imposed on the Brazilian State are organized in the constitution as it follows. First, the constitution establishes in article 23, II,[7] that the governments of all federative entities in Brazil are responsible for taking care of health. It is worth noting that unlike the North American model, the Brazilian federative organization is a three tier structure encompassing not only the division between the Union, the Federal District, and States, but also the Municipalities, as can it be seen from articles 1° and 18.[8]

Secondly, article 24, XII[9] combined with article 30, II and VII[10] present as competing powers between federative entities the duty to legislate on the protection of health and as the duty of the municipalities to provide, with the technical and financial cooperation of the Union and of the State, health services for the population.

Third, the constitution organizes the model to operationalize and finance the provision of the right to health by the so-called Unified Health System (SUS). This system in the constitutional text is described in article 198[11] and it is regulated in Law 8142 of 1990 and Law 8.080 of 1990.

Finally, in order to understand the constitutional legal landscape of the right to health in Brazil, it is necessary to present the issue of the right to health as a subjective right.

In Brazil, legal doctrine establishes classifications of constitutional norms. One of the most popular one is concerned about the legal institute of effectiveness, in other words the effects that these rules will have on the legal and social order.

Therefore among the several existing classifications, we will present the most famous among our legal jurists, since it is the one adopted by the Brazilian Supreme Court—STF,[12] which is authored by José Afonso da Silva (1998, p. 262). According to Silva the Constitutional rules are classified as: full effectiveness standards, contained effectiveness standards, and limited effectiveness standards.

The rules of full effectiveness are those that are capable of producing all their effects since the Constitution comes into force. Thus, they do not require infra-constitutional regulation and have immediate, direct, and full applicability. For example: article 5°, II.[13]

The rules of contained effectiveness are those that like the ones of full effectiveness produce all their effects. However, they admit being restricted or contained in their effects by infra-constitutional legislation. Therefore, they have immediate and direct applicability, but since they admit restraint in their effects they might not have full effectiveness if the respective legislation is on force, for instance we can point the rule of article 5°, XIII.[14]

Norms of limited efficacy are those that need an infra-constitutional norm that will complement them for the broad production of their effects. Therefore, as long as the infra-constitutional legislation does not exist, they will not produce full effects, therefore, its applicability is indirect, mediated and reduced. For example: article 37, VII.[15]

Norms of limited effectiveness, such as institutional norms are still divided into (i) norms of an organizational principle in the structuring of public bodies, e.g. article 37, VII; and (ii) programmatic norms, in other words, norms that establish objectives to be achieved by the Constitution and which effectiveness is complemented with a set of actions or programs of the State, by the executive branch (public policies) and by the legislative branch (legislation), for example, right to housing or to health (article 6º).

Therefore it can be seen that the norms of social rights in general have the character of a programmatic norm due to their nature of requiring a set of positive benefits from the State to achieve housing for all or health for all, for example. However, it is not because they are programmatic that, due to the normative force of the constitution, in particular attributed to fundamental rights in article 5º§1º,[16] one should not attribute high effectiveness to these norms.

Thus, the right to health is not merely programmatic; it is a subjective right, subject to legal requirements. Sarlet explains (2018, p.646):

> Furthermore, as with fundamental rights in general, social rights also have a dual subjective and objective dimension. With regard to the first, that is, when social rights operate as subjective rights, the possibility of being enforceable (in favor of their respective holders) in relation to their recipients is at stake. Despite the difficulties and objections that are registered in this sphere (e.g., lesser density of the rules that define social rights, limits to the judicial control of public policies, dependence on the availability of resources, in other words, the impact of the so-called reserve of the possible) , there is, in the Brazilian case, a strong doctrinal and jurisprudential tendency (with emphasis here on the STF jurisprudence) towards the recognition of a definitive subjective right (therefore, generating an obligation of performance by the recipient) in terms of the existential minimum, conceived as a (fundamental) guarantee of the minimum material conditions for a life with dignity, which, in terms of greater incidence, is especially true in the cases of the right to health and to education.

This perspective is still reinforced by the Brazilian Supreme Court (AgR-RE 271.286-8 / RS):

> The subjective public right to health represents an unavailable legal prerogative guaranteed to most people by the Brazilian Constitution itself (article 196). It translates a constitutionally protected legal good, whose integrity the Government must, in a responsible manner, ensure that it is incumbent on formulating—and implementing—suitable social and economic policies aimed at guaranteeing access to citizens, including those with the HIV virus, the universal and equal treatment to pharmaceutical and medical-hospital assistance.

THE BRAZILIAN SUPREME COURT

Judicial institutions play important roles in complex societies, such as providing jurisdictional provision to citizens and managing conflicts in society. Weaknesses in their permanent duties can contribute to conflict becoming explicit violence and often unmanageable by law and the courts. This circumstance alone indicates the need for investigations into the social functions of the judiciary, especially those concerning the role of the judiciary in democratic societies and how this power builds its decisions and influences the effectiveness of the rule of law.

The Brazilian Supreme Court[17] is the highest court in Brazil with national jurisdiction over constitutional matters and its rulings cannot be appealed. The language of the Constitution states that the STF has "primary responsibility for safeguarding the Constitution.

Article 102[18] of the 1988 Constitution provides for the court jurisdiction and regarding matters of constitutionality, the court decides on extraordinary appeal, cases decided in sole[19] or last instance and the court has as well the power to try and to decide, as matters of original jurisdiction, direct actions of unconstitutionality of federal or state normative acts, or declaratory actions of constitutionality of federal laws or normative acts.

As Rosenn (2000, p. 293) explains:

> Brazilian judicial review combines the decentralized, incidental form of judicial review of a common law country like the United States with the centralized, abstract form of judicial review of civil law countries such as Germany and Italy.' Brazil's Constitution provides for both forms of judicial review. The constitutionality of federal, state, or municipal laws or decrees may be challenged incidentally in the course of litigation before any state or federal court. In addition, the constitutionality of any law or decree may be challenged in the abstract directly before the Supreme Federal Tribunal (STF), Brazil's highest court, or, in certain cases, before the state supreme courts (Tribunals of Justice).

As the Brazilian Supreme Court itself explains

> General repercussions—Procedural institute by which the STF reserves the judgment of subjects brought in extraordinary appeals that present relevant issues from the economic, political, social, or legal aspect and that go beyond the subjective interests of the cause. It was included in the legal system by Constitutional Amendment no. 45/2004 and regulated by articles 322 to 329 of the Internal Rules of the Brazilian Supreme Court and by articles 1,035 to 1,041 of the Civil Procedure Code (Law no. 13,105 / 2015). 2. Demonstration—The

> relevance of the constitutional issue that the appellant intends to assess must be demonstrated clearly and objectively in the extraordinary appeal and its analysis is the exclusive competence of the Brazilian Supreme Court (§ 3 of article 102 of the Constitution of the Republic and § 2 of article 1.035 of the Code Civil Procedure). 3. Representatives of the controversy—They are those appeals in which the legal issue discussed is identical and is reasonably repeated in the courts of origin, which can highlight them and identify them as representative of the controversy so that, forwarded to the higher courts, they have a uniform solution. The rapporteurs of these appeals in the higher courts are not, however, linked to them, being able to select other appeals as representative of the controversy (§§ 1, 4 and 5 of article 1.036 of the Code of Civil Procedure). 4. Paradigm Appeal—Extraordinary appeal—RE or extraordinary appeal with interlocutory appeal—ARE in which the question of law is brought up, highlighted or not by the courts of origin, and transformed into a topic of general repercussion by the justices of the Brazilian Supreme Court. 5. Theme—Autonomous procedural category, object of general repercussion, which arises with the judgment of the preliminary general repercussion. The information on existing themes and paradigm resources can be found on the STF website. 6. Judgment of the preliminary general repercussion—Judgment made by the STF on the existence, or not, of general repercussion of a given theme. The vote is usually held in the Virtual Bench, starting with the inclusion of the topic by the rapporteur, followed by the fields "constitutional issue," "general repercussion" and "reaffirmation of jurisprudence," which must be analyzed and voted on. The insertion of the theme in the Virtual Bench always takes place on Fridays and the other justices have a period of twenty days to vote (article 324 of the STF Internal Regulations). The general repercussion can be declared with a simple majority, that is, four votes are enough to define if the question has general repercussion. The absence of general repercussions, on the other hand, requires a qualified quorum, requiring eight votes to recognize it (§ 3 of article 102 of the Brazilian Constitution). The omissions are computed in favor of the existence of general repercussions. The result obtained at the Virtual Bench in the sense of affirming that the matter under judgment is of an infra-constitutional nature observed the simple majority of votes. This rule was modified by the Regimental Amendment n. 47/2012. Since then, according to the new wording of paragraph 2 of article 324 of the RISTF, the statement that a given issue has an infra-constitutional nature is verified based on the votes of 2/3 of the voting justices."

In short, the Brazilian system can be seen as a broad and complex scheme of judicial review, one might even say a quite complicated one.

On the other hand, the Federal Supreme Court caseload is a very heavy one. According to the *Supremo em Ação 2018 Report*[20] between 2009 and

2016, there were 723,579 cases in the court. In December of 2016, 57,437 were not decided yet. But in this same year, the court gave 117,426 rulings.

THEMES AND CASES REGARDING HIGH COST MEDICINES AND MEDICAL TREATMENTS IN THE BRAZILIAN SUPREME COURT

As we have stated earlier, we will explore the themes and their respective cases arising from the general repercussions[21] related to the issues of high cost medicines and medical treatments are since they represent the debate that goes under the court.

Altogether there are five themes to be dealt with as follows in sequence:

Theme 6—Duty of the State to supply high-cost medication to patients with serious illnesses who cannot afford to buy it.
Rapporteur: Min. Marco Aurélio
Leading Case: RE 566471

The problem exposed in this theme is in the leading case RE 566471. The question here is whether it would be constitutional in face of the principle of universality of health and protection of life for the public authorities to supply high-cost drugs to those who cannot afford them.

The court's position with the issuing of a thesis has not yet been defined, as the case files have been concluded for the decision since March 20, 2020.

Theme 345—Reimbursement to the Unified Health System—SUS of expenses with services to beneficiaries of private health plans.
Rapporteur: Min. Gilmar Mendes
Leading Case: RE 597064

The problem exposed in this topic reached the Supreme Court in RE 597064. According to article 32 of Law No. 9656/98. According to article 32 of Law No. 9656/98, the public authorities may be reimbursed by private health plans if any insured patient has used medical treatment by SUS.

It turns out that health plans refused to pay for treatment on the grounds that according to the Brazilian Constitution their participation in health would be supplementary and that of the public authorities would be primary. In other words, the government is obliged to provide treatment to those who seek it, with no obligation to reimburse the plans. In addition to this argument, the aforementioned article 32 was creating a form of costing for social security, which would depend on its own regulation so that it could become mandatory.

On the other hand, the public authorities argued that despite the medical treatment provided by SUS being universal, if it had occurred in a private hospital, it would be possible to recover it under penalty of illicit enrichment of health plans. In addition, article 32 did not create a tax source of funding, but a civil obligation to reimburse the public budget for the fulfillment of the contractual provision between the health plan and the beneficiary patient.

The Supreme Court, based on the theme of general repercussion, which summarizes the legal problem, established the following thesis which is equivalent to a binding decision: "The compensation provided for in article 32 of Law 9,656/98 is applicable to medical, hospital, or outpatient procedures funded by SUS and after 6/4/1998, ensuring the contradictory and broad defense, in the administrative scope, in all legal frameworks."

Theme 500—Duty of the State to supply medication not registered by ANVISA.
Rapporteur: Min. Marco Aurélio
Leading Case: RE 657718

This theme is present in the leading case RE 657718. The question is whether it would be the duty of the state, and may be authorized by the judiciary, given the duty to provide health, to supply medication not registered by the autarchy linked to the Ministry of Health ANVISA (National Health Surveillance Agency, in English), a body that, according to Brazilian legislation, is responsible for regulating, inspecting and approving the use of medicines in Brazil (article 8, paragraph 1 of Law No. 9782/99 and articles 1 and 12 of Law No. 6360/76).

The Supreme Court's thesis for the issue of this theme was:

> 1. The State cannot be compelled to supply experimental drugs. 2. The absence of registration with ANVISA prevents, as a general rule, the supply of medication by judicial decision. 3. It is possible, exceptionally, the judicial granting of medication without health registration, in the event of ANVISA's unreasonable delay in considering the request (a period greater than that provided for in Law No. 13,411 / 2016), when three requirements are met: (i) the existence request for registration of the drug in Brazil (except in the case of orphan drugs for rare and ultra-rare diseases), (ii) the existence of a drug registration with renowned regulatory agencies abroad; and (iii) the absence of a therapeutic substitute registered in Brazil. 4. Actions that demand the supply of drugs without registration with ANVISA must necessarily be filed with the Federal Government.

Theme 579—Improvement of the type of accommodation for inpatients by the Unified Health System—SUS through the payment of the respective difference.

Rapporteur: Min. Dias Toffoli
Leading Case: RE 581488

Another theme related to the costs of medical treatment concerns the so-called class difference that allowed an SUS patient to pay the differences in the values of standard treatment in order to have more privileged conditions for medical care.

This difference was prohibited by Ordinance No. 113/97 of the Ministry of Health. However, the issue reached the Supreme Court questioning the constitutionality of the ban.

The binding thesis defined by the leading case RE 581488 was: "It is constitutional the rule that prohibits, in the scope of the Unified Health System, hospitalization in superior accommodations, as well as differentiated care by a doctor from the Unified Health System itself, or by an accredited doctor, upon payment of the difference in the corresponding amounts."

Theme 793—Joint responsibility of federated entities for the duty to provide health care.
Rapporteur: Min. Luiz Fux
Leading Case: RE 855178

As we explained at the beginning of this text, the Brazilian Constitution of 1988 established the duty of providing health to citizens as a common competence (article 23). It appears that this constitutional command is, therefore, jointly and severally liable to appear as co-plaintiff in actions that demand health benefits.

In this theme of the leading case RE 855178, the Supreme Court established the following thesis which is biding:

> The federation entities, as a result of common competence, are jointly responsible for the provision of health care demands, and in view of the constitutional criteria of decentralization and hierarchization, it is the responsibility of the judicial authority to direct compliance in accordance with the rules for the division of powers and to determine reimbursement, who has borne the financial burden.

CONCLUSION

This work aimed to provide an overview of how the Brazilian Supreme Court has been deciding issues related to the fundamental right to health in the specific context of the provision of medicines and high-cost treatments.

As a conclusion, we would like to bring the theoretical category of semantic field that is constructed with the help of the Semilinguistic Discourse Analysis, of French origin, which has inspired our researches related to the decisions of the Supreme Court.

The Semantic Field

The idea of semantic field is related to the set of different meanings that a word (or a group of words) presents through the contexts in which it is used, revealing that words can refer to different realities within the same concept.[22] Considering that the same term has or can have several different meanings in the same text, depending on how it is used and which other words accompany it, the semantic field is formed by a group of words and their associated meanings. This is linked to the concept of polysemy. The semantic fields are often related to cultural attitudes about the objects that field describes.

In our research, considering the general repercussions themes and their cases we have studied, we identify the following terms that integrate the semantic field which informs the concept of high cost medicines and medical treatments in the Brazilian Supreme Court:[23]

> joint responsibility of federative entities for the implementation of health—duty of the state to provide medicine and/or treatment—health is presupposed to the life and to the dignity of the human being—medicine is on the list of ANVISA—reserve the possible as a state thesis for not implement the right to health—equal treatment of citizens' health.

NOTES

1. This paper is part of a broader context of research in which we are looking for the various meanings of Human Rights in Brazil, trying to establish its discursive significance and social representation through the use of legal lenses, especially tailored by the courts.

2. An English version of Brazil's Constitution of 1988 (with Amendments through 2014) is offered by Constituteproject.org with content generously provided by Keith S. Rosenn. https://www.constituteproject.org/constitution/Brazil_2014.pdf (last visited Mar. 14, 2020). A more current version is available from Brazil's Supreme Federal Court on http://www.stf.jus.br/repositorio/cms/portalStfInternacional/portalStfSobreCorte_pt_br/anexo/BrazilFederalConstitution_atualizadaataemenda99de2017Eletrni.._.pdf (last visited Mar. 14, 2020).

"CHAPTER II Social Rights Article 6. Education, health, food, work, housing, leisure, security, social security, protection of motherhood and childhood, and assistance to the destitute are social rights, as set forth by this Constitution. (CA No. 26, 2000; CA No. 64, 2010. SECTION II Health Article 196. Health is a right of all and a duty of the State and shall be guaranteed by means of social and economic policies aimed at reducing the risk of illness and other hazards and at the universal and equal access to actions and services for its promotion, protection and recovery. Accessed in: (https://www2.senado.leg.br/bdsf/bitstream/handle/id/243334/Constitution_2013.pdf?sequence=11&isAllowed=y).

3. "The General Repercussion is a procedural instrument inserted in the Federal Constitution of 1988, through Constitutional Amendment 45, known as the "Judicial Reform." The purpose of this tool is to enable the STF to select the Extraordinary Appeals (REs) that it will analyze, according to criteria of legal, political, social or economic relevance. The use of this appeals filter results in a decrease in the number of cases referred to the Supreme Court. Once the existence of a general repercussion is found, the STF analyzes the merits of the matter and the decision resulting from this analysis will be applied later by the lower levels, in identical cases. The preliminary of General Repercussion is analyzed by the STF Plenary, through a computerized system, with electronic voting, that is, without the need for a physical meeting of the members of the Court. In order to refuse the analysis of an RE, at least 8 votes are required, otherwise the matter must be judged by the Court. After the appeal's rapporteur launches his statement on the relevance of the topic, the other ministers have 20 days to vote. Abstentions in this vote are considered to be favorable to the occurrence of general repercussions in the matter." Reference: STF (Glossário Jurídico). Accessed in: (http://www.normaslegais.com.br/juridico/Repercussao-geral.htm).

4. Article 102. The STF is responsible, essentially, for safeguarding the Constitution, and it is within its competence: (CA No. 3, 1993; CA No. 22, 1999; CA No. 23, 1999; CA No. 45, 2004) Paragraph 3. In an extraordinary appeal, the appealing party must demonstrate the general repercussion of the constitutional issues discussed in the case, under the terms of the law, so that the Court may examine the possibility of accepting the appeal, and it may only reject it through the opinion of two thirds of its members. Accessed in: (http://www2.senado.leg.br/bdsf/bitstream/handle/id/243334/Constitution_2013.pdf?sequence=11&isAllowed=y).

5. Regarding the way statutes are cited, the Brazilian "article" would be equivalent to "section" in the United States. We have opted to use the Brazilian term "artigo" simply translated as the English "article," though without implying an intercultural approach to the meaning of the words in both legal cultures.

6. "The first generation of rights has also been complemented historically by the legacy of socialism, it is worth saying, by the claims of the underprivileged to a right to participate in "social welfare," understood as the goods that men, through a collective process, accumulate over time. It is for this reason that the so-called second generation rights, provided for by the welfare state, are the individual's credit rights in relation to the community. Such rights—such as the right to work, health, education—have the State as a passive subject because, in the interaction between government and governed, it was the collectivity that assumed the responsibility of serving them … Hence the complementarity, in the perspective ex parte populi, between the rights of first and second generation, since the latter seek to ensure the conditions for the full exercise of the former, eliminating or mitigating the impediments to the full use of human capabilities." (Lafer, 2006:127).

7. Article 23. The Union, the states, the Federal District and the municipalities, in common, have the power: (CA No. 53, 2006) II—to provide for health and public assistance, for the protection and safeguard of handicapped persons. Accessed in: (https://www2.senado.leg.br/bdsf/bitstream/handle/id/243334/Constitution_2013.pdf?sequence=11&isAllowed=y).

8. Article 1. The Federative Republic of Brazil, formed by the indissoluble union of the states and municipalities and of the Federal District, is a legal democratic state and is founded on: I—sovereignty; II—citizenship; III—the dignity of the human person; IV—the social values of labor and of the free enterprise; V—political pluralism. Sole paragraph. All power emanates from the people, who exercise it by means of elected representatives or directly, as provided by this Constitution. Article 18. The political and administrative organization of the Federative Republic of Brazil comprises the Union, the states, the Federal District and the municipalities, all of them autonomous, as this Constitution provides. (CA No. 15, 1996) Paragraph 1. Brasília is the federal capital. Paragraph 2. The federal territories are part of the Union and their establishment, transformation into states or reintegration into the state of origin shall be regulated by a supplementary law. Paragraph 3. The states may merge into each other, subdivide or dismember to be annexed to others or to form new states or federal territories, subject to the approval of the population directly concerned, by means of a plebiscite, and of the National Congress, by means of a supplementary law. Paragraph 4. The establishment, merger, fusion and dismemberment of municipalities shall be effected through state law, within the period set forth by supplementary federal law, and shall depend on prior consultation, by means of a plebiscite, of the population of the municipalities concerned, after the publication of Municipal Feasibility Studies, presented and published as set forth by law.

9. Article 24. The Union, the states and the Federal District have the power to legislate concurrently on: XII—social security, protection and defense of health. Accessed in: (https://www2.senado.leg.br/bdsf/bitstream/handle/id/243334/Constitution_2013.pdf?sequence=11&isAllowed=y).

10. Article 30. The municipalities have the power to: (CA No. 53, 2006) II—supplement federal and state legislations where pertinent; VII—provide, with the technical and financial cooperation of the Union and the state, health services to the population; Accessed in: (https://www2.senado.leg.br/bdsf/bitstream/handle/id/243334/Constitution_2013.pdf?sequence=11&isAllowed=y).

11. Article 198. Health actions and public services integrate a regionalized and hierarchical network and constitute a single system, organized according to the following directives: (CA No. 29, 2000; CA No. 51, 2006; CA No. 63, 2010; CA No. 86, 2015) I—decentralization, with a single management in each sphere of government; II—full service, priority being given to preventive activities, without prejudice to assistance services; III—participation of the community. Paragraph 1. The unified health system shall be financed, as set forth in article 195, with funds from the social welfare budget of the Union, the states, the Federal District and the municipalities, as well as from other sources. Paragraph 2. The Union, the States, the Federal District, and the Municipalities shall apply each year, to health actions and public services, a minimum amount of funds derived from the application of percentages

calculated upon the following: I—in the case of the Federal Government, the current net revenue for the respective financial year, which may not be less than 15% (fifteen percent); II—in the case of the States and of the Federal District, the proceeds from the collection of the taxes mentioned in article 155 and of the funds mentioned in articles 157 and 159, item I, subitem a, and item II, after deducting the portions remitted to the respective Municipalities; III—in the case of the Municipalities and of the Federal District, the proceeds from the collection of the taxes mentioned in article 156 and of the funds mentioned in articles 158 and 159, item I, subitem b, and paragraph 3. Paragraph 3. A supplementary law to be revised at least every five years shall establish: I—os percentuais de que tratam os incisos II e III do § 2º; II—the criteria for the sharing of funds of the Union earmarked for health and assigned to the States, the Federal District, and the Municipalities, and of funds of the States assigned to their respective Municipalities, with a view to a progressive reduction of regional disparities; III—the rules for supervision, assessment, and control of expenditures on health at the level of the Union, the States, the Federal District, and the Municipalities; IV—(revoked).Paragraph 4. The local managers of the unified health system may hire community health workers and endemic disease control agents by means of a public selection process, taking into account the nature and complexity of their duties and the specific requirements of their activity. Paragraph 5. Federal legislation shall provide for the legal regime, a nationwide professional minimum salary, the guidelines for Career Schemes, and the regulation of activities of community health workers and endemic disease control agents, and it shall be incumbent upon the Federal Government, under the terms of the law, to provide supplementary financial support to the States, the Federal District, and Municipalities, to achieve compliance with said minimum salary. Paragraph 6. In addition to the cases set forth in paragraph 1 of article 41 and in paragraph 4 of article 169 of the Federal Constitution, an employee whose activities are equivalent to those of a community health worker or an endemic disease control agent may be dismissed if he does not comply with the specific requirements stipulated by law for such activities. Accessed in: (https://www2.senado.leg.br/bdsf/bitstream/handle/id/243334/Constitution_2013.pdf?sequence=11&isAllowed=y) and (http://www.planalto.gov.br/ccivil_03/constituicao/constituicao.htm).

12. RE 249.970-RS. Rapporteur: Min. Celso de Mello. This precept of the Brazilian Federal Charter qualifies as a typical norm coated with restrained or restrictive efficacy, since, due to its own material content, it contemplates the possibility of the common legislator limiting the scope of the constitutional prohibition pertinent to civil prison, authorizing it o to exception the prohibitory clause in two unique cases: (a) non-payment of maintenance obligation and (b) depositary infidelity.

It should be noted, therefore, that the special qualification of this constitutional precept is considered, defined as a rule of contained effectiveness—as proclaimed by the magisterium of the doctrine (José Afonso da Silva, "Applicability of Constitutional Norms", p. 97, 1968, RT; Maria Helena Diniz, "Constitutional Norm and its Effects," p. 101, 1989, Saraiva, vg)—that the legal possibility for the National Congress to institute civil prison in cases of depository infidelity is based on the Constitution itself, whose normative authority cannot and nor should it be exposed to limitation mechanisms set out in international treaties, such as the San José Pact of

Costa Rica (American Convention on Human Rights). Accessed in: (http://www.stf.jus.br/arquivo/informativo/documento/informativo158.htm).

13. Article 5. All persons are equal before the law, without any distinction whatsoever, Brazilians and foreigners residing in the country being ensured of inviolability of the right to life, to liberty, to equality, to security and to property, on the following terms: (CA No. 45, 2004) II—no one shall be obliged to do or refrain from doing something except by virtue of law. Accessed in: (https://www2.senado.leg.br/bdsf/bitstream/handle/id/243334/Constitution_2013.pdf?sequence=11&isAllowed=y)

14. Article 5. All persons are equal before the law, without any distinction whatsoever, Brazilians and foreigners residing in the country being ensured of inviolability of the right to life, to liberty, to equality, to security and to property, on the following terms: (CA No. 45, 2004) XIII—the practice of any work, trade or profession is free, observing the professional qualifications which the law shall establish. Accessed in: (https://www2.senado.leg.br/bdsf/bitstream/handle/id/243334/Constitution_2013.pdf?sequence=11&isAllowed=y).

15. Article 37. The governmental entities and entities owned by the Government in any of the powers of the Union, the states, the Federal District and the Municipalities shall obey the principles of lawfulness, impersonality, morality, publicity, and efficiency, and also the following: (CA No. 19, 1998; CA No. 20, 1998; CA No. 41, 2003; CA No. 42, 2003; CA No. 47, 2005) VII—the right to strike shall be exercised in the manner and within the limits defined by a specific law. Accessed in: (https://www2.senado.leg.br/bdsf/bitstream/handle/id/243334/Constitution_2013.pdf?sequence=11&isAllowed=y).

16. Article 5. All persons are equal before the law, without any distinction whatsoever, Brazilians and foreigners residing in the country being ensured of inviolability of the right to life, to liberty, to equality, to security and to property, on the following terms: (CA No. 45, 2004) Paragraph 1. The provisions defining fundamental rights and guarantees are immediately applicable. Accessed in: (https://www2.senado.leg.br/bdsf/bitstream/handle/id/243334/Constitution_2013.pdf?sequence=11&isAllowed=y).

17. Considering its members, the Court has 11 Justices, which are called in Portuguese as *Ministro,* chosen from citizens between the ages of thirty-five and sixty-five, with notable legal knowledge and unblemished reputations. The Justices are nominated by the President after the Senate's approval. They serve on the bench for lifetime but there is mandatory retirement at the age of 75, which is a general rule for all the judges in Brazil. Justices can be impeached by the Senate, according to article, 52, subsection II, of the 1988 Constitution.

Every two years, the members of the Supreme Court elect the Chief Justice (which is called the President of the Court) by secret ballot within its peers. A Vice-President is elected as well. Re-election for a consecutive term is not allowed.

The President of the Supreme Court is the third in the line of succession in the event of impediment of the President and Vice-President, or a vacancy in the respective offices.

The President of the court is also the President of the National Council of Justice (*Conselho Nacional de Justiça—CNJ*) which is in charge of controlling the administrative and financial functioning of the Judiciary and performance of judges' functional duties nationwide.

18. It is important to bear in mind that the court has jurisdiction over other criminal and civil cases too which could be considered as alien duties compared to its position as the defender of the Constitution. Altogether, article 102, has three subsections with 22 items. For example, in subsection I, "n" the Court has original jurisdiction over case in which all members of the Judiciary have a direct or indirect interest, and those in which more than half the members of the tribunal of origin are disqualified or have a direct or indirect interest. In subsection I, "o": the court is the mediator of Tribunals, arbitrating conflicts of jurisdiction between Brazilian national Higher Courts, such as the Superior Tribunal of Justice and any other tribunals, between Superior Tribunals, or between the latter and any other tribunal. On the other hand, in subsection I "b": the court has original criminal jurisdiction to try charges of common criminal offenses against the President of the Republic, the Vice-President, members of the National Congress, the Tribunal's own Ministers, and the Procurator General of the Republic. Accessed in: (https://www2.senado.leg.br/bdsf/bitstream/handle/id/243334/Constitution_2013.pdf?sequence=11&isAllowed=y).

19. According to the way jurisdiction is designed in Brazilian courts, "decided in sole" refers to a decision made by a higher court at first and in respect of which there is no provision for appeal, meaning that the case starts and finishes at the same court.

20. This report was produced by CNJ. Accessed in: (https://www.cnj.jus.br/wp-content/uploads/2017/06/fd55c3e8cece47d9945bf147a7a6e985.pdf).

21. On the STF website for the research entry "Repercussão Geral" (which might roughly be translated into English as general repercussions: http://portal.stf.jus.br/repercussaogeral/), we have used the keywords *medicamento de alto custo* e *tratamento de alto custo* (high cost medicines and high cost treatment). We have checked our results three times in order to avoid missing cases. (Dates: April 13th, April 17th, April 25th 2020).

22. A semantic field does not just reflect the ideas, values and perspectives of contemporary society; it crystallizes and perpetuates them too, socializing to future generations an already elaborated analysis of the experience through which the world will be understood. *See* Stephen Ullmann, *Principles of semantics* (1957) and Stephen Ullmann, *Semantics: an introduction to the science of meaning* (1962).

23. As possible development of this research, for instance, would be to focus on discussion of the meaning of these words in context, revealing the values, perspectives and representations adopted by the Supreme Court that could disclose the court's attitude towards religion and the law.

REFERENCES

Amado, Frederico. (2018). *Direito Previdenciário*. Salvador: Jus Podivm.

Barata, Rita Barradas; Chieffi, Ana Luiza. (2009). Judicialização da política pública de assistência farmacêutica e eqüidade. *Cad. Saúde Pública, Ago*, vol. 25, no. 8, pp. 1839–1849.

Barroso, Luís Roberto. (2018). *Curso de direito constitucional contemporâneo: os conceitos fundamentais e a construção do novo modelo.* São Paulo: Saraiva Educação.

Branco, Paulo Gustavo Gonet. (2018). *Curso de Direito Constitucional.* São Paulo: Saraiva Educação.

Brazil. Constitutional of the Federative Republic of Brazil. (1988). https://www2.senado.leg.br/bdsf/item/id/243334. Accessed 06 Apr. 2020.

Brazil. Conselho Nacional de Justiça. (2015). II Jornada de direito da saúde. Disponível em: https://www.cnj.jus.br/wp-content/uploads/conteudo/destaques/arquivo/2015/05/96b5b10aec7e5954fcc1978473e4cd80.pdf. Accessed 06 Apr. 2020.

Brazil. Lei n. 6360. Lei de Vigilância Sanitária sobre Produtos Farmacêuticos. (1976). http://portal.anvisa.gov.br/documents/33864/284972/lei_6360.pdf/5330c06d-1c17-4e1e-8d21-d7e3db4d3ce4. Accessed 06 Apr. 2020.

Brazil. Lei n. 8.080. Lei Orgânica da Saúde. (1990). http://www.planalto.gov.br/ccivil_03/leis/l8080.htm. Accessed 06 Apr. 2020.

Brazil. Lei n. 12.864. (2013). http://www.in.gov.br/materia/-/asset_publisher/Kujrw0TZC2Mb/content/id/30045029/do1-2013-09-25-lei-n-12-864-de-24-de-setembro-de-2013-30044994. Accessed 07 Apr. 2020.

Brazil. Lei n. 8.142. Dispõe sobre a participação da comunidade na gestão do Sistema Único de Saúde (SUS) e sobre as transferências intergovernamentais de recursos financeiros na área da saúde e dá outras providências. (1990). https://www.saude.mg.gov.br/index.php?option=com_gmg&controller=document&id=1444. Accessed 06 Apr. 2020.

Brazil. Lei n. 13.1305. Código de Processo Civil. (2015). http://www.planalto.gov.br/ccivil_03/_ato2015-2018/2015/lei/l13105.htm. Accessed 08 Apr. 2020.

Brazil. Ministério da Saúde. Portaria n. 113. (1997). http://bvsms.saude.gov.br/bvs/saudelegis/sas/1997/prt0113_04_09_1997.html. Accessed 07 Apr. 2020.

Carvalho Filho, José dos Santos. (2019). *Manual de Direito Administrativo.* São Paulo: Atlas.

Charaudeau, Patrick. (2006). *Discurso Político.* São Paulo: Contexto.

Charaudeau, Patrick. (2001). Uma teoria dos sujeitos da linguagem. In: Mari, H.; Machado, I. L; Mello, R. (eds.). *Análise do Discurso: fundamentos e práticas.* Belo Horizonte: NAD/FALE/UFMG, 2001, pp. 23–38.

Charaudeau, Patrick; Maingueneau, Dominique. (2004). *Dicionário de Análise do Discurso.* São Paulo: Contexto.

Charaudeau, Patrick. (2011). *Dize-me qual é teu corpus, eu te direi qual é a tua problemática.* Revista Diadorim/Revista de Estudos Linguísticos e Literários do Programa de Pós-Graduação em Letras Vernáculas da Universidade Federal do Rio de Janeiro. Volume 10, Dezembro 2011. http://www.patrick-charaudeau.com/Dize-me-qual-e-teu-corpus-eu-te.html. Accessed 29 Jan. 2020.

CNJ. (2017). *Supremo em Ação 2018.* https://www.cnj.jus.br/wp-content/uploads/2017/06/fd55c3e8cece47d9945bf147a7a6e985.pdf. Accessed 16 Jan. 2020.

Duarte, Fernanda; Iorio Filho, Rafael Mario (2005). *Supremo Tribunal Federal e Sociedade Brasileira: legitimando a desigualdade jurídica ou a diferença?* ANAIS da 25ª Reunião da Associação Brasileira de Antropologia.

Duarte, Fernanda; Iorio Filho, Rafael Mario. (2007). *Supremo Tribunal Federal: uma proposta de análise jurisprudencial- a igualdade jurídica e a imunidade parlamentar.* ANAIS do Conselho Nacional de Pós-graduação em Direito.

Duarte, Fernanda; Iorio Filho, Rafael Mario. (2009). *Imunidade parlamentar e análise de discurso jurisprudencial do STF*. Revista da Seção Judiciária do Rio de Janeiro. Rio de Janeiro, n. 25, pp. 353–375.

Duarte, Fernanda; Iorio Filho, Rafael Mario. (2010). *A gramática das decisões judiciais: entre a igualdade e a desigualdade jurídica.* ANAIS da Associação Brasileira de Ciência Política, Recife, 7o. Encontro.

Fausto, Boris; Fausto, Sérgio. (2014). *A concise history of Brazil.* Cambridge: Cambridge University Press.

Holmes, Stephen; Sunstein, Cass. (1999). *The cost of rights: why liberty depends on taxes.* W. W. Norton & Company: New York.

Iorio Filho, Rafael Mario; Duarte, Fernanda. (2010). *Por uma gramática das decisões judiciais.* ANAIS do Conselho Nacional de Pós-graduação em Direito, Fortaleza XIX Encontro.

Iorio Filho, Rafael Mario; Duarte, Fernanda. (2016). *A lógica do contraditório: ainda somos medievais.* In: Silva, Mário Luis Villarruel da (ed.). *Direito, discurso & poder* : plexos pela linguagem. Niterói PPGSD/UFF. https://www.academia.edu/14300522/A_lógica_do_contraditório_ainda_somos_medievais. Accessed 31 Jan. 2020.

Jacob, Cesar Augusto Alckmin. (2013). A "reserva do possível": obrigação de previsão orçamentária e de aplicação da verba. In: Grinover, Ada Pellegrini; Watanebe, Kazuo (eds.). *O controle jurisdicional de políticas públicas.* Rio de Janeiro: Forense, pp. 237–289.

Lafer, Celso. (2006). *A reconstrução dos direitos humanos: um diálogo com o pensamento de Hannah Arend*t. 6 ed. São Paulo: Companhia das Letras.

Levine, Robert M.; Crocitti, John J. (editors) (1999). *The Brazil reader: history, culture, politics.* Durham: Duke University Press.

Levine, Robert M. (1999). *The history of Brazil.* New York: Palgrave MacMillan.

O'Donnell, Guillermo. (1998). *Polyarchies and the (un)rule of law in Latin America.* Paper presented at the Meeting of the Latin American Studies Association, Chicago, September. http://lasa.international.pitt.edu/LASA98/O%27Donnell.pdf. Accessed 21 Jan 2020.

Pietro, Maria Sylvia Zanella Di. (2019). *Direito Administrativo.* Rio de Janeiro: Forense.

Mendes, Gilmar Ferreira; Branco, Paulo Gustavo Gonet. (2018). *Curso de direito constitucional.* São Paulo: Saraiva Educação.

Moraes, Alexandre de. (2018). *Direito Constitucional.* São Paulo: Atlas.

Ribeiro, Darcy. (2000). *The Brazilian people. The formation and meaning of Brazil.* Gainsville: University Press of Florida (translated by Gregory Rabassa).

Rosenn, Keith S. (2000). Judicial review in Brazil: Developments Under the 1988 Constitution. *Sw. J. L. & Trade Am.* vol. 7, p. 291. https://repository.law.miami.edu/cgi/viewcontent.cgi?referer=https://br.search.yahoo.com/&httpsredir=1&article=1169&context=fac_articles. Accessed 15 Jan. 2020.

Sarlet, Ingo Wolfgang; Marinoni, Luiz Guilherme; Mitidiero, Daniel. (2018). *Curso de direito constitucional*. São Paulo: Saraiva Educação.
Schwarcz, Lilia; Starling, Heloisa M. (2018). *Brazil. A biography*. New York: Farrar, Straus & Giroux.
Skidmore, Thomas. (2010). *Brazil. Five centuries of change*. New York/Oxford: Oxford University Press.
Silva, José Afonso da. (2005). Curso de Direito Constitucional Positivo. São Paulo: Malheiros.
Silva, José Afonso da. (1998). Aplicabilidade das normas constitucionais. São Paulo: Malheiros.
Ullmann, Stephen. (1957). *Principles of semantics*. Oxford: Blackwell.
Ullmann, Stephen. (1962). *Semantics: An introduction to the science of meaning*. Oxford: Blackwell.
World Health Organization. (1946). Constitution. https://www.who.int/about/who-we-are/constitution. Accessed 06 Apr. 2020.

Chapter 13

The Presumption of Innocence

José Duarte Neto

INTRODUCTION

There is a Brazilian tree with a smooth four to six-meter stem and small leaves that produces a berry-shaped fruit with a black peel and a white pulp. Its scientific name is *Myrciaria cauliflora*, and its fruit is known as *jabuticaba*. This name comes from *yawoti'kawa*, a native Brazilian language, and it is said to be produced only in Brazil. It is often invoked as a synonym, or a symbol, for what is both exuberant and unusual. Our judicial procedural system, the organization of our courts and judges and the powers and decisions taken by our high court, the Federal Supreme Court, are *not different* from other countries around the world. However, there are some particularities that, *among us* and in a symbolic common sense, are called *jabuticabas*. They are unique, unusual for other countries, and exuberant. For this reason, for a better comprehension of these specificities, the presumption of innocence will be contextualized in the constitutional text, in the Brazilian judicial appeals system and in the model of judicial review. These are subjects developed in the first three chapters. The last ones are intended to present the jurisprudence of our constitutional court on the subject and which, by the way, has been inconstant for the past thirty-one years, since the promulgation of the Brazilian Constitution of 1988.

The expressions in Portuguese for some procedural instruments and legal institutes are preserved in the text because some terms have no correspondence in English, and there was a risk of giving a different meaning to how our system works. The same happened to the abstract of the courts' decisions. There is not always an equivalent term to maintain the literality of the proclamations of the Judges or the Court. They are preserved in Portuguese as notes. When it was necessary, the institute was explained. Abbreviations were transcribed.

THE PRESUMPTION OF INNOCENCE AND THE FEDERAL CONSTITUTION OF BRAZIL

The Brazilian constitutional organization has produced eight enacted texts in its history in the years 1824, 1891, 1934, 1937, 1946, 1967 EC-1/69, and 1988. The presumption of innocence, or non-guilt, expressly entered only in the last enacted text. This is not to say that the previous Brazilian legal system did not know other democratic criminal procedural principles. The Federative Republic of Brazil adhered to the Universal Declaration of Human Rights of 1948 (article XI.1) and to the American Declaration of Rights and Duties of Man, which also makes it explicit (atricle XXVI). Both of them provide the presumption of innocence. There were other principles of a democratic criminal procedural law in the previous constitutions, in the previous ordinary legislation, and in the previous enforcement of decisions of the courts. The due process of law summarizes all them.

The presumption of innocence was confirmed alongside other rights in the second chapter of the Federal Constitution. The previous constitutions enunciated the rights after the chapters of the organization of powers. In the current constitution, the declaration of rights precedes the provisions on the organization of powers. The constituent's preference is at least symbolic. It symbolizes the option for overcoming an autocratic past, in which the quantity and quality of the positivized rights mark the democratic option and are placed as protection against an autocratic return. It is an explanation for the fact that it was only from 1988 onwards that the principle rose to constitutional hierarchy.[1]

For the same reason, in the Declaration of Human Rights of 1948 the "principle of the presumption of innocence" or "non-guilt" is proclaimed so that *"Everyone charged with a penal offence has the right to be presumed innocent until proved guilty according to law in a public trial at which he has had all the guarantees necessary for his defense"* (emphasis added), while in the Brazilian Federal Constitution it is stated in a way that *"no one will be found guilty until the* res judicata *of the condemnatory criminal sentence"* (atricle 5, item LVI), understanding *the res judicata* as the immutability of the condemnatory criminal sentence for the extinction due to exhaustion of the appeals (formal *res judicata*) and that has as a consequence the immutability of what is decided in the same and in another process (the external reflection of the decision's effects preventing that another litigant comes to discuss the same matter).[2]

It is not just a matter of semantic, because as it will be seen—impacted by our procedural and appeals system and by our judicial organization—the Federal Supreme Court will alternate the meaning of the presumption of innocence. Sometimes restricting constitutional freedom to a procedural moment, under the scrutiny of due legal process, when there is evidence that the defendant is guilty. Other times, extending it until the exhaustion of the different appeals in the Brazilian procedural system (*res judicata*).

The changing of meaning of the presumption of innocence in thirty-one years of constitutional jurisdiction is a constant, and the possibilities of a new hermeneutic shift can be real soon. The procedural period once the defendant is understood as guilty is an open question. It was always decided by the majority, and the question is not just theoretical, but also practical in essence. It affects the quality of the defendant's arrest (a procedural detention[3] or a detention due to the conviction) and the moment of the conviction sentence enforcement (from the factual demonstration of guilt or the exhaustion of appeals). It impacts the criminal justice system and the effectiveness of its decisions in a complex scenario in which an intricate appeals system converges, prisons overcrowded by prisoners without the formation of guilt (procedural detentions), decisions that take decades to pass judgment, and crimes that leave to be punished. There is frequent criticism in part of Brazilian society that the number of arrests is high, but the global analysis of decisions, which determines the deprivation of liberty, produces almost a consensus that its high number does not make criminal justice policy any better. It is not the best criminal policy to prevent and repress crimes.

At the center of this dispute, which is not only a problem of interpretation of the law, but also a criminal judicial policy, is the "presumption of innocence," At least it has a very relevant role.

THE PRESUMPTION OF INNOCENCE AND THE BRAZILIAN JUDICIAL APPEALS SYSTEM

The meaning of presumption of innocence (nonculpability) requires, for the reader not versed in Brazilian law, an understanding of its judicial organization, its appeals system, and its model of judicial review. As a fundamental right, the presumption of innocence is invoked, interpreted, and applied by the different courts. Sometimes, different interpretations occur due to a structure in which the principle of *stare decisis* does not predominate. Where the obedience of the appellate court and judges to the authority of precedents of their High Court occurs exceptionally. The procedural system of appeals also has an impact. As a general rule, the binding of judges and appellate courts to the precedents of their superior bodies occurs exceptionally. The appeals procedure is also a relevant variable. The existence of more or less appeals is linked to the brief or lengthy end of the process. The effects in which the appeals are received imply the possibility or not of the provisional enforcement of a conviction sentence. Finally, the judicial review model gives greater or lesser stability to the decision taken on the presumption of innocence. These are variables to be considered in order to understand it.

The Constitution (article 92, I–VII) establishes that the organs of the Judiciary are: a) Federal Supreme Court; b) National Council of Justice; c) Superior Court of Justice; d) Federal Regional Courts and Federal Judges; e) Labor Courts and Judges; f) Electoral Courts and Judges; g) Military Courts and Judges; h) Courts and Judges of the States, the Federal District and the Territories. The structure is composed at its apex by Courts, largely with appeal function (review) and at its base, generally, by judges with original jurisdiction to the disputes. Among the courts there is in the summit the Federal Supreme Court, which serves as guard of the Constitution and the defense organ of the Federation. Below it is the Superior Court of Justice with residual jurisdiction to protect federal law.[4] Besides that, there are the *appellate courts*, with jurisdictional review powers and the judges of first instance, mostly with original jurisdiction: the judicial systems of the States and the Federal District, and the federal, labor, electoral and military judicial systems. Most crimes, except military ones, are tried by the judges and Courts of Justice of the States and the Federal District or by the judges and the appellate courts of the Federal Justice. In this structure is important to highlight that a criminal case, in principle, can go through four judicial instances. The existing filter mechanisms cannot prevent them from easily reaching the Superior Court of Justice, with jurisdiction to protect federal law, and the Federal Supreme Court, with jurisdiction to guard the Constitution. Therefore, the definitive solution to a criminal controversy (*res judicata*) is time-consuming and costly.

Our procedural system supports two ways of reforming judicial decisions: appeals and lawsuits. Appeals are procedural instruments, addressed to other judicial authorities, within the same procedural legal relationship, searching for a new decision in order to modify the previous one; lawsuits consist of opening a new procedural legal relationship, different from the one in which the decision was attacked. There are two kinds of appeals to attack a judicial decision within the criminal proceeding: ordinary appeals and extraordinary appeals (*latu sensu*).

Ordinary appeals operate on factual and legal grounds. By factual nature, it is understood the occurrence of the criminal fact, the authorship, the illegality of the conduct, the guilt of the defendant and the punishment; by legal nature it is understood the interpretation of the criminal law and the constitution. Ordinary appeals are brought before Courts of Justice of the States and the

Federal District, Regional Federal Courts, Regional Electoral Courts, and Military Courts of Justice, depending on the subject. They are provided for in ordinary legislation (Penal Procedure Code—CPP) and not in the constitution. Ordinary appeals during the process are: the interlocutory appeal, or *recurso em sentido estrito* (articles 581–592 of the CPP), the appeal, or *apelação* (articles 593–692 of the CPP), the appeal requesting clarification of the decision, or *embargos de declaração* (articles 382–619 of the CPP), request for reconsideration, or *embargos infringentes* (article 690, CPP sole §), and the appeal to bring an appeal to a Court, or *carta testemunhável* (article 639). The difference among the appeals is marked by the type and nature of the decision, by the procedural moment when it is brought to the court (appeal or interlocutory appeal), by the refusal to admit the appeal (the appeal to bring an appeal to a Court) and by the existence of unanimity or majority when the decision is rendered by at en bench or panel (request for reconsideration).

The extraordinary appeals (*latu sensu*) perform on legal grounds and are filed to the Superior Court of Justice and the Federal Supreme Court. Facts are not part of the argument. The Federal Constitution provides for them. There are two extraordinary appeals: special appeal (Resp), filed to the Superior Court of Justice, and extraordinary appeal, filed to the Federal Supreme Court. The special appeal is undertaken to have a decision reconsidered about the interpretation of the federal legislation, while the extraordinary appeal is brought when it affirms an affront to the Constitution. The argument on appeals is limited to offending legal or constitutional rules.

The appeals in the procedural system have a double effect: the effect of giving back to the appellate court the possibility of modifying a given decision and the suspensive effect of preventing consequences with the decision pending the statement of the review court. Ordinary appeals generally have a double effect. The extraordinary appeals system, special and extraordinary, affords only with the devolutive effect. The existence of a suspensive effect on an appeal is important because it has the ability to bar the order of detention from a conviction.[5]

The criminal procedural system also has the presence of lawsuits to review decisions in the criminal process. *Revisão criminal* is one of them and lends itself to invalidate the condemnatory decision that became *res judicata* (articles 621 to 631 of the CPP—Penal Procedure Code). The most important of these, due to its historical nature as a speedy instrument for guaranteeing freedom, is the constitutional lawsuit of habeas corpus (article 5, LXVIII of the CF).

In a few words, when the Federal Supreme Court decides on the presumption of innocence, it decides on the procedural moment when a defendant ceases to be presumed innocent. In fact, it decides on the quality of the judicial organization and the criminal procedural system. It is not just a decision in the abstract, but about whether a judicial organization and a procedural system have technical capacity to guarantee the freedom of the defendant in the face of the accusation. In this sense, the reading of the judicial organization and the appeals system in the light of the clause of the presumption of innocence consists in understanding what the principle of due process of law represents (article 5, LIV da CF).

THE PRESUMPTION OF INNOCENCE AND THE MODEL OF JUDICIAL REVIEW OF CONSTITUTIONALITY

The Federal Supreme Court is the highest court of Brazilian Judiciary and its main function is to guard the Constitution (article 102 CF). In the exercise of its constitutional jurisdiction, by means of a historical series of decisions, with indisputable impact, it decided the content of the principle of the presumption of innocence (nonculpability): (a) right to freedom of movement for defendants in general, (b) decree of the arrest during the processing of procedural legal relationship, (c) exercise of jurisdiction by judges and court, (d) use of legal lawsuits and appeals, and (e) establishment of a judicial policy.

The understanding of its decisions recommends the comprehension of the exercise of constitutional jurisdiction by the Federal Supreme Court. The importance of constitutional jurisdiction is presented as an instrument to monitor the respect for constitutional supremacy and as a means of adjudging the correspondence between the constitutional text and the facts. The Constitution opted for a complex hybrid model of judicial review, which includes categories from both American and Kelsen system. The former is an abstract review: the textual interpretation of the rule rather than its application to real and legal controversies. The jurisdiction of abstract review is centralized in Federal Supreme Court. The latter has been exercised since the Constitution of 1891. The Court set aside the legislation considered incompatible with the constitution to solve a concrete controversy, which is why it is called concrete or incidental. The concrete judicial review is diffused and exercised for all courts. Depending on the model of judicial review, the effects of the decision are different. If in the incidental and diffuse model the decision taken has an indicative and a suggestive force for the other courts, in the abstract and concentrated control it has a binding effect, similar to *stare decisis.*

The Constitution of 1988 absorbed the advance of almost a century of judicial review. It provided for the incidental judicial review in article 102, III, conferring jurisdiction on the Federal Supreme Court to hear in extraordinary appeal cases decided in single or last instance, when the decision: (a) contradicts the Constitution, (b) declares an unconstitutional treaty or federal law,

(c) considers valid the law or act of local government contested in the light of the Constitution. The extraordinary appeal is the procedural instrument par excellence for the decision of the constitutional case. It is carried out as a conditioning issue of a dispute. The number of extraordinary appeals and habeas corpus are quantitatively relevant. It occupies a large part of the jurisdictional activity of the Federal Supreme Court.[6] The observation is important because the change in the jurisprudence on the presumption of innocence had occurred in habeas corpus filed. The main thesis is centered on the need or not to handle the extraordinary appeal and the special appeal to recognize the guilt to justify the issuance of an arrest warrant. The thesis would only be tried in an Abstract lawsuit in 2019.

In the abstract judicial review, the original wording of the constitution text created the Direct Action of Unconstitutionality, or ADI (article 102, I CF). Beside it, a lawsuit focused on deciding unconstitutional omissions, the Direct Action of Unconstitutionality by Omission, or AIO (article 103, § 2). The system of judicial review established already indicated a propensity or preference of the constituent for abstract judicial review. Under the Constitution enacted in 1988, this system evolved, being enriched and endowed with a growing tendency to this model of abstract judicial review. The first major transformation occurred with the Constitutional Amendment no. 3 of 1993. The Declaratory Action of Constitutionality (ADC) was created with jurisdiction concentrated in the Federal Supreme Court (article 102, I, a CF / 88), whose object was to declare the constitutionality of a federal law or normative act. There was an indispensable requirement for filing the lawsuit: the demonstration of a judicial controversy over the interpretation of a federal law or rule, which was not required in the Direct Action of Unconstitutionality (ADI). Still in 1999, the Allegation of Disobedience of Fundamental Precept (ADPF) was created, and the model of judicial review was complete.

The jurisprudence on the presumption of innocence is outlined in several habeas corpus in the years ranging from the enactment of the Constitution to HC 84.078/MG in 2009, when there was a change in understanding, what would also change in HC 126.292/SP (2016). A criticism that can be made to the decisions undertaken in this habeas corpus is the same that can be made to the incidental judicial review. The consequences of the decision, as a general rule, produce effect between the litigants involved in the dispute. It is the result of *res judicata*, and, for that reason, it does not supplant the case. They are not binding on other jurisdictions. Unlike in abstract judicial review, the decision that recognizes it produces *erga omnes* effects and it is binding on the other organs of the judiciary and public administration (article 102, § 2 of the CF). The final solution to the understanding of the presumption of innocence clause would only come with the judgment on the merits of ADCs 43 and 44, as will be seen next.

THE PRESUMPTION OF INNOCENCE FROM 1988 TO 2009

The clause of the presumption of innocence brought to the jurisprudence of the Federal Supreme Court the need to balance two variables: the need for the effectiveness of criminal jurisdiction and the protection of individual freedoms by the presumption of nonculpability while the criminal proceedings are in progress. As the procedural system has always had a large number of appeals and a complex judicial organization, in practice, the discussion was about the possibility and the conditions for the provisional judgment execution of a conviction sentence. In other words, the execution of a conviction judgment before *res judicata*.

The leading case was the HC 68.726, judged on June 28, 1991, under the report of Justice Nery da Silveira. The contention in the judgment was that the conviction judged on appeal by appellate court had been sufficient to issue an arrest warrant. The provisional execution of the sentence to the deprivation of liberty did not offend the presumption of innocence, provided that the principle of *due legal process* had been obeyed, because extraordinary and special appeals did not have suspensive effect. Both, without suspensive effect, did not have the strength to prevent the execution of the conviction. The based condemnatory decision was sufficient to promote the beginning of criminal execution. The procedural legislation that authorized the provisional sentence was approved by the Constitution of 1988, that is, it was in accordance with the principle of the presumption of innocence. The procedural legislation was constitutional.[7]

The two panels of the Federal Supreme Court, in successive trials, maintained the precedent. It issued two Abstracts that pacified the understanding,[8] summarizing the comprehension of the Court in its various jurisdictions. There was no need for *res judicata* to carry out acts of enforcement of the custodial sentence: the progression or application of a less severe regime of enforceable conviction. This precedent persisted in the Federal Supreme Court until 2009.

THE PRESUMPTION OF INNOCENCE AND HABEAS CORPUS 84.078/MG

In 2009, the jurisprudence of the Federal Supreme Court would undergo a new change that would also come from a habeas corpus. The action was brought to the first Panel of the Court and forwarded it to *trial at the bar*. The argument for the eleven justices' knowledge of the issue was that the two panels that make up the Federal Supreme Court differed under the exact interpretation of the presumption of innocence principle (or not culpability). While the second Panel followed Abstracts 716 and 717, some decisions issued by the first Panel understood that it would only be possible to start the execution of the conviction sentence after the final judgment (*res judicata*). The Federal Supreme Court, by a majority of votes, decided that the Penal Execution Law (L. 7,210/84) established that the enforcement of the custodial sentence would only take place after the *res judicata*. It was the legislation that, in principle, contradicted the Code of Criminal Procedure in the provision that, by not giving suspensive effect to the extraordinary and special appeal, made possible the provisional enforcement of the sentence. The wording of the provisions of the Penal Execution Law was compatible with the clause 5, LVII of the Federal Constitution (presumption of innocence), which would derogate from the possibility of provisional execution. Only *procedural detention*, with procedural reasons, could be enacted in the course of the process and before the final judgment. The right to ample defense encompasses all procedural stages, including extraordinary and special appeals. The execution of the sentence before its exhaustion implies undue restriction on the right to ample defense. The argument that the prohibition of arrests, after confirmation of the conviction by the second instance (appellate courts), allows the multiplication of appeals to the Federal Supreme Court, only serving the convenience of judges and justices, ignoring the interest of the defendant. In another trial, the Federal Supreme Court had the opportunity to judge that the suppression of civil servants' salaries was unconstitutional before the due legal process was exhausted and the sentence was final. If what is decided is applicable to property issues, greater weight is given to issues involving freedom. Criminals, under a democratic constitutional regime, are subject to law and are not procedural objects. The enforcement of custodial sentences is only after the final judgment.

Once again, the decision did not definitively closed the exact understanding of the presumption of innocence, it was made in the case of incidental judicial review and for a majority of votes, resulted from new appointments that changed the Justice in the Court.[9]

THE PRESUMPTION OF INNOCENCE AND HABEAS CORPUS 126.292/SP AND ARE 964246

In February 2006, the theme came back to the attention of the Federal Supreme Court in a hermeneutic turn. The question was raised legally due to the amendment of clause 283 of the Code of Criminal Procedure. The provision, as amended, added to the criminal procedural law the following words: *No one shall be arrested except in* flagrante delicto *or by written and reasoned order of the competent judicial authority, as a result of a final sentence or, in the course of the investigation or the process, by virtue of temporary imprisonment or preventive detention.* The previous article dealt with the time and place of detention and respect for the inviolability of the home. The reporter argued that even before the Federal Constitution of 1988, the Brazilian State had maintained the principle of the presumption of innocence, especially by adhering to the Declaration of Human Rights of 1948. The principle of the presumption of innocence requires that relevant doubts remain about the behavior contrary to the legal order. Before the conviction sentence by the judge, the principle of the presumption of innocence generates all the broadest effects, including as a burden of incrimination. At the time of the conviction, there was fragile, but existent, guilty plea arising from the evidence produced. For the judge only, the presumption of innocence is overcome, because he analyzed the facts and the evidence brought to the file. It is the condition for the conviction itself. However, the presumption of innocence persists when an appeal is made to the appellate court as a judicial review body. In the end, the assessment of the appeal exhausts the knowledge of the facts and the evidence produced. The issue is no longer taken up in special and extraordinary appeals. They do not authorize the review of facts and evidence and the justice or injustice of the specific case, serving only to guarantee the completeness of the system of norms of the legal system. These are objective, legal questions that transcend the litigant's subjective interest. As they do not open up the possibility of reviewing facts and evidence, they make relative the understanding of the presumption of innocence within the procedural legal relationship. The essential core of the presumption of innocence remains intact because it is exhausted during the production of evidence and its appreciation by the judges and appellate courts. From the end of the evidence stage and the assessment of the fact attributed to the defendant by judges and appellate courts, extraordinary and special appeals do not prevent the execution of the arrest warrant as established in a reasoned decision. England, United States, Canada, France, Portugal, Spain, and Argentina—according to a study by Luiza Cristina Fonseca Frischeisen, Mônica Nicida Garcia, and Fábio Gusman—admit the beginning of the enforcement of their conviction sentence after the decision of ordinary appeal. The overture to appreciation of extraordinary and special appeals, after the exhaustion of the ordinary appeal, does not ensure the presumption of innocence. On the other hand, it makes the criminal jurisdiction ineffective, which would be up to the Federal Supreme Court to rescue by changing its precedents. Finally, if there were any mistakes, they could be reviewed by handling appeals or suspending the effects of the sentence. It was time to regain the prestige and the traditional understanding of the Federal Supreme Court.

The majority of justices followed the reporter's vote and restored an old understanding of the principle of the presumption of innocence in the Federal Supreme Court.[10] The same understanding would be reflected in ARE964.246 of the reporter Justice Teori Zavaschi.[11]

THE PRESUMPTION OF INNOCENCE AND CONSTITUTIONALITY DECLARATORY ACTIONS (ADC) 43, 44 AND 54

The declaratory action of constitutionality was inserted in the constitutional text by the Constitutional Amendment no. 3 of 1993, which promoted an emergency tax reform. It is an abstract lawsuit destined to the declaration of constitutionality of law or federal norms,[12] considered a kind of direct action of unconstitutionality in reverse.[13] The declaratory action of constitutionality requires the evidence of a judicial controversy about the interpretation of federal law or norms. The need for judicial controversy, as an indispensable requirement for the filing of the lawsuit, had the ADC no. 1 as leading case, otherwise the court would be a mere consultation court. The L. 9,868/99 in clause 14, III establishes the need to demonstrate the judicial controversy for the filing of the lawsuit.

One characteristic of the declaratory action of constitutionality—as it is of the Direct Action of Unconstitutionality—is the possibility of issue a preliminary injunction about the application of the treated law (21 of L 9.868/99). The preliminary injunction implies the preventive suspension of processes and judgment in other jurisdictions. The purpose of the preliminary injunction is to promote legal certainty and guarantee the effects of the final decision.

As there was a serious judicial controversy over the application of 283 of the Code of Criminal Procedure and the presumption of innocence clause, three declaratory actions of constitutionality were proposed. The ADCs 43 and 44 were proposed in May 2016 by the National Ecological Party (PEN) and the Federal Council of the Brazilian Bar Association, and the third one was proposed in April 2018 by the Brazilian Communist Party (PCdoB). As they had the same object, they were gathered for joint judgment. The lawsuits were distributed to Justice Marco Aurélio who historically, since 2009, has maintained a broad and consistent interpretation with the extension of the presumption of innocence clause.

The lawsuits were taken to the bench to decide about the preliminary injunction. The reporter, Justice Marco Aurélio, was accompanied by the votes of Justices Rosa Weber, Ricardo Lewandovski, Celso de Mello, and Dias Toffoli. Justices Edson Fachin, Teori Zavaschi, Roberto Barroso, Luiz

Fux, Gilmar Mendes, and Carmen Lúcia. The majority of Justices reaffirmed the jurisprudence of habeas corpus 126.292/SP and ARE 964246.

Later, in May 2017, Justice Teori Zavascki died in an aircraft accident, and Justice Alexandre de Moraes was appointed to replace him. Taken the lawsuit to the decision of its merit, also by majority of votes, the court would return to the judgment in November 2019. The winning vote was of Justice Marco Aurélio accompanied by Justices Rosa Weber, Ricardo Lewandovski, Gilmar Mendes, Celso de Mello, and Dias Toffoli.

The judgment was neither published nor made available on the Court's website until the date of this writing (April 2019), but the decision is known for all. According to the winning vote, to make it possible to anticipate the enforcement of a conviction sentence is the same as to anticipate guilt. Guilt is condition of a conviction sentence and, according to the literal wording of article 5, LVII, its finding only occurs after the final judgment. The anticipation of enforcing a sentence always requires the guarantee of the return to the *status quo ante*, what is never possible when there is a criminal detention. Article 283 of the Code of Criminal Procedure is a mere reproduction of clause 5, LVII of the Constitution, inserted by the legislator in the criminal procedural law in 2011 due to the judgment in HC 84.078/MG. Meta-legal arguments cannot subvert the constitutional guarantee and arrest during the processing of the case happens only by procedural detention and upon reasoned decision. *The res judicata* is the safest framework for the beginning of the execution of the conviction sentence, but the problem grows when observing overcrowded prisons, recognized as an unconstitutional state of affairs in ADPF 347/2016. Article 283 of the Penal Procedure Code was constitutional because it complies with article 5, LVII of the Constitution. The Court, then, ordered the suspension of the provisional execution of the sentence and the release of those who were arrested due to the confirmation of the conviction at second instance (appellate court).

CONCLUSION

The objective developed in this chapter was to present how the presumption of innocence, a constitutional principle, is understood by the Federal Supreme Court. In the end, it is clear that there is no firm normative sense that gives certainty about the future of liberties and criminal jurisdiction in Brazilian society. Two positions were established and, due to the intensification of the debates in the trials, they can be said to be antagonistic. Between them, the Court has alternated its jurisprudence three times in ten years. In all of them, decisions were taken by a majority of votes. An unstable majority, of only one vote of difference, which explains the fear that alternating the composition of the Court may justify another turning point. It is known that the Court decides in the face of different variables: normative, institutional, ideological, political, economic, and social. There is a vast literature on. It was not what was pursued in this. The aim was to provide the foreign reader with a clear, systematic and understandable view of the presumption of innocence before the Federal Supreme Court and according to legal dogmatic canons. The purpose was achieved since it is concluded that, between two antagonistic understandings, the question is still open. Especially knowing that even if the decision was rendered in the abstract judicial review, the Federal Supreme Court is able to reconsider its jurisprudence, as long as there is "*a significant change in the factual circumstances or a significant change in the legal dominant concepts.*" One thing is right: every defendant has an entitlement to due legal process and is presumed not guilty until a judicial decision that substantiates their culpability is made. It still opened the question about the moment when a reasoned decision will have legal force to erode the presumption of innocence and justify the issuance of an arrest warrant (after the decision in an appeal or after the *res judicata*). Presumably, if there will be transformations in the conditions that justified the decision in ADC 43, 44 e 54, the meaning of the presumption of innocence can change.

NOTES

1. Canotilho, José Joaquim Gomes, et al. *Comentários à Constituição do Brasil* São Paulo: Saraiva, 2013, pp. 440–445; Bastos, Celso Riberto; Martins, Ives Gandra. *Comentários à Constituição do Brasil: promulgada em 5 de outubro de 1988*. São Paulo: Editora Saraiva, 1988–1989, v. II, pp. 277–279; Ferreira Filho, Manoel Gonçalves. *Comentários à Constituição Brasileira de 1988*. São Paulo: Saraiva, 1990, v. I, p. 70.
2. Grego Filho, Vicente. *Manual de Direito Processual Penal*. 9 ed. São Paulo: Saraiva, 2012, p. 753. ebook. Marques, José Frederico. *Manual de Direito Processual Civil*. São Paulo: Saraiva, 1974, v. III, pp. 231–235; Miranda, Pontes de. *Comentários ao Código de Processo Civil—articles 444 a 475*. 3rd ed. Rio de Janeiro: Editora Forense. Tomo V. pp. 96–116.
3. The procedural system provides for two forms of procedural detention. These are arrests that happen not on the basis of proof of guilt, but for reasons that are liable to guarantee the greater or lesser effectiveness of the criminal process. They guarantee to make the result of the process effective. Temporary detention (prisão temporária) is provided for the purpose of criminal investigation or when the perpetrator of the criminal fact does not provide evidence to identify him (L. 7.960/90). The preventive detention (prisão preventiva) is imposed during the process when the defendant's freedom threatens to harm public order, economic order, the application of criminal law or the probative evidence (Articles 311 to 316 of the Criminal Procedure Code).

4. Beside the Superior Court of Justice there are the Superior Labor Court, the Superior Electoral Court and the Superior Military Court with the same to defend national objective law specifically in matters of labor law, electoral law and military law.

5. Beside the Superior Court of Justice there are the Superior Labor Court, the Superior Electoral Court and the Superior Military Court with the same to defend national objective law specifically in matters of labor law, electoral law and military law.

6. The court itself produced statistics. Between 2000 and 2019, 414,902 (four hundred and fourteen thousand, nine hundred and two) extraordinary appeals and 58,545 habeas corpus were brought. In the same period, 36 Declaratory Actions of Constitutionality (ADC), 1639 Direct Actions of Unconstitutionality (ADI) and 355 *Allegation of Disobedience of Fundamental Precept* (ADPF) were brought Cf. Brasil. Federal Court of Justice. FTS statistics. Available at http://www.stf.jus.br/portal/cms/verTexto.asp?servico=estatistica&pagina=pesquisaClasse. Captured on 24/04/2020, at 8:00 am.

7. Habeas corpus. Sentença condenatória mantida em segundo grau. Mandado de prisão do paciente. Invocação do art. 5o, inciso LVII, da Constituição. Código de Processo Penal, art. 669. A ordem de prisão, em decorrência de decreto de custódia preventiva, de sentença de pronúncia ou de decisão e órgão julgador de segundo grau, é de natureza processual e concernente aos interesses de garantia da aplicação da lei penal ou de execução da pena imposta, após o devido processo legal. Não conflita com o art. 5o, inciso LVII, da Constituição. De acordo com o § 2o do art. 27 da Lei no 8.038/1990, os recursos extraordinário e especial são recebidos no efeito devolutivo. Mantida, por unanimidade, a sentença condenatória, contra a qual o réu apelara em liberdade, exauridas estão as instâncias ordinárias criminais, não sendo, assim, ilegal o mandado de prisão que órgão julgador de segundo grau determina se expeça contra o réu. Habeas corpus indeferido (STF—Tribunal Pleno—HC 68.726/DF—j. 28/06/191—votação unânime—rel. Néri da Silveira).

8. Súmula no 716: Admite-se a progressão de regime de cumprimento da pena ou a aplicação imediata de regime menos severo nela determinada, antes do trânsito em julgado da sentença condenatória.

Súmula no 717: Não impede a progressão de regime de execução da pena, fixada em sentença não transitada em julgado, o fato de o réu se encontrar em prisão especial.

9. Ementa: Habeas Corpus. Inconstitucionalidade da chamada "Execução Antecipada da Pena". Art. 5º, LVII, da Constituição do Brasil. Dignidade da Pessoa Humana. Art. 1º, III, da Constituição do Brasil. 1. O art. 637 do CPP estabelece que "[o] recurso extraordinário não tem efeito suspensivo, e uma vez arrazoados pelo recorrido os autos do traslado, os originais baixarão à primeira instância para a execução da sentença". A Lei de Execução Penal condicionou a execução da pena privativa de liberdade ao trânsito em julgado da sentença condenatória. A Constituição do Brasil de 1988 definiu, em seu art. 5º, inciso LVII, que "ninguém será considerado culpado até o trânsito em julgado de sentença penal condenatória". 2. Daí que os preceitos veiculados pela Lei n.º 7.210/84, além de adequados à ordem constitucional

vigente, sobrepõem-se, temporal e materialmente, ao disposto no art. 637 do CPP. 3. A prisão antes do trânsito em julgado da condenação somente pode ser decretada a título cautelar. 4. A ampla defesa, não se a pode visualizar de modo restrito. Engloba todas as fases processuais, inclusive as recursais de natureza extraordinária. Por isso a execução da sentença após o julgamento do recurso de apelação significa, também, restrição do direito de defesa, caracterizando desequilíbrio entre a pretensão estatal de aplicar a pena e o direito, do acusado, de elidir essa pretensão. 5. Prisão temporária, restrição dos efeitos da interposição de recursos em matéria penal e punição exemplar, sem qualquer contemplação, nos "crimes hediondos" exprimem muito bem o sentimento que EVANDRO LINS sintetizou na seguinte assertiva: "Na realidade, quem está desejando punir demais, no fundo, no fundo, está querendo fazer o mal, se equipara um pouco ao próprio delinqüente". 6. A antecipação da execução penal, ademais de incompatível com o texto da Constituição, apenas poderia ser justificada em nome da conveniência dos magistrados—não do processo penal. A prestigiar-se o princípio constitucional, dizem, os tribunais [leia-se STJ e STF] serão inundados por recursos especiais e extraordinários e subseqüentes agravos e embargos, além do que "ninguém mais será preso". Eis o que poderia ser apontado como incitação à "jurisprudência defensiva", que, no extremo, reduz a amplitude ou mesmo amputa garantias constitucionais. A comodidade, a melhor operacionalidade de funcionamento do STF não pode ser lograda a esse preço. 7. No RE 482.006, relator o Ministro Lewandowski, quando foi debatida a constitucionalidade de preceito de lei estadual mineira que impõe a redução de vencimentos de servidores públicos afastados de suas funções por responderem a processo penal em razão da suposta prática de crime funcional [art. 2º da Lei n.º 2.364/61, que deu nova redação à Lei n.º 869/52], o STF afirmou, por unanimidade, que o preceito implica flagrante violação do disposto no inciso LVII do art. 5º da Constituição do Brasil. Isso porque—disse o relator—"a se admitir a redução da remuneração dos servidores em tais hipóteses, estar-se-ia validando verdadeira antecipação de pena, sem que esta tenha sido precedida do devido processo legal, e antes mesmo de qualquer condenação, nada importando que haja previsão de devolução das diferenças, em caso de absolvição". Daí porque a Corte decidiu, por unanimidade, sonoramente, no sentido do não recebimento do preceito da lei estadual pela Constituição de 1.988, afirmando de modo unânime a impossibilidade de antecipação de qualquer efeito afeto à propriedade anteriormente ao seu trânsito em julgado. A Corte que vigorosamente prestigia o disposto no preceito constitucional em nome da garantia da propriedade não a deve negar quando se trate da garantia da liberdade, mesmo porque a propriedade tem mais a ver com as elites; a ameaça às liberdades alcança de modo efetivo as classes subalternas. 8. Nas democracias mesmo os criminosos são sujeitos de direitos. Não perdem essa qualidade, para se transformarem em objetos processuais. São pessoas, inseridas entre aquelas beneficiadas pela afirmação constitucional da sua dignidade (art. 1º, III, da Constituição do Brasil). É inadmissível a sua exclusão social, sem que sejam consideradas, em quaisquer circunstâncias, as singularidades de cada infração penal, o que somente se pode apurar plenamente quando transitada em julgado a condenação de cada qual Ordem concedida (STF—Tribunal Pleno—HC 84.078/MG—j. 05.02.2009- maioria de votos—rel. Eros Grau).

10. Ementa: Constitucional. *Habeas Corpus*. Princípio Constitucional da Presunção de Inocência (CF, Art. 5o, LVII). Sentença Penal Condenatória Confirmada por Tribunal de Segundo Grau de Jurisdição. Execução Provisória. Possibilidade.

1. A execução provisória de acórdão penal condenatório proferido em grau de apelação, ainda que sujeito a recurso especial ou extraordinário, não compromete o princípio constitucional da presunção de inocência afirmado pelo artigo 5o, inciso LVII da Constituição Federal.

2. Habeas corpus denegado (STF—Tribunal Pleno—HC 126/292/SP—j. 17.02.2016– maioria de votos—rel. Teori Zavaschi).

11. The acronym ARE comprises an interlocutory appeal in the extraordinary appeal. In the case, it was decided on the general repercussion. The general repercussion is a requirement for appeal admissibility inserted by Constitutional Amendment 45/2004. As a requirement for admissibility, it is inserted as a matter of procedural order to be considered before analyzing the merits of the appeal. Absent the general repercussion, decided by 2/3 of the votes, the extraordinary appeal is not known. The general repercussion, alleged by the appellant and recognized by the STF, must be relevant and transcendent (beyond the interest of the litigants). Relevant from a political, social, economic and legal perspective and transcending from a qualitative and quantitative point of view. The general repercussion requires that the issue resolved transcend the interests conveyed in the procedural legal relationship (Sarlet, Ingo Wolfgang; Marinoni, Luiz Guilherme; Mitidiero, Guilherme. *Course on Constitutional Law*. 2012, pp. 837–843.

12. The Direct Action of Unconstitutionality has the object of declaring the unconstitutionality of a state and federal law or norm.

13. There were doubts as to whether it was possible to bring a Direct Action of Unconstitutionality to declare the constitutionality, although historically it has admitted a double result, in other words, for the declaration of constitutionality or unconstitutionality (Mendes, Gilmar Ferreira. *Direitos Fundamentais e Controle de Constitucionalidade: Estudos de Direito Constitucional*. 2ª ed. São Paulo: Celso Bastos Editor, 1999, pp. 233–264).

REFERENCES

Barroso, Luís Roberto. *O Controle de Constitucionalidade no Direito Brasileiro: exposição sistemática da doutrina e análise crítica da jurisprudência*. São Paulo: Saraiva, 2004.

Bastos, Celso Riberto; Martins, Ives Gandra. *Comentários à Constituição do Brasil: promulgada em 5 de outubro de 1988*. São Paulo: Editora Saraiva, 1988–1989. v. II.

Brasil. Supremo Tribunal Federal. Disponível em http://portal.stf.jus.br/.Capturado em 04/04/2020, às 8:00 horas.

Brasil. Supremo Tribunal Federal. Ação Declaratória de Constitucionalidade nº 1, do Tribunal Pleno do Supremo Tribunal Federal. Brasília, DF, de 27 de outubro de 1993. Revista Trimestral de Jurisprudência, Brasília, nº 157.

Canotilho, José Joaquim Gomes et al. *Comentários à Constituição do Brasil*. São Paulo: Saraiva/Almedina, 2013.

Cléve, Clèmerson Merlin. *A fiscalização abstrata da constitucionalidade no Direito brasileiro*. 2ª ed. São Pauulo: RT, 2000.

Duarte Neto, José. *Rigidez e estabilidade constitucional*. Belo Horizonte: Del Rey, 2010.

———. Independência e accountability judiciárias. In Pretto, Renato Siqueira De; Kim, Richard Pae; Teraoka, Thiago Massao Cortizo [Coord.]. *Federalismo e Poder Judiciário*. São Paulo: Escola Paulista da Magistratura, 2019.

Ferreira Filho; Manoel Gonçalves. *Comentários à Constituição Brasileira de 1988*. São Paulo: Saraiva, 1990. v. I.

Garner, Bryan A. [Editor in Chief]. *Black's Law Dictionary*. 7ª ed. St. Paul, MN: West Group, 1999.

Grego Filho, Vicente. *Manual de Direito Processual Penal*. 9ª ed. São Paulo: Saraiva, 2012. ebook.

Goyos Júnior; Durval de Noronha. *Dicionário Jurídico Noronha: inglês-português, português-inglês*. 5ª ed. São Paulo: Observador Legal Editora, 2003.

Marques, José Frederico. *Manual de Direito Processual Civil*. São Paulo: Saraiva, 1974. v. III.

Mendes, Gilmar Ferreira. *Direitos Fundamentais e Controle de Constitucionalidade: Estudos de Direito Constitucional*. 2ª ed. São Paulo: Celso Bastos Editor, 1999.

———. Controle Abstrato de Constitucionalidade: ADI, ADC e ADO: comentários à Lei n.º 9.868/99. São Paulo: Saraiva, 2012.

Mendes, Gilmar Ferreira; Branco, Paulo Gustavo Gonet. *Curso de Direito Constitucional*. 11ª ed. São Paulo: Editora Saraiva, 2016.

Miranda, Pontes de. *Comentários ao Código de Processo Civil—arts. 444 a 475*. 3 ed. Rio de Janeiro: Editora Forense. Tomo V.

Moraes, Alexandre de. *Jurisdição Constitucional e Tribunais Constitucionais: garantia suprema da Constituição*. São Paulo: Atlas, 2000.

Ramos, Elival da Silva. *Controle de Constitucionalidade no Brasil: perspectivas de Evolução do Controle de Constitucionalidade no Brasil*. São Paulo: Saraiva, 2010.

Sarlet, Ingo Wolfgang; Marinoni, Luiz Guilherme; Mitidiero, Guilherme. Curso de Direito Constitucional. 2012.

Veloso, Zeno. *Controle Jurisdicional de constitucionalidade: atualizado conforme as Leis 9868 de 10/11/1999 E 9.882 de 03/12/1999*. 2ª ed. Belo Horizonte: Del Rey, 2000.

Chapter 14

The Unconstitutional State of Affairs in Brazil's Prisons

Emerson Ademir Borges de Oliveira

THE STATE OF AFFAIRS

The expression "unconstitutional state of affairs" arises from a judgment of the Constitutional Court of Colombia, and it develops there, having been imported into Brazil in the judgment of ADPF 347, before the Federal Supreme Court.

Roughly speaking, it can be said that the "unconstitutional state of affairs" reveals a situation of political omission requiring a legal solution. "The generalization of illegality, that is, the illegality that is repeated round and round in the operations of the system of law, is a problem of law. The state of affairs identified as unconstitutional is, in fact, diffuse illegality."[1]

The "state of affairs" reveals a real situation, that is, a social contextualization, like a vivid photograph of that moment on a given theme, identifying all its characteristics. The expression itself is not political or legal, but merely descriptive about how things are, although it is still influenced by the observer.

In borrowing the expression of Germanic philosophy, what is intended is to identify that the contextualized object is in complete disagreement with the constitutional rules. That is, the factual characteristics of that system attack the Constitution in several different ways, drawing a model of diffuse violations to the point of making simple and feasible solutions impossible immediately. That is to say, solutions to be lent to the system require a series of measures to be gradually implemented.

"The Unconstitutional State of Affairs is characterized by the massive and widespread vulnerability of several constitutional rights that affect a significant number of people, and by the omission of the authorities that should act to stop the violations and adopt measures to guarantee and repair the violated rights."[2]

The problem with a major structural dispute, such as the questions that, as will be seen, involve the recognition of an unconstitutional state of affairs, is to establish contours about the performance of the Powers. The Judiciary, recognizing it, in fact has an awareness of the need to determine the adoption of certain measures, but in order to preserve executive and legislative autonomy. Thus, there is a borderline to circumvent judicial activism, preventing the recognition of the situation of diffuse unconstitutionality from generating judicious decisions that are intertwined in the realm of politics.

THE ORIGINAL COLOMBIAN CASES

The expression "unconstitutional state of affairs" appears for the first time in a decision handed down by the Constitutional Court of Colombia, in 1997, in *Sentencia de Unificación* 559/1997. Later, it was resumed in the *Sentencia de Tutela* 153/1998 and in *Sentencia de Tutela* 025/2004.

In the first decision to use the aforementioned expression, the Constitutional Court of Colombia operated a judgment involving the territorial distribution of teachers in the public network and the existence and connection of teachers to the *Fondo Nacional de Prestaciones Sociales del Magisterio,* a social security entity, intended to pay specific health benefits and actions to teachers.

Throughout the decision, the Court asserted the existence of several violations of the constitutional text, especially with regard to the inequality in the geographic distribution of teachers, with municipalities with a higher proportion and others with a smaller proportion, the use in greater or lesser scale of national treasury revenues to defray education expenses and the absence, in many places, of a social security system, despite the realization of discounts on teachers' salaries to, according to many municipalities, defray medical expenses. The lack of connection to the fund would imply a violation of the right to life, health, social security, and work.

In this assessment, the Court highlighted:

> The above figures show, then, that until now a very small percentage of teachers of the territorial order have been affiliated to the National Fund for Social Benefits of Teaching, a situation that allows us to warn that the irregularity reported by the teachers who are applicants here is not limited to the municipalities of Zambrano and Maria la Baja, but it betrays a general state of affairs. In this regard, it is important to mention that the Ministry communicates that of the 1,061 municipalities and 4 existing districts in the country, only 126 municipalities and the Capital District of Santa Fe de Bogotá have legally affiliated their

> educators to the Fund, which means that 935 municipalities and 3 districts have not yet complied with the necessary procedures for the registration of their teachers to the mentioned Fund.[3]

The issue that leads to the trial is the identification of various constitutional violations that could not be changed immediately, simply by virtue of the judicial decision. The broad and repeated state of violations would require, first of all, a gradual program of modifications, starting with the Court's warning to political powers about the need to adopt measures aimed at eliminating the factors that generate such a state of affairs in the most soon as possible.[4]

This would happen, especially, given the recognition that "a significant group of educators would be suffering unworthy treatment," which is difficult to solve and that would lead to the massive use of judicial demands, justifying the need for the Court to notify the irregular situation to public authorities, so that it can be remedied in a reasonable time.[5]

On a second occasion, the theme could be better developed by the Court, in the judgment of the *Sentencia de Tutela* 153/1998, when the Colombian prison system was on the agenda. According to the Court, the terrible conditions to which prisoners were subjected, including overpopulation, prevented them from enjoying minimum conditions of dignified life, such as the existence of adequate cells, sufficient water, health services, medical assistance, family visits in decorous conditions, among other rights.[6]

According to the Colombian Court, resocialization depends on the provision of means that guarantee their social reintegration, which is an obligation of the State, established in the Constitution and in the Penitentiary Code, including conditions for rest, work, education, health, communication with the visits and so on.

As pointed out, this time more precisely, the unconstitutional state of affairs, in this case, would remain clear in the face of general and structural violations: this corporation has made use of the figure of the unconstitutional state of affairs in order to seek remedy for situations of violation of fundamental rights that are of a general nature—insofar as they affect a multitude of people—and whose causes are structural in nature. That is to say that, as a rule, they do not originate exclusively from the requested authority and, therefore, their solution requires the joint action of different entities. In these conditions, the Court has considered that since thousands of people are in the same situation and that if they all came to the guardianship they could unnecessarily congest the administration of justice, the most appropriate thing is to issue orders to the competent official institutions with the in order for them to put into practice their powers to eliminate this unconstitutional state of affairs.[7]

Urges to stress that, for the Court, the situation, characterized by the serious deficiency in matters of public and essential services, violence, corruption, and other absences, results from a total omission by the State in the face of a clear and unequivocal situation, before which there was no effort solution, preferring to maintain the established social problem.

In *Sentencia de Tutela* 153/98, the Court decided to notify public authorities of the unconstitutional state of affairs, in addition to other more specific determinations, such as the need for the Ministry of Justice and Law to present a prison reform plan to "guarantee prisoners conditions of dignified life in its penalties."[8]

In addition to these, the decision handed down in *Sentencia de Tutela* 025/2004 stands out, in which the rights of displaced persons were discussed, that is, the internally displaced population, removed from their place of residence due to the violence. For the Court, the high rate of violation of constitutional rights for such a population indicates the need for urgent preferential treatment by the State. In addition, the Court has allowed associations representing such a population to take legal action to protect the rights of these people.[9]

According to the Colombian Court's recognition, the widespread violation of constitutional rights, capable of establishing an unconstitutional state of affairs, derived from several factors, such as the massive and widespread violation of constitutional rights affecting a high number of people, the prolonged omission of public authorities, adoption of unconstitutional practices that would hinder access to the Judiciary by these people, the absence of legislative and administrative measures to prevent the violation of such rights, the existence of a broad social problem requiring the intervention of several entities, coordinated actions and high level of resources and the risk of judicial congestion if all those affected sought individual protection from the Judiciary.

Several elements confirm the existence of an unconstitutional state of affairs regarding the situation of the internally displaced population. First, the gravity of the situation of violation of rights faced by the displaced population was expressly recognized by the same legislator when defining the condition of displaced person and highlighting the massive violation of multiple rights. Secondly, another element that confirms the existence of an unconstitutional state of affairs regarding forced displacement is the high volume of tutelage actions filed by the displaced to obtain the various aids and their increase. Thirdly, the processes accumulated in the present tutelage action, confirm that unconstitutional state of affairs and indicate that the violation of rights affects a large part of the displaced population, in multiple places in the national territory and that the authorities have omitted to adopt the required corrections. Fourth, the continuation of the violation of such rights is not attributable to a single entity. Fifthly, the violation of the rights of displaced persons rests on structural factors set forth in section 6 of this providence, among which the lack of correspondence between what the regulations say and the means to comply with them stands out, an aspect that acquires an especial importance when looking at the insufficient resources given the evolution of the displacement problem and the magnitude of the problem is seen in the face of the institutional capacity to respond in a timely and effective way. In conclusion, the Court will formally declare the existence of an unconstitutional state of affairs regarding the living conditions of the internally displaced population. For this reason, both national and territorial authorities, within the scope of their powers, will have to adopt corrective measures to overcome such a state of affairs.[10]

Likewise, the decision rendered by the Court established obligations for the public power, such as the establishment of a public policy to protect the fundamental rights of such population, indication of the percentage of resources of the national treasury to be applied and to establish a contingency plan in the case of insufficient resources.

It is important to emphasize that these are not the only three decisions in which the Court has recognized the unconstitutional state of affairs, deserving mention, the *Sentencia de Tutela* 68/1998, *Sentencia de Unifcación* 250/1998, *Sentencia de Tutela* 525/1999, and the *Sentencia de Tutela* 153/1998. However, even for a better definition of the scope of this analysis, we were careful to work with the first to deal with the theme and two others relevant in content and rationale.

In any case, as can be seen and as we have already seen, the decisions basically establish three requirements for the configuration of an unconstitutional state of affairs: i) the existence of a structural dispute, the mere inefficient protection of rights is not enough; ii) the occurrence of massive violation of fundamental rights, far beyond occasional affront; and iii) the deliberate omission of the Public Authorities regarding the cessation of this massive violation.[11]

THE CASE SUBMITTED TO TRIAL AT THE BRAZILIAN SUPREME COURT

On May 27, 2015, the Brazilian STF of Appeal was filed with the Fundamental Precept of Non-Compliance (ADPF),[12] which had come to receive number 347, by the Socialism and Freedom Party (PSOL), which had received the rubric of the constitutionalist Daniel Sarmento.

Based on the construction of Colombian jurisprudence, especially in *Sentencias de Tutela* 153/1998 and 025/2004, the action questioned the state of affairs of the Brazilian prison system, in the face of which patent, deep, and widespread violations of the Constitution fall. Brazil's prison system presented, as it were, the perfect laboratory for the identification of an "unconstitutional state of affairs," On August 27, 2015, the Court began the analysis of the Precautionary Measure, ending the trial on September 9 of the same year. The merits of the lawsuit, however, have not yet been analyzed.

Initially, based on the analysis of the Rapporteur, Minister Marco Aurélio, there is a catastrophic situation with regard to the Brazilian prison system, with violations not only to the Federal Constitution of Brazil, but also to the Law of Penal Executions, and to Articles 9.3 of the Pact International Civil and Political Rights Convention and 7.5 of the Inter-American Convention on Human Rights.

The list of situations giving rise to the state of affairs is extensive: overcrowding of cells, proliferation of contagious diseases, unhealthy and high temperature cells, absence of beds and mattresses for all prisoners, very low food quality, usually with supply of spoiled food or sour, lack of drinking water, lack of basic hygiene products, internal crime, including homicides, beatings, torture and sexual violence, serious offenses against minorities, such as sexual abuse practices, violent practices by state agents, absence of legal aid, education, health and work, existence of prisoners who have already served their sentences.[13]

The sum of offenses perpetrated, also, makes Brazilian prisons become "schools of crime," inserting common criminals in criminal factions from which they cannot escape until their own death, which, without a doubt, makes the recidivism index remains very high and the objective of social reintegration is frustrated. This is also due in large part to the lack of separation of prisoners according to their crimes and dangerousness.

According to data attached to the process, Brazil has the third largest prison population in the world, close to 600 thousand people in 2014 (currently around 800 thousand prisoners). As highlighted in the report, over twenty-five years there was a 650% increase in the prison population, generating a deficit of more than 200 thousand vacancies in the system. It urges to stress that the Brazilian prison population is made up of 41% of pre-trial prisoners, that is, who still await the judgment of sentence and appeals.

Women are presented with an even more serious situation, especially for pregnant women and mothers, with no nurseries, places suitable for pregnant women and new mothers, day care centers for children, absence of medical care and prenatal care, as well as newborns, lack of gynecological monitoring, and provision of basic hygiene items to inmates.

The clairvoyant state of affairs would attest to frontal violations of the Brazilian Constitution: principle of human dignity (article 1, III, CF); prohibition of torture and cruel, inhuman or degrading treatment (article 5, III);

prohibition of cruel penalties (article 5, XLVII, "e"); violation of the determination that sentences are served in different establishments, according to the nature of the offense, age, and sex of the convict (article 5, XLVIII); violation of respect for the physical and moral integrity of the prisoner (article 5, XLIX); violation of the presumption of innocence (article 5, LVII) and violation of social rights, such as health, education, and food (article 6).

In addition to constitutional violations, there is a violation of the Law on Criminal Executions (Law 7,210/1984), especially with regard to the absence of a wholesome individual cell with a minimum area of six square meters; Complementary Law 79/94, given the nonuse of resources from the National Penitentiary Fund—FUNPEN, in the activities for which it was intended; and also the International Covenant on Civil and Political Rights, the Convention against Torture and other Cruel, Inhuman and Degrading Treatment and Punishment and the Inter-American Convention on Human Rights (Covenant San Jose de Costa Rica).

It is important to establish that, as recognized by the Federal Supreme Court, the "picture is not exclusive to this or that prison. The situation is similar in all units of the Federation, and the unequivocal bankruptcy of the Brazilian prison system must be recognized."[14]

As Barcellos (2010, 39) points out, "the inhuman treatment given to prisoners is not just a problem for prisoners: the free society receives the reflexes of this policy in the form of more violence."[15]

Under the Precautionary Measure, recognizing the responsibility of the Public Power for systemic violations and the role of the STF as guardian of the Constitution, including implying determinations when other Powers are violating the Constitution, a series of administrative measures were determined.

First, judges and courts were ordered, based on article 9.3 of the International Covenant on Civil and Political Rights and article 7.5 of the Inter-American Convention on Human Rights, to hold custody hearings within ninety days, which they would make it possible for the prisoner to be presented before a judicial authority within a maximum of twenty-four hours after the arrest was made. The main objective of the custody hearing is to avoid the maintenance of unnecessary prisons, especially when other precautionary measures can be taken, such as activity limitations, installation of electronic anklets, prohibition from attending certain places, or from approaching certain people, and so on.

The first custody hearing was held on October 14, 2015, in the Federal District, with Minister Ricardo Lewandowski, President of the Federal Supreme Court at the time.

Custody hearings or the immediate presentation of the prisoner to the judicial authority allow a better implementation of items LXV and LXVI of article 5 of the Constitution. First, because the judge, having contact with the case and the person, will be able to relax the illegal prison (hypothesis of illegal prison). Secondly, in case of unnecessary arrest, the judge will admit that the person is placed on temporary release, with or without bail, depending on other circumstances.[16]

Second, the Federal Supreme Court ordered the Union to release the balance of the National Penitentiary Fund so that it could be used for the purpose for which it was created, prohibiting the realization of new contingencies. Thus, the Fund's balance could be used to implement improvements in the prison system.

Finally, according to a proposal by Minister Roberto Barroso, the Court determined that the Union and States, in particular the State of São Paulo, forward information about their prison situations to the Court.

Despite the precautionary measures determined, and all the developments regarding the unconstitutional state of affairs, the lawsuit is still pending judgment on the merits.

CONSTITUTIONAL BASES OF THE DECISION

One of the most tormenting questions about the unconstitutional state of affairs concerns the limits on the Court's action, as an organ of the Judiciary, on legislative and administrative activities, that is, on the Legislative and Executive Powers.

The issue is, however, much deeper. Modern constitutionalism ends, as it were, the pursuit of the realization of the revolutionary triad—equality, freedom and fraternity—advancing on it and establishing the constitutional position very clearly and above the rest of the legal system. Along this same path, constitutional principles, rooted in constitutional supremacy, place the Constitution at the top of the Kelsenian pyramid.[17]

In this context of "constitutional totalitarianism,"[18] constitutional supremacy means that the rules below you must keep you compliant, as well as administrative acts. If, at first, the Constitution sought to limit the power of the monarch, nowadays it intends to guarantee rights to all, without distinction, including demanding from the State itself.[19] Hence, it is said that "the interpretation of the norm has meaning only if it is in tune with the social and organizational proposal of the Constitution."[20]

Faced with a picture of diffuse violations to the natural Constitution that classifies the situation as a very serious constitutional affront, hoping that the Judiciary will act beyond the mere acknowledgment of violation, but determine the adoption of public policies to remedy the unconstitutional situation.[21]

It is important to emphasize that, as the Colombian Court pointed out, in the *Sentencia de Tutela* 025/2004, the decisional content, when establishing obligations to the Public Power, would not constitute intervention in another Power:

In order to correct this situation, it is necessary that the different national and territorial entities in charge of caring for the displaced population fully comply with their constitutional and legal duties and adopt, within a reasonable time, and within the orbits of their competencies, corrective measures that ensure sufficient budget appropriation. By ordering this type of measure, the Court is not disregarding the separation of powers established by the Constitution, nor displacing the other authorities in the performance of their duties. On the other hand, the Court, taking into account the legal instruments that develop the policy of attention to the displaced population, as well as the design of the policy and the commitments assumed by the different entities, is appealing to the constitutional principle of harmonious collaboration between the different branches of power, to ensure compliance with the duties of effective protection of the rights of all residents in the national territory. That is the competence of the constitutional judge in a Social State of Law with respect to rights that have a clear performance dimension.[22]

The same logic had guided the judgment of the Brazilian Supreme Court. According to a report by Minister Marco Aurélio, "the technique of declaring the 'unconstitutional state of affairs' allows the constitutional judge to impose on the public authorities the urgent and necessary actions to remove massive violations of fundamental rights, as well as to supervise the effective implementation."[23]

Likewise, Amaral[24] asserts, to whom the allegation of reserve of the possible should be dismissed, from the economic point of view and the scarcity of resources, as well as of possible interference by the Judiciary on the other Powers. The realization of citizens' rights must be guaranteed by the Judiciary when not fulfilled administratively.

It is evident that special parsimony in judicial activity is recommended, especially in the case of an exceptional institute, since public policies are originally the responsibility of the other Powers. But when they fail to act and their inaction violates the Constitution, the Constitutional Courts are called upon to act and, as has been said, merely recognizing violations of the constitutional rule will not suffice.

Hence, we have already said that the application of the unconstitutional state of affairs, and its legal consequences materialized in the decision, must obey three criteria: i) the cases to be justified are exceptional; ii) the Judiciary must not establish determinations that, in practice, address strictly political contexts, being restricted to structural issues; iii) the measures determined are in the context of effective dialogue between public agencies, both in terms of their implementation and in terms of their inspection.[25]

It is necessary that the Constitutional Courts are guided by balance. The serious and repeated violations of fundamental rights do not justify the Judiciary taking ownership of the full elaboration of public policies. But it is essential that they act to unlock the channels for the realization of rights.

NOTES

1. In original: "A generalização da ilegalidade, ou seja, a ilegalidade que de volta em volta se repete nas operações do sistema do Direito, é um problema do direito. O estado de coisas apontado como inconstitucional trata-se, na verdade, de ilegalidade difusa." De Giorgi, Raffaele, and Diego de Paiva Vasconcelos. 2018. "Os fatos e as declarações: reflexões sobre o Estado de Ilegalidade Difusa". *Revista Direito & Práxis*, v. 9, n. 1, p. 490.

2. No original: "O Estado de Coisas Inconstitucional é caracterizado pela vulnerabilidade massiva e generalizada de vários direitos constitucionais e que atingem número significativo de pessoas, e pela omissão das autoridades que deveriam agir para fazer cessar as violações e adotar medidas para garantir e reparar os direitos violados." Taquary, Eneida Orbage de Britto, and Wangle Samuel Costa Leão. 2019. "O diálogo entre Colômbia e Brasil sobre o 'estado de coisas inconstitucional.'" *Revista de la Secretaria del aTribunal Permanente de Revisión*, y. 7, n. 13, p. 197.

3. In original: "Las cifras anteriores dejan ver, entonces, que hasta ahora un porcentaje muy reducido de los docentes del orden territorial ha sido afiliados ao Fondo Nacional de Prestaciones Sociales del Magisterio, situación que permite advertir que la irregularidad que denuncian los docentes aquí demandantes no se circunscribe a los municipios de Zambrano y Maria la Baja sino que delata um estado de cosas de carácter general. Al respecto es importante mencionar que el Ministerio comunica que de los 1.061 municipios y 4 distritos existentes en el país, únicamente 126 municipios y el Distrito Capital de Santa Fe de Bogotá han afiliado legalmente a sus educadores al Fondo, lo cual significa que 935 municipios y 3 distritos aún no han cumplido con los trâmites necesarios para la inscripción de sus docentes al mencionado Fondo." Colombia, Corte Constitucioanal de Colombia. 1997. "Sentencia de Unificación 559/1997", p. 15.

4. Colombia, Corte Constitucioanal de Colombia. 1997. "Sentencia de Unificación 559/1997", p. 26–27.

5. Colombia, Corte Constitucioanal de Colombia. 1997. "Sentencia de Unificación 559/1997", p. 28.

6. Colombia, Corte Constitucioanal de Colombia. 1998. "Sentencia de Tutela 153/1998", p. 1.

7. In original: "Esta Corporación ha hecho uso de la figura del estado de cosas inconstitucional con el fin de buscar remedio a situaciones de vulneración de los derechos fundamentales que tengan un carácter general - en tanto que afectan a multitud de personas -, y cuyas causas sean de naturaleza estructural - es decir que, por lo regular, no se originan de manera exclusiva en la autoridad demandada y, por lo tanto, su solución exige la acción mancomunada de distintas entidades. En estas condiciones, la Corte ha considerado que dado que miles de personas se encuentran en igual situación y que si todas acudieran a la tutela podrían congestionar de manera innecesaria la administración de justicia, lo más indicado es dictar órdenes a las instituciones oficiales competentes con el fin de que pongan en acción sus facultades para eliminar ese estado de cosas inconstitucional." Colombia, Corte Constitucioanal de Colombia. 1998. "Sentencia de Tutela 153/1998", p. 2.

8. Colombia, Corte Constitucioanal de Colombia. 1998. "Sentencia de Tutela 153/1998", p. 84.

9. Colombia, Corte Constitucioanal de Colombia. 2004. "Sentencia de Tutela 025/2004", p. 1.

10. In original: "Varios elementos confirman la existencia de un estado de cosas inconstitucional respecto de la situación de la población internamente desplazada. En primer lugar, la gravedad de la situación de vulneración de derechos que enfrenta la población desplazada fue expresamente reconocida por el mismo legislador al definir la condición de desplazado, y resaltar la violación masiva de múltiples derechos. En segundo lugar, otro elemento que confirma la existencia de un estado de cosas inconstitucional en materia de desplazamiento forzado, es el elevado volumen de acciones de tutela presentadas por los desplazados para obtener las distintas ayudas y el incremento de las mismas. En tercer lugar, los procesos acumulados en la presente acción de tutela, confirma ese estado de cosas inconstitucional y señalan que la vulneración de los derechos afecta a buena parte de la población desplazada, en múltiples lugares del territorio nacional y que las autoridades han omitido adoptar los correctivos requeridos. En cuarto lugar, la continuación de la vulneración de tales derechos no es imputable a una única entidad. En quinto lugar, la vulneración de los derechos de los desplazados reposa en factores estructurales enunciados en el apartado 6 de esta providencia dentro de los cuales se destaca la falta de correspondencia entre lo que dicen las normas y los medios para cumplirlas, aspecto que adquiere una especial dimensión cuando se mira la insuficiencia de recursos dada la evolución del problema de desplazamiento y se aprecia la magnitud del problema frente a la capacidad institucional para responder oportuna y eficazmente a él. En conclusión, la Corte declarará formalmente la existencia de un estado de cosas inconstitucional relativo a las condiciones de vida de la población internamente desplazada. Por ello, tanto las autoridades nacionales como las territoriales, dentro de la órbita de sus competencias, habrán de adoptar los correctivos que permitan superar tal estado de cosas." Colombia, Corte Constitucioanal de Colombia. 2004. "Sentencia de Tutela 025/2004", p. 4–5.

11. Lazari, Rafael de, and Emerson Ademir Borges de Oliveira. 2018. "Estado de coisas inconstitucional e ativismo judicial". In *Constituição Federal: 30 anos*, edited

by Ives Gandra da Silva Martins, Adolfo Mamoru Nishiyama and Rafael de Lazari, 387–93. Belo Horizonte: D'Plácido, p. 387–388.

12. In original: "Arguição de Descumprimento de Preceito Fundamental."

13. Brasil, Supremo Tribunal Federal. 2015. "Medida Cautelar na Arguição de Descumprimento de Preceito Fundamental n. 347", p. 9.

14. Brasil, Supremo Tribunal Federal. 2015. "Medida Cautelar na Arguição de Descumprimento de Preceito Fundamental n. 347", p. 24.

15. In original: "o tratamento desumano conferido aos presos não é um problema apenas dos presos: a sociedade livre recebe os reflexos dessa política sob a forma de mais violência." Barcellos, Ana Paula de. 2010. "Violência urbana, condições das prisões e dignidade humana". *Revista de Direito Administrativo*, v. 253, p. 39.

16. In original: "As Audiências de Custódia ou a apresentação imediata do preso à autoridade judicial permitem uma melhor efetivação dos incisos LXV e LXVI do artigo 5º da Constituição. Primeiro porque o juiz, tendo contato com o caso e com a pessoa, poderá relaxar a prisão ilegal (hipótese de ilegalidade da prisão). Segundo porque, em caso de desnecessidade de prisão, o juiz admitirá que a pessoa seja colocada em liberdade provisória, com pagamento ou não de fiança, a depender de outras circunstâncias." Oliveira, Emerson Ademir Borges de. 2020. *A Constituição brasileira ao alcance de todos*. Belo Horizonte: D'Plácido, p. 139–140.

17. Kelsen, Hans. 2012. *Teoria pura do direito*. São Paulo: Martins Fontes.

18. Carvalho, Kildare Gonçalves. 2008. *Direito constitucional: Teoria do Estado e da Constituição – direito constitucional positivo*. Belo Horizonte: Del Rey.

19. Lazari, Rafael de, and Emerson Ademir Borges de Oliveira. 2018. "Estado de coisas inconstitucional e ativismo judicial." In *Constituição Federal: 30 anos*, edited by Ives Gandra da Silva Martins, Adolfo Mamoru Nishiyama and Rafael de Lazari, 387–93. Belo Horizonte: D'Plácido, p. 389.

20. Oliveira, Emerson Ademir Borges de. 2015. *Ativismo judicial e controle de constitucionalidade: impacto e efeitos na evolução da democracia*. Curitiba: Juruá, p. 127.

21. Lazari, Rafael de, and Emerson Ademir Borges de Oliveira. 2018. "Estado de coisas inconstitucional e ativismo judicial." In *Constituição Federal: 30 anos*, edited by Ives Gandra da Silva Martins, Adolfo Mamoru Nishiyama and Rafael de Lazari, 387–93. Belo Horizonte: D'Plácido, p. 388.

22. In original: "Con el fin de corregir esta situación, es necesario que las distintas entidades nacionales y territoriales encargadas de la atención de la población desplazada, cumplan a cabalidad con sus deberes constitucionales y legales y adopten, en un plazo razonable, y dentro de las órbitas de sus competencias, los correctivos que aseguren una suficiente apropiación presupuestal. Al ordenar este tipo de medidas, no está desconociendo la Corte la separación de poderes que establece nuestra Constitución, ni desplazando a las demás autoridades en el cumplimiento de sus deberes. Por el contrario, la Corte, teniendo en cuenta los instrumentos legales que desarrollan la política de atención a la población desplazada, así como el diseño de la política y los compromisos asumidos por las distintas entidades, está apelando al principio constitucional de colaboración armónica entre las distintas ramas del poder, para asegurar el cumplimiento de los deberes de protección efectiva de los derechos

de todos los residentes en el territorio nacional. Esa es la competencia del juez constitucional en un Estado Social de Derecho respecto de derechos que tienen una clara dimensión prestacional." Colombia, Corte Constitucioanal de Colombia. 2004. "Sentencia de Tutela 025/2004".

23. Brasil, Supremo Tribunal Federal. 2015. "Medida Cautelar na Arguição de Descumprimento de Preceito Fundamental n. 347", p. 12.

24. Amaral, Mariana Alves Zanelli. 2018. "A audiência de custódia e o estado de coisas inconstitucional: uma análise da lotação do sistema carcerário brasileiro." *Revista de Artigos Científicos dos Alunos da EMERJ*, v.10, n. 1, p. 978.

25. Lazari, Rafael de, and Emerson Ademir Borges de Oliveira. 2018. "Estado de coisas inconstitucional e ativismo judicial". In *Constituição Federal: 30 anos*, edited by Ives Gandra da Silva Martins, Adolfo Mamoru Nishiyama and Rafael de Lazari, 387–93. Belo Horizonte: D'Plácido, p. 392–393.

REFERENCES

Amaral, Mariana Alves Zanelli. 2018. "A audiência de custódia e o estado de coisas inconstitucional: uma análise da lotação do sistema carcerário brasileiro." *Revista de Artigos Científicos dos Alunos da EMERJ*, v. 10, n. 1: 972–986.

Barcellos, Ana Paula de. 2010. "Violência urbana, condições das prisões e dignidade humana." *Revista de Direito Administrativo*, v. 253: 39–65.

Brasil, Supremo Tribunal Federal. 2015. "Medida Cautelar na Arguição de Descumprimento de Preceito Fundamental n. 347." Accessed May 1, 2020. http://redir.stf.jus.br/paginadorpub/paginador.jsp?docTP=TP&docID=10300665.

Carvalho, Kildare Gonçalves. 2008. *Direito constitucional: Teoria do Estado e da Constituição—direito constitucional positivo*. Belo Horizonte: Del Rey.

Colombia, Corte Constitucioanal de Colombia. 1997. "Sentencia de Unificación 559/1997." Accessed May 1, 2020. http://www.corteconstitucional.gov.co/relatoria/1997/SU559-97.htm.

Colombia, Corte Constitucioanal de Colombia. 1998. "Sentencia de Tutela 153/1998." Accessed May 1, 2020. http://www.corteconstitucional.gov.co/relatoria/1998/T-153-98.htm.

Colombia, Corte Constitucioanal de Colombia. 2004. "Sentencia de Tutela 025/2004." Accessed May 1, 2020. http://www.corteconstitucional.gov.co/relatoria/2004/t-025-04.htm.

De Giorgi, Raffaele, and Diego de Paiva Vasconcelos. 2018. "Os fatos e as declarações: reflexões sobre o Estado de Ilegalidade Difusa." *Revista Direito & Práxis*, v. 9, n. 1: 480-503. DOI: 10.1590/2179-8966/2018/32819.

Kelsen, Hans. 2012. *Teoria pura do direito*. São Paulo: Martins Fontes.

Lazari, Rafael de, and Emerson Ademir Borges de Oliveira. 2018. "Estado de coisas inconstitucional e ativismo judicial." In *Constituição Federal: 30 anos*, edited by Ives Gandra da Silva Martins, Adolfo Mamoru Nishiyama and Rafael de Lazari, 387–93. Belo Horizonte: D'Plácido.

Oliveira, Emerson Ademir Borges de. 2020. *A Constituição brasileira ao alcance de todos*. Belo Horizonte: D'Plácido.

Oliveira, Emerson Ademir Borges de. 2015. *Ativismo judicial e controle de constitucionalidade: impacto e efeitos na evolução da democracia*. Curitiba: Juruá.

Taquary, Eneida Orbage de Britto, and Wangle Samuel Costa Leão. 2019. "O diálogo entre Colômbia e Brasil sobre o 'estado de coisas inconstitucional.'" *Revista de la Secretaria del aTribunal Permanente de Revisión*, v. 7, n. 13: 193–212. DOI: 10.16890/rstpr.a7.n13.p193.

Chapter 15

Expanding Constitutional Dialogues in the Judicial Review

What Are the Institutional and Behavioral Challenges of the Brazilian Supreme Court as a Human Rights' Guardian?

Flavia Santiago Lima

INTRODUCTION

The Brazilian Supreme Court (STF) is considered a key element in the Brazilian institutional arrangement, because of the remarkable universe of themes submitted to its appreciation and for its willingness to interfere in relevant causes of the national political life. The relevance of the "guardian" of the Federal Constitution of 1988 (CRFB) is often attributed to the reconformation of the Court in the democratic transition, with the expansion and concentration of competences, by combining the diffuse judicial review (American model) with the abstract control of constitutionality (European inspiration), in addition to ordinary jurisdictional powers, that justify the discussion of three distinct "courts," three *personae*, merged into just one institution: constitutional, appellate, and ordinary court.[1]

Furthermore, article 60, paragraph 4, establishes an intangible core: the Federation, direct, secret universal, and periodic voting; separation of powers and individual rights, and guarantees, which cannot be abolished. The *stone clauses* authorize the claim to hold the "last word" on the constitution, regarding the manifestations of the legislative power—constitutional amendments included—and acts of the executive power. The Court still has control over political processes and dynamics between authorities and parliamentarians, judges important authorities criminally, and evaluates intervention mechanisms in the economy.[2] So, in an extensive and analytical constitution, that has 250 articles and 114 articles on Temporary Constitutional Provisions Act (*sic*), it is up to the STF to guarantee a system of rights that allows it to address almost all major issues.

Under the light of the Court's main role, since the enactment of the CRFB, a research agenda has been consolidated around the Court's activity (and omissions), with attention to institutional and behavioral factors that explain its functioning, in interaction with other political actors, among the procedures and decisions taken. The STF's vaunted willingness to appreciate the most diverse themes and interfere in other branches of government, however, it is not accompanied by statistics regarding its judgments, which shows that its performance is concentrated on procedural aspects and, in the analysis of the merits, the effective declarations of unconstitutionality correspond to a low percentage of the decided lawsuits.

If the judicialization of politics—or mega politics—seems to be a characteristic of the Brazilian constitutional arrangement, it is important to question about the obstacles for fundamental rights in order to constitute the main agenda of the Court in charge of guarding the so-called Constitution of Citizenship.

To answer that, we will explore the characteristics of the judicial review exercised by the Brazilian Supreme Court, based on its normative conformation (plus scholarly expectations)[3] and the praxis of its activity. Thus, it is suggested the combination of institutional approaches—starting point of the initial research about judicialization of politics in Brazil[4]—with political dynamics—exploring empirical data produced around the actions and omissions of the court and its judgments.[5]

In this sense, the following sections propose—and suggest further research—that judicial review be studied as a sum of the subjects brought to court, debates after the filing of the lawsuits, and judging. The objective is to analyze how the Court, based on its internal dynamics, can decide (or not) the issues, in view of a cooperative and dialogical dimension necessary for the exercise of a legal activity with undeniable political repercussions.

THIRTY YEARS OF JUDICIALIZATION OF POLITICS IN BRAZIL: EXPANDING THE SCOPE OF ANALYSIS, ESTABLISHING A NEW RESEARCH AGENDA

Judicialization, despite semantic divergences and the different points of scientific observation common in any interdisciplinary phenomenon, is an expression that would characterize the process under which rules, procedures, and judicial discourse come to pervade many aspects of life. From a political point of view, it would correspond to the transformation in the means of government, with the progressively crucial role of justice in the field of public policies and in its central character for the functioning of democracies.[6] It is about the second aspect that, in a more specific approach, the judicialization of politics, thus, pertains to the new dynamic between courts and the political environment. It examines their interactions in institutional aspects and analyzes their impact on the behavior of political and judicial actors, elements that were subsequently distributed on different research agendas.

There is a consensus on the necessary connection between judicial discourse and political aspirations.[7] At the same time, the institutional configuration of the courts is attractive to minority groups. The courts' duty to examine certain claims with a degree of independence enables them to go forward in themes of difficult-to-reach consensus between political actors and social sectors.

Regardless of local circumstances, there has been a global movement towards directing to the judicial system conflicts and tensions inherent to the political process, and the same holds true for Brazil. The CRFB, as one of the instruments of the democratic restoration in the country, has attempted to redefine its national politics. Among other measures, it has empowered courts and other authorities and judicial organizations, such as the Public Prosecution, Public Legal Defence, Advocacy General of the Union and even the Legal Profession. The search for the courts is not just explained by social mobilization, but it is the result and can be instrumentalized by the dynamics between the non-majority state institutions themselves, which has repercussions not only on competition relationships and reciprocal overlaps, but also on agreements and identities of preferences, based on corporate interests and individual political agendas.

CRFB has adopted an analytic model for the democratic transition, allowing the "translation of political demands into judicial language, making them justicialisable."[8] It is a constitution with a broad guarantee of rights, ~~and~~ which adopts different semantics for legal protections: rights recognized therein are called "fundamental rights" (Title II, article 5, paragraph 1), constitutional rights and freedoms (article 5, LXXI), or individual rights and guarantees (article 60, paragraph 4, IV), whereas there is an opening clause in the provision of article 5, paragraph 2, which establishes the interaction between The National Law and international human rights treaties.

But the Constitution also brings extensive regulation of the separation of powers, federalism, organization of state structures and guarantees of public servants, economic and social activities. So, constitutionalizing policies would have "strong implications for the *Brazilian political system´s modus operandi*": (i) constitutional amendments as a necessary means for implementing the political agenda of government officials, (ii) the need for broad legislative majorities to pass them in the National Congress, and (iii) the judicialization of these decisions in the Supreme Court to control the constitutionality of laws and other acts of government.[9]

As a legal framework for the transition to democracy, there was a clear Iberian (especially Portuguese) influence guiding a democratic and communitarian constitutional view and high expectations from social actors, vulnerable groups and political minorities. Optimism about judicial review and its potential to promote constitutional values also prevailed in the legal academy, with a so-called "Brazilian constitutionalism,"[10] the description of a combination between theoretical efforts and an action perspective, for the "elaboration of dogmatic categories of constitutional effectiveness."[11]

Given that context, judicial institutions have become a relevant study subject for legal scholars and political scientists, who have affirmed the judicialization of politics and social relations. It is a process that has been observed in the entire Brazilian judicial system, from smaller lawsuits (concerning specific individual rights), to public class action suits, challenging the tenets of public policy in the STF.[12]

In recent years, the validity of the judicialization of politics as a category applicable to the Brazilian case has been discussed not only by the theoretical assumptions that support it, but also by the methods and approaches suggested to researchers. For Avritzer and Marona, this is a research agenda that "operates, fundamentally, from the liberal tradition, both in the field of constitutionalism and in that of democratic theory."[13]

In this chapter, we assume the criticisms already formulated, which allow to expand the focus of analysis, taking into account the data and elements already available to advance the diagnosis, and debate of the STF. Taking the judicialization of political themes, traditionally directed at representative bodies, as a perspective of approach, it is possible to address the various issues involved in judicial review, distinguishing important phases and arrangements between the actors and institutions involved in constitutional adjudication. Authors like Andrei Koerner also privilege the interactions and the contingency of the debate, depending on different political circumstances. The combination of institutional and factors, considering the various interests involved, would offer a more complete explanation of judicialization in Brazil.[14]

For Ribeiro and Argueles, in the joint analysis between institutional design of the judiciary, political dynamics or conjunctural variables, and motivations of the actors, it would be possible to assess the intensity of judicialization, since "an important part of the variation of what will be the object of a judicial challenge, that will sue the STF and how, when and how much the court will be mobilized is explained by factors that are contingent on political dynamics."[15]

Based on this renewed analytical scope, we will explore the topics submitted by political actors, the agenda-setting, the characterization of the selectivity of STF´s activism and its option for self-restraint.

INSTITUTIONAL ACTORS AND DEMOCRATIC PARTICIPATION IN BRAZILIAN JUDICIAL REVIEW: BETWEEN LEGISLATION AND CONSTITUTIONAL PRAXIS

Thus, in order to understand the STF's performance, it is necessary to evaluate the issues that are brought to its appreciation and the Court's strategies for including (or not) public sphere in its dynamics. So, results of the research carried out on abstract judicial review will be presented (especially direct actions of unconstitutionality–ADI´s). It is important to highlight that, more than 30 years after the enactment of the CRFB, there is a long trajectory of judicialization, with advances and setbacks in the interpretative praxis of the Court. This has an important impact on the legal mobilization of social and political actors.

Considering that the research covers different periods (with possible overlapping of temporal analysis), different objects (procedures) and specific approaches, we will try—whenever possible—to make the pertinent observations, remembering that the most relevant is to evaluate trends and to confront the different perceptions about STF´s performance.

The exercise of jurisdiction, according to the principle of *inertia*, depends on the provocation. In the Brazilian constitutional design, the (relative) "opening" of judicial review is an important cause of judicialization of politics, by *facilitating* the access of various political groups to the Court, breaking with the attorney-general's monopoly in the previous Constitution, when it had the function of defending the Executive Power.[16]

It is interesting to note that although the STF´s Justices were quite active in the constituent process, they did not mobilize efforts against such enlargement at that time, nevertheless expressed disagreement in the media. Concerns about excessive litigation, especially among civil society actors, had repercussions on the Court´s later performance, with the establishment of strict requirements for filing lawsuits.[17]

In this sense, talking about access to abstract judicial review implies a distinction between those who can litigate on any topic and those who are submitted to the "filter" of the thematic pertinence, the jurisprudential creation of the STF that establishes the need to identify the link between the contested rule and the institutional activities of the applicants as a condition for admissibility" of the lawsuits. In practice, a state (or the Federal District) governor, the Directing Board of a State Legislative Assembly and a confederation of labor unions or a national professional association access are limited by this *ruling*. The thematic limitation of the latter shows that, except for political parties and the Brazilian Bar Association, representatives of civil society are bound to mobilize their own priorities.

After the claim has been received, authorized participants in the constitutional adjudication process at the Court must be called. There are those public agents who have the duty to integrate the action, but there are also possibilities for calling on social actors or by broadcasting parts of the sessions on "TV Justiça" and "YouTube," so that the Justices and their debates are carefully monitored by the public and the media.

During the judgment, initially, the Rapporteur must open a deadline for information from other agencies or entities, which bring elements that justify the adoption of the contested rule/act. After this period, the summons of the advocate general of the Union (AGU) and the attorney general of the Republic (PGR) must be determined, so that they can respond to the lawsuit, successively.

The CRFB expressly provides that when the STF examines the unconstitutionality in abstract the advocate general of the Union "shall defend the impugned act or text," but despite the literalness, for a long time it has been discussed the distinction between the functions of the "defensive" AGU, who would not be in a position to give an opinion, and that of the PGR, which is supervisory. The conversion of the mandatory defense into a duty to demonstrate the constitutionality, finally, was enshrined in the judgment of ADI 3916/2010 and the AGU´s "right of manifestation" must be compatible with constitutional guidelines (not necessarily of the contested law) and must be focused on Federal Government´s priorities—although state legislation can also be contested in ADI (*sic*).

The PGR, in addition to being able—at its discretion—to file a lawsuit, "shall be previously heard in actions of unconstitutionality and in all suits under the power of the STF" (article 102, paragraph 1, CRFB). Thus, there is a "double position"—possible author and advisor—that guarantees active participation in the judicial review and high success rate in judgments.

If the constitution guaranteed the presence of institutional actors in the (judicial) procedures, the ordinary legislation—Laws 9.868 / 99 and 9.882 / 99—when regulating constitutional actions, expanded the technical and social participation, establishing: requests for information from entities that promulgated the contested rule, possibilities to summon additional information from specialists to issue an opinion (*amicus curiae*) and the call for public hearings.

The "opening of the constitutional proceedings" was widely celebrated by Brazilian academia, with expectations about their effective conditions to influence decision-making dynamics. According to the Justice Gilmar Mendes, who collaborated in the legislative process, these tools would transform the STF into a "house of the people, just like the parliament," due to their strong democratic potential (ADI 3,510).

According to Law 9,868/99, the admission of *amicus curiae* is subject to the assessment of the relevance of the matter and representativeness of candidates. However, the admission, procedure, participation, and powers do not have precise regulations therefore the parameters can be set by the Justice. In fact, the "friends of the court" are present in almost all classes and procedural instruments. As a consequence, there is an upward curve of requests in the universe of actions that "have at least one organization that manifests itself as *amicus*, which jumped from just over 13% in the period from 1999 to 2005 and reached 30% between 2006 and 2014." This performance is surrounded by hope, especially from advocacy organizations, in mobilizing strategic litigation.

However, surveys show (1990–2015) that, although admitted, they "are not heard, considering that 62% of the judgments informed the entry of the *amici curiae* in the deed, but only 6% explained the arguments produced," demonstrating the court's low permeability to information brought by them.[18]

Legislation also provided holding public hearings, summoned by the Rapporteur, that has the power to select the qualified participants and organize the speeches, guaranteeing the plurality of the opinions presented, "whenever he deems necessary." Surrounded by attention, the hearings are broadcast, to ensure debate publicity. Justices and exhibitors adhere to a plurality discourse, in the "conceptual tripod: legitimacy, participation, and information."[19]

In practice, Justices' participation is considered timid, eminently passive, and they ask few questions (often none).[20] As reported in a book about the STF´s background, the hearings would be another tool for Justices to interfere in the Court's agenda, "saving time until the trial" or the Justices simply "supply themselves with supposedly technical arguments to justify already consolidated positions.

Therefore, although the relevance of these opening instruments is emphasized, the low impact on final judgments and its use would not allow to affirm that the STF is a court in which social participation prevails.

INPUTS AND OUTPUTS: IS THE STF GUARDIAN OF ITS OWN AGENDA AND PRIORITIES?

Considering the prevalence of institutional actors in the STF decision-making process, on what themes does the Court focus its activity? Once again, understanding the Court's choices depends on its design and the behavior of the actors who mobilize its performance.

There are two issues that emerge from the thousands of cases received each year by the STF: the significant number of lawsuits awaiting judgment and the overlapping of formal and procedural aspects over material criteria in the court's decision-making process. There is a long time between filing and the STF's response, in which "a lawsuit is rarely judged in less than 2 years and the average time of these judgments is more than 5 years, that is, it is longer than a legislature."[21]

Docket control is an important element to understanding a court and the most successful ones would make better use of it, to ensure "specific support" or "diffuse support" and to avoid excessive interventions.[22] In Brazil, it is said that the STF "would be a political Court not only because it agrees or disagrees with the Executive or Congress (…) but rather because it controls the time to agree or disagree."[23] And in this decision-making process, the individual role of the Justices stands out, because the Rapporteur may not submit the process to the plenary for judgment or a Justice, if not convinced, or he/she can interrupt the plenary session and request a hearing in order to clarify points and better support his/her decision.

Considering the expressive number of lawsuits awaiting judgment, we have argued in previous works if the supervening "lack of grounds" in abstract judicial review can be a strategy for the STF, because "in the universe of 5,546 ADIs presented over 27 years, a significant number of 743 were deemed impaired by supervening lack of grounds (13.4% of the total)."[24]

However, it is expected that the Court decides the lawsuit, not exempting itself from appreciating the alleged injury or threat to constitutional provisions. To exercise its self-restraint, the STF has a wide range of arguments that combine the North American and European traditions, being able to move between them and use them selectively, without establishing a priori the contours of its performance. It is possible to organize and categorize the Brazilian self-restraint as material and formal, as tools available to the Court to interact at the political level, basing their express or tacit dialogue with the majority institutions. As criteria for material self-restraint, respect for the separation of powers is frequent, with the recognition of Parliament's *interna corporis* acts and "administrative discretion" of Executive branch, political question doctrine and recognition of its role as a "negative legislator" without the power to create law. There is formal self-restraint (or passive virtues), represented by specific criteria for filing actions, such as thematic pertinence, subsidiary actions, and others. In this way, the reduction in the degree of intervention and respect for representative institutions denote a flagrant institutional restriction, both in terms of interpretation and behavior.[25]

After controlling the time to decide and what deserves to be judged, it is relevant to analyze which themes are the target of the STF action and which are its preferred partners in the judicialization. Despite the assurance of a wide range (list) of plaintiffs, the confederations and professional associations, state governors, political parties and the Attorney General stand out in the ADI's practice, with at least 15% shares each and, which together, filed more than 90% of these lawsuits.[26] And the role of institutional actors must be distinguished again, which demands recognition of the influence of the profile—political and legal preferences—of office holders on the lawsuits brought.

In the case of Governors, the STF is used as a tool to mediate their disagreements with State Legislative Assemblies. The Court presents the tendency, in assessing the merits, of maintaining the *status quo* at the regional level, whose political and economic costs of overriding fiscal and tax policies that have already been sedimented by time are too high, and protects the Federal Government at the national level."[27]

The PGR is the head of Public Prosecution of the Union, reconfigured by CRFB, independent of the other powers to fulfill the "duty to defend the juridical order, the democratic regime and the inalienable social and individual interests" (article 127). Considering the consolidation of the institutional "defense of society" discourse, expectations would suggest an agenda focused on fundamental rights. The data, in turn, show a preponderance—80%—of the theme "Public Administration" for questioning state laws. It is the plaintiff with the higher success rate and, of its 144 lawsuits with a positive result (unconstitutionality), 100 dealt with guarantees for public servants' careers, in particular those given to the Public Prosecution itself and the judiciary."[28]

With regard to the civil society, although the requirement of thematic pertinence can be affirmed as a limitation on the inclusion of these groups in the constitutional dialogue, there is a greater "presence of associations of civil servants and of businessmen."[29] The role of the Brazilian Bar Association (OAB) also stands out because it can bring any topic to the STF. Although initially focused on the consolidation of professional practice and guarantees of lawyers, more recently, the OAB began to question issues of greater repercussion as elections and political parties.[30]

As a consequence, on the universe of lawsuits effectively judged, there is a predominance of the themes "public servant," "tax law" and "social security," especially directed against acts of the Executive Power—above all, alleging "defects of initiative" in bills of private competence of other political agents.[31] And, moreover, part of the judgments corresponds to the organization of the Judiciary, the Public Prosecutor's Office and advocacy.[32]

CONCLUSIONS

The Brazilian Supreme Court, in its daily judicial review activity, makes an important docket control and is very selective, predominating self-restraint. On the merits, certainly conditioned by the actions that are filed, the STF favors themes related to horizontal and vertical relations of power, based on the constitutionalization of public policies. So, despite famous decisions on important matters (e.g., electoral system, same-sex marriage, right to health, and education), there is a disconnection between the STF's performance and one of the main arguments for legitimizing its activity: protection and effectiveness of fundamental rights and social participation.

The history of a court cannot be told only through quantitative data, taking into account that the political, economic, social, and even symbolic impacts can result from just one decision or a set of them. Judicial affirmation of rights can be the starting point—or the arrival—for many conquests of vulnerable groups and those excluded from the majority political processes, collaborating with the strengthening of constitutional democracies.

Successes and tragedies often depend on a particular judgment in a given context and the Justices know it. The gradual affirmation of a court in a political system depends on the interactions it establishes with other actors and institutions, in a dynamic process that involves actions and reactions. They are inherent in the political game, but also important for the enforcement of decisions and preservation of the court's authority, protecting it from outside interference.

The STF has among the institutional actors—justice system above all—its main interlocutors, for the lawsuits filed and also for their participation in the decision-making process. The constitutional commitment to legal professions anticipated this connection, which makes part of the Court's agenda dependent on the interests mobilized by the office holders, of the relationships they establish with their own corporations and with other political agents.

The Constitution expanded access to the Court by civil society, the legislation ensured instruments for sharing debates in public hearings and *amici curiae*; STF´s jurisprudence limited this access with the creation of formal requirement and, in public sessions and votes, Justices show little disposition to listen those who intend to expose information and aspirations.

It is important that, based on this diagnosis, the academy and actors focus their attention not only on criticizing the omissions and selectivity of the Court's agenda but for new institutional means that would allow the forwarding of the Brazilian society' demands to the STF.

Institutional designs can shape courts, but the consolidation of a constitutional culture among the agents who interpret it is the vector that points the way for the judicial review. And, in Brazil, it is up to the "guardian of the Constitution" to create and offer, in its judgments and praxis, the conditions for cooperation and the necessary dialogue to maintain the constitutional agreement that ensures its power.

NOTES

1. Falcão, Joaquim; Cerdeira, Pablo de Camargo; Arguelhes, Diego Werneck. *Relatório Supremo em números - o múltiplo Supremo*. Rio de Janeiro: Fundação Getúlio Vargas, 2011, p. 16.
2. Lima, Flávia Danielle Santiago. *Jurisdição Constitucional e Política: ativismo e autocontenção no STF*. Curitiba: Juruá, 2014. On the particularities of the judicial review of constitutional amendments in Brazil, Jairo Lima's pioneering work brings surprising conclusions. Lima, Jairo. *Emendas constitucionais inconstitucionais: democracia e supermaioria*. Rio de Janeiro: Lumen Juris, 2018.
3. Jackson, Vicki C.; Greene, Jamal. Constitutional Interpretation in comparative perspective. In: Ginsburg, Tom; Dixon, Rosalind (orgs.). *Comparative Constitutional Law*. Cheltenham: Edward Elgar Publishing, 2011, pp. 599–623, p. 616.
4. In previous works, we discussed the institutional explanations for the strengthening of the STF and the disfunctionalities on its performance. Lima, Flávia Danielle Santiago; Garbaccio, Grace Ladeira; Cyr-Moreau, Sophie. Cartographie d'une Super Cour: approches institutionnelles de la Cour Fédérale Suprême brésilienne. *Sequência*, v. 39, n. 78, pp. 37–62, abr. 2018.
5. So, we will start from Judicial Politics, combining methodological approaches of Law and Political Science. V. G. Whittington, Keith E.; Kelemen, R. Daniel; Caldeira, Gregory A. (eds.) *The Oxford handbook of law and politics*. Oxford: Oxford University Press, 2008.
6. Commaille, Jacques; Dumoulin, Laurence. Heurs et malheurs de la légitimité dans les sociétés contemporaines. Une sociologie politique de la "judiciarisation". *L'Année Sociologique*, v. 59, n. 1, pp. 63–107, 2009, pp. 65–70.
7. Stone Sweet, Alec. *Governing with judges – constitutional politics in Europe*. Oxford: Oxford University Press, 2000, p. 206.
8. Lima, Flávia Danielle Santiago. *Jurisdição Constitucional e Política: ativismo e autocontenção no STF*. Curitiba: Juruá, 2014, p. 221.
9. Couto, Cláudio Gonçalves; Arantes, Rogério Bastos. Constituição, governo e democracia no Brasil. *Revista Brasileira de Ciências Sociais*. São Paulo, v. 21, n. 61, pp. 41–62, jun. 2006, pp. 44–58.
10. "The objective of this movement of legal and political dimensions is to develop dogmatic and procedural mechanisms for the realization of the constitutional text, with the acceptance of its emancipatory character. It is assumed, therefore, that the political "struggle" for constitutional effectiveness is also a legal struggle." Souza Neto, Cláudio Pereira de. Teoria da constituição, democracia e igualdade. Bercovici, Gilberto *et al*. *Teoria da constituição: estudos sobre o lugar da política no direito constitucional*. Rio de Janeiro: Lumen Juris, 2003. pp. 1–73, pp. 14–17.

11. Barroso, Luis Roberto. *O direito constitucional e a efetividade de suas normas – limites e possibilidades da Constituição Brasileira*. Rio de Janeiro: Renovar, 2009, pp. 354–355.

12. Vg. Vianna, Luiz Werneck, et al. *A judicialização da política e das relações sociais no Brasil*. Rio de Janeiro: Revan, 1999, pp. 147–ss.

13. Avritzer, Leonardo; Marona, Marjorie Corrêa. Judicialização da política no Brasil: ver além do constitucionalismo liberal para ver melhor. *Revista Brasileira de Ciência Política*, v. 1, n. 15, pp. 69–94, dez. 2014.

14. Koerner, Andrei. Ativismo Judicial? Jurisprudência constitucional e política no STF pós-88. *Novos Estudos CEBRAP*, v. 1, n. 96, pp. 69–85, jul. 2013.

15. Ribeiro, Leandro Molhano; Arguelhes, Diego Werneck. Contextos da judicialização da política: novos elementos para um mapa teórico. *Revista Direito GV*, v. 15, n. 2, p. e1921, 2019, p. 5.

16. Carvalho Neto, Ernani Rodrigues de. A ampliação dos legitimados ativos na Constituinte de 1988: revisão judicial e judicialização da política. *Revista Brasileira de Estudos Políticos*, v. 96, pp. 293–325, jul./dez., 2007, pp. 322–323.

17. Lima, Flávia Danielle Santiago. Revisitando os pressupostos da juristocracia à brasileira: mobilização judicial na Assembleia Constituinte e o fortalecimento do Supremo Tribunal Federal. *Revista da Faculdade de Direito UFPR*, v. 63, n. 2, pp. 145–167, ago. 2018, p. 161.

18. Ferreira, Débora Costa; Branco, Paulo Gustavo Gonet. Amicus curiae em números. Nem amigo da corte, nem amigo da parte? *Revista de Direito Brasileira*, v. 16, n. 7, pp. 169–185, jan./abr. 2017, pp. 174–175, 182.

19. Ferreira, Débora Costa; Branco, Paulo Gustavo Gonet. Amicus curiae em números. Nem amigo da corte, nem amigo da parte? Revista de Direito Brasileira, v. 16, n. 7, pp. 169–185, jan./abr. 2017, pp. 174–175, 182.

20. Leal, Fernando; Herdy, Rachel; Massadas, Júlia. Uma década de audiências públicas no Supremo Tribunal Federal (2007–2017). *Revista de Investigações Constitucionais*, v. 5, n. 1, pp. 331–372, jan./abr. 2018, p. 354.

21. Benvindo, Juliano Zaiden; Costa, Alexandre Araújo (coords.). *A quem interessa o controle concentrado de constitucionalidade? O descompasso entre teoria e prática na defesa dos direitos fundamentais*. Brasília: UnB, 2014, p. 20.

22. Fontana, Davis. Docket control and the success of constitutional courts. In: Ginsburg, Tom; Dixon, Rosalind (orgs.). *Comparative Constitutional Law*. Cheltenham: Edward Elgar Publishing, 2011, pp. 624–641, pp. 626–629.

23. Falcão, Joaquim. *O Supremo: compreenda o poder, as razões e as consequências das decisões da mais alta Corte do Judiciário no Brasil*. Rio de Janeiro: Edições de Janeiro, Fundação Getúlio Vargas, 2015.

24. Lima, Flávia Danielle Santiago; Gomes, José Mário Wanderley; Barbosa, Leon Victor Queiroz. Exploring the wonderful mystery of time: "lack of grounds" in the constitutional judicial review as an evidence of passive virtues in the Brazilian Supreme Court (STF). Revista Direito e Justiça: *Reflexões Sociojurídicas, Santo Ângelo*, v. 18, n. 30, pp. 21–36, jan./abr. 2018, p. 29.

25. Lima, Flávia Danielle Santiago; Gomes Neto, José Mário Wanderley. Autocontenção à brasileira? Uma taxonomia dos argumentos jurídicos (e estratégias

políticas?) explicativo(a)s do comportamento do STF nas relações com os poderes majoritários. *Revista de Investigações Constitucionais*, Curitiba, vol. 5, n. 1, pp. 221–247, jan./abr. 2018, p. 244.

26. Gomes, Kelton de Oliveira. *Em defesa da sociedade? Atuação da Procuradoria Geral da República em controle concentrado de constitucionalidade (1988–2012).* Dissertação de Mestrado. Brasília: UNB, 2015, p. 73.

27. Barbosa, Leon Victor de Queiroz. *Ativismo judicial e federalismo fiscal: o comportamento do Supremo Tribunal Federal.* Recife: UFPE (Dissertação de Mestrado), 2009, p. 113.

28. Gomes, Kelton de Oliveira. *Em defesa da sociedade? Atuação da Procuradoria Geral da República em controle concentrado de constitucionalidade (1988–2012).* Dissertação de Mestrado. Brasília: UNB, 2015, pp. 85–91.

29. Vianna, Luiz Werneck; Burgos, Marcelo Baumann; Salles, Paula Martins. Dezessete anos de judicialização da política. *Tempo Social (Revista de Sociologia da USP)*, v. 19, n. 2, pp. 39–85, 2007, pp. 61–62; p. 42.

30. Carvalho, Ernani; Barbosa, Luis Felipe Andrade; Gomes Neto, José Mário Wanderley. OAB e as prerrogativas atípicas na arena política da revisão judicial. *Revista Direito GV*, v. 10, n. 1, pp. 69–98, jun. 2014.

31. Sundfeld, Carlos Ari, et al. *Controle de constitucionalidade e judicialização: o STF frente à sociedade e aos Poderes.* Belo Horizonte: Faculdade de Filosofia e Ciências Humanas, 2010, pp. 27.

32. Progrebinsky, Thamy. *Judicialização ou Representação? Política, Direito e Democracia no Brasil.* Rio de Janeiro: Elsevier, 2011, pp. 67–68.

REFERENCES

Avritzer, Leonardo; Marona, Marjorie Corrêa. Judicialização da política no Brasil: ver além do constitucionalismo liberal para ver melhor. *Revista Brasileira de Ciência Política*, v. 1, n. 15, pp. 69–94, dez. 2014.

Barbosa, Leon Victor de Queiroz. Ativismo judicial e federalismo fiscal: o comportamento do Supremo Tribunal Federal. Recife: UFPE (Dissertação de Mestrado), 2009.

Barroso, Luis Roberto. *O direito constitucional e a efetividade de suas normas—limites e possibilidades da Constituição Brasileira.* 9 ed. Rio de Janeiro: Renovar, 2009.

Benvindo, Juliano Zaiden; Costa, Alexandre Araújo (coords.). *A quem interessa o controle concentrado de constitucionalidade? O descompasso entre teoria e prática na defesa dos direitos fundamentais.* Brasília: UnB, 2014.

Burgos, Marcelo Baumann; Salles, Paula Martins. Dezessete anos de judicialização da política. *Tempo Social (Revista de Sociologia da USP)*, v. 19, n. 2, p. 39–85, 2007.

Carvalho Neto, Ernani Rodrigues de. A ampliação dos legitimados ativos na Constituinte de 1988: revisão judicial e judicialização da política. Revista Brasileira de Estudos Políticos, n. 96, p. 293–325, jul./dez., 2007.

Carvalho, Ernani; Barbosa, Luis Felipe Andrade; Gomes Neto, José Mário Wanderley. OAB e as prerrogativas atípicas na arena política da revisão judicial. *Revista Direito GV*, v. 10, n. 1, p. 69–98, jun. 2014.

Couto, Cláudio Gonçalves; Arantes, Rogério Bastos. Constituição, governo e democracia no Brasil. *Revista Brasileira de Ciências Sociais*. São Paulo, v. 21, n. 61, p. 41–62, jun. 2006.

Commaille, Jacques; Dumoulin, Laurence. Heurs et malheurs de la légitimité dans les sociétés contemporaines. Une sociologie politique de la "judiciarisation." *L'Année Sociologique*, v. 59, n. 1, p. 63–107, 2009, p. 65–70.

Falcão, Joaquim. *O Supremo: compreenda o poder, as razões e as consequências das decisões da mais alta Corte do Judiciário no Brasil*. Rio de Janeiro: Edições de Janeiro, Fundação Getúlio Vargas, 2015.

Falcão, Joaquim; Cerdeira, Pablo de Camargo; Arguelhes, Diego Werneck. *Relatório Supremo em números—o múltiplo Supremo*. Rio de Janeiro: Fundação Getúlio Vargas, 2011.

Ferreira, Débora Costa; Branco, Paulo Gustavo Gonet. Amicus curiae em números. Nem amigo da corte, nem amigo da parte? *Revista de Direito Brasileira*, v. 16, n. 7, p. 169–185, jan./abr. 2017.

Fontana, Davis. Docket control and the success of constitutional courts. In: Ginsburg, Tom; Dixon, Rosalind (orgs.). *Comparative Constitutional Law*. Cheltenham: Edward Elgar Publishing, 2011, p. 624–641.

Gomes, Kelton de Oliveira. *Em defesa da sociedade? Atuação da Procuradoria Geral da República em controle concentrado de constitucionalidade (1988–2012)*. Dissertação de Mestrado. Brasília: UNB, 2015.

Jackson, Vicki C.; Greene, Jamal. Constitutional Interpretation in comparative perspective. In: Ginsburg, Tom; Dixon, Rosalind (orgs.). *Comparative Constitutional Law*. Cheltenham: Edward Elgar Publishing, 2011, p. 599–623.

Koerner, Andrei. Ativismo Judicial? Jurisprudência constitucional e política no STF pós-88. *Novos Estudos CEBRAP*, v. 1, n. 96, p. 69–85, jul. 2013.

Leal, Fernando; Herdy, Rachel; Massadas, Júlia. Uma década de audiências públicas no Supremo Tribunal Federal (2007–2017). *Revista de Investigações Constitucionais*, v. 5, n. 1, p. 331–372, jan./abr. 2018.

Lima, Flávia Danielle Santiago. *Jurisdição Constitucional e Política: ativismo e autocontenção no STF*. Curitiba: Juruá, 2014.

Lima, Flávia Danielle Santiago. Revisitando os pressupostos da juristocracia à brasileira: mobilização judicial na Assembleia Constituinte e o fortalecimento do Supremo Tribunal Federal. *Revista da Faculdade de Direito UFPR*, v. '63, n. 2, p. 145–167, ago. 2018.

Lima, Flávia Danielle Santiago; Garbaccio, Grace Ladeira; Cyr-Moreau, Sophie. Cartographie d'une Super Cour: approches institutionnelles de la Cour Fédérale Suprême brésilienne. *Sequência*, v. 39, n. 78, p. 37–62, abr. 2018.

Lima, Flávia Danielle Santiago; Gomes, José Mário Wanderley; Barbosa, Leon Victor Queiroz. Exploring the wonderful mystery of time: "lack of grounds" in the constitutional judicial review as an evidence of passive virtues in the Brazilian

Supreme Court (STF). *Revista Direito e Justiça: Reflexões Sociojurídicas,* Santo Ângelo, v. 18, n. 30, p. 21–36, jan./abr. 2018.

Lima, Flávia Danielle Santiago; Gomes Neto, José Mário Wanderley. Autocontenção à brasileira? Uma taxonomia dos argumentos jurídicos (e estratégias políticas?) explicativo(a)s do comportamento do STF nas relações com os poderes majoritários. *Revista de Investigações Constitucionais,* Curitiba, v. 5, n. 1, p. 221–247, jan./abr. 2018.

Lima, Jairo. *Emendas constitucionais inconstitucionais: democracia e supermaioria.* Rio de Janeiro: Lumen Juris, 2018.

Marona, Marjorie Corrêa; Rocha, Marta Mendes da. Democratizar a jurisdição constitucional? O caso das audiências públicas no Supremo Tribunal Federal. *Revista de Sociologia e Política*, v. 26, n. 62, p. 131–156, jan. 2017.

Nejaime, Douglas. The legal mobilization dilema. *Emory Law Journal*, v. 61, p. 663–736, 2012.

Ribeiro, Leandro Molhano; Arguelhes, Diego Werneck. Contextos da judicialização da política: novos elementos para um mapa teórico. *Revista Direito GV*, v. 15, n. 2, p. e1921, 2019.

Progrebinsky, Thamy. *Judicialização ou Representação? Política, Direito e Democracia no Brasil.* Rio de Janeiro: Elsevier, 2011.

Recondo, Fernando; Weber, Luiz. *Os onze—o STF, seus bastidores e suas crises*. São Paulo: Companhia das Letras, 2019.

Souza Neto, Cláudio Pereira de. Teoria da constituição, democracia e igualdade. Bercovici, Gilberto et al. *Teoria da constituição: estudos sobre o lugar da política no direito constitucional*. Rio de Janeiro: Lumen Juris, 2003, p. 1–73.

Stone Sweet, Alec. *Governing with judges—constitutional politics in Europe*. Oxford: Oxford University Press, 2000.

Sundfeld, Carlos Ari, et al. Controle de constitucionalidade e judicialização: o STF frente à sociedade e aos Poderes. Belo Horizonte: Faculdade de Filosofia e Ciências Humanas, 2010. p. 27.

Vianna, Luiz Werneck, et al. *A judicialização da política e das relações sociais no Brasil*. Rio de Janeiro: Revan, 1999.

Vianna, Luiz Werneck; Burgos, Marcelo Baumann; Salles, Paula Martins. Dezessete anos de judicialização da política. *Tempo Social (Revista de Sociologia da USP)*, v. 19, n. 2, p. 39 85, 2007, p. 61–62; p.42.

Whittington, Keith E.; Kelemen, R. Daniel; Caldeira, Gregory A. (eds.) *The Oxford handbook of law and politics*. Oxford: Oxford University Press, 2008.

Index

Note: Page numbers with "n" refer to endnotes.

About the Authors

Rubens Becak is full Professor at the Universidade de São Paulo. He is a visiting professor at the University of Salamanca's Brazilian Studies Center and co-editor of the Journal of Brazilian Studies. In the Universidade de São Paulo he headed the Center of Rights (Núcleo de Direitos) and worked as the general-secretary of the University (2010–2014). He hasseveral works in Theory of State, Constitutional Law, and Human Rights

Jairo Lima is professor at the Universidade Estadual do Norte do Paraná. He obtained his PhD degree in Constitutional Law at the Universidade de São Paulo with a thesis on unconstitutional constitutional amendments. In 2016, he was a visiting researcher at the University of Glasgow.

Cristina Godoy Bernardo de Oliveira is professor of Legal Theory at the University of São Paulo. Academic visitor at the Faculty of Law of the University of Oxford. Postdoctoral Researcher at the Université Paris I Panthéon-Sorbonne. PhD at the Faculty of Law of the University of São Paulo. LLB at the Faculty of Law at the University of São Paulo

Emerson Ademir Borges de Oliveira is post-doctorate in Democracy and Human Rights by the Universidade de Coimbra. PhD and Master in State Law from the Universidade de São Paulo. Assistant coordinator of the Master and Doctorate Program in Law at the Universidade de Marília. Lawyer and appraiser.

Estefânia Maria de Queiroz Barboza is adjunct professor of Law at the Federal University of Paraná and at the Centro Universitário Internacional, undergraduate and graduate programs. PhD in juridical science—Pontifical Catholic University of Paraná. Vice-President of Italo-Brazilian Association of Professors of Constitutional and Administrative Law. Visiting researcher at Osgoode Hall Law School (2009). Visiting professor at Università degli Studi di Palermo and Università degli Studi di Messina (2019).

Fernanda Duarte is professor of Law at the Federal Fluminense University, Niterói and at the Estácio de Sá University, Rio de Janeiro, Brazil. Faculty of Law Researcher (Senior PhD) of INCT-InEAC—Institute of Comparative Studies in Institutional Conflict Management/UFF (Niterói, Brazil). Organizer of the Collaborative Research Network of the Law and Society Association/ LSA—CRN1: Comparative Constitutional Law and Legal Culture: Asia and the Americas, USA. Federal Judge.

Fernando de Brito Alves is associate professor and coordinator of the Masters and Doctorate Program in Legal Science at the State University of Northern Paraná (Universidade Estadual do Norte do Paraná—UENP).

Flavia Santiago Lima is professor of Political and Law Theory at State University of Pernambuco and Graduate Program of Damas Catholic College. PhD in Public Law. Researcher at Juspolitica (coordinator). Advocate of the Union, since 2003, working with public policies and judicialization.

João Andrade Neto is lecturer at the Pontifical Catholic University of Minas Gerais (PUC Minas) and Padre Arnaldo Janssen Faculty of Law (Brazil); Court Legal Advisor at the Regional Electoral Court of Minas Gerais (TRE-MG); PhD with the highest distinction (summa cum laude) at the University of Hamburg 2016; Brazilian federal prize for a monograph in election law in 2012; author of the book *Borrowing Justification for Proportionality: On the Influence of the Principles Theory in Brazil* (Springer, 2018); member of the Brazilian Academy of Electoral and Political Law (ABRADEP).

José Duarte Neto is a PhD in Constitutional Law. Master in Constitutional Law. Assistant professor of Constitutional Law at the Faculty of Human and Social Sciences (FCHS)—UNESP—Campus de Franca. Professor at the Graduate Program at UNESP—Campus de Franca. Head of the Department of Public Law at FCHS—UNESP—Campus de Franca (mandates 2013/2014 and 2015/2016). Coordinator of the Graduate Program in Law. Judge in the State of São Paulo—Brazil.

Lucas Catib de Laurentiis is full professor at PUC-Campinas. Coordinator and member of the permanent faculty of the Post-Graduation Program stricto sensu in Law (PPGD). PhD in Constitutional Law at the Faculty of Law of the University of São Paulo.

Maria Paula Dallari Bucci is professor at the Faculty of Law of the University of São Paulo, State Law Department. She was a Legal Counsel (2005–2008) and Secretary of Higher Education (2008–2010) of the Ministry of Education of Brazil. She participated in the Public Hearing held at the STF in March 2009, presenting the position of the Ministry of Education in favor of the constitutionality of affirmative actions.

Melina Girardi Fachin is adjunct professor of Law at the Federal University of Paraná, undergraduate and graduate programs. PhD in juridical science—Pontifical Catholic University of São Paulo. Visiting researcher at Harvard Law School (2011). Visiting Professor at Coimbra University (2019/2020).

Murilo Gaspardo is dean of the School of Human and Social Sciences of São Paulo State University (UNESP), Campus of Franca—SP—Brazil and full professor of State Theory at the Department of Public Law. PhD in Law by University of São Paulo (USP).

Nina Beatriz Stocco Ranieri is Adjunct Professor at the State Law Department of the Law Faculty of the University of São Paulo. Coordinator of the UNESCO Chair in the Right to Education at the Faculty of Law of the University of São Paulo.

Orides Mezzaroba is a Master and Doctor in Law from the Federal University of Santa Catarina. Professor and Coordinator of the Professional Master's Program in Law at the Federal University of Santa Catarina. CNPq Productivity Researcher.

Rafael Mario Iorio Filho is Professor of Law at the Federal Fluminense University, Niterói and at the Estácio de Sá University, Rio de Janeiro, Brazil. Faculty of Law Researcher (Senior PhD) of INCT-InEAC- Institute of Comparative Studies in Institutional Conflict Management/UFF (Niterói, Brazil). Organizer of the Collaborative Research Network of the Law and Society Association/LSA—CRN1: Comparative Constitutional Law and Legal Culture: Asia and the Americas, USA.

Simone Cristine Araújo Lopes is Bachelor of Law at the Universidade Federal de Minas Gerais. Specialization Degree in Taxation Law and Master Degree in Public Law at Pontifícia Universidade Católica de Minas Gerais. Ph.D in State Law at Universidade de São Paulo. Lawyer and Professor at Universidade Federal de Juiz de Fora, campus Governador Valadares.

www.ingramcontent.com/pod-product-compliance
Ingram Content Group UK Ltd.
Pitfield, Milton Keynes, MK11 3LW, UK
UKHW041841031026
15587UKWH00002B/934

9 781793 623690